OUT OF WEAKNESS

OUT
OF
WEAKNESS

HEALING THE WOUNDS THAT
DRIVE US TO WAR

Andrew Bard Schmookler

BANTAM BOOKS
Toronto • New York • London • Sydney • Auckland

OUT OF WEAKNESS

A Bantam Book / September 1988

*"Bantam New Age" and the accompanying figure design as
well as the statement "the search for meaning, growth
and change" are trademarks of Bantam Books.*

Library of Congress Cataloging-in-Publication Data

Schmookler, Andrew Bard.
  Out of weakness.

  "Bantam new age books."
  Bibliography: p.
  Includes index.
  1. Aggressiveness (Psychology) 2. Control
(Psychology) 3. War—Psychological aspects.
4. Civilization. 5. Social evolution. I. Title.
BF575.A3S35   1988   302.5'4   88-47511

ISBN 0-553-05329-9
ISBN 0-553-34477-3 (pbk.)

Published simultaneously in the United States and Canada

*Bantam Books are published by Bantam Books, a division of Bantam Doubleday Dell Publishing
Group, Inc. Its trademark, consisting of the words "Bantam Books" and the portrayal of a rooster, is
Registered in U.S. Patent and Trademark Office and in other countries. Marca Registrada. Bantam
Books, 666 Fifth Avenue, New York, New York 10103.*

PRINTED IN THE UNITED STATES OF AMERICA

FG   0 9 8 7 6 5 4 3 2 1

To my brother
Who went with me up the mountain
And helped me come back down
A more whole man

CONTENTS

PROLOGUE

Out of Weakness

I. The Warrior Spirit

War and the Search for Security

War is both the parent and child of fears. For the people of the world today, the expansion of our powers of destruction has increased the scope of our fears. As before, each nation worries about impingement or conquest by rival powers. But a new element has been added. We are haunted by the possibility that in a fit of bellicose passion we human beings may self-destruct. This danger casts a shadow over everything we love.

To avoid this new and cataclysmic danger, we must master an ancient problem. To end the plague of war, we must understand both the adaptive and the maladaptive dimensions of our fears and our efforts to protect ourselves.

For human beings to live in fear is nothing new. Insecurity has been the common lot of civilized peoples: as far back as the written record reaches, societies have preyed upon one another. This has been part of the cost of civilization. Among civilized societies, the struggle for power has continued from the dawn of civilization without relent.

The ceaseless struggle for power has structured the living energies of civilization into the form of fear. Two images of civilization illustrate the structure that fear has imposed: the image of the warrior, whose vital

3

energies of flesh and blood are encased in armor; and that of the fortress city, whose social life is surrounded by thick defensive walls. Fear drives what is alive into a hard, dead shell; it mandates that love is turned inward, while distrust and enmity guard the approaches from the world outside.

This structure governed by fear is adaptive in a world plagued with insecurities. To survive, human societies have made themselves ready to fight, amassing armed forces and adopting a martial spirit in defense of fatherland and national honor. It is the great warriors who have traditionally been sung as heroes, for they have been the peoples' protectors. And nations have recorded their histories as the chronicles of battles, for these bloody encounters have been the most visible molders of peoples' collective destinies. In a world shaped by chronic and inevitable armed conflict, it has been adaptive for civilized peoples to have their values shaped by the demands of war.

The search for security goes on in our times. Where earlier peoples sought stronger metals for their swords, we strive for more accurate missiles. The fortress walls of ancient cities are replaced now by dreams of "Star Wars" bubbles to make us impervious to enemy attack. The technology is new, but the fear and the adaptive strategy are quite ancient.

The nuclear arms race, however, reveals that adaptation is not the whole story. Adaptation means finding the way toward survival. An uncontrolled race for superiority in weapons of mass destruction is clearly not the best strategy for assuring survival for anyone. The inability of the warriors of two mighty nations to seize upon their overriding common interest suggests that dark passions have clouded their reason. Each side may legitimately fear the danger posed by the other. But the greater readiness of each superpower, for the past forty years, to attend to the fear of its dangerous enemy than to reduce the catastrophic danger created by their enmity suggests that maladaptive forces are also at work. A few decades ago, who would have thought that nations armed with such apocalyptic powers could continue their desperate, headlong dash to arm still further? In the 1950s, a comparative handful of nuclear weapons, ready for cumbersome delivery, held the world in terror; now there are tens of thousands of warheads poised minutes from their targets. Yet, both superpowers strive for more weapons with an anxiety and a determination that show no sign of abating.[*] Something is amiss in our ostensibly self-protective efforts.

---

[*]As this work goes to press, some most welcome signs of such abatement may be last becoming visible.

There is a saying that when the clock strikes 13 we must question not only the 13th ring but all those that have gone before. For us, the present spectacle of barely restrained escalation in nuclear arms can serve as the 13th ring in the chronicles of the civilized warrior.

Doubtless, part of our present problem is that the nuclear arms race is an atavistic attachment to a strategy that is no longer adaptive. After thousands of years when killing one's enemies enhanced one's security, it is difficult to grasp the implications of the possibility of nuclear winter. In this new kind of war, the blow may ultimately strike him who delivered it as hard as him on whom it falls.

But the problem goes much deeper than the intellectual inertia of strategists always fighting the last war. The persistence of the combative mode in the face of the possibility of mutual annihilation also reveals with striking clarity an irrationally destructive strain that has been present throughout the saga of human strife. There is an attachment to the struggle for preeminence, the need for an evil enemy, a "lust to annihilate."[1] Our means of self-protection have long also been a source of our own endangerment.

The clock has struck 13. It is time to reexamine the warrior spirit that has been shaped and manifested by ten thousand years of civilization.

Images of Imbalance

We like to have our truths simple: yes or no. Either we need to be warriors in a dangerous world or it is our warrior posture itself that endangers us. The problems that seem to produce the most intractable and futile of debates are those that require more complicated truths: yes *and* no. Our warrior spirit has been both a necessity and a danger. It is therefore crucial to be balanced in our reexamination of the warrior spirit, scorning neither those who seek security through a posture of strength—thus biting the hand that protects us—nor those who call for an end to the whole pattern of war.

Balance is essential to our inquiry, for it is balance that the warrior spirit within us has lacked. The world does pose dangers, but we have often been driven to exaggerate and exacerbate them. Realism combines with excess. The history of societies' efforts to defend themselves presents a curious mixture of sanity and madness. As we stand ready in the name of self-defense to destroy ourselves, it behooves us to peer deeply into this strain of irrationality in the warrior spirit.

Let us consider now three dimensions in which the legitimate pursuit of security is distorted by irrational excess.

THE SAMURAI AND THE FLEA

In an anarchic environment, every actor is in danger of being disregarded as inconsequential, of being swept aside by others who want what is his. The world has not been a safe place for those who have no sense of their own worth, and who are unwilling to protect their entitlements against those who would challenge them. Anarchy creates an environment in which each actor (group or individual) must be the guarantor of his own security. Thus *honor* has been considered of paramount importance. This has been true in the feudal societies of Japan and medieval Europe, in the fragmented village societies of the Balkans, in the tribal systems of the Middle East, and in the gunfighter culture of the American West. This dimension of the warrior spirit endures in that last frontier of anarchy, the international system of sovereign states. In such an environment, survival as an autonomous entity has required a readiness to fight in defense of one's honor.

But it seems that an element of excess can easily creep into this essential defense of one's worth and position. This is well illustrated in the samurai story about an unfortunate and well-intentioned servant who reached out to flick a flea from the back of his master, a samurai warrior. The great warrior, drawing his sword, wheeled on his servant and struck off his head. The servant's crime? Fleas are a problem for beasts. In the eyes of the samurai, the servant's gesture constituted the intolerable insult of likening the great warrior to a mere beast. A capital offense, as the samurai's swift and sure retribution demonstrated.

The warrior's cult of honor has always been given to such excess. It is not enough to defend what is essential. The most trivial slight can become an occasion for the shedding of blood: the warrior exhibits a hypersensitivity to insult and a tendency to retaliate out of proportion to the offense. This overdefense of honor and this insistence upon a grandiose self-image have characterized the ethics of aristocratic warrior classes. They have also shaped the conduct of nations, with their prickly sense of national honor.

What, we want to know, underlies this imbalance—this excessive defense of pride—in honorable men? This question is a central subject of parts 1 and 2, "Winning: The Worship of Strength" and "Winning: A World of Scarcity."

FINAL SOLUTION

In an intersocietal system of chronically competing groups, it has been important for each group to enlist the support and loyalty of its members. The group's struggle to survive both creates and mandates a sense of group identity, an image of the world in which a boundary is drawn between "us" and "them." It is essential for the members to feel cohesive because, as Benjamin Franklin once said, members of a society that do not hang together will surely hang separately.

But the tendency to divide the world into "us" and "them" can be carried to pathological lengths. To the Nazis, the extermination of the Jews was an act of self-defense against a pernicious and mortal threat to the identity and survival of the German nation. In the name of self-defense, the Nazis committed the most unspeakable aggression. In the name of purification, the Nazis fouled the whole image of civilization.

The Final Solution was an especially monstrous instance of an ancient problem in human conflict: the spirit of righteousness in the defense of the group. The boundaries around the group divide not only us from them but also good from evil. If we are all good, even our evil deeds are sanctified. If you are all evil, nothing we do to you can be worse than you deserve. Across the world's disputed boundaries, great crimes are committed with a feeling not of criminality but of righteousness: between Turks and Greeks, Arabs and Israelis, Protestants and Catholics. And the President of the United States, to meet the threat from "the focus of evil in the modern world," now builds "Peacekeeper" missiles, each one capable of incinerating the inhabitants of ten Soviet cities.

To penetrate to that heart of darkness that pumps the blood onto the pages of human history, we will investigate this pathology of "Boundaries" in part 3.

INQUISITORS AND CRUSADERS.

Group consensus helps forge group cohesiveness: the group that prays together stays together. Thus, societies tend to generate and instill some kind of social ideology, each orienting its members to a shared system of belief and motivation. This helps to explain the tendency to establish orthodoxies of belief, along with the corollary intolerance for heretical deviations.

But the need for cohesiveness is not adequate to explain the tortures and burnings of an Inquisition. The Grand Inquisitor guarded his Truth with the excessive zeal of the flea-flicked samurai avenging the insult to his sense of stature: "My truth is God's truth, and I shall not suffer any other beliefs to exist." The destructive intolerance of the inquisitor within his domain is practiced by the crusader across intersocietal boundaries: "Believe as I do, or else." Medieval Christian armies and fanatical followers of Muhammed the Prophet differed in their beliefs but were alike in their use of the sword as an instrument of persuasion. In the name of what is sacred, heads will roll. As they still do in our times—in the liquidation of Trotskyites by Stalinists, in the Cultural Revolution of Maoist China, in the violence fomented by Khomeini's Iran, and so on.

What leads to this zealous certainty, combined with an inability to respect others' truths, or even to tolerate the errors of others? Part 4, "God's Truth," will delve into this question.

These examples illustrate dimensions of the warrior's historical and enduring tendency toward excess. In each case, it is clear that the warrior becomes violent in response to some profound sense of threat. But that threat is of a different kind from the objective, physical insecurity that has made the warrior spirit necessary for civilized peoples. We must ask: what is the nature of the fears that lead to such excess?

The Flight from the Human Condition

People go to war to defend many things. It is sane to defend our lives and homelands against those who would take them from us. But the engines of destruction in human affairs are often fueled by a defensiveness of a different kind.

Contrary to rationalist and materialist assumptions about human motivation, what we human beings seem most ferocious in defending are certain beliefs we hold—or want to hold—about ourselves. We are not weak, we insist, nor are we insignificant. We most emphatically are not evil. Nor, we declare, are we confused or bewildered. It is in defense of these beliefs that we have so often been ready to kill and to die. This helps explain why the warrior spirit has been tinged with madness. *For these beliefs about ourselves we defend so zealously we inwardly sense to be false.*

We feel our confusion, but we insist on denying it because it is frightening. Even less are we prepared to acknowledge the painful guilt from the sense of our own evil. And, outraged by our condition as mere specks at the mercy of forces beyond our control, we fight to uphold a grandiose sense of our importance and power. The human condition can be terrifying, and we fight to protect our flight from that reality. The fact that we are struggling against what we unconsciously feel is true only makes us more desperate and destructive, and ultimately more self-destructive. *

This, then, is the threat that leads to excesses of violence: the threat that we will have to confront unbearably frightening aspects of our experience of ourselves. This idea of flight from the human condition helps to illuminate each of the images of imbalance just discussed.

THE BURDEN OF BEWILDERMENT [SEE PART 4; "GOD'S TRUTH"].

Who are we to be so certain of our truth? Of the earth's creatures, we are the only ones prone to the agony of uncertainty. Life developed for several billion years before an animal emerged that could wonder. Only with the development of the human mind did living creatures confront the overwhelming mysteriousness of existence. What are we doing on this earth? What is our place in this cosmos that looms before us silent, unexplained? What will become of us? In human beings, the spark of awareness gives a ray of light to reveal the galactic vastness of darkness. Only for an animal whose genes do not chart its destiny is it necessary to ask: how are we to live? We call ourselves Homo sapiens—"man knowing"—expressing our wish more than our reality. For it is the human condition not so much to possess answers as to be confronted with bewildering questions. This perpetual confrontation with the unknown can be frightening. So we retreat from it, preferring certainty to truth.

The posture of zealous certainty is therefore a denial of part of what it is to be human. The zealot-warrior's approach to the overwhelming task of unraveling the mysteries of existence is exemplified by Alexander the Great's solution to the challenge of the Gordian knot. Confronted by the famous knot, which for centuries had defied all who attempted it, Alexander drew his sword and cut it in two. Thus was the Gordian knot "untied." The blade, the stake, the rack—by the tools of coercion can reality be compelled to recant.

---

*In focusing on the issues constellating around the flight from the reality of our condition, this work does not pretend to be an exhaustive psychology of war and peace—just to explore a vital dimension of the problem. Conversely, the problem of our flight from the human condition has ramifications far beyond the issues of war and peace. Indeed, our inability to embrace fully what we are and what we experience distorts everything we do. In this work, however, the focus will be on the implications of our flight from reality for the problem of human destructiveness.

THE FLIGHT FROM BAD CONSCIENCE [SEE PART 3, "BOUNDARIES"].

Then there is the problem of evil. As Genesis shows, of all the creatures in the Garden there is only one that eats of the Tree of the Knowledge of Good and Evil. That myth also shows that we have gained this knowledge at great cost. Paradise lost is the loss of innocence, and in the place of innocence comes guilt. We are freed of the tight regimen of instinct that governs other animals, but we must nonetheless be governed. Therefore we learn to govern ourselves, bringing into ourselves a social law in the form of a conscience (or superego). This internalized law monitors our impulses in order to condemn and restrain those impulses that would run us afoul of our social environment. To be human, therefore, has seemed to mean to be at war with ourselves, to judge a part of our natural being as evil.

When this internal war rages with an intensity and brutality too painful to bear, we may abandon all efforts to reconcile our social and natural selves. Identifying only with our "good" part, we banish our forbidden desires to "otherness." Freud reflected this third-person separateness when he named the reservoir of natural impulses the "id," the "it." Not *I*, but *it*: the evil is not part of me, but is "out there."

This false boundary eases the burden of trying to reconcile the irreconcilable, but it does not bring peace. The war rages still between the law and the desire; the evil that we do not acknowledge as our own still lurks as an unceasing threat. To preserve the comforting illusion that we are only good, we need to find out there an embodiment of our denied evil. We must cleave the world with boundaries to protect the lie of our evil denied.

The warrior may thus have need of his enemy. Consider the prototypical warrior Achilles as portrayed in that masterpiece of warrior literature, the *Iliad*. Achilles, sulking because of an injury to his overweening pride, sets in motion a drama that leads to the death of his much-beloved friend Patroclus at the hands of Hector, the Trojan hero. Achilles' suffering is intense, for his grief is compounded by remorse. Then he finds his release from the pain of guilt. Achilles moves from accusing himself to blaming Hector, venomously pouring upon him "accusations he shortly before inflicted upon himself . . . And Achilles not only kills Hector, he utterly degrades him . . . And through this violence, Achilles is redeemed."[2]

The enemy is a kind of savior: he too can die for our sins.

THE MYTH OF OMNIPOTENCE [SEE PARTS 1 AND 2, "WINNING"].

Shelley's famous poem recounts the inscription on the fabled monument of Ozymandias:

> And on the pedestal these words appear:
> "My name is Ozymandias, King of Kings:
> Look on my works, ye mighty, and despair!"
> Nothing beside remains. Round the decay
> Of that colossal wreck, boundless and bare
> The lone and level sands stretch far away.

We are born more helpless than virtually any other animal. Yet, according to psychologists, we emerge into consciousness with a feeling of omnipotence. We believe the cosmos is ruled by our thoughts and feelings. Tiny, quivering bundles of fears and desires, we enter the world with a boundless egocentrism: we are each the center of our universe. What a painful shock to learn of our true place in the order of things. We are small, and prey to hostile forces we cannot control. Other people, with power over us, may be indifferent to our needs. And the final insult: we learn that we are mortal.

Like our fellow creatures, we must die. Unlike them, we know it. With the important ability to conceive of the future comes the unwelcome insight that our own future is limited. These limits are not easy to bear.

Mere mortals: our being subject to death is the quintessence of our limitations. It is telling that among the Greeks the gods were the same as we mortals—in motives and morals—save in their power and their immortality. This concept of the gods reveals the thrust of the aspirations of a warrior people. While men cannot be gods, warrior peoples have often held out to their men a compensatory kind of "immortality": in the achievement of heroic status on the battlefield. It is one of those paradoxes in which our species specializes: the warrior hero can become an "immortal" through his proficiency as an agent of death.

The serpent in Genesis had it right: people will do anything to be as gods. Behold the warrior, godlike in his power and glory. He is more than flesh and blood. His shiny armor renders him invulnerable, and his iron will will not be turned aside. The serpent promised—falsely—that our act of hubris would bring eternal life. But if we cannot be immortal, then we can at least enjoy the illusion of controlling death by inflicting it on others. Hitler, with his obsession with and fear of death, played the lord of destruction. Now, on launching pads on both sides of the world, great rockets are ready to spurt forth not the seeds of life but the fires of death.

The power of life and death is a godlike power. The warriors of the nuclear giants will not easily give up their power over the earth's survival, even under the threat of annihilation by the other. For ingrained in the warrior is the denial of vulnerability, and the compensatory lust for the power to destroy. Afraid to be mere men, the warriors yearn for the apotheosis of omnipotence.

On witnessing the first atomic explosion, Robert Oppenheimer declared, quoting the *Bhagavad Gita*:

> If the radiance of a thousand suns
> Were burst at once into the sky
> That would be like the splendour of the Mighty One.[3]

And to think: we are its Creators!

Thus does the sword deliver us from the human condition. Our will be done, it says, assuaging the suppressed pain of our impotence. It cleaves the world into the righteous and the infidel, leaving us on the right side. And it cuts through the knotty problems of existence, laying to rest visions other than our own.

It appears we are at war because we would otherwise have no peace.

A WORD ABOUT "US."

I speak of "us" human beings, then I use some monster like Hitler as an illustration of "our" condition. Some, I imagine, will object to such a connection. What has a Hitler to do with *us*? Nothing, many would like to believe. But though it is an understandable temptation to regard the likes of Hitler or Pol Pot or Idi Amin as totally "other,"* it is a dangerous error to succumb to that temptation.

The monsters among us provide a valuable insight into the human condition. The inner demons that make a Hitler monstrous are to be found in the rest of us as well. As I have studied these pathologies of destructiveness, everything I have found in these destroyers resonates with some part of myself. The difference is partly a matter of degree, but, more important, it is a matter of the way in which the elements are organized. What differentiates Hitler is that the demonic elements that you and I also have within us *gained possession* of him. What we may keep hidden and under control, in a Hitler or a Stalin showed its naked face to the world.

---

*This temptation is discussed further in part 3, "Boundaries."

The value of these extreme and monstrous examples lies in the opportunity they provide to learn the faces of the demons that lurk also in us. Then we might recognize those demons for what they are if they should come to us at some stressful moment and bid us allow them to take charge of our "protection." Hitler was a destroyer who would have brought the whole world down with him. As we try to preserve our survival in an age of nuclear weapons, it behooves us to come to know the face of the world-destroying impulse, and to recognize that this impulse might rise also in us.

This is not, therefore, a book about "them," but about "us." Much of the work that is done in the name of peace these days is done by an "us" seeking to overcome "them," those bad people in this or that government who perpetuate strife. Of course, there are moral distinctions to be made among people, but sometimes the most morally profound act is to let go of the preoccupation with those distinctions. Psychology makes important and interesting analytic distinctions between this personality type and that, while the anthropologists tell us of the profound differences in the ways that different cultures interpret their worlds. But I believe there is also an important intellectual understanding to be gained by setting those distinctions aside to look at the plight of "the civilized human animal."

Out of Weakness, therefore, while in no way denying the validity of the differences among us, will largely disregard those differences in an effort to gain some larger insight into the nature of the human condition. My intent is to hold up not so much a window before the panorama of human destructiveness displayed out there in history, as a mirror in which we can peer into our own heart of darkness—and light.

II. THE HUMAN PSYCHE
AMONG THE FORCES OF HISTORY

The Tragedy of History

T he preceding section, in arguing that we fight because we are in flight from "the human condition," is misleading in one important respect. It implies that the distress from which we strive to escape is a part of our birthright, inextricable from our inherent nature. True, we did not begin with perfect peace, any more than we were created in a perfect paradise. But with the unfolding of the destiny of our species, something of both peace and paradise was lost. It is not "the human condition" per se that our warrior spirit seeks to deny. What we cannot bear is the human condition as it has been rendered by our tormented history. This correction implies both a blessing and a tragedy concerning human destiny.

All human beings are fallible and vincible, and all must control their impulses. Were this enough to set us at war with our condition and with one another, we all would be conduits of destruction. But some of us know peace. If it were incompatible with peace to be intelligent, social, and mortal, there would be scant basis to hope for the survival of our species. But there *is* ground for hope. We are capable of living at peace. This is the blessing.

The tragedy lies in the way social evolutionary forces beyond our control have compounded the inevitable stresses of human life and made them more than we can bear. This is the tragedy described in my book, *The Parable of the Tribes: The Problem of Power in Social Evolution.* That work shows how the very strength of our species became transmuted into the means of our undoing. When, with our creativity, we extricated ourselves from the regime of biologically evolved nature by developing civilization, we seemed to become free. But, by a tragic irony, the rise of civilization only subjected us to new and harsher necessities.

I will very briefly show how this is so.

The regime of nature is closely governed. Though each creature is free to follow the law of its own nature, the evolutionary process that has inscribed that law also ensures that this law fits into an overarching order that protects the whole living system. The biological order of nature, though it has no ruler, is far from anarchic. For nature imposes limits.

With the rise of civilization, the limits began to fall away. Hunting-gathering societies, though fully human, were still compelled to occupy a niche essentially the same as that in which our species evolved. In their size and structure, and in their dependence upon what nature spontaneously provided, such societies were continuous with our primate past. But when, ten thousand years ago, human beings began rearranging the ecosystem for their own purposes, they became the first creatures to invent their own way of life. Suddenly, all things seemed to become possible for the creative animal: larger and more settled societies, greater division of labor and social complexity. The breakthrough in man's relationship with nature created open-ended possibilities for social innovation. The new civilized forms of society possessed an unprecedented capacity for unlimited growth as a living entity.

But this apparent freedom is not what it seems. What seems to be freedom for any one society is anarchy in an interacting system of such societies. For the first time in the three-billion-year history of life, living entities were compelled to interact unregulated by any life-serving order. This is anarchy, the condition the great English philosopher Thomas Hobbes misnamed but analyzed correctly. Hobbes called it the state of nature, whereas in fact it is a state of unnature, peculiar to civilization. But he was right about what anarchy dictates to those who live in it: they are compelled to engage in the fearful "war of all against all."

Thus, civilized peoples have inevitably been condemned to a ceaseless struggle for power. This inescapable struggle, combining in a deadly way with the open-ended possibilities for innovation, has engendered a new evolutionary process: the selection for the ways of power.

This is the parable of the tribes:

> Imagine a group of tribes living within reach of one another. If all choose the way of peace, then all may live in peace. But what if all but one choose peace, and that one is ambitious for expansion and conquest? What can happen to the others when confronted by an ambitious and potent neighbor? Perhaps one tribe is attacked and defeated, its people destroyed and its lands seized for the use of the victors. Another is defeated, but this one is not exterminated; rather, it is subjugated and transformed to serve the conqueror. A third, seeking to avoid such disaster, flees from the area into some inaccessible (and undesirable) place, and its former homeland becomes part of the growing empire of the power-seeking tribe. Let us suppose that others observing these developments decide to defend

themselves in order to preserve themselves and their autonomy. But the irony is that successful defense against a power-maximizing aggressor requires a society to become more like the society that threatens it. Power can be stopped only by power, and if the threatening society has discovered ways to magnify its power through innovations in organization or technology (or whatever) the defensive society will have to transform itself into something more like its foe in order to resist the external force.

I have just outlined four possible outcomes for the threatened tribes: destruction, absorption and transformation, withdrawal, and imitation. *In every one of these outcomes the ways of power are spread throughout the system.*[4]

Of all the many conceivable cultural options apparently open to the civilized creature, only the ways of power can survive. Ways of life that bring weakness in the inescapable competitive struggle—however intrinsically valuable and humane—are swept aside. Power is like a contaminant which, once introduced into this system of competing societies, spreads inexorably.

This reign of power is dictated not by human nature but by the anarchy into which we are inadvertently plunged. Any creature whose cultural evolution brought it across the threshold of civilization would have to contend with this agonizing evolutionary process. Any such creature would be condemned to engage in a ceaseless struggle in which destruction is not part of a larger, harmonious order that protects sacred living systems. And the resulting process of selection would magnify the worst of that creature's potentialities into laws of its cutural existence.

This is the tragedy of the human experience so far: because of human creativity but not because of human choice, the thrust of civilization's development has been toward the ways of power and destruction. Our wonderful qualities of mind and imagination have condemned us to live in chronic fear and insecurity.

This view of the dynamics of the evolution of civilization puts a new light on our problems in coping with "the human condition." The inescapable problem of power that arose with civilization has both intensified the burdens of our condition and weakened our capacity to bear them. It is the wounds inflicted upon us by history that have made us so uncomfortable being what we are. Were the world around us not so threatening, we would not be so defensive.

Imbalance in a World
Where Power Reigns

PRIDE IN AN INSULTING WORLD [SEE PARTS 1 AND 2, "WINNING"].

Most animals, in their natural state, comport themselves with dignity and poise. Not only the regal lion, but also the grazing deer; not only the elephant, but also the shy gorilla. Anthropologists dwelling among the few hunter-gatherer societies remaining in our times have noted the dignity of their informants. To feel craven and of little worth is not our birthright. But neither were we fashioned to strut with bloated pride.

The hypertrophic ego of the warrior is a sign of a perturbation of the natural human instrument. Like a musical string pulled from its place, injured human pride oscillates between extremes. The inflated narcissism of the warrior is one extreme of an oscillating spirit; it is a rebound from the other extreme, the experience of being degraded.

At the core of this narcissism is the feeling of having been wronged.[5] Not that being wronged enhances one's self-esteem—it injures it. From bad treatment one absorbs the feeling that one is bad. However, mistreatment can also engender the insistence on the opposite, compensatory image of oneself as superior. Conscious megalomania, as Jung observed, is the visible companion of unconscious feelings of inferiority. We may surmise that when the samurai's servant plucked the flea, he plucked also a raw and deeply wounded nerve. It is not for nothing that boot camp, to mold warriors, humiliates and terrorizes the recruits. To make "a few good men," first treat them worse than dogs. Thus does the warrior gain his pride.

The social evolutionary theory of *The Parable of the Tribes* helps show why history has pulled the cord of dignity and poise in the human spirit toward the side of degradation, creating the reactive spring to the other extreme. Historical forces that disregard human needs push people toward defensive grandiosity. The inevitability of the rule of power makes it inevitable that people will worship power. A species caught up in a destructive spiral out of its control will place control inordinately high among its values. People will seek occasions where they can impose their will to compensate for the epidemic experience of impotence. In a process where everyone is losing, it is a sweet balm to prove oneself a winner.

The world insults us by not letting us embody our humanity. Forced to be less than by nature we are, we posture as if to be more. We would accept being weak in a safe world. But it is unacceptable to be weak in a world where the mighty rule by force. It would be tolerable to be a mortal creature whom time will allow to ripen like fruit and let fall. But it is a crushing burden to live under the constant threat of annihilation.

MYSTERY MADE SINISTER [SEE PART 4, "GOD'S TRUTH"].

The same sense of peril that places a premium on control also makes the sense of certainty most welcome. We are frightened to peer out into the darkness not only because our limited knowledge cannot illuminate it but because we have reason to believe that dangers await us there. The more the landscape is strewn with traps, the greater our need for reliable maps. The sense of mystery that, in a more benign world, we might have apprehended with wonder and awe now creeps toward us with terror mounted upon its back.

By condemning civilized peoples to inescapable insecurity, civilization has therefore greatly intensified the temptation to cling to false certainties. The experiments of social psychologists show that the greater the stress, the less tolerance for ambiguity. Over thousands of years of civilization, the larger human experiment has demonstrated the same relationship. The more one senses that a false step may mean disaster, the more impelled one feels to know with certainty that one is walking on the true path. Dogma is the child of anxiety.

THE WAR WITHOUT, THE WAR WITHIN [SEE PART 3, "BOUNDARIES"].

The way the intersocietal struggle for power intensifies our intrapsychic war of good and evil is less obvious, but the connection is just as strong.

To survive, a society needs power enough to withstand threats from its competitors. The level needed in a given competitive system rises over time as the surviving societies innovate to tap new sources of power. The sources of power lie in all dimensions of culture: in technology, in political organization, in economic productivity—and in the psychological structure of its members. Because of our wonderful ability to learn, we can be trapped into learning the ways of power. Because of human malleability, we can be bent to fit into the machinery of power.[*]

Regrettably, the inner peace of civilized human beings can be incompatible with the survival of their societies struggling in the toils of

---

[*]For an extended portrait of how human beings have been shaped to meet the demands of power systems, see chapter 5 of *The Parable of the Tribes.*

intersocietal anarchy. For the demands of power are often opposed to the needs of the human organism. The more intense the struggle for power, therefore, the more fiercely will the demands of society make war upon the natural inclinations of the human animal. Internalizing these demands, which are the fruits of the war outside, thus exacerbates, if it does not entirely engender, the war within the human psyche.

The greater the gap between the internalized social demands and human nature, the more painful will be the intrapsychic conflict. We are more likely to be taught to regard our natural desires as evil; the warring parts within us will be less reconcilable. To deliver ourselves from pain, to experience ourselves as more whole and harmonious within, we will be tempted to deny our evil. But since the sense of evil does not simply disappear, we will project our forbidden desires out into the world, and reconstrue the war inside us as a war out in the world.

Thus does anarchy in the world cycle conflict into and back out of the human organism. The struggle for power doubly inclines civilized people toward paranoia: it thrusts us into the insecure Hobbesean "state of nature" that provides so ample a supply of potential enemies, and it drives us to see in others what we cannot bear to acknowledge in ourselves.

Out of Weakness

Thus also are many of the heroic postures of human greatness revealed in a new light. Just as many of the impressive edifices of civilization are shown, by the parable of the tribes, as defensive adaptations to unwelcome necessities, so are much of the power and glory of the warrior now seen as compensations for weakness. We posture to display our power and purity and certainty; but, in Hamlet's phrase, we do protest too much. We pretend to be godlike because our inner torment has rendered us the sickest of animals. It is not because we are free of fear that we charge the enemy, but because we are fleeing inner demons. We assume the posture of might to keep from caving in under the weight of the burdens history has imposed on our species. We are warlike not out of power, but out of weakness.

Chicken and Egg:
Bad History Makes Bad People
Make Bad History . . .

The destructive forces at work in human systems, and those in human beings, thus work in a chicken-and-egg fashion. Each unfolds into the other. But here there can be an escape from the paradoxical dilemma of "which came first?" The solution is provided by *The Parable of the Tribes*.

The anarchic circumstances that emerge when a creature's cultural development crosses the threshold of civilization can explain the "chicken" of the chronic systemic struggle for power without requiring any prior existence of the egg of irrational bellicosity or destructiveness in that creature's nature. That is, circumstance is a *sufficient* explanation of the rise of war. Any creature whose behavioral repertoire includes aggressiveness (and that is virtually any creature) and whose psychic makeup can allow the development of neurotic conflict (and the susceptibility to such a malady is probably an inevitable concomitant of the malleability required for the development of culture) could emerge onto the stage of its history as maddened as we find the warriors of the human chronicle.

BEYOND PSYCHOLOGICAL REDUCTIONISM

Many of those who are most sensitive to the psychological issues involved in human destructiveness have construed the problem in terms of a different logic. People are not shaped by history, the reasoning goes, but by their childhood experiences in the microcosm of the family. The problems in the macrocosm are outgrowths of the dynamics within the microcosm: i.e., chickens have to begin as eggs.

According to this view, if we find in some culture a pathological insistence on the triumph of their will, look to the upbringing of the young: there we may discover a parental campaign to break the will of the child. Where there is a growth of narcissism, the root will likely lie in maternal care that neglected many of the child's important emotional needs. If we find that patriarchal societies produce men more inclined toward violence and toward a Manichaean view of the world, the source of the strife may lie in the tendency of patriarchal families to withhold from their infants the kind of gentle touching and nursing infants need.[6] Andrew Jackson told the story that when, as a little boy, he went crying to his mother, she gave him not solace but the rebuke that little girls were made to cry, and little boys to fight: it is mothering like this that gave America a culture fit for the fighting and killing of Indians.[7] In short, because the warriors begin as babies, the problem of belligerent passions *must* begin with the way those babies are treated.

This approach to the problem is indispensable to an understanding of the experiential core of the human dilemma, but it is also misleading as an explanatory guide to human history. Tracing the genesis in the individual human soul of the passions that disturb us is essential to disclosing their true nature. But the logic is false that underlies the assumption that only a "Genesis" like this can tell the story of the creation of the historical pattern of war.

Consider, for example, the vivid and profound portrait of violence in ancient Greek culture found in Eli Sagan's *The Lust to Annihilate.* Sagan argues persuasively that among the Greeks a passion for vengeance was the fruit of the tyrannical and spiteful treatment of sons by fathers. The poisonous pattern perpetuates itself through the generations, as the sons grow up to be fathers who deal with their sons the same way their fathers had dealt with them. The family pattern is seen as *necessarily* the prime mover in the cultural dynamic of violence, as if the vicious cycle could begin in no other way.

But the poison might have seeped into the family system from an altogether different realm. One could begin with a society where the family pattern was healthy and loving. Next, subject that society to terror and oppression from outside, humiliating the men and filling them with a rage that cannot be expressed toward its legitimate object. The results are likely to include major alterations in the family system, for these men will not remain the kind of fathers they were before. The parable of the tribes shows how just such poisons inevitably spread among civilized peoples, once the contaminant of power-maximization is introduced. Because the structure of the overarching system allows power free reign, the tyranny of a destructive few can crush the more humane ways of many others, including their gentle and loving family systems.

Indeed, a macrocosm that allows only the ways of power to survive can transform a pattern of family violence from mere pathology into an indispensable contributor to social survival. The breeding of fighters becomes, however lamentably, an adaptive strategy. (Without harsh mothers like Andrew Jackson's, North America might now be dominated by members of a different culture.) This suggests a different perspective on the observation made by some that where we find patriarchy we find also war and violence. The connection may not be, as some assume, that the domination of society by men is evil and creates the evils of war. More likely, the relationship is in the opposite direction. Where circumstance has made the struggle for power acute, the martial virtues become more important to social survival. The ascension of the martial virtues inevitably means an increase in the status of men—and not just of men as they existed in some peaceful bygone period, but of men filled with the passions required of fighters. Out of the evils of war, therefore, can arise the domination of society by men, the transformation of men into warriors, and a pattern of child rearing that perpetuates the brutality and rage conducive to success in the business of killing. Indeed, the struggle for power not only produces injuries as byproducts, it can make the side effects of injuries requirements for survival.

THE ROLE OF THE EGG

To say that there is madness at work in history is not necessarily to say that the root cause of the madness is psychological. But to acknowledge this, in turn, is not to deny that it is of compelling importance to heal our emotional and familial wounds. Although forces on a more than human scale may have determined our overall social evolutionary course, forces within the human soul have played a necessary role in the perpetuation of that course. And that course will change only if humankind can achieve a change of heart.

For one thing, the psychological patterns, once begun, have a momentum of their own. From generation to generation, for better or worse, we tend to replicate the form of humanity to which we have been exposed. The cycle of child abuse illustrates this.* As the world has sown in us, so does it reap from us. Thus it is that the "egg" of our psychological structure tends to perpetuate itself through the generations, even independently of reinforcement from the chicken of macrocosmic forces.

Another factor bears reiteration. The egg does grow again into a chicken. Even as the destructive aspects of social evolution make us mad, our madness drives us to act destructively upon the stage of

---

*"Without exception in our study group of abusing parents, there is a history of having been raised in the same style which they have repeated in their pattern of rearing their own children."[8] The way we recapitulate what we have received, and the impediment this constitutes to moral progress for humankind are the themes of my book *Sowings and Reapings: The Cycling of Good and Evil in the Human System*.

history. While the brutal and authoritarian pre-Nazi German family pattern may be the fruit of historical forces, the toxic fruit once ripened and fallen would sprout forth into the death camps to poison history still further. Although Russian paranoia may derive from the traumas of historical experience, such a world view in the minds of a few men in the Kremlin may bring on a final cataclysm of destruction that breaks all the eggs and incinerates the chicken. It is one of the tragedies of the human saga that the very wounds that history inflicts upon us make us all the more suitable players in the drama of violence and pain.

Taken together, these two points—the self-perpetuation of psychological patterns and the role of these patterns in channeling the currents of history—suggest that a psychological or spiritual transformation of civilized peoples is a *necessary* element in redeeming our civilization. Without a new kind of egg, we will be condemned to keep hatching fighting cocks.

OPPORTUNITY KNOCKS

The importance of the spiritual dimension in governing human destiny is growing. This is because social evolution has now progressed to a point where it is increasingly possible for mankind to begin to control the destructive forces *endemic to our systems* that heretofore have largely controlled mankind. Human choice can have a correspondingly greater role in guiding social evolution; wisdom, if we can develop and tap it, can shape a more humane world.

What is changing? The root of our problem, according to the parable of the tribes, is anarchy. Civilization inevitably arose in a fragmented state, and under such circumstances inevitably it was power and not collective human choice that ruled our common destiny. With no escape from the struggle for power, the world was rendered unsafe for our most humane and gentle values. The spirit of love could not rule except within special sanctuaries, such as within monastery walls. The understanding that all men are brothers could not redeem the world, but could only ameliorate its viciousness as long as the anarchic world order allowed evil to spread like a contaminant, enabling one Cain to slay a dozen Abels or to force them to become like him in self-defense.

But now this anarchy can begin to fade away, replaced by a more integrated world order. Now, for the first time in history, it is possible for representatives of the world's peoples to meet together to address the problems that we face as one species on one planet. As the original fragmentation diminishes with the rise of an interconnected global system, it becomes possible for humankind to cooperate in formulating and exercising its collective will. By freeing itself from the unwanted reign of power, our species can gain the power to govern its own destiny. An enlightened, peace-loving human consciousness can begin now to create a world safe for its own way of being to thrive in security—not in special sanctuaries alone, but all across the open face of the earth.

But it seems that civilized peoples are not yet prepared to realize these emerging possibilities for a more peaceful world order. Our spiritual maladies, the scars of our tormented history, linger on to perpetuate the torment. Again and again we see nations with the opportunity to make peace, but preferring instead to cling to strife. (Iran and Iraq are now bleeding each other to death along the rivers where civilization was born.) Wars too readily seem holy. (For an Arab leader, even to talk directly with Israel of the possibilities for peace remains a dangerous step to take, as the example of the late Anwar Sadat lamentably demonstrates.) To draw the line gives deeper satisfaction than does overcoming divisions. (Hardliners in the current U.S. administration argue that negotiations and agreements with our ruthless adversary can only render us more insecure, and that the best way to preserve security is an American victory in an unrestrained arms race.)

The destructive logic of our evolving civilized system has tragically narrowed the range of cultural options open to humankind. But it is the destructive illogic of the human soul that hinders us from choosing the wisest of the options available to us. Even if, as the parable of the tribes argues, our dilemma did not originate in human folly or wickedness, much of what now stands in the way of resolving that dilemma lies in the domain of human consciousness.

It is necessary, therefore, to explore the irrational passions that divert us from the path where our true good lies.

III. THE SPIRITUAL CHALLENGE

Are we up to the task of turning our civilization away from the path of destruction?

The Human Crossing

We are compelled to live in a time of continuous crisis, "crisis" in the literal sense of a time of decision. We stand at a crossing of the roads. In the coming centuries, human history must go in one of two directions: toward destruction or toward a radically healing transformation. The powers we wield—with our weapons of destruction and in our continuous impact on the environment—are now so great that either we must attune ourselves to the life-serving order around and within us, or we must perish for our errors and our crimes. Utopia, as Buckminster Fuller once said, is becoming the only viable option open to us. To live at this crossroads, with all life at stake, poses for us a considerable spiritual challenge.

FALSE HOPE, COMFORTING DESPAIR

It seems a tendency of the modern temperament to demand a ready solution to any problem. The problem of war and peace will surely frustrate that demand.

The nineteenth-century capitalists believed the rewards of the open market had rendered war obsolete; Marxists later assured themselves that the comradeship of collective ownership would eliminate the causes of societal bellicosity. These two beliefs were fatally misguided, as the carnage of two world wars and the harsh expansionism of the Soviet empire all too clearly demonstrated. In today's peace movement, there is the idea that war is simply a species of mistake, a consequence of unfortunate misunderstanding that more open communication could prevent. This belief is as naive as its predecessors, and we may but hope that history will spare us its catastrophic refutation. The problem of war and peace runs too deep to admit of any easy answer.

Things could be worse: the matter of war and peace could be not difficult but hopeless. Our need to fight and kill could be as ineradicable a part of our nature as is our need for food and water. Some believe this is in fact so, and, were they right, it is hard to conceive how the cycle of violence could ever be broken as long as human beings people this planet with no zookeeper placed above us to hold us in awe and to keep us from satisfying our lust for one another's blood. But even if violence is not an inherent and unalterable part of our nature, the sources of war are deeply ingrained in the human condition as we find it, and they will not quickly be uprooted.

According to the analysis presented here, the problem of war has two principal sources: it is an inevitable result of the fragmented and anarchic form in which our civilization has arisen; and it is an expression of the war, engendered by our tormented history, between ourselves and the conditions of our lives. Neither source will be quickly eliminated. We have begun to diminish the fragmentation of civilization, but an end to anarchy and its dangers is difficult to imagine in less than a century, even with history's ever-accelerating pace. A spiritual transformation of humankind is hardly an easier undertaking, nor more quickly accomplished. None of us alive today will dwell in the promised land, or even see it clearly on the horizon.

To face the problem in this form is a central part of the spiritual challenge we face. To insist that there be some "quick fix," on the other hand, is a manifestation of the same spiritual deficiency it seeks to solve. Like the sources of the warrior's excess described earlier, the need to believe that the New Age is almost at hand shows a refusal to confront the reality of our condition. As our false pride and false certainties drive us to make war, so can our false hopes disable us from undertaking the proper work of making peace. Those who underestimate the magnitude of the task will focus on momentary tactics where a long-term strategy may be needed. More important, they will lack the spiritual stamina to persevere when they discover that their efforts leave the problem not greatly diminished.

Facing how entrenched is the problem of war, however, constitutes just the first step. The second is to maintain hope in spite of it. If on one side of our path is the trap of false hope, on the other is the abyss of despair.

Despair, like false hope, represents a deficiency of courage. The idea, often heard, that mankind is surely doomed to exterminate itself is not the brave acceptance of unpleasant truth it pretends to be. Rather, it is a comforting abdication of responsibility. The pessimistic certainty of failure, like the Panglossian certainty of quick success, gives a kind of comfort: if it is hopeless, we need do nothing; if the issue is resolved already, we can ignore it. The truth is that the future remains for us to write—or to obliterate. To avoid plummeting from our perilous path will take all the strength and wisdom we possess.

Faith

But how are we not to lose heart, with the dangers so great and with the redemption of history and the salvation of humanity so far from accomplishment? A special kind of courage is required of us, one with an ancient name: faith.

There is a power that emanates from those who make the leap, thrusting themselves into the current of history with an assurance that the bridge to the promised land will form. Faith like this is a species of strength within a healthy organism. In *The Biology of Hope*, Lionel Tiger shows how we are molded by our evolution to move into the future with hope. Faith is an embodiment of organismic strength, and is in turn a source of strength.

Through our acts of faith, our kind can make the crossing. In the jungle, huge columns of ants cross great streams because those in the vanguard do not turn back but go forward into the perilous current, making a bridge with their flesh over which the many coming after them can safely cross.

Strength at the Core

This is an inquiry about humanity's moving "out of weakness" in two senses: first, in the sense that it is "from weakness" that we have infused irrational excess into our legitimate efforts as warriors to protect ourselves; second, in the sense that it is "beyond weakness" that humankind must go.

FALSE STRENGTH AND TRUE

Our species has made itself mighty, but our strength resides not at the core of our being. We can destroy the earth, but we lack the solid strength of a healthy creature comfortable with itself. War is a test of strength. But the war against our bondage to war is a test of another, truer kind of strength.

We have understandably worshiped the might of the warrior, for his sword has governed much of our history and has divided those who shall live from those who shall die. Behold him, glorious and proud in his armor. Yet, we can see beyond the armor to the weakness. Armor, though a form of strength, is a signal of vulnerability concealed beneath: what is secure does not need to be covered with dead layers of protection. The body of the warrior, even stripped of its metal protection, stands before us "armored." The Reichians speak of "body armor," the bunchings of muscle that tighten the body, blocking the flow of life energy, in an effort to keep what is threatening from penetrating into one's experience. In the statues of the warrior through history, we see that the body of the warrior wears such armor of flesh and blood. His body bears the imprint of fear, which makes his body rigid and closed.

Another kind of strength is imaged in the representations of Jesus and Buddha. Jesus's body shows vulnerability. It is not that he is more vulnerable than the warrior, but rather that he is comfortable enough with his vulnerability not to hide it. The Buddha too appears unguarded. His belly is not the warrior's scrubboard of abdominal muscles, but a fullness and openness to what may come in. Vigilance has yielded to receptivity. Both Buddha and Jesus are represented frequently with hands open and outstretched, expressing at once receptivity, generosity, and unthreatening goodwill. These are bodies governed by love, with its openness to flows that dissolve boundaries. These are bodies that rest on a foundation of true strength—strength at the core.

The polarity of love and fear is not the equivalent of good versus evil. We have amassed our awesome destructive powers in response to true dangers. The world has been and remains a threatening place, and we are equipped to experience fear because fear is an adaptive response to danger. But when we come to worship this defensive kind of strength, it indicates that we have lost touch with the possibility of true security—such as that embodied by the tranquil Buddha. When we are so enthralled with our defenses that we deny our vulnerability, we only bring the danger closer. It is the power of a Jesus or a Gandhi, with their courage to display vulnerability, that can move us to build upon our common humanity, that community of peace that we ultimately need for our protection.

Although trying to move from our present condition toward true strength is all too much like trying to lift ourselves by the bootstraps, it is useful at least to envision our goals. In providing us with these models of strength at the core, the spiritual traditions of many of our cultures have, for several thousand years, helped us toward such envisioning. Humanity, struggling with the problems of violence and destruction, has had the wisdom to create and to hold before its sight images of unfrightened vulnerability and gentle power.

Never have these ancient visions so urgently demanded our attention as in the nuclear age. Vulnerability is now an inescapable fact of planetary proportions. Yet we persist in denying it. We pursue ever-greater power to destroy our enemies, as if their more thorough annihilation would increase our security. With bravado we brandish our weapons and display our resolve, participating in a two-sided game that only increases the tensions for everyone. We strive for illusory airtight defenses, refusing to accept that we depend for our survival on our hated enemies, as if what we find intolerable must necessarily be remediable. Our insistence on being invulnerable can create the crisis instability in which desperate fear can more readily trigger a nuclear holocaust. The fears we deny can end in devouring us.

The way to security lies less in achieving greater technological sophistication than in working toward a transformation of the spirit of our relationship with our potential adversaries. The tasks of diplomacy are surely not simple, and the mutual distrust and hostility between the superpowers will not readily be eliminated. But it must remain our unshakable goal to be able to deal with our potential adversaries on a different, spiritually more truthful basis, one where the acknowledgment of our mutual vulnerability and common humanity overrides the preoccupation with our mutual suspicion and competing interests. As we work for this change, it behooves us to maintain those tools of fear that preserve deterrence. But as we assume our warrior's posture of vigilance, we must not forget that what will truly keep the peace is a very different power from the thrust of our rockets.

It was one of Jesus's teachings that we will not make the passage into the kingdom of heaven bloated with the wealth of our possessions, but in a less pretentious form like little children. Likewise, it is not as strutting heroes that we will be able to usher onto this earth the kingdom of peace, but when we more modestly embody our true condition, acknowledging ourselves to be but vulnerable creatures who know and accept that we are not God.

BUILDING BRIDGES IN THE MIND

The task of making peace, therefore, is not just a matter of realpolitik; it is a matter also of the spirit. It requires us not only to deal with the practicalities of our place in the mundane world, but to confront our place in the cosmic order of things. We must *know* who we are and what we are doing—know not only with the intellect but with our whole being, in the way that mystics have always achieved the knowledge that has given our species its deepest guidance.

This work, therefore, attempts to bring together the levels of sophisticated analysis and spiritual understanding. For though we will not be able to build peace without grasping the realities of our contemporary world, neither will we be able to transform the face of our civilization unless we are moved by the force of some ancient spiritual truths. The attempt to bridge these levels in itself addresses part of the core of the problem of making peace, which is the task of making ourselves whole.

To look at real world problems in spiritual terms runs contrary to the way the "best minds" in our advanced societies are educated to think. To talk, therefore, of love and fear, of faith and despair, may seem to some insufficiently sophisticated to be of much help in addressing the challenges of the nuclear age. But such a judgment is itself a manifestation of the weakness at the core from which much of our difficulty arises. We need to know more about knowledge.

KNOWING AT THE CORE

In those circles in our culture where ideas are taken seriously, there is a strong emphasis on the importance of new and "original" ideas, and a disdain for dwelling on old ideas, and for what are regarded as spiritual platitudes. This prejudice against old ideas and traditional spiritual wisdom derives from a shallow understanding of what it means to know.

Human understanding occurs at many levels, rational and mythopoetic, of the head and of the heart, of thought and of feeling. Only when the abstract idea engages with the deeper levels of emotional meaning does knowledge gain the power to move us. The special nature of spiritual truths—those that can penetrate and integrate the whole and provide a lever for true human power—does not register on the two-dimensional map of disembodied knowledge. The reiteration of old truths therefore seems platitudinous, for the repetition does not deepen their resonance but just makes them tinny.

One can know the importance of love in the same way one knows the depth of Death Valley: a cognitive knowing. But if this is the only level of one's knowing of a spiritual truth, then that truth will be as little able to drive one's life as putting the accelerator to the floor will move a car whose clutch is disengaged. Thus it is that in a course of psychotherapy months or years may go by before the time is ripe for the therapist to impart a truth that the client could have been told at the outset: were the seed to fall only on the shallow soil of the intellect it would not bear the fruit of knowledge of the kind that changes lives. So it is also with the psychotherapeutic journey our species must undertake: certain insights—e.g., about projection and denial, self-acceptance and love—can become quite commonplace notions before they become widely known truths.

The really important truths require a deeper kind of knowledge. "In the shadow of the nuclear bomb," said Albert Einstein, "we see more and more clearly that all men are brothers. If we can recognize this simple truth and act accordingly, then humanity can move on to a higher plateau." Surely we do know that all men are brothers, but that knowledge does not lead us to act accordingly until it resides in our hearts.

Our quest for knowledge must be more than that accumulation of new information and ideas that since the Enlightenment has been the redemptive ideal of scientific progress. While the advance of coolly rational and objective knowledge surely can help empower us to engineer a better world, the rather ancient and not so altered problem of how to be a whole human being still stands near the center of our task. And here the goal is not so much onward into uncharted territory as inward toward the core that many have explored before us.

Knowledge is alive. Like all living things, it must be continually renewed, or it dies. We do not say of food, I have eaten before, therefore I will eat no more. We eat every day to renew our strength. What is important to know must regularly be known afresh. One may have eaten, but then starve to death; one may have known, but then lose one's spiritual bearings.

The old truths must continually be made new. Unless they are rewoven every generation into the conditions and understandings of the living present, they will not quicken in our lives. Conversely, unilluminated by basic spiritual insights, the events of our times will seem mere sound and fury, signifying nothing; and our systems of intellectual knowledge will lack the overtones that would lend them depth of meaning. The understanding required for the building of peace, therefore, involves a process of integration, bringing together the domains of our knowledge. The quest for peace in the geopolitical realm must be seen in relation to the fundamental spiritual struggles of the human creature caught in history. The illuminating insights of modern depth psychology need to be shone into the heart of our own personal experience and beamed outward onto the drama on the global stage. Our knowledge of the currents of history should be brought together with some vision of the meaning of human destiny in the cosmic evolutionary process. When our understanding is unified, and the channels of our knowledge are open to flow to the core of our being, then our truths will have the power to move the mountains that block our way. This is part of the path toward peace.

Shalom

The word *shalom* means "peace." It also means "fitting together." The word itself thus helps show the way.

Opening the channels within us to achieve greater unity of experience is part of the process of "fitting together." The cause of peace is served by our integrating our analytical and our spiritual knowledge.

Gaining the strength at the core to be able to embrace the reality of our experience is the essence of making ourselves whole human beings. Only people who can make peace with their own sense of vulnerability, of moral imperfection, of confusion, will possess the power to make peace with the rest of humankind.

Creating a harmonious order out of the continuing intersocietal anarchy in which our civilization arose is part of that same process of *shalom*. Anarchy is fragmentation, and it mandates the war of all against all; while peace requires that humankind end that anarchy with some unifying world order.

All these are part of the domain of *shalom*, the knitting together of living human energies into a harmonious whole.

For three and a half billion years, the way of *shalom* has been the way of life, as the evolutionary process knitted together harmonious wholes at every level from cell to biosphere to protect the sacred stuff of life. Now we—the creatures with the creativity to break out of that life-serving order—are challenged to create *shalom* at a new evolutionary level.

It is to contribute to that process of integration that *Out of Weakness* is written.

PART 1

Winning:
The Worship of
Strength

1

DAMAGED
IN THE MALE

P arts of the wall still stand in northern Britain, after two thousand years. The Romans built it as a barrier against the intrusions of the tribes of Scots and Picts. Carved into the stone of part of the surviving wall, pointing outward as a threat or warning, are a phallus and testicles.[1] An image of flesh and blood, made hard as stone, rendered into a weapon. The male energy that transmits life is translated into a threat of death.

Power and violence are human concerns, but they are especially important for the male. This orientation is inscribed in the flesh.

Written in the Flesh

The structures of living things represent intricately crafted strategies for the perpetuation of their genetic heritage. The greater size and muscle mass of the male primate is no exception. The requirements of reproduction place fewer constraints upon the male body than upon the female; nature has thus had greater latitude in structuring the male to make him useful in other ways. Also because of reproductive facts, adult males can be regarded as more dispensable than females in a strategy for species survival. These facts, plus the inevitability of threats to the group in a dangerous world, have led nature to fashion in the male primate the rudimentary ingredients of the warrior.

In the primate group, the males generally play an important protective role. On the savanna, when a leopard threatens, the baboon troop
forms itself into a phalanx with the dominant males forward to face the
danger and the females and young protected within the formation. In
form and in spirit, the male primate is given the resources for effective
fighting in the service of the species.

The different sex hormones instill different spirits: female monkeys,
given male hormones in utero, display in their childhood playing the
aggressiveness and competitiveness generally exhibited by the young
males of their species. Male and female God made them, a cleavage that
divided labor not only in the act of procreation but in other dimensions
of social life as well.

In the human species, compared with baboons, the specialization of
the male in the capacity for effective violence is less pronounced. The
fact that the ratio of male body size to female body size is smaller among
humans than among baboons is evidence that the division of role and of
character between the sexes is naturally less stringent in our species.
Nonetheless, there are differences in size, and from this we can infer
that role differences between the sexes are innate.

It is extremely difficult to discern what might be called the outlines
of a "natural" human society and to answer a question such as, "What is
the natural role of men within human society?" For one thing, we are
cultural animals. There is no single way for human society to be. But
that does not mean there are no tendencies around which cultural
variations tend to cluster. There are, for example, many culturally
determined diets in different societies; nonetheless, an analysis of our
teeth and our digestive tracts can say something important about our
"natural diet" and the mix of vegetable and meat foods within it.
Another problem—illuminated by the parable of the tribes—is that,
generally, human societies as we find them in our times are greatly
warped by forces independent of human nature. So we must be wary of
the sociobiologists' error of inferring human nature too directly from the
way we behave in the zoo of our civilization. But we can find at least
suggestive evidence in the societies of our nearest primate relatives and
the societies of hunters and gatherers, whose structure is probably closest
to the form in which our species evolved.

Because physical strength has been essential to the male contribution to the survival of primate society, those societies have evolved to
reward and foster such strength. Strength has been an important deter-
minant of a male's status within the male dominance hierarchy. Strength
also gives males as a group some dominance in the social order. In some

species, the most dominant males enjoy preferential access to females—i.e., a favored role in the creation of the next generation. Strength may also contribute to a male's sexual attractiveness, so that sexual selection by females reinforces the molding of the male primate, through the generations, in the image of strength. In a variety of ways, the structure of primate social relationships encourages the evoluton of males who most fully embody qualities most useful for social survival. And among these qualities are not only such physical properties as strength but also the corresponding motivational structures (such as physical courage and aggressiveness)—the rudimentary bases of the warrior spirit.

I have suggested that power is particularly a male concern. This does not mean that human society naturally revolves around the male: the paternalistic structures that have dominated much of civilization are not simply human nature made manifest. In some respects, it may be that it is natural for females to stand closer to the core of human society, and for males to be more peripheral. In chimpanzee societies, for example, the bond between the female and her young (and among the females) seems to be at the center of the social network, with males more marginal, sometimes coming in and sometimes going off. This centrality may represent a kind of female "power" in society, derived from the crucial role of creating and nurturing life. There is, at the same time in these societies, another kind of power that operates, this kind having to do with "dominance." Along this dimension, the males are primary. Dominance clearly is not the same as importance. But this kind of power, based on strength and intimidation, exists because it too plays an important role for the species. And this power—which is most germane to our investigation of the warrior—would seem in our species as well to be the natural province of the male.

While there are variations among primate societies, there is no reason to doubt that forces like those just described have been operative in the evolution of the nature of the human male. And while biology does not determine human destiny, it does play a role in shaping it. It is therefore probably in the nature of the beast for men to be more involved than women in certain basic issues. These include: (1) *Strength*, the capacity to protect, the achievement of invulnerability; (2) *Winning*, the ability to establish one's superiority, to be chosen (as by a female, who has considerably greater reason to be choosy about her sexual contacts than does a male), to prevail over rivals; (3) *Will*, to have one's way, to control, and to possess. These are the issues parts 1 and 2 will explore.

These issues matter to all human beings, but nature made them stand out somewhat more prominently in the total emotional landscape of males than in that of females. This does not mean, however, that the issues surrounding power are naturally at the heart of the male emotional world. Males in primate society play a multidimensional role in which protection is simply a part, and the qualities those societies require their males to embody are correspondingly diverse. If we find in history that men have been preoccupied with power, it is evidence less of our inheritance from nature than of our trauma in civilization. The historical male assertion of power in civilization stands out swollen not with pride or pleasure, but like an injury—like a sore thumb.

Injuries

The destructive process described by the parable of the tribes represents a direct attack upon the foundations of manhood. This is true even while, at another level, the selection for power has led to the ascendancy of the male, and indeed to his tyranny over women and children. In fact, the unjust and pathological masculinization of human culture derives directly from the pathological assault on men by the unjust dynamic of cultural evolution.

Even for the strong, since the rise of civilization, there has been no security. The inexorable movement of civilization toward power maximization has mandated strength without limit. Today's victor is not only the likely heir of historic humiliations and violations; he must also look anxiously over his shoulder, fearful that what is strength enough today will not suffice tomorrow. The war of all against all allows no one to feel secure in the protection of what he values. An anarchy unknown in the state of nature turns a world that holds some dangers into an acutely dangerous world. As in a circus mirror, all the familiar human elements remain but are distorted into hideous shapes: power's magnified role twists the mild natural structures of human dominance into a grim contest of life and death.

The free play of power in the intersocietal system has condemned the overwhelming majority of men to be the victims of power more than its possessors. The male in civilized history has retained his natural role as protector, but history too often has robbed him of the possibility of fulfilling that role. A fitting image of this has been given us by the movies: the brave warriors with their spears at the ready are mowed down by the intruders' guns, their lands and families coming under the exploitive domination by the alien power.

The world becomes ever more full of losers. The selective process is all too much like an NCAA basketball tournament, in which every team but one loses its final game and is forced to the sidelines. The lingering taste of defeat is nearly universal. The pride of manhood is rendered a scarce commodity, with only a very few left able to stand tall and to raise a finger before the camera of history and declare, "We're Number One!"

Unmanned. Defeat in the struggle for power often entails a kind of castration. Sometimes literally, as in the sexual mutilation of fallen foes. Sometimes more figuratively, in the appropriation of the women of the vanquished, and the murder of their young sons—a process heart-rendingly depicted in Euripides' *Trojan Women*. This too is a kind of castration: in the Hebrew of the Old Testament, to be "cut off" means to be left without descendants.[2]

And then there can be unmanning without a drop of blood shed. The conqueror may impose on the men of the group he dominates a status below adulthood: thus, whites in Africa and in North America have called full-grown black men "boy." In the wake of conquest, the women of the vanquished seem more likely to be accorded their adult status than are their men.

It could be argued that the women of the vanquished are less quashed because the status to which they are admitted—adult womanhood—is less than a fully adult role, even among the dominant group. The male conquerors can therefore allow full "womanhood" of this sort without creating a threat to their predominance. There is validity to this perspective: when the free play of power injured human manhood, it also distorted the relations between men and women, as injured and insecure men compensated for their wounds at the expense of women. Injured men have abused their mates and their offspring. At the same time, dominance being less a female issue, women are also somewhat exempt from the struggles over who shall dominate and who shall be humiliated. Castration is an issue only among the men. For this reason, too, conquest entails less of an assault on womanhood than on manhood.

Conquest emasculates and, in the debris of shattered cultures, it is often the men who are most clearly broken. We see them hunched in their posture and lost in an alcoholic fog. Meanwhile, strong women of the vanquished people carry their people forward into the future, sustaining the next generation and perhaps bearing the seeds of an eventual cultural renaissance.

While history is told as the story of winners, the nearly universal experience to which we are heir is that of the vanquished. The "we" of patriotic history was more often than not created by force, when one group managed to bring under its domination its neighbors and their lands in the creation of a "nation." Even the creation of the free British nation entailed an invasion by France, and subsequent subjugation of Scots, Welsh, and the still-restive Irish. And who now within the Soviet Union is not more fundamentally the heir of the experience of defeat and vanquishment than that of victory and domination? Although official histories may lead us to identify with the few who succeed—and who can impose upon the rest their version of history—through the generations the meaning and burden of the real experience of our ancestors is inevitably handed down.

The coming of civilization also created a problem of power *within* societies. Whether the emergent social hierarchies derived from conquests between previously independent groups or from a purely internal development of exploitive class relations, the workings of power in social life have entailed the same ubiquitous insult to manhood. The rise of stratified societies transformed the mass of men from creatures who could look straight across at the world to underlings compelled to look up to a ruling class.[3] The peasant is considerably more typical of the civilized man than the Jeffersonian farmer: what makes Jefferson's vision so noble is that it restores a vision of manly existence with nothing above one but the trees and the sky. In the modern world, we are not peasants who till the earth and answer to armed lords above us, but the vast bureaucratic structures of industrial society still demand a peasantry of a sort. Almost all in these organizations must look to those above them for direction, functioning as instruments of the will of others.

The free play of power in the overarching system strangles the free play of the human will for individuals. Power is the capacity to impose one's will over another's. The building of empires and the development of stratified societies have compelled the many to submit to the will of the few. If autonomy and the free exercise of the will are by nature especially central to the expression of an adult male identity, then the power structures of civilization are directly injurious especially to the male spirit. To all human beings it is an insult to be compelled to submit; to men it is a violation. Around the world, men fight against their oppressors—almost always in the name not of power but of freedom. The world is filled with "freedom fighters" because freedom means coming out from under the weight of another man's will.

It is obvious that the wielders of power are, with few exceptions, men. What is less obvious are the injuries that the play of power inflicts especially upon men. Pathologies of the will afflict not only those on the bottom, but also—and in some cases especially—those who ride them on top. Even the dominant do not begin on top. Even members of the ruling class begin as children, often subject to a socialization process of systematic (if subtle) deprivations and humiliations. In most systems, no one will get to the top without a pathologically exaggerated involvement with will. From the men on the bottom, with their injured will, the world gets rapists and muggers eager to give back to the world the violation and theft of dignity they have suffered. Often the same spirit imbues those who rise to the top. And the mighty men of the earth display their pathological insistence on the triumph of their will as they violate the sovereignty of their weaker neighbors; as they rape the earth, bending Mother Nature to yield her bounties to their greed; as they rob the masses of their liberty and property.

What is afflicted by disease will spread the disease. Thus, injured by the pathological workings of power, men become pathological in their use of power. Constrained by the structures around them from embodying the natural nobility of a man, they become twisted into the form of monsters.

Men are thus most directly involved with the pathologies of civilization. This is not because men are by nature worse than women (or children), or because men are more important. It is, rather, because the inevitable problems of civilization are intertwined with issues that naturally involve the male spirit. Any creatures that extricate themselves from nature will stumble into anarchy. The systems they create will be infected with the diseases of anarchy—violence and the struggle for power. Because these inevitable problems of civilization draw especially upon male energies, their cancerous growth has been intertwined with the maiming of men in body and spirit.

2

The Demand for Invulnerability

In a benign world, our dreams may be of happiness and fulfillment. Life has positive possibilities. But in a dangerous world, the avoidance of pain and terror assumes priority. The crueler the world, the more our most cherished dream will be to find a way to avoid the nightmare.

The worship of strength reflects this aspiration. Strength is a shield against victimization. Weakness is intolerable because it puts one at the mercy of other forces. Were these forces merciful, were they kind and caring, weakness might be as good as strength. A baby in the loving arms of its mother may know bliss despite its utter helplessness. A baby who is abused, whose mother's arms not only hold but strike it, discovers the terror of its helplessness. From such fear arises a desire for strength: "If I were strong enough, no one could hit me again."

Since the beginning of civilization, people have lived in fear, knowing that the blow might fall upon them. The perpetual anxiety of the war of all against all has bred into the warrior spirit of civilized societies a love of strength. When an abused child, as both Hitler and Stalin were, comes to rule a nation that feels itself to have been the victim of abuse, such as Germany or Russia, all other values may fade in relation to the worship of strength.

The Doer and the Done For

One must not only be strong, one must be *active*. To be active is to do; to be passive is to be done to. Passivity is the road to victimhood, and to be a victim is to be nothing. From the world's cruelty, one man who learned this lesson well was Menachem Begin. He wrote in his autobiography:

> Just as "the world" does not pity the thousands of cattle led to the slaughter-pens in the Chicago abattoirs, equally it did not pity—or else it got used to—the tens of thousands of human beings taken like sheep to the slaughter in Treblinka. The world does not pity the slaughtered. It only respects those who fight. For better or worse, that is the truth.[1]

"All the world," says Begin, "knew this grim truth except the Jews." But in men like Menachem Begin, the Jews come to know it too in the post–Holocaust era. One does not wait to be done to. As their enemies, the Iraqis, progressed (in 1981) toward the possession of nuclear weapons, Begin as the leader of the Jewish state struck first. The Iraqi reactor was destroyed. Do unto others before they do unto you.

By gaining the strength and resolution to strike, the previously disregarded victim now can demand that he be taken into account. Begin entitled the chapter in which he described how the British in Palestine did not take the Jews and their threats seriously: "We Fight, Therefore We Are." The ubiquity of terrorism in today's world is, in part, testimony to the fact that the same lesson is being taught. The world is filled with groups that are oppressed and exploited. Too often, those who refrain from imposing their suffering on others will find no help or comfort. The great powers, in formulating their policies, do not use their influence to rescue those whose plight has no impact on them. But when a group starts planting bombs and hijacking airplanes, the root causes of their rage suddenly are explored, their possibly legitimate demands considered. The cruel world teaches, as Begin says: fight or be nothing.

Better to inflict suffering than to endure suffering oneself. In a tribe of head-hunters, "When a chief's son died, the chief set out in a canoe. He was received in the house of a neighboring chief, and after the formalities he addressed his host, saying, 'My prince has died today and you go with him.' Then he killed him. In this, according to [their tribe's] interpretation, he acted nobly because he had not been downed, but had struck back in return."[2]

In the warrior ethic, the fear of passivity and victimhood outweighs even the value placed on courage and the discipline of will. Gandhi once posed a challenge that clarifies the warrior ethic's preoccupation with the avoidance of passivity: "Wherein is courage required—in blowing others to pieces from behind a cannon, or with a smiling face to approach a cannon and be blown to pieces?"[3] Although in this instance, as Gandhi implies, it is the passive resister who shows greater courage, a display of such courage counts for little among warriors for whom the central issue is the humiliation of passive victimhood. Better to blow than to be blown. According to the warrior ethic that developed around this abhorrence of passivity, one can become a hero in death, but only if one is active. The brave men of the Alamo are heroes, for they died fighting to their last breath against an overwhelmingly larger enemy force. Take one (or more) with you. The prisoner in enemy hands can be a hero by passively enduring their tortures, but only if he does not yield to their pressures—to cooperate, to divulge information. Ultimately, therefore, this victim is not passive: his will has successfully fought against theirs. Unlike cattle led to the slaughter, he did not let others have their way with him. *

---

*This last example may provide a bridge back to Gandhi's passive resistance. The difference emotionally between Gandhi's approach and that of the warrior is not as great as may at first appear. From Gandhi's writings it is clear that he proposed not so much an alternative to fighting as another way of fighting. For Gandhi, too, it was important that he not simply be disregarded. Whether the Gandhian passivity would be satisfying depended, therefore, on the impact of his conduct on his adversary. Just as Saint Paul says, in expounding the Christian teaching of overcoming evil with good, that "in so doing thou shalt heap coals of fire on [thine enemy's] head,"[4] so also Gandhi required that his passive resistance be disturbing to his adversary. With the comparatively humane British, under those particular circumstances, it worked. One must wonder, however, whether it would have worked at Treblinka or in the Gulag, and whether there were Gandhis who disappeared unavailingly in those death systems. And one wonders whether Gandhi would have been satisfied to be a mere victim the power of whose moral stance did not even register upon those who struck him down. Gandhi wrote as one who has achieved a kind of invulnerability. But a part of that is because his experience—in his family and in the wider world—had been in moral universes in which his pose of passivity conferred stature and power.

The early Christians had a similar solution, but one less contingent upon the other actors, their persecutors. In their concept of martyrdom, the early Christians posited an unworldly moral universe that transmuted their victimization into victory. Whatever the attitudes of their oppressors, there was assumed to be a divine audience to approve and reward their suffering. Their assumptions transformed their persecutors into the unwitting agents of their own side of the moral struggle.

The Unassailable Character

Another dimension of invulnerability is a sense of being *blemish-free*, with no chink in the armor. The insistence on perfection is an attribute of the extremely defensive personality. Where the world is experienced as hostile and intrusive, any point of entry can be the means of one's undoing.

An apt image of the warrior's sense of vulnerability through even the smallest imperfection is found in the myth of Achilles. According to the story, as a child Achilles was dipped by his mother, Thetis, into the waters of the river Styx to render him invulnerable. The dipping covered his entire body—except for his heel, by which his mother held him. Eventually, an arrow from the Trojan, Paris, struck Achilles in that very spot, inflicting a fatal wound. Because the defensive coating is less than perfect, the world intrudes and destroys.

The warrior spirit is preoccupied with the defense against threat. The story of Achilles symbolizes the sense of dread in the warrior spirit. To the extremely defensive personality, any imperfection, any opening to criticism, can be an Achilles' heel. Stalin showed "intolerance of anything short of perfection in himself."[5] Similarly, Hitler "could not abide the thought of his own mistakes."[6]

> One evening during the war, Hitler was whistling a classical air. When a secretary had the temerity to suggest that he had made a mistake in the melody, the Fuehrer was furious . . . [He shouted] angrily, "I don't have it wrong. It is the composer who made a mistake in this passage."[7]

The insistence upon perfection appears to be an intrinsic element of the cult of power. It is not just that the narcissistic rulers pretend to be without fault. Their followers, who look to the rulers as embodiments of their own power, make similar demands. Whatever represents *us* cannot be wrong. This immunity from error may apply to our nation or to our leader, both of which represent our efforts to identify with the invulnerability we crave. In 1934, Hermann Hoess said in a speech: "We note with pride that one man remains beyond all criticism, and that is the Fuehrer. This is because everyone senses and knows: he is always right, and he will always be right."[8]*

---

*Our leader must be perfect. This requirement may be expressed in terms of physical perfection. In his study of the origins of tyrannical kings, Eli Sagan writes that "any

In the emotional economy of those who worship power and crave invulnerability, the admission of fault represents weakness, and criticism from others is an assault. Such assumptions permeate the patriotism of the Right. Along with militarism and a cult of the unassailable leader often comes a kind of chauvinism that exempts one's society from criticism. Sometimes to the chauvinist, the process of national self-criticism engaged in by others is tantamount to treason. To them it does represent an attack upon vital defensive structures. We must maintain ourselves to be blemish-free or these defenses are in danger of crumbling.

Such defensive structures, erected against an external world seen as threatening violation and destruction, are regarded as strength; anything that diminishes that solid front against the outside world brings weakness. It is in this context that we may understand a statement of Ariel Sharon. In the wake of the national report, condemnatory of him and others in the Israeli Defense Forces, on the massacres at the camps of Sabra and Shatila, Sharon declared that "a wave of weakness is sweeping the country."†

---

physical imperfection barred a person from becoming king." Once, in the African kingdom of Dahomey, for example, the first-born son of the king was disallowed from the succession because one of his toes overlapped another. "As late in history as the Byzantine Empire, an incumbent emperor would cut off the nose of a potential rival for the throne, since physical disability disqualified the victim."[9]

†I hesitate to draw upon Israel and its leaders as examples of the warrior's excess. In the moral calculus embedded in official propaganda, much of the world is singularly unfair to Israel: a few allegations of Israeli brutality in the West Bank seem to evoke greater moral condemnation than the Syrian slaughter of thousands in Hama; of all Lebanon's many massacres, those in Sabra and Shatila in 1982 are the ones the world attends to, and then the condemnations are directed less at the Christian executioners than at those who looked the other way; the nationalisms of most nations are lauded, while that of the Jews is branded a form of racism. Whether due to the numerousness and wealth of those who want to take back the lands of the Jewish state, or to the ancient strains of anti-Semitism, this chorus of hypocrisy should not be strengthened by fair-minded people. Nonetheless, as the most democratic and humanistic of the countries embroiled in this area of chronic conflict, Israel's shortcomings stand out against the backdrop of its better possibilities. And to me, as a Jewish American, Israel is one of the countries to which I look with the greatest hope of finding wisdom in its policies. Thus I have watched the pathologies of contemporary Israeli policy more closely than those of its adversaries, just as I have scrutinized current American practice and utterance more than Soviet. This inevitably is reflected in my choice of examples.

Better Dead Than Yellow

The invulnerable man is also *fearless*. If one were invulnerable, there could be nothing to fear. Fear is therefore an admission of vulnerability, and thus an intolerable sign of weakness.

To be a coward is to be less than a man. The great warrior General Patton slaps the coward, the soldier who is in the hospital for his "nerves." In one war movie after another, the hysterically frightened soldier is slapped by one of his more manly comrades, as if the blow will bring him to his senses. The blow drives home the fear of fear. The sensible warrior suppresses his fear. With fear beneath the surface in everyone, its outbreak might prove contagious. Sometimes when one soldier turns and runs, another will follow, and another, until a whole army panics, making itself vulnerable to wholesale destruction. The socialization of the warrior thus includes making him afraid of nothing so much as of fear itself. He is taught, to paraphrase the old slogan: better dead than yellow.

So great is the fear of fear that even recklessness can become a badge of manhood. In many adolescent male subcultures, to achieve high status boys must take entirely gratuitous risks. In the cowboy subculture of the United States, spontaneous games of "chicken" occur on the highways, with cars rushing toward each other on the same lane: "At stake is the issue of who will 'give in' first; the one to capitulate is thereby less the man. With manliness thus at stake, it is inevitable that many head-on collisions occur—as is indeed the case."[10] Such violent outcomes are particularly frightening when one recalls that certain elements of the nuclear posturing of the superpowers have been likened to the game of chicken.

Connected with fearlessness is an *imperviousness to pain* and injury. The manly man never shows his pain. The "strong, silent type" who embodies the heroic image of the American warrior actually gets injured often, but he pays no more attention to his injury than is required to get him back into the fight. (Perhaps he will tie his bandanna as a tourniquet to stanch the bleeding, and then resume firing.) Those around him do not learn of his injury until they see the blood on his saddle when he stiffly—but strongly and silently—dismounts.

This ethic is part of the socialization of every American male, especially clearly so in athletics, that arena of symbolic combat. The development of sports medicine may be changing this ethic, encouraging athletes to take better care of their bodies, but I doubt that the change is fundamental. It is only a few years since I saw, on television, a college wrestler of the first rank lauded as a hero for continuing a match after suffering a severe dislocation of the knee: it was heroic to strive for a victory in one match, even at the risk of permanent disablement. When I was involved in competitive athletics over two decades ago, it seemed that physical suffering was regarded by the coaches as so valuable a part of training that even avoidable stress was not avoided. In summer football practice, young men wearing ponderous equipment would work out for two hours in 95-degree temperatures without water or other liquids. My teammates and I survived, but all suffered. Sometimes someone would pass out or suffer from heat stroke. In the newspapers, one would occasionally read about a player somewhere dying. It would have been easy, and it would have made us better football players, to make rehydration possible. But: no pain, no gain..

For the coaches, athletics was clearly based on the military model. They were molding men, men who would fight to win, tough men inured to pain. On the other end of the temperature spectrum, football in late autumn in Minnesota could get very cold. My hands would grow so numb and slippery from the cold that, aside from being very painful, they became useless for grabbing on to the runner I was tackling, or for catching a loose ball. I suggested to my coach that I might wear gloves and play better. The coach, a former marine sergeant (as he often reminded us), responded: "Sure, Andrew, why don't you wear lace gloves." The meaning was clear: to attend to the vulnerability and pain of one's body was to be unmanly, like a girl—the worst possible insult in such a setting. The subject of gloves never arose again. I suffered in silence and became, no doubt, more manly for it. (This was, unfortunately, before the effeminate hulks of the NFL took to wearing gloves for cold-weather play.)*

This is but a modern remnant of the ancient male ethic of warrior societies. Among the Rwala Bedouins, a father is supposed to punish his adolescent son by cutting him with a dagger—a practice that not only punishes the sons "but hardens them for their future life."[12]

---

*Horst-Eberhard Richter writes of the power-oriented patriarchal society: "Boys learn to regard suffering as a sign of weakness and thus as a quality that can appropriately be manifested only by girls; so they relinquish their suffering to the female."

The Confidence Game

Finally, a particular variety of fearlessness is *confidence* of success. Humanity would probably do better to have a greater attachment to reality, but as we have seen it is reality from which we want to escape. Thus we blur the line between hope and belief. Las Vegas becomes a rich city because so many will go there believing they will win, although in the long run it is only the house that wins. What the house is for gamblers, death is for the makers of war. Those who lead us into battle must exude a certainty of victory. In World War I, power went to those leaders who, like the British general Douglas Haig, possessed "an irrepressible and totally unrealistic optimism."[13] Clearly it cannot have been reasonable for the leaders of *both* sides of that bloody struggle to be certain of victory—indeed, the expectations of both sides were quite unrealistic—but to be reasonable at such a time was "to risk the label of 'defeatist,' with potentially dire penalties."[14]

Both sides in World War I, confident that victory was at hand, lost the flower of a generation. Only Death won. To be optimistic in that way is indeed to be sanguine.

Again, on the issue of certainty of success and fear of failure, leaders put their male parts on the block. There are times when it is sensible to be afraid, and only sane to be cautious. But if these qualities are deemed weak and unmanly, one might feel compelled to do what is senseless and insane to preserve manly appearance. As President of the United States, John F. Kennedy evidently bore the imprint of such an ethic: those who advised caution he described as "grabbing their nuts in fear"; and JFK and his inner circle gave the green light to the disastrous Bay of Pigs invasion without consulting Bowles, Rusk, and Stevenson, from whom criticism was anticipated and who "were counted too 'ladylike' to be consulted on the manly scheme . . ."[15] Better dead than unmanned.

Our insistence on maintaining delusions of invulnerability perverts especially the process of leadership, for leaders have a special role to play for us in relation to danger. Fear makes us regress to become more like children. And like children, we want others—bigger and stronger than ourselves—to stand between us and the danger that threatens us. This is why our "greatest" leaders are those we have at times of gravest crisis: both because at those times we choose leaders who are ready to play a powerful role, and because the more dangerous our situation, the more—out of fear—we will project an image of power onto whoever is leading us. We want Daddy to reassure us that everything will be all right: we have nothing to fear but fear itself. The more afraid we are, and the less able we are to confront the danger realistically, the more we will insist that our leaders radiate an aura of confidence and invincibility.

Nowhere is our insistence on unrealistic optimism more regularly on display than in the process by which we democratically select our leaders. The language makes clear the connection with war: "campaigns," we call them, conjuring up images of warriors engaging in a succession of battles on the fields of combat. In one primary battle after another, we see even the losing candidates rallying their troops with expressions of confidence that—whatever tonight's results, whatever the polls say—victory will ultimately be theirs. Until a candidate is compelled to admit defeat, we never hear him admit its possibility. The demands of our political ritual make such an admission taboo. In our leaders, we appreciate confidence more than realism.

The majority of these statements of confidence prove to be unfounded. Most of the contestants are defeated. But the magic of the political process is that the one we end up electing was right: he did end up a winner, just as he said he would. Never mind how many other times he may have run and lost, exuding all the while the same confidence he did this time. We like a man who knows he will succeed. He is the kind of man we want to lead us forward into the future, which, for all our professed belief in its brightness, frightens us with its uncertainties.

This may seem a harmless charade, but it is not. At best, the unrealistic optimism is a lie our leaders convey without believing it themselves. But this means that among the criteria for ascension to political leadership is the capacity to lie convincingly. It also means that we put barriers in the way of our leaders' communicating with us in a way that genuinely confronts our real problems. When President Carter tried to speak to us of a national "malaise," he evidently violated the Commandment of Optimism we impose on our leaders. The political costs of that violation were considerable. The nation then turned for leadership to Ronald Reagan, who assured us of our greatness and of our limitless capacity for strength and for prosperity without sacrifice. America will stand tall again among the nations. In the context of feeling diminished stature and increased vulnerability in the world, the American electorate turned to Reagan and his grade-B movie get-tough patriotism.

Surely, optimism is an asset.* It can help give us strength to achieve the possible. But when the insistence on a rosy view means an unwill-

---

*See remarks on the biology of hope in "The Spiritual Challenge," in the prologue.

ingness to grab the bull by the tail and look the facts squarely in the face, it can disable us from meeting danger effectively. President Reagan's unflagging commitment to it evidently can overrule a balanced assessment of the facts. As the nation was heading into the deepest recession since the Great Depression, the *Washington Post* reported:

> "It's remarkable," said an aide. "You can show him five charts of decline and he will inevitably find the one blip that shows the economy is getting better."
> Reagan's own spirits remain high. His health is remarkable except his deafness has increased noticeably.

Under any circumstances, the well-being of a nation is jeopardized by leadership that can believe that, regardless of realities, our enterprises will always succeed and our battles will always bring us victory. But in a nuclear age, this choice of optimism over realism could be catastrophic. The war that must now be avoided is a war that cannot be won. It is among those most attached to the myth of invulnerability that this epochal change in the nature of warfare has been slowest to sink in. They go on planning for how to "prevail" in a nuclear exchange.

A General Douglas Haig in our times might not only cut off the flower of a generation, but pluck up the whole plant by the roots for all generations to come.

The Apotheosis of Power

Finally, the idea of the "worship" of strength brings to mind the image of the Almighty God who is the object of worship of half the people of the world. There are many factors that shape people's concepts of God. One of these is that in the image of God people erect a representation of the ideal they themselves yearn to embody. As the immortality of the Greek gods expressed the ambitions of that warrior people, so also is the omnipotence of the one God of Western religions a manifestation (among other things) of the craving for invulnerability. "A mighty fortress is our God, a bulwark never failing . . . On earth is not His equal." To this condition of invulnerability, His worshipers fervently aspire.

This God is not only almighty, He is untouchable. He is abstracted out of the material realm altogether into the invulnerable realm of spirit. The body—the receiver of wounds and the source of pain—is no problem at all for the disembodied God. He has achieved, in other words, the condition to which men, in their desperation to escape the realm of pain and vulnerability, have long aspired and toward which—in their relationship with their minds, bodies, feelings, and technology—they have ceaselessly striven. *

---

*The possibility that God, with all His/Her/Its power and majesty, might be otherwise conceived, that God might also be vulnerable, and not just for a one-time crucifixion, will be discussed at the end of chapter 5.

3

THE CONFUSION OF VALUES

L ife offers much of great value: the world is filled with beauty; we may be open to the goodness of love's flow. But the more we are traumatized by the brutal workings of power, the less do we orient toward these positive values. It requires openness of spirit to let the pleasure and beauty flow through. The blows of injury cause us to cringe, turning inward and closing off those possibilities. Less able to experience goodness, we come to value most highly whatever will protect us from pain. The ambition to be invulnerable, therefore, brings with it a warping of our values: what is good is what is strong.

The brutality of the world thus instills in some of its victims the perverted notion that *might makes right*.

Might Makes Right

This notion, like the struggle for power, has all too long a history. Even once-noble Athens proclaimed this cruel and amoral idea. Racked by chronic war, the Athenians proclaimed to the Melians, before they slaughtered them: "You know as well as we do that right, as the world goes, is only in question between equals in power, while the strong do what they can and the weak suffer what they must."[1] This amoral philosophy was echoed by Thrasymachus in Plato's *Republic*, where he argues that "justice" is simply the interest of the stronger party.

The idea that strength is its own justification recurs in our own time. It gained ascendancy especially during the past century in Germany. The Germans, feeling too often the victim of others' aggression, became worshipers of power, sacrificing all other values on the altar of strength. The German historian Hermann Ocken justified the German violation of Belgium during World War I:

> "The fate Belgium has brought upon herself is hard for individuals, but not too harsh for the Belgian state. For the historic destiny of the immortal great nations is so important that in case of necessity it must overrule the right-to-exist of states which cannot defend themselves."[2]

The German nation is justified in its aggression because it is an immortal great nation, which is to say it has a *right* to do it because it *can* do it. The Belgian nation deserves its fate because it cannot prevent it. Might makes right. This same perversion of values resurfaced—with a vengeance, so to speak—in Nazi Germany. Nathan Leites describes the Nazi character type: "objects which are deemed powerful tend to be loved . . . while objects deemed powerless tend to be hated . . . [M]oral valuations follow the same pattern: the powerful object is morally good, the weak one, morally bad."[3] Just as Thrasymachian justice reduces right to strength, so does the extreme power-worshiper reduce the criteria of lovability and goodness to mere functions of power.*

---

*With the allegiance to power fundamental, all other bonds are rendered unstable. Loyalty becomes contingent upon the successful display of power, upon victory. When the coming defeat of the Nazis became clearer, the Fuehrer was ready to consign them to destruction. "For the people has [sic] proven to be the weaker," Hitler tells Albert Speer, "and the future belongs exclusively to the stronger Eastern people."[4] Meanwhile, a similar transference of loyalty according to the dictates of power-worship was taking place among the German troops. "Their attitude toward their major enemies tended to grow more or less favorable in direct relation to their estimate of these enemies' power . . . Enemy victories were frequently followed by mellowed feelings. 'They can't be as bad as that.' "[5]

This suggests that the argument that might makes right may not always be simply hypocrisy or self-serving rationalization. To him who truly worships strength, even the might of his enemy may inspire his awe and his loyalty. Perhaps, had Belgium smashed Germany, that German historian Ocken would have bowed before the immortal great Belgian state.

The Adaptive and the Mal

On one level, this convergence of strength and goodness represents a *positive adaptation*. We have evolved to be "valuing" animals because values are in the service of survival. We have been structured by a selective process so that by nature we are inclined to value positively what nurtures and protects our survival and to value negatively what threatens it. Value is the basis for choice, and our own values are a kind of mirror of the natural process of "choosing" that created us. The selective process of biological evolution chooses what can live over what cannot, and it molds us to choose likewise. By a natural system of values,* we are drawn to seek those pleasures of food and sex that perpetuate our form of life; and, on the other side, that same inborn structure of valuation impels us to avoid stubbing our toes and falling off cliffs. It is natural also for us to adapt the basic thrust of our natural values to the opportunities and dangers of our environment. Where the dangers are particularly acute, we will naturally tend to stress in our system of values those that have a defensive or protective function.

Where weakness means death, therefore, and strength means survival, it is adaptive for strength and goodness to converge. The underlying, inherent equation of life with goodness is converted, in an environment with a fierce struggle for power, into an equation of the strong with the good. It is like the transitive function in mathematics, where if $a = b$ and $b = c$, then it follows that $a = c$.

Viewing this equation as an adaptation, however, does not mean denying the enormous costs of this warping of human values: the amoral worship of strength still appears as a sign of sickness in the human system. What this view does, rather, is to imply a different way of looking at those costs. To the extent that these values are required for survival, we would see their distortion of our humanity less as a sickness in human beings than as one of the costs of people having to live in a pernicious environment.†

---

*On this subject, see chapter 4 of *The Parable of the Tribes*.

†Thus we see that the collapse of the good into the strong is not equally characteristic of all human systems, but particularly so of those systems where anarchy reigns. It is in the intersocietal arena, for example, that the idea that might makes right—as represented in amoral concepts like "reasons of state"—is afforded most legitimacy. Pertinent here also is the observation that of moral systems that operate within societies, it is in those based on *honor* that the domain of value is most likely to be engulfed by the worship of

But again, adaptation is not the whole picture. Again there is an element of excess that alerts us to the presence of disease. Again there is a need for healing ourselves as well as the fragmented world around us.

In a sense, most of what we call "mental illness" is "adaptive." The neurotic patterns we learn make sense as a means of surviving under circumstances that are highly stressful: lessons learned under the impact of trauma are deeply imprinted upon our being lest we forget what our survival requires. It is especially in our formative years, when we are in fact most helpless and thus most vulnerable to trauma, that we are most likely to establish our life-long neurotic patterns in self-defense. Yet all years are "formative," and not only for us as individuals but for us as collectivities or nations. Thus a Pearl Harbor can induce traumatic learning, and "the lesson of Munich" can make an indelible impression on the consciousness of nations shocked by historical trauma. Such shocks can make us declare, with the Jewish survivors of the Holocaust, "Never again!"

Traumatic Overlearning

But even if the patterns we learn through trauma can be regarded as "adaptive," oriented toward survival in a world like that which taught us, it is also appropriate to regard those patterns as illness. This is because we overlearn them, applying them universally, as if every circumstance posed a threat just like the one we experienced at the time of our traumatic learning. We may be disabled from taking risks in love relationships as adults because, when we were small and helpless, painful experience in our families taught us that such risks were too dangerous. Trauma can do the same in our collective experience: in the historical shadow of Munich, for example, we may turn away from opportunities to make peace with potential adversaries, seeing all concessions on our part as dangerous appeasement.

We overlearn because the experience that taught us was more than we could handle. The problem with traumatic learning is that it leads to a

---

strength. Honor, as was said in the prologue, tends to be regarded as the highest virtue in the circumstances where each actor must be the guarantor of his own security, i.e. where the social system is still largely anarchic. And moral systems of honor tend to declare strength to be the highest virtue, whereas "all forms of weakness are shameful. So the weak, the humble, the modest, even the merely good-hearted and cooperative, are not virtuous."[6]

kind of "autoimmune" response to our own experience, in which panic drives us to employ in a dangerously excessive fashion mechanisms that usually serve to protect us. An exaggerated and unceasing response to a perceived danger can end up crippling us. Overwhelmed with fear, we can see nothing but threat and thus can value nothing but what protects us from that threat.

Our inability to handle our overwhelming and injurious experiences means therefore, that we learn in some sense more than the world itself has taught us.

The human face has been disfigured, therefore, not by objective necessity alone. The struggle for survival has required human beings to distort the face of human life, but nowhere has our larger environment by itself been so pernicious as to make wholly untenable the preservation of our humanity. Even in the anarchic intersocietal system, in which survival unfortunately has required some capacity for ruthlessness, there is room for compassion and fairness: the concept of honor deals not only with the value of strength but with that of "honorable" conduct. Even in the most inhuman of environments, the Nazi concentration camps, those inmates who had sufficient inner strength were able to maintain human values. And those who established the camps are themselves proof that the sacrifice of our humanity may far exceed the true requirements for survival. The worshipers of power who organized the systematic murder of millions of helpless and innocent people were warding off a threat that was real only in their deluded imaginations; their pursuit of their immoral program, far from required to assure their survival, proved actually a hindrance to their prosecution of the war they had provoked.

It is our weakness that leads us beyond necessary adaptation into maladaptive excesses of adaptation. The collapse of values into the worship of strength is a sign of the collapse of the living structures of our humanity under the blows of traumatic injury. Thus, while some of the costs of the worship of strength should be charged directly against our onerous environment, many of these should be seen as growing out of this organic injury to the human spirit. *

---

*Here is a chilling example of how the trauma of victimhood leads to the collapsing of all other values into the worship of strength. It is the case of Juergen Bartsch, described by Alice Miller. As a growing boy, in postwar Germany, Bartsch had himself been subjected to incredible torments, seductions, and other abuses from parents and other adult authorities. As an adolescent, Bartsch came to public attention as the perpetrator of a series of grisly crimes in which he had molested, tortured, and finally murdered and butchered small boys. These crimes Bartsch could describe with a kind of pride, since he

Although we are foolish, when in a dangerous environment, not to place a high value on the capabilities that protect us, trauma may lead us into folly of a different sort: losing sight of what it is we are trying to protect. We need to have the means to survive, but what kind of life have we gained if all we can love is power, if we have no moral sense of right or justice that goes beyond the amoral workings of raw might? The worshiper of power has a problem with means and ends. This problem goes deeper than the old issue of whether the end justifies the means. The power-worshiper clings so desperately to what should be only a means to an end that the means becomes an end in itself.

As the idea of goodness disappears into the idea of strength, so the goal of survival overwhelms concerns about the quality of life. The preoccupation with the external threat means neglect of the interior life. We can see this effect of threat-orientation at both the individual and social levels. The manly values of the warrior are anaesthetic, away from feeling. Toughness includes the capacity to disregard pain, which might otherwise distract the warrior from combating the external threat. But the barriers to the experience of pain cannot function so selectively; thus, blocking the path of pain means turning away from the realm of experience generally. Warrior discipline means putting the *uses of* the self above the *caring for* the self. The territory inside, where life is lived, is neglected in favor of the territory outside, where survival must be won.

At the macro level, the politics of the warrior Right are similarly skewed: a trillion for defense, and cutbacks in social welfare. "Domestic" programs are not, in the conservative perspective, infused with meaning because life is not lived, as it were, "domestically"—at home, within—but rather out at the periphery, on the barricades, on the boundary with the outside world whence come the threats to survival. Just as strength—the armor that surrounds one's living being—becomes the locus of moral value, so is the MX missile seen as contributing to the security of the nation, whereas the nurturing of "women, infants and children" (WIC) is not.

In part, again, this is adaptive. It is true, as the hawks on the Right argue, that we cannot live well if we do not manage in the first place to

---

saw himself "in the murder scenes as a powerful person with a strong feeling of self-confidence, although he knows everyone will condemn him for these actions and attitudes." It was very difficult for him, however, to describe other scenes where he had been in a weak position, for in these "the warded off pain of the humiliated victim comes to the surface and causes him unbearable feelings of shame."[7]

survive. "The demand for invulnerability" began with the idea that positive aspirations are most possible in a benign world, whereas in a dangerous world we aspire to be spared pain and horror. It is therefore an adaptation, regrettable but necessary, to take a negative, threat-oriented approach to life. But again, there is also a tendency toward pathological excess.

The preoccupation with threat is learned from injury, and from injury can come not only adaptive lessons but organic damage as well. The turning away from the quality of life toward mere survival can reflect not only the necessity for strength but the *incapacity* for experiential richness. Too traumatic a pain can destroy our ability for pleasure. Traumatized to the core, we leave the core not only to ward off further blows but to escape the pain that lies within.

The more we are incapacitated to live fully, the more we will be driven to accumulate the symbols rather than the substance of living. Strength is one of these symbols; money is another. Money can be described as coagulated happiness, for it embodies consumption (or gratification) that has been postponed or, in the capitalist ethic, canceled forever, with all profit perpetually reinvested to make still more money and never directly enjoyed at all.[8] Strength also can serve a symbolic function, for if we are unable to enjoy life, the strength we amass can provide consolatory testimony to our capacity at least to survive. The senseless accumulation of ever more missiles and warheads may be akin to the pursuit of endless wealth in being essentially symbolic consolation: the money represents pleasure we cannot enjoy, the weapons the preservation of life we cannot live.

The Girl Who Can't Dance

One can see, therefore, a certain connection between the excessive preoccupation with threat (and therefore with strength) and a hostility toward positive aspirations about life. An example of this is *Commentary* magazine, a journal of considerable intellectual depth and occasional brilliance. *Commentary* has two principal themes: the Nazi Holocaust, and the threat posed by the Soviet Union to the United States. The first of these is perhaps the scene of traumatic learning, the case of a grotesque and deadly threat against which one was unprepared to defend oneself. As a result, one is now acutely, perhaps excessively vigilant against the second, the Soviet threat. The continuous message is that the threat is greater than we suppose, and that our defenses against it are inadequate. (The annihilatory threat of the Arab nations against Israel is monitored with the same fierce attention.)

Commentary wages an ongoing war of polemic against the illusions of what might be called the cultural Left in the United States. These are the people who think we can be chummy with the Soviets and who advocate the joys of sex, cooking, and unpolluted water. The writers in *Commentary* point out with devastating effect the tendency of the cultural Left to *deny* the threat, to refuse to see some unpleasant realities of this dangerous world. Survival is not to be guaranteed by smiles and good vibes.

Commentary is preoccupied with survival, but one looks in vain for a positive vision of the possibilities of human life. What is striking to me is that no less vituperative than its attack on dovish illusions is *Commentary*'s assault on the positive values and aspirations of the cultural Left. The gradual but unmistakable impression that arises from this magazine is that the vision of life as containing possibilities for joy and beauty and love is *itself* experienced as a threat. It is apparently necessary to preserve a view of life as bleak and grim, not only because of threats from the outside but, it seems, because of an incapacity on the inside.

In Yiddish, there is a saying that the girl who can't dance says the band can't play. To which it might be added, to the cripple there is comfort in the idea that there is no dance at all.

Come Sweet Death

In the most extreme cases, the wages of traumatic injury are not just an incapacity for life but an attraction to death. Although we are designed by nature to place life at the core of our values, if we are so crippled by injury that life is torment, death becomes a desirable release.

This is one factor that helps to explain the paradox that so many people die from their ostensible efforts to ensure their survival. What at one level is a frantic effort to protect oneself against external threats may at another represent a determination to end one's existence. Suicide is far from always conscious, a fact that demands attention in the age of nuclear deterrence. The same crippling trauma that directs our living energies to protect ourselves from a dangerous world can attenuate our desire to stay in that world at all. "Better a horrible end than a horror without end."[9]

Thus, in its extreme forms, the worship of strength can be part of a complete perversion of our values, values serving death over life. Injury and the threat of injury can make us warriors for the protection of life. Severe injury that cripples the spirit can make us warriors in the service of Death.

Those of us who wish to preserve life and all the sacred values that enhance its meaning must be careful whose counsel we follow in the search for security. The most extreme of the doves would endanger us because they ignore the reality of danger and deny the need for strength. But because the most extreme worship of strength can combine with the love of death, the most hawkish of voices may not lead us even toward the grim survival they promise. While the superdove unconsciously refuses to confront the reality of the world, the superhawk unconsciously wishes to destroy that world.

There is a story about the Spanish fascist general Millan Astray. Maimed and crippled by war, General Astray had as his motto, *Viva la muerte!* ("Long live death!") In 1936, on the eve of the carnage of the Spanish Civil War, he gave a speech at the University of Salamanca, during which one of his followers shouted out, *"Viva la muerte!"* After the speech, Miguel de Unamuno, then rector of the University, rose to say, "This outlandish paradox is repellent to me. General Millan Astray is a cripple. Let it be said without any slighting undertone. He is a war invalid. So was Cervantes. Unfortunately there are too many cripples in Spain just now. And soon there will be even more of them if God does not come to our aid."[10]

The worship of strength and the love of death are connected by Erich Fromm in his description of a character type he calls the necrophile, the lover of death.

> Just as for the lover of life the fundamental polarity in man is that between male and female, for the necrophile there exists another and very different polarity: that between those who have the power to kill and those who lack this power. For him there are only two "sexes": the powerful and the powerless; the killers and the killed. He is in love with the killers and despises those who are killed.[11]

In the Garden, He made them male and female. After the Fall into the struggle for power came the sickness that transformed the life-giving phallus into the death-disseminating sword.

Mortal Wounds

We are born into the Garden, where the fundamental principle is life and the creation of life. Adam (the Earth) is incomplete without Eve (life). Thus male and female He made them, quickening the dust of the earth with life. But it is not paradise that we live in. We suffer injury and with each injury some of our life's blood spills from its proper channel and returns to the earth. If our wounds fester, the corruption of Death gains a foothold in us. Injury attenuates our attachment to life. And injured animals, with paradise painfully lost, may willingly play a role in the tragic drama of death. War is not only the parent of injury but the child of injury as well.

In the fallen human condition, we pass along not only the principle of life, but of death as well. The wounds pass from generation to generation, like a kind of original sin.

There is a scene in *Oedipus at Colonus* where Oedipus meets with his son, Polyneices. Polyneices comes to his father for help, but Oedipus, remembering past wrongs done him by his son, rebuffs him with great harshness. Far from forgiving Polyneices, Oedipus rejects and curses him: "I abominate and disown you! Wretched scum! . . . [Y]ou shall die by your brother's hand, and you shall kill the brother who banished you. For this I pray."[12] Immediately thereafter, Polyneices refuses, in his conversation with his sister Antigone, to turn back from the path of destruction. "Do not go to your own death and your city's!" his sister entreats him. But Polyneices chooses the path of death, saying that despite his father's curse, "I cannot give way." Antigone perceives that Polyneices "go[es] with open eyes to death."[13]

This scene, as Eli Sagan interprets it, affords an insight into the dynamics of the warrior culture's love of war and killing: it is fed by "the failure of love in a fundamental situation of love—between father and son . . . The father's curse makes the son a lover of death."[14] Oedipus, who as an infant was sent off by his royal father to die on the mountainside, now inflicts upon his own son that wound that drives him off into battle. This war will be, for Oedipus's two sons, a battle of mutual fratricide. For the male line of Oedipus considered as a unit it is a fall into suicide: the line of life is "cut off," as the ancient Hebrew phrase puts it. From father to son it is not the generation of life through the shaft of the flesh that here prevails, but the cutting off of life by the death-dealing shaft of iron.

We all, of course, suffer injury. Consequently, the principle of life does not rule us unchallenged. The love of life and the love of death are probably best understood not as being neatly divided between two groups of people—the biophiles and the necrophiles—but as being present in us all. Life not being paradise, some ambivalence toward life is to be expected. This helps explain the widespread attraction of war. It helps explain the frequently observed phenomenon that the outbreak of war brings to many people an unprecedented feeling of vitality.*

It may seem a paradox that war, the carnival of death, makes people feel so acutely alive. But paradox is the natural child of ambivalence. This is part of the power of tragic drama. In tragedy, the enactment of one side of an ambivalence releases the full experience of the other side. Only after we have witnessed and relished the punishment of hubris by the cosmic order are we free to experience our admiration for the heroic daring. Only after the hero has been struck down for his transgressions is the grandeur of his spirit reborn in our own souls. We enter the theater with ambivalence, and leave with a clear distillation of heroic feelings, because the enactment on the stage of one side of the drama releases the other side to be played out freely in our hearts. Thus tragedy's famous paradox of death and rebirth.

What tragic drama is on the stage of the theater, war can be on the world stage. War represents, in part, our enactment of our love of death. With that side of our ambivalence enacted, those necrophiliac feelings no longer stand as a check to our love of life. Thus in the midst of war, the drama of death, people report feeling a surge of vitality. Many people may remember their wartime experiences with nostalgia. Never as much as then, they say, did they feel so alive.

But most of us, even if we are willing in some sense to participate in the tragedy, have no compelling need to play it out. It is a possible but not a necessary script for us. Those who drive the drama of death are themselves driven to it. As Adam was incomplete without Eve, the true necrophile is incomplete without his carnage.

Part of what distinguishes the necrophile is the depth of the wound. When "the father's curse made the son a lover of death," it is because a wound was inflicted at the core of his being. Something "died" in him then, we often say of people who suffer such deep wounds but go on living. When the organic damage is fundamental enough, the creature whose living flesh was meant for the Garden of life may become instead an architect for the landscape of Death.

---

*I do not claim that the factors discussed here are the only ones involved in a full explanation of the invigoration people experience in times of war and other situations of great danger.

Like so much of Erich Fromm's thinking, the concept of the necrophile was inspired in large part by the Nazis. Many have been drawn to
study the Nazis, for they demonstrated that the advancement of civilization might mean not the elevation of human life but the greater
empowerment of death. In their study of Nazi war criminals, Florence
Miale and Michael Selzer used projective tests to bring out the underlying condition of the Nazi personality. What they found was that these
Nazis described "aspects of their personalities . . . in such terms as dead,
mounted, hard, rough, cold, dry, bones, torn, ragged, and so on . . ."[15]
Here, then, are people who already were bearing death inside them.
The cruel experiences of their lives had already in great measure killed
them. The psychological tests were one way of making manifest what
was inside; history, unfortunately, was another. In creating a cruel world
strewn with rubble and corpses—a landscape of death—the Nazis made
the world into their own image. These were people in whom the
attraction to death was uncommonly strong because Death had already
established an outpost in the core of their being.

The Big Lie

But there is another element that helps drive the tragedy. It is not just
that Death, given a foothold in the wounded core of the necrophile,
can rule. It is that the rule of Death is well concealed. Perhaps Polyneices
goes off to war to achieve destruction, his own and others'. But his
ostensible aim is to possess the throne that was his father's. In the name
of his advancement, he works his undoing; outwardly seeking a place in
the sun, he brings himself back to dust. It is similar with the Nazis. In
the name of *Lebensraum* (room for living), they turned Germany into a
chamber of death. Their drama of survival was a tragedy of destruction.
The Fuehrer who claimed to be building a thousand-year Reich in
reality engineered the devastation of his country. A campaign for unpar-
alleled excellence and nobility led to unprecedented depravity.

Lies are at the core of our dramas of destruction. The outward contradictions between the necrophile's ostensible goals and real results are a
reflection of a central untruth in his relationship to his own experience.
So painful are his wounds that he will not suffer them. He insists on
turning his unbearable reality into its opposite. But reality will not forgive
this, and it retaliates by subverting all the necrophile's appearances into
their opposite. What is denied returns with a vengeance; what will not
be given admission as simple truth returns as the hidden master.

The strength that was to protect from danger is transmuted into but another source of danger. Ostensibly a worshiper of Power in defiance of Death, he becomes an agent of Death. At the center of the tragedy, therefore, is the Big Lie. Not the one that Hitler wrote about in *Mein Kampf*, but the one that he unwittingly embodied. It is the lie that true strength can be built upon the denial of weakness.

In truth, the wage of denial is death.

4

THE WAGES OF DENIAL

The Bent Hnau

In C. S. Lewis's novel *The Silent Planet*, the wise extraterrestrial being Oyarsa says that a "bent *hnau* [sentient creature] can do more evil than a broken one."[1] So it is with the necrophiliac worshiper of strength. His use of denial serves to keep him from breaking, but it only makes him more dangerous.

Denial makes the bent *hnau* dangerous first because it infuses him with energy. This energy is not the energy of health, for he is not whole. He is wounded unto death, but, not yet crushed by his injury, he is maddened and enraged by it. Bent but not broken. Although Polyneices' heart may be broken, his spirit is enflamed. The necrophile is like a mad dog: although he carries death within him, he is animated with a peculiar intensity. The carrier of death is intense because he is running scared. Frightened of the pain that lies within him, the one who drives the drama of destruction is himself driven by fear.

Another consequence of denial further augments the dangerousness of the bent *hnau*. For it is what we run from that we are driven by.

There is an old Sufi story: A man is working in a garden and sees Death come in. Then he notices Death looking at him rather strangely. Fearing that Death has come for him, he throws down his tools and flees, intending not to stop until he has reached Baghdad, many miles away. Another worker in the garden approaches Death and asks, "Why were you looking so intently at that man?" And Death replies: "It is just that I was so surprised to see him here. For I have it written down that I have an appointment to meet him tomorrow in Baghdad."

This seems an apt metaphor for the consequences of running from the frightening dimensions of our experience: we run right into the arms of what we are most eager to deny. Joe Louis said about one of his opponents, "He can run but he can't hide." The same is true of our own experience of pain and terror. If it is there, it will find us one way or another. And our denial ultimately serves only to strengthen the forces from which, in our terror, we run away.

It is what we will not own that possesses us.

Death has claimed a part of the bent *hnau*, but the creature denies this. The denial only strengthens death's dominion over him. What we will not face will ride us from behind. Thus it is often he who is (often unconsciously) most afraid of death who courts it, he who is terrified by death for whom death has the greatest attraction.* Hitler was both terrified of death and fascinated with it, determined to survive and drawn to self-destruction. A contradiction? Yes, and also no, for it mirrored the contradiction in his structure of denial. What is repressed returns, strengthened with new demonic powers. It is he who runs from his fear of death whom death will possess.

The denial of the dark side of our experience thus allows the forces of darkness both to energize and to enslave us. A combination that makes the bent *hnau* dangerous indeed.

The Worship of Strength and the Denial of Weakness

It is frighening to be what we are; but it is disastrous to pretend to be anything else. What we are is flesh and blood. We are mortal creatures, prone to injury.

We are not, however, defenseless. Along with our soft tissues, we were also given teeth as hard as stones, and hands that can clench into bony fists or grasp a wooden club. It is natural for us to defend ourselves

---

*Horst-Eberhard Richter writes that "the demonstration of contempt for death is, as a rule, merely a form of overcompensation for just the opposite feeling—namely a particularly acute fear of death."[2]

and, as the threats to us have grown in magnitude, natural for us to craft greater defenses to compensate for our heightened vulnerability. Over his fragile skin the knight places a skin of metal. The warrior extends his arm with a blade of steel or with a gun that spits deadly pellets of lead across great distances.

But it is important to remember that we develop our strength to compensate for our feelings of vulnerability, that our armaments are less fundamentally a manifestation of our power than of our anxiety. Consider the imagery of the film that has often accompanied the TV sign-off in the United States.[3] As "The Star-Spangled Banner" is played, the screen shows us the flag, interspersed with the most advanced military aircraft streaking across the sky, soldiers marching with relentless rhythm and determination, marines making amphibious landings. All this, the film says, is ours. But more to the point, all this is protecting us. It is significant that this ritual affirmation of the relationship between the citizen and his or her nation's armaments occurs late at night, presumably in the moments before sleep. Night—a time of vulnerability, a time when fear is ascendant—is when the child wants to be tucked in, to be reassured of the parental bond that is his or her protection. It is therefore fitting and important that night, the time of terrors, is the time we remind ourselves of the protective strength we have constructed between ourselves and a dangerous world.

It is also important to remember that the armor around us is not ourselves but is a hard coating of metal that we interpose between us and peril. We remain but flesh and blood. It is between remembering this and forgetting this that compensation becomes denial, that the adaptive uses of strength become the necrophiliac worship of strength.

Consider the metallurgical images of this century's two great destroyers, Stalin and Hitler. As a child, Stalin was named Iosif Dzhugashvili. He was a Georgian under Russian oppression. After he reached manhood, he renounced his Georgian identity to identify instead with his oppressors, whom he had hated. He then took on a new name, Stalin, a name that in Russian means "steel." I am not made of flesh and blood, but of hard, unyielding metal. Stalin saw threats from every quarter, and with a pathological edge from the denial of consuming fear, this steel shed the blood of millions.

Hitler, too, liked steel.

> Max Planck remembered a remarkable interview with Hitler in which he shouted that it was "libelous" for anyone ever to accuse him of having weak nerves. "I tell you," he screamed, "I have

nerves of steel!" When he said that, Planck recalled, "He pounded his knee, spoke ever faster, and worked himself into such a fury that there was nothing for me to do but . . . to excuse myself."[4]*

This is the man who, at the decisive moment, on the night of the famous *putsch* that led to his imprisonment in the 1920s, "sank into despondency and seemed incapable of taking any effective action . . . He was heard to mutter morosely, 'If it comes out all right, well and good; if not, we'll hang ourselves.' "[6] Some nerves of steel.

The transmutation of flesh into the hard material of weaponry reminds us of the phallus of stone sticking out of the ancient Roman wall. Just so for the German nation was this Fuehrer, he who stood out from the body of the German people with his stiff-armed salute, and who declared of himself, "I am the hardest man that Germany has had for centuries."[7]

But these fantasies of male omnipotence are desperate attempts to deny the experience of weakness. The male identity involved is as tenuous as it is exaggerated. The jack-booted, goose-stepping, iron-fisted Nazi typically assumed his masculine identification in self-defense in a traumatic situation. The typical family constellation, as described by Nathan Leites, had a father persecuting the son over the ineffectual objections of a weak mother. The identification with the father is therefore an identification with the aggressor, a psychic mechanism whereby the victim can magically escape the experience of persecution. "If I am the object I fear, then I need not be afraid."[8] The identification with the aggressor is like a kind of armor that is adopted to cover the true inner core, while that vulnerable inner core is denied. By such psychic sleight-of-hand, the brutalized son can escape, at one level, his traumatic experience. But the experience remains there at the core. It is the experience not of possessing masculine strength but of having been compelled to submit, having been raped, by brutal male power.† Thus

---

*In the context of these images, it is interesting to note that the man who, more than any other, built the foundation for the German ambition and power that proved so destructive in our century was Bismarck, known as the "Iron Chancellor." Of him, Waite reports: "The man who boasted of his *Herrschernatur* (commanding presence) could not sleep at night until he was tucked in by his favorite doctor, who held his hand 'like a mother with the restless child.' Comforting the Iron Chancellor and putting him to bed became a nightly routine."[5]

†Identification with the aggressor helps explain the easy shift of allegiance of the worshiper of power with the shifting tides of victory. The child, identifying with the power that abuses him, establishes the archetypal precedent for this disloyalty: for the embrace of one's tormentor, though a desperate form of self-defense, is also, at a fundamental level, a betrayal of the self.

the hypermacho Nazi fantasy of omnipotence is constructed, Henry Dicks concludes from his study of Nazi SS men, as a defense "against inner feelings of constraint and submissiveness."[9] The solution is to gain power through submission. Willing obedience to the Fuehrer's commands at once reenacts the submissiveness and opens the way, through identification, to participate in the leader's great potency. Goering said it rather clearly: "[O]nly with the Fuehrer standing behind one is one really powerful, only then does one hold the strong powers of the state in his hands; but against his will, or even just without his wish, one would instantly become totally powerless."[10]

The deification of the leader gives the followers an imaginary escape from their nightmarish experience of powerlessness. But the leader, too, according to the Jungian analysis, "is compensating for a deep-seated impotence."[11]•

•The belief in the omnipotent God may have a thread of kinship with the need for an omnipotent leader. Dan Jacobson observes that it was as the Israelites were increasingly victimized by neighboring empires that the biblical writers ascribed ever more global powers to their God.[12] The character of this God, too, like the underlying structure the Jungians attribute to the deified leader, carries across its face dark shadows of underlying compensation. The jealousy of the Almighty, His proclivity to lash out in punitive rage in response to any slight or disobedience, is reminiscent of the fragility of the narcissist, with his precarious and injured ego structure. It is not the behavior we would expect of a mature human being who acted from inner security, let alone of a Being who had been Almighty since the beginning of time.

But the worship of an omnipotent God does not carry the dangers of the deification of an omnipotent leader. For the God may serve to draw some of the urges of narcissistic violence out of the human system, up safely out of the way—somewhat like the kind of promotion we describe as being "kicked upstairs." True, some people who designate themselves the prophets or messengers or anointed of such a God may appropriate to themselves the right, in His name, to express the divine wrath. But the idea that omnipotence lies beyond the human realm may help restrain the presumption of mere mortals to godlike powers. The Hebrews may have made a moral contribution to the species with the concept of an omnipotent God, whose presence kept their kings mere mortals while the rulers of their neighbors, like the pharaohs of the Egyptians, had pretensions of divinity and were unlimited in the thrust of their assertion.

In this light, the Hebrew institution of circumcision might be interpreted more appreciatively than it frequently is these days. Many have condemned circumcision as a symbolic form of castration, signaling the Father's hostility toward the son's growth toward manhood. But perhaps it should be seen not so much as an assault upon our true manhood as an inhibition upon the phallic excess of our warrior civilization.

Those right-wingers may have a kernel of truth, therefore, who see an especial danger in regimes that are "godless." In our century at least, despite all the bloodletting that historically has been done in God's name, the greatest butchery has been perpetrated by

However much Hitler might inflate himself with his rhetoric and his posturing, there was something crushed at the core. The sexual practices of this omnipotent leader, for example, are believed to have focused on the particularly humiliating perversion of having women squat over his face and excrete upon him.[13]†

The followers hold onto the leader to keep from collapsing into their denied feelings of weakness, while the leader clings just as desperately to his followers to keep from falling into the pit of his impotence. But there is no foundation, and so the gravity of reality brings down the structure of denial.

The insistence on being more than human derives from the incapacity to bear the pain of being human. In the Nazi lexicon, as Nathan Leites' linguistic analysis discloses, the word *menschlich* ("human") was associated with *Schwache* ("weakness"). Worshiping strength was joined with denying and despising one's humanity. The idea of *Starke* ("strength") was associated with *keine Nerven haben* ("to have no nerves").[15] Beyond nerves of steel to no nerves at all. The body freed from the messengers of feeling. With no nerves, he feels no pain. To crave such strength is like praying for death: Deliver me from this body and its suffering. Ultimately what we wish to deny is suffering. The weakness, the vulnerability, the submissiveness to victimization—these must be denied because of the unbearable suffering that attends them.

"Ultimately, it is their own inability to endure suffering which forces people to make others suffer," writes the contemporary German psychiatrist Horst-Eberhard Richter.[16] To be human is to be vulnerable to pain; to be unwilling to suffer is to become like the strong, godlike Nazi hero. Himmler congratulates the SS for their heroic work in exterminating the Jews:

> "Most of you will know what it means to see a hundred corpses lying before you . . . Having stood up to that and—apart from

---

regimes (like Nazi Germany, and like communist regimes in the Soviet Union, China, and Cambodia) that deified the leader and/or the state itself.

The world might be safer, therefore, if all nuclear nations were, in some sense, "under God." For while necrophiliac prophets on the fundamentalist right in the United States may happily await the Lord's bringing the Apocalypse onto the world, a necrophile like Hitler who deified himself, had he possessed the nuclear means, would gladly have brought on the Apocalypse himself.

†The hardest man in Germany seems not to have been very impressive to his lovers, a disturbing number of whom seem to have committed or tried to commit suicide sometime after their contact with him.[14]

some exceptional cases of human weakness—having remained decent has made us hard. This is an unwritten and never to be written page of glory in our history."[17]*

From our humanity, we can run but we cannot hide. What is denied will return in its most corrupt form. In denying our humanity we become not gods but monstrosities of inhumanity. Flesh and blood denied may return as shit and piss. And always, around the worshipers of invulnerability, the stench of death.

Denial and the Nuclear Challenge

I had a personal encounter with the denial of vulnerability not long ago. It involved the idea of space-based defensive systems against nuclear attack, the system nicknamed "Star Wars." I was involved with a project to explore our national options on the nuclear defense issue. My job was to travel around the country interviewing the experts, the best minds on all sides of the issues, to seek out their ideas and to uncover the assumptions underlying their positions. I conducted over forty such interviews. Many of these conversations—with hawks and doves—were stimulating explorations both for me and for my interlocutors. All were cordial and pleasant, except one.

The gentleman in question was a retired military man who had held high rank in both a military service and in U.S. intelligence. I will call him the General. His work at that time—early 1984—was as a vocal advocate of the Star Wars defense. He promised me an hour's interview, the minimum required to get beyond practiced position statements to the underlying beliefs, and I traveled to meet him at his office.

Part of my method with each interviewee was to present him with the arguments of those who disagreed with him and to invite him to respond to those challenges. This helped uncover the true areas of disagreement, usually on matters much more fundamental than those that are debated in the political process. I believed it would not be difficult for me to probe the General's positions in this way, for I had

---

*Pitilessness has long been a positive value in the perspective of the pathological power-worshipers. In his book on the origins of tyranny and oppression, Eli Sagan recounts that one of the "praise names" for the *kabaka* ("king") in the Buganda kingdom of Africa was "He who does not pity the parents of the man he kills."[18] This, remember, is a name of praise. Worshipers of power love hardness of heart.

already interviewed a great diversity of experts, and one of the few things on which there was a semblance of consensus among them was that the hopes for an effective Star Wars defense were based on illusions. They agreed that nothing approaching meaningful protection was technically possible and that the expense of trying for one would be exorbitant. Many also argued that the pursuit and eventual deployment of such systems would be highly destabilizing, intensifying the arms race, militarizing space, destroying the arms-control process, and finally increasing crisis instability. This last point means that it would create a condition where there is an advantage in striking first, thus making it more likely that either side might fire its missiles first in a crisis out of fear of being second. In other words, the striving for an illusory invulnerability arguably might have the very real consequence of helping bring about the nuclear holocaust.

The General and I never got to those issues.

I found him behind his desk, chain-smoking. He began going through his argument, offhandedly, as if he had said it all so many times before that it not only must be true but must be obvious that it was true. It boiled down to this: we cannot trust the Russians to be "co-guarantors" of our security, so we should construct defenses so they can't hurt us. Mutual assured destruction is intolerable, so we should choose assured survival instead.* We were about ten minutes into our interview. I was gently probing some of his collateral points—such as his contention that Soviet treaty violations should make us abandon arms control efforts altogether, and that the Soviets' ruthlessness and indifference to their civilian casualties made it doubtful that the threat of a retaliatory strike would deter them from making a first strike on the United States—when he abruptly terminated the interview.

Shocked, I reminded the General of his promise of an hour's time. "I've changed that," he said. I replied that at least I would like to know why he was terminating me. "I don't have to explain anything to you," he said. "The interview is over." I looked at him, and saw him eyeing me from under his eyebrows, as if I were the enemy. I had a thought: I

---

*Critics of Star Wars agree that mutual assured destruction (or nuclear deterrence, or the balance of terror) is "intolerable," but they say that it is also inevitable (for the foreseeable future) and that therefore we have to accept it. Living with deterrence, which is to say with vulnerability, "is like living with the law of gravity," said one of my interviewees. "There is no escaping it." To talk of constructing defenses to make us invulnerable, said another, is "like discussing what we will do on our 200th birthday. It isn't going to happen."

assured him that my questioning his positions had nothing to do with whether I agreed or disagreed with him. It was not my job to take sides on these controversies; it was my job to explore experts' views, and this was my way of doing it. The better I understood his positions, the better I could use them later to challenge the ideas of people who disagreed with him. "Get out of my office!" he commanded.

My blood chemistry was changing, turning from that of one who is comfortably engaged in a mutual exploration into that of one who is under attack and mobilizing to deal with it.

Then I saw the connection among his positions. "I don't have to justify my conduct. I don't have to respond to counterarguments challenging my opinions. I don't have to be vulnerable to Soviet missiles." They were all part of the same thing, the same insistence on being out of reach, invulnerable.

I rose, almost quivering from all the things I was not letting my body do. "Well, General," I said as I left, "I see what you mean by good defenses."

It felt good to deliver that line. But I did not enjoy the turmoil in my guts.

The General's approach to defense may have been based on a denial of reality, but there is no denying that his approach remains a powerful shaper of our global realities in the nuclear age. Illusion or not, the Star Wars dream has recently dominated the world of security. Notwithstanding the virtual consensus I discovered among the experts against the idea, the vital debate in the U.S. government about security in the nuclear age now focuses on Star Wars (or the Strategic Defense Initiative). This subject is at the center also of discussions between the United States and its NATO allies. But, most important, this fantasy of invulnerability has helped to bring about an impasse in the efforts of the superpowers to contain the nuclear arms race. Beneath these headlines, knowledgeable people still provide glimmers of the underlying reality that no system we can build will provide protection against catastrophic destruction. But the present U.S. administration, temperamentally ill-equipped to seek security through cooperation with its enemies based on mutual interest, persisted until recently on the basis that a truth that is unacceptable cannot be true. Meanwhile the Soviets, presumably knowing at one level the illusory nature of the Star Wars dream, panicked on the basis that a delusion that would be disastrous to them if it were true must be fought as if it were true.

Mutual assured destruction (MAD) is generally described as a policy. But those experts who, in wide-ranging discussions, best impressed me with their understanding of nuclear realities declare that it need not be a policy, for it is a fact. Whether or not it is acceptable, whether or not we accept it, both sides are inescapably vulnerable to virtual annihilation by the other, and neither can preemptively destroy the other's capacity to annihilate it in retaliation. Nonetheless, the denial of facts is also a fact. The Soviets, according to some persuasive experts on Soviet strategic doctrine, have not embraced MAD as a fact.* Hence, their continual refusal to adopt a more stable force structure, namely to diminish their reliance on land-based ICBMs (70 percent of the Soviet force, versus roughly 33 percent of the U.S. force). These missiles have simultaneously the two unfortunate characteristics of being best able to threaten the retaliatory ability of the other side (because of their accuracy and throw-weight), and of being most vulnerable themselves to destruction by a first strike from the other side (because their locations are known). Both characteristics reward a first strike. Now, with Star Wars (and other measures) the Reagan administration joins the Soviets in approaching nuclear defense as though vulnerability were escapable and as though one could guarantee one's survival by one's own strength. Both sides also "know" they are vulnerable, but their strategic policies show that at the same time both deny it. For each finds intolerable the truth that its survival depends on the restraint of its enemy.

Policies, clearly, need not be based on fact; but policies based on illusions can bring about disasters that are all too real.†

---

*This, as well as other aspects of Soviet military doctrine, may now be changing under the new Soviet leadership.

†In fairness, two points about the Strategic Defense Initiative should be noted. First, that it appears possible that the Soviets, because of their anxieties about American technological capability, might be willing at last to make substantial reductions in their own first-strike capability in exchange for American abandonment of the SDI. Thus, two bad ideas might end up canceling each other. Second, that the SDI includes some defensive concepts that, rather than striving for national invulnerability, confine themselves to protecting retaliatory weapons. Such defenses could contribute to the stability of deterrence.

It should also be added that this critique of certain of the strategic policies of the superpowers is not based on the sweeping assumption, common in dovish circles, that the destructive capacities of the superpower arsenals have rendered all development of new weapons systems superfluous. The question, "What is required for deterrence?" does not admit of an obvious, a priori answer. Nor will one answer necessarily suffice for every conceivable scenario of conflict. Consequently, responsible planners must take into account a range of uncertainties and prepare for a variety of contingencies. The problem of deterrence is more complex both militarily and psychologically than many in the peace movement seem to comprehend.

The Truth Also Costs

The other day I saw a poster of a doll-like figure, apparently female, hung over some kind of machine that might have been a medieval torture device or perhaps an old-fashioned clothes wringer. The caption reads: "The truth shall set you free. But first it will make you miserable."

We avoid painful truths for good reason: they hurt. The ability to bear pain is another illustration of that ubiquitous and unfair principle, "Them that has, gets." The more whole we are, the more we can bear the pain, and come out through it more whole still. Those whom life has wounded most profoundly lack the strength to confront reality honestly. The patients most desperately in need of surgery may be ineligible for it, because they are so weak they would die on the operating table. The less intact we are, and the more injurious and threatening the world is, the more difficult it is for us to bear embracing our true pain and peril.

This has ramifications for the nuclear age, which exposes us all to such shatteringly unthinkable dangers. The need and the difficulty grow together: what is unthinkable we recoil from confronting, yet nothing is so necessary for us to face together openly and with humility. The perils of the nuclear age thus impose on us the question whether the urgency of the challenge will bring us to our senses and compel us to deal with one another as vulnerable creatures, or whether the pain of our vulnerability will drive us on a dangerously insane search for illusory security through an unusable strength.

This perspective does not solve the problem, but it helps show part of the nature of the solution. If we are to choose life, we must be whole enough to choose all of life. What is excluded will turn demonic and work against life. Everything, therefore, that strengthens us at the core will help to preserve us. All the ways that we can truly nourish ourselves and one another will better equip us for the making of peace: the building of friendship, the creation of beauty, the reduction of tensions—all such things help build the foundations of peace.

Nonetheless, I am convinced, from my conversations with a wide range of experts, that the building of weapons more useful for a first strike than for retaliation and the effort to extricate ourselves from the condition of vulnerability to the weapons of the other side are both misguided and dangerous.

5

THE STRENGTH OF WEAKNESS

Problems and Solutions

T his book is about not only the problem of war but also the possibility of peace. Not only our dilemma but its solutions.

With the systemic problem of power in the evolution of civilization, two things are true: there is no solution, and the solution is obvious. There is no solution in that we will always be dangerous animals. We cannot go back, we cannot undo our breakthrough into power like returning a jinni to the bottle. Unlike other living things, we will always have the possibility and the temptation to do evil. No matter how we order our world, there will be no guarantee that the order will not break down and unleash the destructive play of power.

On the other hand, the solution is clear. The baneful reign of power arises out of anarchy, out of the emergence of our species into a condition where action is constrained by neither natural nor human law. The solution, therefore, is to end the anarchy. We must work forward to a new overarching order that constrains the play of power. Many effective designs for world order are conceivable, while in the absence of some such order the destructive process described by the parable of the tribes will persist.*

---

*Those interested in designs and strategies for world order may wish to explore the work of, among other groups, the World Policy Institute in New York City and of the World Federal Association.

The creation of a world order (which need not be a single world state) is both an obvious and a meaningful part of the solution to our problem. But many are not satisfied with a "solution" like this. For some, a desirable solution must tell us clearly what to do, and perhaps must promise immediate results. Of solutions like this, unfortunately, there are none to be offered.

In the first place, it is impossible to judge now just what the form may be of an effective order that our species might achieve in the coming centuries. Like the political structures we see around us now, such a future global order will bear the imprint of numerous historical accidents and unforeseeable circumstances. What combinations we may arrive at of global, national, and tribal entities, federated or confederated in what ways, with what kind of central armed forces and/or collective security structures—these cannot be foreseen. We can only bear in mind what the general directions of our long-term movement as a species must be.

In the second place, the day-to-day management of our national and international affairs can only partially be governed by our long-term goal as a species. Meanwhile, we are compelled to protect our values and interests in the short term. One standing on a mountain may point to the next mountain as his destination, but as he begins his descent he must watch his feet. And the course down the mountain is sure to be winding, including some stretches where the climber must turn his back on his goal. Similarly, we cannot safely march toward the world order we need. The United Nations represents part of a beginning of our species' efforts to solve the problem of anarchy in the international system. But as long as most of the member governments of the United Nations are themselves gangster regimes embodying the fruits of anarchy, it would certainly be folly for us to surrender to that body all those sovereign powers by which we now protect ourselves.

We are compelled, therefore, to grope in considerable darkness, trying at once to survive in the world as it is while trying also to take steps toward the world as it must become. To insist upon a solution that is better illuminated is to close our eyes to the nature of the challenge we face, and thus to deepen the darkness.

But it is different when it comes to knowledge of the spiritual alternatives to the sickness of soul described in this book. To solve the problem of the parable of the tribes, our species must move forward into *terra incognita*, an evolutionary terrain where no one has been. To be a human being at peace, to achieve spiritual health, is an achievement of a different kind: others through the ages have been there before us. This is inward territory that, to some extent, has been known.

It is true that there is no simple spiritual "solution" to the problem of war. No inner peace is so contagious that achieving it would grant immunity from the destructive passions of others. The "Prince of Peace" could not deter his crucifixion by those who hated him. And I feel sure that no meeting with Gandhi would have deterred Hitler from his murderous war. Indeed, in the case of Hitler, it seems more likely that if anyone could have turned him from his course it would have been not a lamb of peace but a snarling lion like Churchill, had it been he and not Chamberlain across the table from Hitler in 1938. Mystic traditions have promulgated the notion that great saints bring peace by their very presence; but I think that doves are often sacrificed, and that we have need of both hawks and doves in our aviaries. In this domain, too, we are compelled to grope, heading in different directions even as our ultimate goal remains unchanged.

Still, however complex the task, there is a place of strength and wholeness within us that better enables us to use both love and force in the service of peace. About that place, I can give only limited testimony, for I have spent more of my life escaping bondage in Egypt and wandering in the wilderness than drinking milk and honey in the promised land.

Although I wish I could live in the promised land, I console myself with the thought that anyone for whom the state of grace came more easily would have little comprehension of the toils in which we generally are ensnared. The legacy of our tormented history I see also in myself. Thus, when I write of the demons that have possessed the likes of Stalin and Hitler, I can draw upon my knowledge of my own demons. Our need is not only for pictures of the promised land but also for guides through the wilderness.

Of the promised land, my glimpses have been as of a landscape illuminated at night by flashes of lightning. These images are etched upon my mind and serve as guides to all my groping steps. I will tell what I can of what I have seen.

Embracing Fear

Most of this chapter is about the weakness of strength, the compensatory and defensive quality of much that manifests in the world as might. This work is inspired by my direct experience of the opposite condition:

the strength of weakness, the power and freedom that come from embracing the true vulnerability of one's condition.

One such experience was in a dream. I was in a sunlit and sandy place, crouched by the earth, holding in my hands a bowl of nourishing soup. A feeling rose in my heart and I cried out, "Oh Lord! Help me! I am afraid! I'm afraid of everything! Just *being* scares me!" And as I opened my heart to this admission of fear, I felt something healing flow in. It was not as if I were being given something from the outside. Rather, it was as if the very act of opening was itself the help I sought. By willing *fully* to embrace my fear, I was led beyond it to what could be called a state of grace.

So powerful was this dream that it awakened me in the middle of the night. For ten or fifteen minutes I lay in bed absorbing the blessing of that experience. By then I was wide awake, and I got up. I drew upon the openness of my heart to address a place in my life which, at that point, was not at peace: I wrote a letter to a friend with whom I had recently exchanged angry communications. I had complained of his unwillingness or inability as a friend to meet my needs, and he had complained of my inability to understand the problems that disabled him. The letter I wrote that night related to us both as vulnerable and needy creatures, rather than as judge and judged. It did not work miracles—I still cannot rely on him as I would like to—but it did bring peace between us.

That dream was a renewal of a previous, bone-shaking, heart-changing experience.

I had long hoped for a vision that would extend my understanding beyond the scope of the vision that underlay my book *The Parable of the Tribes*. That first vision was bounded by this earth, and dealt with that precious film of life that covers this planet. For years I had been aware, when I looked up at night into the stars, that in some fundamental way they lay beyond the reach of my worldview. I knew some astronomy and cosmology, but in my gut I lived only on this cozy earth, and not also in a vast universe.

Then one day I went up a mountain with my brother, and the visionary experience of the heavens I had sought came to me. In my mind's eye—and in the gut of my experience—for the first time I saw space in galactic terms. I saw the swirling of the galaxies and grasped the unfolding of time in the billions of years. And I felt, as I never had before, that we are but the tiniest of creatures walking on a speck of dust floating in space. It was a vision that filled me with awe, and an important component of awe is fear.

I was deeply shaken, afraid. In the vision that led to *The Parable of the Tribes*, I had experienced the sacred as having a warm and nurturing energy, a vibrant force that imbues all that lives. This time I sensed an energy that was wholly different. The words *sacred, divine*—these did not fit, for what I had sensed expressing itself in that unspeakable vastness fit no category in my mind, perhaps no category my mind was capable of conceiving. Even "God" seemed too domesticated. It was a force not at all hostile, but of a scope and quality so far beyond human terms that the question of its relation to us could hardly be broached. It was as though the river of energy that infuses life on this planet is, in larger perspective, but a tiny spray up the protected bank away from the raging torrent from which it arises. Like air that is warmed amid the outstretched hairs of a furry creature, the environment in which terrestrial life finds succor is a tiny enclave protected from the cold and howling cosmic wind. It came as an inspiring and terrifying understanding.

Fear had always been something I had held at arm's length, and now it was planted in my gut. The cosmic wind shook me, yet my brother was with me, and if I turned to his loving face I found comfort. For a time I alternated between one experience and the other, and the two combined to teach my heart a lesson that changed it. In the face of the power and vastness of the cosmos, I experienced the truth that we are vulnerable creatures afraid of the overwhelming forces that surround us. In the face of my brother, I discovered that if we embrace this vulnerability as part of what we share as human beings, our hearts can be opened to a kind of divine grace. When I stopped running from the terror that is part of the human condition, my heart opened to receive love. And when I could open my heart, the fear lost its sting. I learned that when I stopped trying to be more than I am, I became more than I had been. I learned that for us humans it is love without pretense of invulnerability that stretches out the furry hairs to warm the cosmic wind around us.

It is that experience that is at the core of this book. It may seem that all this is far removed from the problem of war and peace, but for me the connection is strong and deep. At the root of our enmities and violence is our resistance to our experience of elemental fear. And at the heart of the task of making peace is finding the strength to deal with one another, acknowledging our mutual fear and vulnerability and our shared yearning for love.

This is a utopian vision, of course, far removed from the actual way that nations deal with one another. But it is a mistake to dismiss the utopian as something that does not and cannot exist. It *does* exist as an

element in our reality. And it can function as a beacon toward which
we attempt to turn. Given what we are, we cannot wholly embody our
greatest aspirations. But only by trying to steer toward those aspirations
can we escape plunging into the abyss.

The connection between the experience I have described and the
problem of war and peace is illustrated by a commentary I recently gave
on National Public Radio. Like the dream, and like the vision on the
mountain, this piece was not something I created but something given
me as a gift. As I sat in the Kennedy Center in Washington one evening
in late October 1985, on the eve of the first Reagan-Gorbachev summit
meeting, the piece virtually wrote itself. It remained for me but to write
it down a couple of days later.

To Live Free from the Grip of Terror

I went to the Kennedy Center the other night. On the way in I
noticed that the huge bank of windows around the entrance,
flanked by tall metal columns, formed a visual doorway sixty feet
high. The place was designed at the height of the American
empire. We thought we were bigger than human, so we built
entrances for giants.

The occasion was a concert to celebrate the fortieth anniversary
of the founding of the United Nations. With people from over one
hundred countries in attendance, Elliott Richardson spoke words of
welcome, and spoke as well of the importance of nations resolving
their differences by discussion rather than war. He was followed by
a young black American diplomat—beautiful in his elegance and
eloquence, beautiful too standing as an embodiment of the genuine
possibilities for human liberation. We must, he said, rekindle the
hope that brought the United Nations forth out of the devastation
of World War II, the hope for a new beginning for mankind.

Part of the concert was the 5th Symphony by Shostakovich. I
read over the program notes, and the story they told took my
breath away. The symphony was written and first performed in the
Soviet Union in 1937, at "the height of the Stalin terror." Through
his music, Shostakovich spoke to that unspoken terror, spoke so
deeply that many in that Leningrad audience wept. "The applause
went on for an entire hour," our conductor Rostropovich was
quoted as saying. "People . . . ran up and down through the streets
of Leningrad till the small hours, embracing and congratulating
each other on having been there." They had understood, said
Rostropovich, the symphony's "message of sorrow, suffering and
isolation; stretched on the rack of the Inquisition, the victim still
tries to smile in his pain."

I was moved by the depth of the yearning of those Russians to
live free from the grip of terror. I was moved to remember the
obvious, that more than anything else the Russians are our fellow
human beings. It is those Russians who wept in Leningrad, and
their children, and their grandchildren, whom we are poised to
vaporize by the millions, I thought; and it is they whose weapons
stand ready to annihilate us.

We are all living now in an era over which terror rules. Our fear
we have in common, yet we have allowed our fear to divide us.
From fear of being vulnerable human beings, we make ourselves
into nuclear giants. These giants hide their fear behind the fortifications on which they display their bluster and threat. Bigger than
human, but less than human too.

The true "high frontier" lies not in an outer space to be filled
with still more weapons. It is in our inner space, where we are
challenged to find that common humanity that can bridge over the
walls we have built between us.

As our leaders go to Geneva, like those who first heard
Shostakovich's symphony, we long to hear something that speaks to
our common terror. We too would weep with relief as we ran out
into the night to embrace each other.

The Worship of the Invulnerable

Out of the fear of our vulnerability, we try to make ourselves into gods.
But even our image of God may be a reflection of our fears. Perhaps it is
because we worship strength that the God we envision is omnipotent
and invulnerable. Part 4, "God's Truth," will discuss our knowledge of
God, or more especially the limits to it. But it may be fitting here, at
the end of part 1, "The Worship of Strength," to consider briefly an
alternative view of God to the Almighty one of Western monotheism.

Whatever our reasons for conceiving of God as we have, one of the
consequences of this belief has been confusion about suffering and evil.
For if God is all-powerful, why is the world in such bad shape? There is
no problem here if one sees God as being not only omnipotent but also
capable of cruelty and evil. And, indeed, in many of the biblical stories
God does appear a projection of a cruel parental image. But even in
these, God's cruelty is represented as righteous, the evils He inflicts as
punishments for the evils we humans do. The evil originates in us, and
God is seen as not only all-powerful but also all-good. But then the
question arises: how could it be that a God capable of bringing into
being whatever kind of creation He wished ends up with creatures as

flawed as we? The traditional solution to this discrepancy between a Creator all-powerful and all-good and a creature so permeated with evil has been the idea of "free will." For whatever reason, He wanted us free to choose between good and evil, and we don't choose well.

At greater length elsewhere,[1] I will explain why the idea of free will that might take God off this moral hook in itself makes no logical sense. Free will, rather than removing the confusion, simply becomes the locus of the confusion. Beyond the logical problems with this "solution," however, this way of understanding seems to me to trap us helplessly in an unhealthy relationship with God. Indeed, the whole pattern here looks like a cosmic version of the relationship that abused children can develop with their parents: *they* must be right, and somehow our suffering must be *our* fault. *

What emerges from the idea of God's omnipotence is such a confusion of love and hate, of what sustains us and what destroys us, that it is no wonder that our attempts to orient by what is sacred have often led us straight to the diabolical.

There is another way of conceiving of the force we call "God."

The traditional way splits the cosmos into the Creator on the one hand and the Creation on the other. But the increase of human knowledge has revealed the "creation" to be an ongoing process. Through cosmic evolution, something is continually coming into being. I and others who are working in an evolutionary perspective and with a sense of its spiritual meaning have sensed that this evolutionary process may be the key to a whole new understanding of "God." The Power is there, seething in the universe and driving its evolutionary movement. The Goodness is there: as Jonas Salk writes, "It is my conviction that when good triumphs over evil, it is not for moral reasons alone but as part of the error-correcting process of evolution. Although not preconceived, there appears to be a direction in evolution . . ."[3] It seems as though something much greater than us is trying to come into being, trying to grow toward perfection. Something greater than us,

---

*Lillian Smith expresses the lesson about God ingrained in Protestant children growing up in the American South: "We were told that He loved us, and then we were told that He would burn us in everlasting flames of hell if we displeased Him. . . . [T]hat 'people,' like God and parents, can love you and hate you at the same time; and though they may love you, if you displease them they may do you great injury; hence being loved by them does not give you protection from being harmed by them. We learned that They (parents) have a 'right' to act in this way because God does, and that They in a sense represent God, in the family."[2]

but also something of which we are *part*. Perhaps this "something" is God.

What profound implications such a view of God brings with it! If we are part of it, then our sufferings are also God's. The carnage of the battlefield, the scarred earth where the tropical forests have been swept away—these are wounds also on the vulnerable body of God. And our "sins" are also, in this view, the shortcomings of God. But the evolutionary view changes our perspective on "evil." Because the work of evolution is unfinished, the perfect order toward which It/we are growing remains unaccomplished, and through the gaps in the evolutionary fabric evils may befall us, may issue from us. The question no longer is "How could God allow an Auschwitz?"—a question that has made many a survivor abandon all belief in God, or to reject a God deemed unworthy of worship. Perhaps a part of God, too, died at Auschwitz—a God that, like us, is vulnerable and, like us, not yet able to safeguard all that is sacred.

Evil and suffering, in this view, are to be seen not as part of an economy of sin and punitive wrath but as signs of the unfinished process of cosmic evolution. Truly, it is our sin that brings us much of our suffering, but it comes not as retribution but as natural consequence, like tumbling off the path onto the sharp rocks. And it is God's body that bleeds as well. And truly, our working to create a better order—the order of *shalom*—is doing "God's work." But "God's work" not in the sense of its having been assigned from a taskmaster above, but rather in the sense that our labors are God's way of working.

Out from the power-dominated imagery of ruler and ruled, of whip-holder and slave, of the Almighty and the weak, we are led by this view into a different relationship with our God. This God is still our Creator, but in a different sense because the boundaries change when we are part of God. The boundaries of inclusion, in contrast with the boundaries of division, may create a more open path to serve God. To serve not dutifully in the fulfillment of commandments handed from above, but lovingly with an understanding that God *needs* us. The Something of which we are part can work only through the Creation, and the failures and sufferings of the creatures are simultaneously those of the Creator.

Not the apotheosis of vulnerable flesh into almighty gods; rather, the recognition—in the flesh of our bodies and in the living web of our delicate planet—of the vulnerability of the divine.

PART 2

Winning: A World of Scarcity

6

THE ORIGINS
OF A SENSE OF
SCARCITY

I n a world filled with victims and victimizers, the search for security appears as a competitive struggle. We all want security but we have trouble imagining all of us having it. The capacity to envision this condition of mutual security grows out of the experience of positive mutuality in human relationships. To the extent, however, that we are traumatized by pain and evil in relationship, we come to believe that pain is inevitable and that the only question is who shall suffer it. The desired condition of security is thus rendered a scarce commodity: a chosen few may enjoy it, and their possessing it condemns the rest to insecurity, injury, and indignity. The sense that evil and pain must alight somewhere makes human relationships a zero-sum game.*

Our way of dealing with our fear, therefore, can permeate our experience with a sense of scarcity. *We live in a world of scarcity to the extent that we see all the goods and evils of human life to be in fixed supply, with only their distribution in question.*

The initial effect of our experience of injury is to make us want protection from harm. We have been hurt, and we do not want to be

---

*A zero-sum game is one where every gain for one player implies a corresponding loss for other players, and vice versa. Losses plus winnings always add up to zero.

hurt again. Hence the demand for invulnerability. The safety and comfort we seek constitute an internal condition, not intrinsically bound up with competition. The worship of strength emerges as part of the strategy for the protection of self. If we are strong enough, we will not be vulnerable. But it is but a step from strong to triumphant. What is strong enough depends on the strength of others. Self-protection becomes competition. Those most determined not to be humiliated again as victims may adopt the strategy of degrading and injuring those around them. He who craves being made of steel ends in mangling the flesh of others. The need to be safe is transmuted into the need to win.

The Fact of Scarcity

Clearly, there is a degree of realism in this. The world is finite, and that means that scarcity is a fact: interests inevitably will conflict, claims will overlap.

The original Darwinian vision posits scarcity as a primary ingredient in the evolutionary process. Many are born, few survive to reproduce. The division of creatures into winners (survivors) and losers is fundamental. The structure of life is chiseled with death as its sculptor.

The parable of the tribes takes this grim dimension of life a step further. It reveals the inevitable emergence of unrelenting competition among the societies of a civilized animal. Breaking out of the regime of nature, these societies develop an open-ended capacity for expansion. But, the world being finite and the room for expansion consequently being scarce, such societies inevitably come to confront one another. This, along with the parable of the tribes, helps explain why the places where civilization first fully flowered—places like Mesopotamia, the Nile Valley, the Indus, the Yellow River, Mesoamerica, and coastal Peru—were areas of circumscribed, cultivatable land.[1] The bounded terrain heightened the fact of scarcity, and thus intensified the competitive process with dramatic social evolutionary consequences.

Once this social evolutionary process had begun, sufficient power became a requisite of social survival. But "power" is a *relative* term, and what is relative is necessarily scarce. To survive, what a society needs is not some absolute quantity of power, but enough power to avoid destruction by those societies living within striking distance. An unmatched increase in a rival's power is equivalent to a decline in one's own. The dangerous arms race of our time is but a magnification and acceleration of an anxiety-driven escalatory process that has characterized the evolution of civilization generally. Societies strive to increase their power in absolute terms in order to avoid a perilous diminution of power in the only terms that have mattered throughout history: the relative terms of "who has more?" In a system in which power is both indispensable and scarce, people learn to see interactions not in terms of cooperation and mutuality but as a zero-sum game.

Why do nations fight? The realist will tell you that, in their rational self-interest, nations fight to increase their share of the world's limited wealth; to extend their territory, of which there is only so much to go around; to enhance their power relative to that of other states.

But once again we encounter the combination of realism and excess. Inescapable realities do teach "realism." But when the experiences that do the teaching are traumatic, we are likely to learn the lessons excessively.

To the extent that war is a *given*, a premise of our calculations, then scarcity is a fact. If we have decided to fight Nazi Germany to the death, then every loss of theirs is a gain for us. To kill them seems to be the equivalent of saving ourselves. As in poker, fewer chips for them mean more chips for us. Throughout the history of civilization, the ever-present *danger* of war has been a given, one that requires us to keep an eye cocked toward the competitive dimension of scarcity. But war itself is not always a given, and thus scarcity is not the only reality. The network of human interactions need not be a zero-sum game. Peace, commerce, and cooperation are also historic realities. Before the outbreak of war, and even after it, there is often a mutual interest in preserving (or reestablishing) the peace. History also teaches—although not all in our traumatized species have been able to learn it—that there are games available to us in which all can win.

An excessive preoccupation with competition, therefore, can itself create scarcity. Chess is one partially valid model for human interactions: a zero-sum contest to the death. But another valid model, employed by political scientists and game theorists of the nuclear age, is the Prisoner's Dilemma. This game presents two players with a situation in which it is disastrous for one player to cooperate if the other will not; but it is far better for both players if they both cooperate than if they both try to defeat the other. Anyone who plays at the Prisoner's Dilemma as if it were chess will not fare well and will also hurt those with whom he interacts. Likewise, the sorry pages of human history are filled with the destructive effects of excessive scarcity consciousness. For much of history has been made by frightened and therefore power-hungry individuals who, because they regard human relationships as a zero-sum game, have unnecessarily made their interactions into a minus-sum game—i.e., one where the losses exceed the winnings.

War often produces only losers, while from peace all may gain. This has always been true, but never more utterly so than in our age, where even a society that has been destroyed can unleash annihilatory retaliation, and where the destruction one unleashes upon another can bring upon oneself an age of darkness and famine.

Thus the world watches with anxiety the ongoing confrontation between two nuclear superpowers, each in part possessed by the scarcity mentality that assumes that security and survival are scarce commodities. Nathan Leites, in his study of the structure of Bolshevik thinking, remarked on "the Bolshevik emphasis on annihilatory relationships between men."[2] Their doctrine, he says, "maintains that if one does not annihilate, one will be annihilated." A conversation I had in 1983 with an American Defense Department official in the Reagan administration revealed another dangerous, scarcity-based assumption. He expressed, if not a belief in a kind of scarcity of survival (kill or be killed), then at least a belief in a kind of conservation of insecurity: the more insecure we can make them, the more secure we will be. What is the purpose of building the MX, I asked, if its basing mode does not render it any less vulnerable to a first strike than the Minuteman, and if the only "improvement" it represents over its predecessors is that it can kill Soviet missiles in their silos? If they can threaten our silos, he replied, we'll be more secure if we can threaten theirs too. My efforts to elicit from him a scenario that showed how our security would be enhanced by our being able to threaten their silos were unsuccessful, but he seemed no less sure of his argument for that.

The Creation of Scarcity

Tough-minded "realism" thus not only confronts the harsh realities of human interaction but can help to create them. Our excessive focus on the struggle for scarce goods is itself a potent force for impoverishing the world, and in our era threatens its termination. It is therefore incumbent upon us to separate the reality in realism from the destructive illusion, to uncover the fears and passions that lead us to magnify the role of scarcity's dark spirit in the system of human interactions.

In our culture we are overly inclined to interpret human conduct in terms of objective necessity, ignoring the role of the actors' underlying spiritual condition. We see people as pursuing rational self-interest without discerning the play of darker passions. Concerning the motives behind war, I have found that a great number of people simply assume that people fight because of greed and the desire for wealth. This hypothesis is presented in a spirit of realism: because of the objective realities of limited goods and unlimited human needs, people compete for control of resources. If one explores this idea with those who propose it, two premises are uncovered. First there is the assumption that people derive their happiness and security from the goods they possess. Second, that taking other people's goods by force is a sensible strategy for maximizing one's wealth. As for the second premise, the history of recent centuries has demonstrated that the age-old method of acquisition through plunder is a second-rate route to enrichment. Wealth is far more readily produced than stolen. Consider twentieth-century Japan: the destruction of its imperial apparatus, far from leading to its impoverishment, cleared the way for an unprecedented rise in national wealth.* This refutes the scarcity-based maxim that "property is theft," replacing it with the cooperation-based truth that property comes from production through commerce. Greed is not served best by thievery.

But it is the first of the premises that most needs scrutiny, that it is goods that people want and need for their well-being. Perhaps people do strive for wealth as a principal goal, perhaps especially in societies of the modern era. But some international data call into question whether it is the goods in themselves that people really desire.

Surveys have found that wealth correlates with reported happiness *within* societies but not *between* societies.[4] This striking finding suggests that it is not so much the wealth itself that makes people feel good, but rather the *status* that comes from having more than their neighbors. We evidently would prefer being poorer in absolute terms but richer than our neighbors to being richer in absolute terms but poorer than our countrymen. According to this interpretation, a good portion of the utility of wealth is its symbolic value. Having more than those around us helps us feel good about ourselves and, we believe, makes others regard us more highly. With such a scheme of utility, theft makes more sense.

---

*John Farrell and Asa Smith, writing that "After total military defeat and a complete loss of their great-power status, [both Japan and Germany] achieved unprecedented rates of economic growth, far exceeding the growth of the victors."[3] Moreover, the costs of waging war are themselves impoverishing. Farrell and Smith cite a study of the impact of the Japanese war industry on the national economy that indicates that the Japanese damaged their own economy with their war effort roughly as much as did all the destruction wrought by the American war machine.

The survey's finding is a sad reflection upon the human spiritual condition. Spinoza wrote that "Every man's true happiness and blessedness consist solely in the enjoyment of what is good, not in the pride that he alone is enjoying it, to the exclusion of others. He who thinks himself the more blessed because he is enjoying benefits which others are not, or because he is more blessed or more fortunate than his fellows, is ignorant of true happiness and blessedness."[5] In Spinoza's view, it is a sign of spiritual ignorance to regard goodness as a relative or scarce commodity, and to conceive of one's happiness in terms of whether one has more or less than his neighbors.

There is a possible rejoinder to Spinoza's argument. If the "good" is conceived as "superior status," the good will necessarily be scarce, and cannot be enjoyed except in those terms of relativity that breed competition and envy. But granting that "superior status" is a "good" to be sought is already to concede the assumptions of the scarcity-creating mentality. For if the desired good underlying the craving for superior status is feeling good about ourselves and enjoying the esteem of others, then scarcity and competition are not inevitable. Were we not "ignorant of true happiness and blessedness," we would know that self-acceptance does not require triumphing over others, and that respectful treatment might be enjoyed by all and not only by the privileged few.

It is not mere "realism," therefore, to explain the conflicts among civilized societies in such terms as the desire for scarce goods. For if people are indeed motivated by greed we must inquire further into the spiritual condition that makes acquisition seem the route to happiness; and if people do crave having more than their neighbors, independently of the level, we must ask what it is that makes another's relative poverty feel like one's own enrichment. The same limitations on realism—i.e., on appeals to objective reality—apply to other ideas dominated by the assumption of scarcity. One of these is the idea that war arises out of the struggle to dominate. Even if it is true that the lust to dominate drives some into war-making, we need to explore why it is that some people feel insecure with anything they do not control. When we read, for example, that the "Russians could not grasp the idea" that the governments of postwar Eastern Europe would be freely elected and be "friendly toward the Soviet Union," we who share a three-thousand-mile unguarded border with Canada can see that more than realism is involved: "an autonomous and friendly neighbor" does not have to be an oxymoron. But American "realism" also has its blind spots. We may not always be able to see that our winning does not require that our rival loses. Garry Wills's interpretation of President Kennedy's handling of the

Cuban missile crisis, for example, reveals a scarcity-creating mentality at work: Kennedy "would not, as he put it, let Khrushchev rub his nose in the dirt. Which meant that he had to rub Khrushchev's nose in the dirt . . ."[6] Thus did the world go to the brink.

It is not, therefore, to scarcity per se that we should look for the engines of competition, but to our *feeling of scarcity*. For as the foregoing discussion suggests, although scarcity is a fact, it is also an illusion we create out of a kind of spiritual ignorance. We enter into destructive competition not only because it is required for survival in a biosphere shaped by natural selection and in a civilization molded by the struggle for power, but also because our experience has somehow disabled us from conceiving of "the good" as anything except scarce.

Because of our illusions about the ubiquity of scarcity, we miss opportunities to create and experience abundance. Because of our exaggerating the requirements for security, we conduct ourselves in a way that reduces the security of all, including ourselves.

An important first step, therefore, is to acknowledge the limits to the role of objective scarcity in fomenting war. As J. W. Burton, scholar of social conflict, writes, international conflicts may not be over those material goods that cannot be shared but over other kinds of values of a less material nature, such as security, identity and recognition, and a role in shaping one's destiny. These kinds of values, he notes, "are not in short supply," and with such nonscarce goods a kind of synergy operates so that to give more can mean to have more, not less.

> The more security one party experiences, the more others experience. The more identity a minority ethnic group experiences, the more likely it is to accord recognition to others and to co-operate within an agreed social and political system. Greek Cypriot attempts to impose a constitution that made "nameless people" out of Turkish Cypriots were doomed to failure. Israeli attempts to make second-class citizens out of Palestinians are also doomed to failure. If this is the case then, clearly, it is in the interest of all parties to ensure that the opposing parties achieve these social needs.[7]

This first step, though important, does not take us far enough. Burton's analysis is reasonable, but regrettably we human beings are not governed solely by reason. Burton and Spinoza are looking to us to behave rationally, like the Economic Man of classical economic theorists, for whom more is always better than less and envy is irrelevant. But it is not enough simply to describe what is reasonable; we must also understand the forces of unreason. We must go beyond the recognition of what is objectively scarce and what is not, to gain understanding of the deep psychological forces that project the shadow of scarcity over everything we behold.

Were we not spiritually ignorant, in the sense that Spinoza describes, we would cease to fight over goods that are potentially abundant. But, as we continue in ignorance, we continue to create competition and conflict where it need not be. Although identity and self-esteem are not intrinsically scarce commodities, some people can feel that their identity and their feeling of self-worth are affirmed only when they play the role of the master race enslaving and degrading others. And while it may be true in some objective and rational sense that each is more secure when others are more secure, when people are operating in an emotional universe of scarcity, their own *sense* of security may be incompatible with others having any security whatsoever. A polity may be most healthy and secure when it affords all its members a participatory role, but to some the ability of others to act autonomously is experienced as an intolerable threat to their own autonomy.

Not only does our assumption of scarcity impel us to destroy the blessings of others, so that we may feel more blessed, we also may impose suffering on others in the belief that we will thereby be relieved of the burden of our own suffering. Among the Kwakiutl, reports Ruth Benedict, those mourning the death of a loved one might seek relief through head-hunting. This head-hunting was called "killing to wipe one's eyes," and the aggrieved restored their well-being "by making another household mourn instead."[8]

Hitler gives us an image of our spiritual ignorance:

> Among 30 candidates who applied for the position of personal chauffeur to the Fuehrer, Hitler selected the shortest man in the group and kept him as his personal driver for the rest of his life, even though it was necessary to put special blocks under the seat so that he could see over the steering wheel.[9]

As if the smallness of others might cast our own stature onto a more than human scale.

Something has happened to human beings that has extended the domain of scarcity beyond reason.

As long as our sense of possibility is constrained by an excessive presumption of scarcity, we will be barred from Spinoza's true happiness, and from the blessings of true security. And perhaps the first step in alleviating our spiritual ignorance is to diminish our ignorance of that ignorance.

The issue of scarcity concerns relationship. Chronic conflict in the human system teaches the lesson that human interaction creates winners and losers. Conversely, the belief that the requirements of security are the rewards of a zero-sum game renders the search for security into a struggle among people and among nations. The excessive sense of scarcity is thus both a sign of sickness and an agent of corrosion in the complex web of human relationships. The cruel world inflicts injury, and injured people seek to protect themselves in ways that unnecessarily deprive others of goods that could be abundant.

In the next two chapters we will explore two dimensions of our excessive sense of scarcity. First, the need for *superiority*, to be better than, more favored than, triumphant over others ("On Top: Narcissism and the Quest for Superiority"). Second, the need for *control*, to make others mere instruments of one's own will ("Running the Show: The Paranoid Economy of the Will").

7

ON TOP:
NARCISSISM AND THE
QUEST FOR SUPERIORITY

I. THE PLAGUE OF NARCISSISM IN
EVOLUTIONARY PERSPECTIVE

W e want to understand how it is that nonmaterial goods "not in short supply" come to be experienced as scarce. There is perhaps no concept more pertinent to this question than that of *narcissism*. Narcissism, which engenders a need to feel superior to others, is the fruit of flawed relationships and then becomes itself a source of conflict in human relationships. An investigation of this problem can, moreover, provide a penetrating glimpse into the problematic side of the human condition as it has evolved with civilization.

A Dependence on Relationship

It can be shown that a consequence of chronic conflict in the system of human relationships is that each person growing up in that system is likely to be burdened with an impaired relationship with himself.

Begin with the fact that we have evolved as social animals. Long before our ancestors were anything like human, they were social creatures. This means that the maintenance of the social bond was a key element in their strategy of survival. We evolved to be connected with one another, not as a casual matter but as a matter of life and death. Dependency upon relationship is at the core of our nature.

This dependency, moreover, provided an essential means to allow our transition from social life to a new experiment, cultural life.

In the history of life, the emergence of culture was a major breakthrough. It reduced the role of genetic inheritance in determining behavior and allowed learning and creativity to devise new forms of social life. For the transition into cultural life to work, however, we had also to become, in William Waddington's phrase, the "ethical animal." As ethical animals, we are by our inherent nature prepared to take in, from the people who raise us, moral principles to constrain the free play of appetite. Morality is a necessary aptitude for cultural animals. Without morality the gap in behavioral control—opened when the grip of instinct is loosened—would be filled by a destructive anarchy inconsistent with the demands of social life. The transition to culture thus required us to develop a moral, or evaluative, relationship with ourselves.

To achieve this end, our evolution into culture seized upon our ancient social dependency. As social animals, we already needed to be loved by others. This emotional dependency is especially great during the formative years when we are most helpless, and thus objectively most dependent, and when we are most receptive to learning. Certain biological changes attendant upon the growth of our cultural abilities accentuated our dependency. In order for us to become cultural creatures, our brain size had to increase. Because of limitations on the pelvic size of human mothers, despite widening of the hips, the necessary growth in brain size required human babies to be born at a more immature stage of development. More immature means more helpless, more completely dependent upon caretakers for survival. And then there was a prolongation of childhood compared with other species. (A cat may produce offspring at less than 5 percent of its life span, whereas with humans the figure is over fifteen percent.) We begin more helpless and remain dependent and subordinate longer than other animals. This gives powerful leverage to the socialization process.

Socialization molds us, in part, by bathing us in more love when we do what others want, while giving us less love, or even anger and rejection and pain, when we stray from the approved path. Our extended dependency on others for survival, and for the flow of love that assures we will be cared for, leads us to mold ourselves into the form that best maintains this flow of love. Internalizing our relationship with those on whom we depend, we become "ethical animals."

Our relationship with ourselves, therefore, is an outgrowth of our relationship with others. As W. W. Meissner puts it: "From the very beginning of his experience, the child is dependent on his relationship with significant others for the building and maintaining of his sense of self."[1] Because by nature we must be ethical animals, our sense of our self will have a strong evaluative dimension. In other words, it is a key requirement of our well-being that we feel good about ourselves. "In a child's eyes," writes John Mack, "his sense of self-worth is *essential* to his survival."[2] "The child who does not experience his value in the eyes of his parents will fear their abandonment and its attendant dangers to his existence."[3] Thus it is that the evaluative dimension of our relationship with ourselves—our sense of self-worth—is also internalized from our relationships with others.

Because the ethical animal cannot feel good unless he feels that he is good, and because he derives his feeling of self-worth from the flow of love he receives from significant others, the human creature can be at peace with himself only to the extent that he has received the love and care he needs. The more secure we are in receiving this love and approval, according to Anna Freud, the better established is our "primary narcissism," a secure kind of self-love. A child growing up at peace with himself is thus a sign of harmony in the system of relationships, and of survival needs being met. Conversely, when there is something wrong in the realm of relationship, when basic human needs are not being securely met, the problem will manifest in injury to the self-regard of growing human beings.

Narcissism as the Fruit of Defective Relationship

The immediate nexus of injury is in the child's relationship to those on whom he depends, especially his parents. It is only in relationship, according to John Mack, that people can experience a feeling of positive self-worth.[4] But if relationship fails, painful negative feelings toward the self are internalized. When a child's needs go unmet, the child will internalize the experience as reflecting negatively upon his or her worth. As a protective measure, a new kind of narcissism develops.

This strategy of "secondary narcissism" has two components. The first is a sealing off of the self, so that the disappointing and hurtful connection with the outside world loses some of its sting. Thus, writes

Anna Freud, such "narcissistic defeats" as are suffered in unsatisfying relationships "only serve to turn the infant back toward his self-contained primary egocentricity."[5] The second part of this narcissistic strategy is a denial of the internalized negative image of the self and a compensatory overinflation of that self-image. Thus, Heinz Kohut suggests, defects in maternal care lead to a "grandiose and exhibitionistic self-image."[6] I am not, the individual protests desperately, what the bad treatment I receive makes me feel that I am.

We are so structured as animals that the need to feel good about ourselves is imperative. Unwilling to forgo the fulfillment of this need, we develop one of two kinds of narcissism. If we are truly nourished emotionally, we are fed at the level of "primary narcissism": secure in being loved, we become secure in our love of ourselves and open to give forth love to others. The experience of abundance equips us for participation in a world of abundant goodness. If, on the other hand, we are the victims of defective care, this fundamental level of self-regard is injured and we compensate by developing "secondary narcissism": to drown out the voice that has inferred from bad treatment that we ourselves must be bad, we protest grandiosely that we are the greatest. Having constituted our emotional structure in a world that gave an insufficiency of needed love, we henceforth see the world as a place where goodness is apportioned through a zero-sum game.

Although this secondary, pathological sort of narcissism* defines a particular character type, it is probably *to some degree* characteristic of us all. The unavoidable imperfections in the care we receive imply inevitable narcissistic injury, and from such injury arises some use of narcissistic defense. "All of us," writes W. W. Meissner, "are the possessors of an embattled narcissism."[7] The more profound the injuries we have suffered, the more germane is narcissism likely to be to our way of maintaining our self.

Narcissism and the Crippled Capacity for Relationship

This narcissism, itself the fruit of failed relationship, cripples the capacity for positive, loving relationship. Sigmund Freud's concept of narcissism derives its name, of course, from the mythological Greek character Narcissus. Narcissus was indifferent to the offers of love from the woodland maidens smitten with his beauty, and fell in love instead with

---

*Hereafter, this "secondary narcissism" will be called, simply, "narcissism."

his own image in a pool. The pathological narcissism that grows out of the narcissistic injury inflicted by neglect or abuse likewise manifests an inability to connect meaningfully and constructively with others beyond the self.

First, the retreat into the protective stance of narcissism casts the rest of the world into a shadowy light. It is less valued, less real. Erich Fromm defines narcissism as "a state of experience in which only the person himself . . . [is] experienced as fully real while everybody and everything that does not form part of the person or is not an object of his needs [is] *affectively* without weight and color."[8] Otto Kernberg describes as "shadowy" the narcissist's image of most others. Even being *real* becomes a scarce commodity.

Second, to maintain the protective isolation of narcissism, the narcissist avoids dependency on others. Such dependence is his greatest fear because it would expose the narcissist "to the dangers of being exploited, mistreated, and frustrated."[9] The narcissistic personality says, "I am my ideal image of myself, better than anyone else whom I wanted to love me could be, so if I have the love of myself I need no one else."[10] The emotional bases of mutuality and cooperation, of giving and sharing, are undermined in the formation of the narcissistic personality.

An image of this aspect of narcissism is Nietzsche's Superman. Horst-Eberhard Richter describes the Übermensch, the dominant figure in Nietzsche's philosophy, in this way:

> The Superman no longer even needs the nurturing service and devotion of a woman, for he has, as it were, appropriated her emotional powers by incorporating them into himself. Zarathustra celebrates his triumphant achievement of total autarchy and luxuriates in his self-infatuation, his orgiastic delusions of grandeur. In his megalomaniacal omnipotence, he performs the act of self-deification, turning himself into his own intoxicated and intoxicating lover.[11]

The narcissistic celebration of the isolated and inflated self is an effort to compensate for the closure by injury of the possibility of establishing nurturing relationships with others.

If narcissism simply meant solipsism or autarchy, though, it would not be as dangerous as it is. But the narcissist does have a need for others in his drama, and the role he needs them for is the one he refuses to play himself. This is the role of the worthless one, the loser. The feeling of unworthiness is at the core of his experience, and it will not go away. The category of unworthiness must be represented somewhere. Unable to bear the pain of his own experience of low self-worth, the narcissist erects a fragile structure of grandiosity. Unable to wish the pain of the feeling of unworthiness wholly out of existence, the narcissist requires others to become its repositories. The devaluation of others is required to protect the gratifying but precarious image of the self.* Because the positive image of the self is menaced by its opposite, the feeling of positive self-worth is experienced as a scarce commodity.

Then there is the rage. Injury produces anger, and as we are so constituted that a feeling of positive self-worth is at the core of our needs, so is an injury to that feeling the most profound of injuries. Narcissism thus arises together with profound rage. The narcissistic structures, the fruit of injury, are, because they are precarious, highly vulnerable to further injury. Thus, narcissism comes with a pool of rage, and that pool is readily refreshed. Gregory Rochlin goes so far as to say that "Aggression *always* issues . . . as a reaction to threatened or actually damaged narcissism . . ."[12]

Narcissism is thus not just retreat but is often the prelude to attack. We can recall that the place of Nietzsche's solipsistic hero in history is not confined to the pages of the works of a single individual. The Übermensch, as adopted by a subsequent generation of Nietzsche's countrymen, goose-stepped his way onto the center of the historical stage, leaving the mangled bodies of millions in his wake. The narcissistic wounds suffered by individuals or peoples thus leads to the infliction of other wounds on other people. The crippled capacity for relationship engenders not just withdrawal from relationship but entry into a twisted pattern of relationship.

A world filled with narcissistic injury is thus a world at war.† The fundamental goods of emotional well-being having been experienced as scarce, the narcissist must fight to maintain his sense of self. And because he is fighting against the reality of his experience, the narcissist is prepared to do battle against whatever or whomever does not reinforce his fragile reconstruction of reality. Trying to make the tolerable *part* of his experience of himself serve as *all* of that experience, the

---

*This kind of psychological mechanism will be dealt with extensively in part 3, "Boundaries."

†James W. Prescott's work substantiates this link. Drawing upon cross-cultural data, in which anthropologists evaluated cultural characteristics for a great diversity of societies, Prescott found a marked inverse correlation between two variables: the degree of physical affection given infants and the extent of violence displayed by adults in a culture. This inverse relationship was found to be significant at the $p = .004$ level, or more than ten times as great as is generally required to be regarded as statistically significant.

narcissist experiences scarcity and comes to deal with goods that objectively "are not in short supply"—such as self-respect, identity, etc.—as scarce commodities. Thus it is that a species plagued by "embattled narcissism" easily becomes a species embattled among itself.

These are the themes that will be explored in "Winning" (p. 121).

This leads us back from the problem of a growing child to the problems of a troubled species, from the injury that derives from a defective relationship to an epidemic that plagues human history.

Chicken and Egg Revisited

If narcissism of this kind is the fruit of defective care during childhood, then recent research into the history of childhood reveals why the problems of narcissism are epidemic in human affairs. According to such profound students of the subject as Lloyd deMause (*The History of Childhood*) and Alice Miller (*For Your Own Good*), the problem of abusive and defective parenting has not been manifested simply by idiosyncratically pathological individuals here and there but rather has been a pervasive sickness in historical societies generally.

Miller, for example, reviews the literature of what she calls "poisonous pedagogy." This frightening literature, drawn from various (mostly German) sources over several centuries, expounds not the covert parenting practices of a few criminal parents, but the proudly enunciated recommendations of cultural leaders on the way to bring up children. In the summary of her investigations into this pedagogy, she lists some of the core beliefs that can be inferred from the literature. For example, the belief that "a high degree of self-esteem is harmful," while "a low degree of self-esteem makes a person altruistic."[13] A Herr Hergang is quoted, from 1851, chastising those pedagogues who "awaken and help to swell a child's conceit by foolishly emphasizing his merits . . ."[14] To counteract the child's feeling good about himself, the wise pedagogue will lead him "into situations where he is made aware of his imperfections," given tasks beyond his abilities, etc.[15] Other core beliefs identified by Miller are that "responding to a child's needs is wrong," and that "severity and coldness are a good preparation for life."[16] "*Suppress everything* in the child," wrote Herr Schreber, the highly respected nineteenth-century expert (and father of Freud's Wolf Man, the prototypical paranoid of Freud's theories).[17] One useful exercise "in the art of self-denial," advocated by Schreber, "is to give the child frequent opportunity to learn to watch other people in his immediate vicinity eating and drinking without desiring the same for himself."[18] As another pedagogic expert put it, parental love "is concerned that the child learn at an early age to renounce, control, and master himself, that he not blindly follow the promptings of the flesh . . ."[19]

In other words, the child is taught to regard his very nature as evil, as bad, as something to be transformed. Simply because he is a child, he is treated as unworthy of respect—this too is a core belief identified by Miller as part of the poisonous pedagogy. The injury to the sense of self-worth is continuous, systematic, and by design.

If one turns from the heartrending pages of Miller's book to deMause's, one gets no respite. DeMause documents persuasively that the abuse of children has been systematic in historical societies, even to the point of widespread murder of children. If defective treatment produces narcissistic injury and the compensatory development of secondary narcissism, then there has been an epidemic sickness in the system of human relationships to make such injury and such narcissism seem an intrinsic part of the human condition.

I began this chapter saying that it can be shown that "a consequence of chronic conflict in the system of human relationships is that each person growing up in that system is likely to be burdened with an impaired relationship with himself." We have seen how this is so, and the historians of childhood show that the chronic conflict has been a virtual state of war of parents against their children.

But what are the origins of this cycle of injury? Both deMause and Miller (and other students of child abuse such as B. F. Steele and C. B. Pollock) show how abusive parent-child relationships tend to replicate themselves in the next generation. Abused children become abusive parents. Once begun, the sick cycle of injurious warfare of parents against their children can perpetuate itself. But the question remains unanswered: where did the cycle begin?

This question brings us back to the problem of the chicken and the egg broached earlier, in the prologue. Sick people make sick history, and sick history makes people sick, and so on indefinitely. But how does the sickness become endemic in the system to begin with?

DeMause, who has an entirely psychological approach to causality in human affairs, gives an answer that is the modern equivalent of the doctrine of original sin. Where did the problem begin? At the beginning. It has always been there. Human beings as a species began as psychologically immature creatures, unfit for parenthood. Our original emotional incapacity is gradually diminishing as we as a species mature emotionally. The possibility of our being caring parents is only now emerging; the darkness of the past is unremitting, reaching back into the primeval origins of the species. It is in the domain of psychological development that the cause of our destructive patterns is to be found, although the injurious effects of those patterns are both micro (in growing children) and macro (in the bloody pages of civilized history).

It is impossible to disprove an explanation like deMause's with logic alone, but given certain premises about the nature of life and the way it evolves, his explanation seems to me implausible. The evolutionary process appears incredibly exacting in assuring that the structure and behavior of creatures conform to the requirements for survival. This was the premise that we used to explain our evolving receptivity to socialization, becoming the ethical animal.

Are we to believe that the evolutionary process that molded our bodies with mind-boggling complexity was so careless with the development of our emotional capacities as to leave us dangerously unfinished? Are we to believe that our evolved need to maintain harmonious social bonds made us receptive to socialization as infants but neglected to equip us to be caring as parents? Good parenting has been central to the challenge of human survival, more so probably than with any other species. Are we to believe that, although we can see marvelously nurturing mothering among other mammals, we have for some million years been too immature to care properly for our offspring? It would violate my beliefs about the processes of life to believe that our capacity to parent well would not be provided by our inherent nature, as are all the other capacities on which our survival depends.

Similarly, to conceive of "maturity" as something a whole species could lack for aeons is inconsistent with what seems a reasonable concept of organismic development: the "psychological maturity" that abusive parents lack, other animals seem routinely to possess, and our ancestors living in healthy environments probably did also. And if such maturity was not something that naturally unfolded from our being, given a healthful environment, it is doubtful that we could "learn" to be mature through a process of cultural evolution. There are some things toward which humankind has to mature through cultural learning, such as gaining the intellectual and spiritual understandings required of a creature with our present and emergent powers. These are in areas where new circumstances demand new levels of consciousness. But something that for millions of years has been central to our way of surviving—something so indispensable as the capacity to care lovingly for our young—would not be an area of "immaturity" in the natural creature.

The most plausible premise seems that our species emerged from millions of years of mammalian evolution endowed by nature with essentially healthy patterns of parenting. Here and there, idiosyncratic factors would have produced pathological parents. But it is implausible that the problem of chronically defective parenting could have arisen spontaneously in the micro realm of psychological forces alone. If we reject deMause's recourse to "original sin," we must look to the intrusion of other kinds of forces to account for the emergence of a pattern of injury.

The "egg" cannot have laid itself. Something must have happened to the species to render human parents as antagonistic to their children as we find them in civilized societies throughout history, to thwart their growth into the kind of emotional maturity required for nurturant parenting.

We can here turn again to the parable of the tribes. We saw earlier that this "chicken"—the destructive social evolutionary process described by the parable of the tribes—need not have grown out of any egg to speak of. The circumstances of the emergence of civilization are themselves conducive to destructive competition; and the selective process described by the parable of the tribes can seize upon particular power-enhancing cultural forms that arise idiosyncratically and magnify them into requirements for the human system generally.

This is the great tragedy of human creativity. It was said earlier that the emergence of culture demanded that we become "ethical animals" or else the retreat of instinct would have engendered an anarchy incompatible with the demands of human social life. We made that transition into being moral animals capable of culture, and could therefore live unplagued by that anarchy for many thousands of years. But the breakthrough into civilization a mere ten thousand years ago reintroduced the problem of anarchy at the macro level of intersocietal interactions. This macro level provided anarchy its point of entry because it was a brand-new system—having virtually sprung into existence with civilization's sudden emergence. As a result of this suddenness, no evolutionary process—biological or cultural—had had any opportunity to structure civilization according to the requirements of harmony and survival. At this point, life's experiment with culture at last fell into the pitfall of anarchy, and the war of all against all began.

Chronic conflict at the macro level was inevitable, not because human beings were already sick but because the nature of the overarching system made such sickness, whenever it did break out, irresistibly contagious.

There are several ways in which the parable of the tribes can explain the epidemic of narcissism.

First, the inevitable struggle for power condemned humankind to the chronic experience of injury. I would propose as an axiom that all bad treatment one suffers from the world injures one's feelings of self-worth. When we are small children, just developing a concept of self, we are most vulnerable to such narcissistic injuries. But—as social, cultural, ethical animals—we are structured to continue to regard the receiving of love and the meeting of our needs as affirmations of our value, and the suffering of abuse and the neglect of our needs as messages about our worthlessness. *

The parable of the tribes describes how this inevitably became a cruel world, and a cruel world inflicts narcissistic injury. Adults thus injured will be impaired in their capacity to give full love to their spouses and their children. The sickness begun because of anarchy in the overarching system infects relationships in the intimate system of the family.† Over time, the gradual compounding of injuries can grow into a wealth of pathological narcissism, with people emotionally ill-equipped either to raise children or to make peace in the world.

Second, in a world of unrelenting competition, a degree of narcissistic injury may actually be adaptive. Just as the genetic defect sickle-cell anemia is adaptive to maintain in a population living in areas chroni-

---

*During the Great Purge in the Soviet Union, most Russian people assumed that the victims must be guilty of something. Similarly, the people of Poland assumed that the Jews being gassed in the extermination camps must have done something terrible to bring such a horrific punishment upon themselves. To the extent that we automatically interpret sufferings and misfortune as punishment, we are incapable of giving sympathy to victims, whether the victims are other people or ourselves.

†A horrific image from the film *Shoah* may stand as a hyperbolic emblem of the problem. A Jewish man, who was forced to serve at the Nazi crematorium at Treblinka, told of what was hardest of all to endure: the scene when the doors to the death chambers were opened. The cyanide gas, he explained, rose from the floor. The higher one could get, therefore, the longer one could postpone one's death. Because of the scarcity thus created by the Nazis' brutal death machine, the turning on of the gas unleashed a desperate struggle among the three thousand densely packed men, women, and children to rise to the top. When it was all over and the doors were opened, on the bottom would be the weak—the children and the aged—their faces crushed and bloodied beyond recognizability. In the panic of death brought on by the Nazi destroyers, our witness explained, a man might, in the darkness, push to the top over the shattered skull of his own son.

The destructive play of power creates a desperate sense of scarcity, injuring people and throwing them into a blind panic in which, in their efforts to preserve themselves, they are driven to hurt their own children.

cally infested with malaria, a psychic injury that energizes one for the struggle for preeminence may be conducive to survival in an anarchic world. It is noteworthy that it is in the most anarchic of environments (e.g., "feudal" societies) that the symptoms of narcissism are most likely to be regarded as virtues: they are called by a more glowing name, however—honor.* This adaptive quality of narcissism compounds the spread of the disease. Not only does the struggle for power inflict injuries that engender narcissism, but the selection for power—which spreads whatever enhances competitive ability—tends to impose the advantageous structure on everyone in the system. So often, history has shown that people whose hearts are open and full of peace are trampled by those bent on glory and dominion.

Third, as the structure of power escalates in social evolution, civilized societies tend to make increasingly burdensome demands during the socialization of their members. Not only is the struggle for power chronic, but over time the terms of that struggle tend to escalate. This escalation has exploited the flexibility inherent in the cultural animal to make us able servants of systems antagonistic to our natures.† The escalation of the level of power required for social survival has thus entailed an escalation of the requirements imposed on people raised to serve civilized societies. Therefore, although it may be cruel for civilized pedagogy to make war on the inborn nature we bring into the world as children, it is not only out of cruelty that it does so. The necessities of power have also mandated that the parents and teachers of civilized children not simply nurture their flowering as nature had intended. Because civilization has required us to become something different, children grow up with the narcissistically injurious message that what they are is not all right. Civilization's demand that people reshape themselves in the service of power thus has mandated that the parent-child relationship be the scene of chronic narcissistic injury.‡

---

*The connection between narcissism and honor is explored in "The Honor of the Warrior" (p. 129).

†On this, see chapter 5 of The Parable of the Tribes.

‡An interesting illustration of this is found in Eli Sagan's description of child rearing in the African kingdom of Buganda. Bugandan society had evolved across the crucial threshold that separates the earlier kinship-based society from those with a nonkinship form of political cohesion. (The evolution toward more powerful societies led away from kinship-based order because bureaucratic structures could, among other things, control larger areas and larger and more diverse populations.)

Child rearing among the Baganda included "arbitrary, painful, and aggressive separat-

In all these ways, the "chicken" of an inevitable social evolutionary process has made the problem of narcissism epidemic in our species.

It is the human tragedy that our greatest virtues have been the means of our undoing. I spoke of this earlier with respect to human creativity: the special abilities that enabled us to extricate ourselves from the limits of biologically evolved nature also plunged us into the terrors of anarchy. In the same way, we are the tragic victims of *our inherent sensitivity to relationship.*

By nature we are builders of bonds among people. Living by the synergistic modes of cooperation is our natural way. But our creativity thrust us into a situation where the contagion of strife would overwhelm our capacity to knit together—at least for the first ten millennia of this still unfolding experiment that life is conducting through us. Such chronic strife is particularly distressing to creatures like us who are so sensitive to the quality of relationship. * Where we crave mutuality, the struggle for power gave us competition. Where our nature turns us to the abundance that grows from love, our injured feelings perverted us toward the scarcity-dominated world of narcissism. Were we not so dependent upon harmony in our relationships, we would not have been so crippled by the unbidden entry—at the macro level—of destructiveness in the system of human interactions. It is our being born for love that makes us so vulnerable to being turned, when injured, into channels of hate.

---

ing of the young from its parents." And the "weaning from the breast seemed to be designed to be as traumatic as possible. No effort was made to wean the child gradually; the breast was suddenly withdrawn one day, usually when the child was two or three, and if the child insisted on sucking chili powder was put on the nipple to make it unpalatable."[20]

How do such brutal practices connect with the need to help the child adapt to his world? The Baganda "clearly felt that the infantile attachment should be violently broken, probably so that the child could develop a more separated and individuated ego." Functioning in the bureaucratic structure may indeed have been facilitated by such individuation, but the Bugandan system was not just bureaucratic, it was also the stage for intense and deadly Machiavellian intrigues dominated from the top of the power structure by a narcissistic and infantile tyrant. Sagan cites Mahler's finding that the trauma of separation produces first anxiety and then anger. To this we can add, in Eriksonian terms, that it establishes distrust where nature would have us grow into trust. But the Bugandan tyranny was not a state of nature, and what better set of ingredients to survive a world of Machiavellian power struggles than the anxiety to make one alert, the distrust to prevent one from being stabbed in the back, and the rage to make one ruthless.

* In her analysis of how Hitler's traumatic childhood turned him into a mass murderer, Alice Miller imputes to the child Hitler an acute sensitivity that, perverted by injury, only compounded the evil that later issued through his actions in the world.

II. THE CHOSEN AND THE REJECTED

Chosen People

We need to feel good about ourselves. But the plague of narcissistic injury has transformed our need to feel good about ourselves into the task of feeling better than others. In a world of scarcity, not everyone can be all right. We must thus be special beings. And the others? They must be lesser. The world cloven into the chosen and the rejected is a violent one, as each defends an image of self that he inwardly senses is a lie.

Recall the samurai, a special being above the level of beasts, immune to the ills of flesh and blood, such as fleas. Snuffing out another human life was not too great a price to pay to preserve his cherished illusion.

This narcissism operates at the group level as well as the individual. Indeed, narcissism is so corrosive to human relationships that society could hardly cohere if everyone's private narcissism were given free reign. Where narcissism is allowed—as among aristocratic warriors like our samurai, or among glamorous movie stars on a Hollywood set—the mollification of others' narcissistic needs can be a full-time job, and even then the peace can be hard to maintain. Not every *donna* can be *prima*.

In addition, the narcissistic energy that could be fatal to society if expressed at the individual level can be of positive value to the society if channeled into a collective form of narcissism through identification with the social group. For the society must survive in a hostile environment and, as was said earlier, narcissism supplies energy for that struggle. This narcissism can be channeled into patriotism. As Denis de Rougemont has said: "It is accepted that every form of pride, every form of vanity, and even the most stupid boastings are legitimate and honorable so long as they are attributed to the nation in which one has taken the trouble to get born. What nobody would dare to say of his *me*, he has the sacred duty of saying for his *us*."[21]

But group narcissism is more than just a channel for the private narcissism of the members. In our consciousness, we are not only individuals but also members of larger entities. Our identification with these entities is profound, and made all the more so by our historic and continued dependence upon them for our very survival. Part of human experience, therefore, is *group* experience. And what has been the group experience of civilized peoples? Much of that experience, it is important to note, has been of the kind that engenders narcissism. Just as the growing human being becomes narcissistic from the chronic experience of abuse and disregard in the family, evolving societies have become energized with defensive group narcissism because of the chronic injury inflicted in the family of human societies. The anarchic system of interacting societies has condemned every group to develop in an environment that is hostile and disrespectful, leading each group, in order to preserve its embattled feeling of self-worth, to armor itself with the inflated claims of group narcissism.

So it is that the world is full of "chosen peoples." "All peoples inquire as to their origins and without exception the question finds an identical answer—each makes the independent claim that they are the 'chosen.' "[22] We are special. We are the greatest. God is on our side.

The Chosenness-Rejection Connection

It feels good to be special, but this way of shoring up one's feelings of self-worth is perilous and precarious. For the idea of the "chosen" is inseparable from the idea of the rejected.

What is the chosenness-rejection connection, and what is the danger that derives from it?

Gregory Rochlin observes the first part of the connection, that "the assertion of being an exclusive breed . . . creates an Ishmael . . . [I]f there are to be the 'chosen,' there must be others, the rejected, the unclean, the untouchable, the disbeliever and hence the undesirable."[23] It may seem obvious that dividing the world is "divisive," but the psychological implications of this cleaving of the chosen from the rejected nonetheless deserve to be noted. For if we regard others as our inferiors we will treat them that way; if we treat them that way, the seeds of enmity will be sown. And if it can be assumed that the peoples on both sides of the cleavage alike consider themselves the chosen, they will be all the less tolerant of denigrating treatment. The interaction of competing narcissistic claims is a pattern of mutual insult and frustration in which bitterness and conflict naturally escalate.

A second aspect of the chosenness-rejection connection is suggested by Dan Jacobson, a South African interested in how the sense of being the "chosen people" has influenced the Afrikaners' approach to their world. In his exploration of the idea of chosenness, he turns naturally enough to the Chosen People of the Old Testament. There he discovers an underlying anxiety. While "exulting over Yahweh's choice," Jacobson writes, "the composers of the biblical story could never lose sight of the terrifying possibility that it might be their turn next to join the ranks of the rejected."[24] A world divided into the high and the low is at best an insecure world. If one is among the favored to be exalted upon a peak, the danger is ever-present that one will fall. Life on a pinnacle has little freedom of movement. The arrogance of the chosen is inseparable from their anxiety; and knowing little of peace, they are not adept at building a world at peace.

The root of the connection between chosenness and rejection, however, lies one level deeper. The underlying anxiety is not that one *will be* rejected, but rather that one will have to confront the feeling that one *already has been* rejected. The claim to being the chosen is precarious because it represents an effort to deny the opposite experience. The arrogance is accompanied by anxiety because it is a compensation for that anxiety. The landscape of the narcissist is beset with pitfalls because he has erected his pinnacle in an inevitably futile effort to rise above the reality of his experience.

This is, as we saw, the genesis of narcissism: it is those who have experienced themselves as cast-offs, abandoned in the desert of neglect, who feel compelled to see their neighbors as Ishmaels. It is he who has imbibed with his mother's milk the feeling that he is a damnable creature who will proclaim with arrogant piety that he is among the elect. The height of the narcissist's inflated claims is but a mirror erected over the pit of his despair.

A world of chosen peoples is therefore an unhappy world, not primarily because they cannot get along with one another, which they cannot, but because they cannot come to terms with their own experience. The ubiquitous assertion of our specialness reflects our failure to deal successfully with our experience of vulnerability and rejection.

At one level, the Old Testament is the statement of a people proud to have been chosen of all those on earth to be God's people, blessed with His laws, and protected by a Covenant made with Him. But at another level, it is a study of the problem of rejection. Yahweh might have chosen the Israelites as His people, but more prominent in the ongoing relationship is His repeated rejection of their weaknesses and their transgressions. The Old Testament is not the story of a people getting a lot of applause from their God for doing things right. It is the story of falling short. God says no to more than He says yes to. At the heart of the tale lie the sense of moral failure and the experience of being cast off for that failure. It begins with Adam, who was evicted from paradise by a wrathful God. And for every Joseph, there are eleven other brothers. They too were the sons of Israel (Jacob), and they too would wish to be favored with the special coat of many colors.

The "legacy of Israel" was thus one part favored son and eleven parts the rejected. This may be indicative of the underlying psychological condition. That the story is told from the point of view of Joseph can distract us from the reality as a whole. Overidentifying with Joseph is like the narcissist's identification with his ideal self. But just as Joseph is but one of twelve, our ideal sense of ourselves is but the conscious tip of the unconscious iceberg.

That everyone feels chosen tells us that underlying these claims is the equally widespread feeling of having been rejected.

Compensatory Inflation

The compensatory nature of people's inflated claims lies visible just beneath the surface. Consider the Germans. If their arrogance became proverbial among Europeans, it is because their assertion of an inflated image of their national selfhood endured so long. In 1810, Adam Mueller claimed, "Everything that is great, everything that is thorough, everything that is enduring in European institutions is German."[25] Precisely a century later, the Pan-Germanic League proclaimed, "Our race with its culture is superior to all other nations and races on earth."[26] This German need for an exalted status among the world's peoples found its most exaggerated embodiment in Hitler:

> Germans, he insisted, were superior in all human endeavors from food preparation to music, architecture to dog training, poetry to weight lifting . . . When shown pictures of the Golden Gate Bridge he said that Germany must build a better bridge in Hamburg. Told that a span there would not be as long as the one in San Francisco, he sulked for a long time and then said brightly, "Well, we'll build ours wider." Informed that the widest avenue in the world was in Buenos Aires, he said that his new capital, "Germania," would have a street wider than any other street in the world.[27]

Such insistence on superiority reflects not solid self-assurance but its opposite. In the "sneering arrogance" of the Nazis, Erik Erikson discerns "the old German fear of succumbing to foreign . . . influence."[28] One inflates oneself out of fear of becoming invisible. In their study of the place of the Nazi experience in German consciousness, Alexander and Margarete Mitscherlich write that the "German sense of mission serves to compensate for fears of insignificance and to combat a specifically German feeling of worthlessness."[29]

Narcissists frequently have a mission, and this can be what makes narcissism so dangerous. The effort to deny the inner experience of worthlessness requires a constant campaign, and an essential part of that campaign is to get the world to validate one's inflated self-image. The narcissist needs the world to reflect his precarious version of reality. The myth illustrates the centrality of this mirroring: Narcissus reclines by the pool, looking longingly at the reflection of his own beauty. Likewise, the narcissist turns to the world as a mirror, demanding confirmation that he is identical with his ideal self. But unlike the figure in the myth, the narcissist must work to keep the mirror sending back the required message. Thus does the tyrant surround himself with sycophants, an ever-present chorus of voices to declare that he is unexcelled.* The question must always be asked: "Mirror, Mirror, on the wall,/Who is the fairest of them all?" And the answer had better be the right one.

The narcissist has the "mission" of making the world over into a properly gratifying mirror. This reconstruction job can be more or less damaging to the world. When the narcissist is an opera singer, there are limits to the damage that can be done. When a whole nation suffering from narcissistic injury, like Germany, unites behind a leader, like Hitler, who gives voice to their compensatory demand to be masters over the other peoples of the earth, the damage can be catastrophic.

The world being full of narcissists, the arrogance and chauvinism of every other nation is generally experienced by others as threatening, and thus they evoke antagonism. It is one thing, however, to insist on having the widest avenue—or to use a more current instance, to strive mightily for athletic preeminence in the Olympics, as the Soviets and East Germans do. It is another when the "mission" is for conquest and dominion. Indeed, the Nazis were but the hypertrophy of what European civilization had been doing to the rest of the world for several

---

*One of Napoleon's contemporaries, Marshal Masséna, described the reflecting pool of Napoleon's narcissism: he "never loved anybody in his life—women, men, children—nobody but himself."[30] Napoleon, says Frank Richardson, "disliked and was jealous of successful generals, especially those whose reputation challenged his own." With the narcissist's typical distribution of good and bad elements, Napoleon "saw to it that all successes were attributed to him," while being sure "to throw the blame on others when things went wrong."[31]

centuries: arrogantly claiming to be God's chosen people, treating other cultures with brutality and contempt, and attempting to create a world that confirmed their exalted status. Where the European imperialists were superior was chiefly in the domain of power, and when their power no longer could match their narcissistic claims, their colonial mission receded, leaving a legacy of intercultural bitterness, shattered societies, and disturbed geopolitical order that continues today to threaten the world's peace.*

The expansionism of the Soviet Union is, in part, another such narcissistic mission. Russian culture manifests polarities of grandiosity and inferiority analogous to those of German culture. Alternating between periods of wholesale emulation of admired foreign cultures and periods of xenophobia and chauvinism, the Russian sense of self-worth seems especially precarious. Eastern European diplomats have recently warned that "the West has to see and acknowledge the Soviet Union as 'equal partner' in every sense of the word. It is no use you [in the United States] saying you accept it as a 'military equal' but then ignoring the Russians' position, their prestige, and sensibility, in all other matters of global concern."[33]

A good deal of the U.S.-Soviet struggle is about realities of power, but an important dimension of it also is an effort—arising from narcissistic needs—to gain recognition and acknowledgment from the other, an effort for which power is the tool and the language.

Meanwhile, in the United States, there are contrasting schools of thought on how to deal with the Soviets' claims to status. Some respond to the arrogance of the Soviets by belittling their system, as with President Reagan's imputation of evil to the Soviet empire and his prediction of its eventual fate on "the ash-heap of history." Others advocate attending less to the manifest arrogance and more to the underlying feeling of inferiority. These suggest that we extend empathy

---

*Through the play of power, the plague of narcissistic injury and rage is passed along like a contagion. Consider the reactionary Khomeini revolution in Iran. Under the shah—allied with and, indeed, at the outset installed by the United States—Iranian society emulated the West. But "while the Iranian people were all too eager to adopt Western ways . . . there was always an undercurrent of dismay, disgrace, and even narcissistic injury in the dismantling of Iranian culture in the pursuit of Americanization." This feeling helped fuel the revolution of the mullahs. Khomeini reasserted the traditional Iranian belief in their own superiority among the cultures of the earth. The general belief in one's chosenness, perhaps particularly pronounced in Iranian culture, reemerged with a vengeance, with the vindictiveness being particularly directed against the nation whose great power had inflicted the narcissistic injury.[30]

and respect and recognition in order to establish the basis for a more cooperative relationship.

Both of these approaches to narcissistic needs entail potential problems. Does the granting of respect require giving the Soviets a decisive voice in shaping the world? Wide avenues are different from power, for power concerns genuine scarcity. If such are the perils of the dovish approach, there are perhaps greater dangers from the more bellicose. For the latter, as exemplified through most of his term in office by President Reagan, indulges our own American narcissism at the cost of unnecessarily inflicting further narcissistic injuries on the Soviets. The doves may be insufficiently sensitive to genuine threats; the hawks are studiously unconscious of the role of our own narcissistic arrogance, and of the suppressed self-doubts for which that arrogance compensates. We must decide whether, in our relationship with the Soviets, we are more fundamentally threatened by their *arrogance* in seeing themselves as chosen by history to make the world into their image, or by the *feelings of inferiority* of people who have felt themselves to be the victims of history's cruelty.

It was not long ago that the Soviet Union was run by one who was possessed by the need for absolute preeminence. Just as Hitler epitomized the German mission for superiority, so did Stalin in the Soviet Union. Nikolay Bukharin described Stalin as "unhappy at not being able to convince everyone, himself included, that he is greater than everyone."[34] Stalin made himself into a god, posing as the Great Leader, the Great Thinker, the Great Commander. For the Soviet nation, similarly, he ludicrously claimed authorship of the world's great inventions, and ruthlessly expanded Soviet dominance over as many neighboring countries as he could. Beneath this surface are the agonizing residue of the abuse and terror inflicted on him as a child, and the degradation suffered by the oppressed Georgian people of which he had been a member. Like Hitler, who also imbibed a brutal message of rejection in childhood, Stalin was willing to sacrifice millions of lives to make the world a safer reflection of his cherished illusions about himself.

Fortunately, neither superpower is now ruled by a madman like Hitler, who was given to tantrums of rage at the slightest deviation of events from his narcissistic needs. The talk of "equality" suggests a possibility of a solution, whereas the insistence on being the master race does not. But even "healthy" people, while not as easily possessed by their passions as are narcissistic tyrants, are subject to similar impulses.

Because both the Soviet Union and the United States are activated by narcissistic needs, there is danger. Both see themselves as "chosen"—by

God or by history—to lead mankind into the brighter future; both want acknowledgment of their preeminent status, and do not rest easily with mere equality; both want the world made over into their own image. Narcissism being so central to their interaction, examples of extreme cases like Hitler and Stalin can be quite instructive. For the interactions of wounded narcissisms tend to be escalatory, each pushing the other further into their defensive narcissistic passions. Thus, even with the "healthier" superpower leaders of today, what begins as a minor pertur-bation can become, after a few defensive pushes, a larger swing. And as the swing widens, the passions of narcissism can gain possession.

It behooves us, therefore, to understand those passions. There are two essential and related elements in this comprehension. The first, as we have seen, is that beneath the expression of arrogance is the feeling of unworthiness; beneath the claim to be chosen is the experience of being rejected. The second: to this feeling of having been rejected as unworthy, the essential response toward the rejecting world is *rage*.

A world of "chosen peoples" is thus a world that's mad as hell.

The Rage of the Unchosen

The realm of myth makes clear the fury that comes from the feeling of rejection. "Who is the fairest of them all?" asks Snow White's wicked stepmother. And when the answer is not "You, my queen . . ." but "Snow White," the plan for murder is born. The Stalin of Bukharin's portrait is the same. Unhappy at not being able to convince everyone that he is the greatest, Stalin "cannot help taking revenge on people, on all people but especially those who are in any way higher or better than he. If someone speaks better than he does, that man is doomed! Stalin will not let him live, because that man is a perpetual reminder that he, Stalin, is not the first and the best."[35] When those who need to feel chosen experience rejection, destruction is the likely result. But, as we have seen, beneath the surface, those who need to feel chosen *already* feel rejected. The rage is so intense because the wound is an old one, so painful it could not be faced, but was closed off and allowed to fester. Its reopening allows the deadly gangrene of wounded narcissism to spill into the human system.

The brotherhood of man is a dream about mutual acceptance. But we will not realize this dream of brotherhood until we break the pattern of the chronic experience of rejection. The biblical story of humankind's first two brothers shows what rejection does to brotherhood: its fruits are enmity and death. When God rejected Cain's offering in favor of that of his brother, Abel, "Cain was very angry and his countenance fell." Luring his brother out into a field, Cain then "rose up against his brother Abel and slew him."[36] Here lies uncovered the tragedy of human narcissism. It shows the frustrated rage, but it also shows the bearer of that rage to be first the victim and only after that the wrongdoer. There is no reason given why "for Cain and his offering [the Lord] had no regard." It is no punishment, for he had not yet done wrong. He becomes a killer because God rejects him. In order to achieve the brotherhood of man on earth, we will have to have a vision of a cosmic order in which all are accepted. From a vision of a God who cleaves between the chosen one and the rejected one, we end up with two human roles: the enraged slayer of his brother, and the man lying dead.

As with the rage of Cain, so with the brothers of Joseph. The emotional climate for their throwing their brother into the pit and subsequently selling him into slavery is created by the signs of their being passed over in favor of Joseph. First there is the coat, which is an indication of their father's greater love for the one brother over the others. This painful reality is then compounded by Joseph's dreams, which represented a future in which they would be subordinated to him. " 'Are you indeed to reign over us?' . . . So they hated him yet more for his dreams and his words."[37] Out of rejection, two roles: a group of brothers who lie to their father about their rage and the deed it led them to, and one who is sold into slavery.

The narcissist's world is thus beset by strife for two mutually reinforcing reasons: (a) the claims of narcissism accentuate and create scarcity, and (b) the experience of rejection that creates narcissism creates also rage. Conflict must therefore resolve the conflicting claims, and it allows the discharge of the pent-up fury of the chronically injured creature.

(a) Scarcity is accentuated because the narcissistic claims to preeminence are necessarily mutually contradictory. Just as Gregory Rochlin observes that all peoples claim that they are the chosen, so Elias Canetti says that "There is no nation, it seems, which has not been promised the whole earth, and none which is not bound to inherit it in the course of nature."[38] While each narcissistically driven entity (person or nation) makes extravagant claims about its own entitlement, so also is it excessively threatened by any signs of greatness in others. As with Hitler in his choice of chauffeurs, each claims to be a giant and can tolerate only midgets. It is plain to see how the interactions of such narcissists quickly run up against a sense of scarcity: as the stock line in the Western movies puts it, "There ain't room in this town for both of us." Time for a gunfight in the street.

(b) The underlying feeling of the narcissist also makes the showdown an attractive solution. He feels fundamentally cheated of his birthright.[39] Indeed, if one believes, as I do, that human beings are born naturally heir to the love they need, then the narcissist's feeling of being cheated is valid. Feeling cheated, he is consumed with envy: anyone who has or seems to have what he lacks becomes the object of poisonous feelings. Feeling cheated and envious, hurt and enraged, the narcissist finds in conflict an outlet for his destructive passions.

Conflict as a solution also is a compounder of the problem. The narcissistic rage we have considered thus far is evoked merely by the *existence* of the other. The need to be special is frustrated by the other's very being: Snow White did not need to *do* anything to the wicked Queen to earn her vitriolic enmity, nor did Abel do anything to Cain. Subsequently, the conflicts arising from this injured narcissism provide many more opportunities for narcissistic injury. Now, in "Winning" we will look again at narcissistic rage in the context of the directly competitive struggle to win.

From the "Chosen" to the "Winner"

Conflict serves many purposes. It is cathartic of rage. It is a chance to destroy or humiliate those we envy. "Here comes this dreamer," say Joseph's brothers. "Come now, let us kill him and throw him into one of the pits . . . and we shall see what will become of his dreams."[40] It is a chance to seize more of the world's scarce goodies, and thus bolster one's preeminence. And it is one more thing: it is a chance to test that proposition so central to one's emotional structure, and so insecurely believed—that one is indeed the chosen. Like the mirror on the wall, the battle on the field will tell who is fairest, who is best, who is favored by the gods.

III. Winning

Making Fortune Smile

I proposed earlier as an axiom that all bad treatment by the world is experienced as an injury to one's feelings of self-worth. Thus the child who is neglected feels rejected, and the child who is rejected feels that he must be bad. And the human species, which is compelled to endure ceaseless strife, is plagued by narcissistic injury. This way of interpreting events also helps explain why people, upon suffering misfortune, are likely to ask: "Why me?"

The converse axiom is also true psychologically: whenever one is treated well or favored by events, one absorbs it as an affirmation of one's worth. Good fortune is good food for embattled narcissism.

In this, I believe, lies a central component of the appeal of gambling. The euphoria that accompanies a string of success at the gambling table is not derived from the winnings so much as from the fact of winning. "Winning" implies that one is favored, and being favored helps heal narcissistic injury. Emotionally, we are always in touch with the primeval level of the early relationship, wanting to be well cared for. The experiential relevance of the dimension of relationship is embodied in the imagery surrounding luck. Luck is a lady.* And in the imagery of the Renaissance, *Fortuna* was a woman, and one moreover whose breasts tend to be temptingly on display. We want to be abundantly fed. A wise man once told me that in a person's relationship with the "world" one can see a macrocosmic reflection of his relationship with his mother. Some years of checking on this presumed connection have impressively borne out its validity. The fate that issues out of the order that envelops us is experienced as maternal acceptance and care or rejection and neglect.

Things don't just happen. The card that comes up, the hole the little ball falls in, the side of the die that ends on top—these are messages from the order that surrounds us, messages that tell whether we are

---

*In the musical *Guys and Dolls*, the connection between fortune in gambling and the issue of reliability and trust in relationship is suggested in the song, "Luck Be a Lady Tonight." "Remember, I'm the fella you came in with," the singer reminds Lady Luck.

favored or rejected, and thus whether we are worthy or not. To place one's stake on the gambling table is therefore like putting a question to the world. It is a way of asking the mirror on the wall to settle one's anxieties and self-doubts.

Things don't just happen, for we interpret events as ruled by an order to which we have a vital and personal relationship. The contest can thus be a test, and the results reveal not just who won but whom the order *chose* to be the winner. The German word for "ordeal" illustrates this interpretation beautifully. The word is *Gottesurteil*, literally "God's decision."[41] An ordeal can be something inflicted on the accused to establish innocence or guilt: if the accused survives, he or she was innocent, if not, the handing down of the verdict and the execution of sentence have been accomplished simultaneously.

An ordeal can be a contest or battle, to determine whose side God is on. Things don't just happen. The fight tests not only one's own powers but also one's relationship with the enveloping order. Ernest Becker writes:

> If you kill your enemy, your life is affirmed because it proves that the gods favor you. The whole philosophy is summed up in the lines from a typical "western" movie, when the Indians come upon a cavalry officer and the leader says, "Let's see if his gods protect him—shoot!" The point we moderns miss is that this is not said out of cocky pride or cynicism, as if the Indian knew in advance that the enemy would fall: ancient man really wanted to *see*.[42]

But it is not just *ancient* man who looks to fate in battle to learn the judgment of the cosmic forces. In modern states as well, the national fortune in international conflict can be crucial determinants of public mood and of the perceived legitimacy of rulers. At the outset, the Argentine misadventure in the Falklands (the would-be Malvinas) brought forth an enormous outpouring of patriotic fervor as the nation put its narcissism on the line. Had Argentina won, it would have been as if God had put His seal of approval on the military junta. And it is entirely likely that—despite the economic shambles and the thousands of the "disappeared"—the junta would still be in power. But the grab for the Falklands proved disastrous, and there are now civilians in power and military men have been tried for crimes committed long before the seizure of the islands. The fortunes of war reflect a judgment not just on military strength and weakness, not just on good or bad strategic decisions, but on the goodness of the national order.

This is why the defeat in Vietnam proved so traumatic for the United States. In objective terms, it appears that the American interests at stake were not so vital. But we had put our national honor on the line, which is to say we had put to the test our narcissistic self-image.* Peace *with honor* was experienced as emotionally necessary. Winning, or at least not losing, became a "vital" interest in itself. Thus, Richard Nixon declared "I'm not going to be the first American president who loses a war."[43]

When the "peace" we achieved proved to be "without honor," a severe narcissistic wound was inflicted on the national psyche. How else to explain why a defeat in a military campaign in a small country on the other side of the world would lead to years of what has been described as national "self-doubt," "loss of confidence," and the like. At stake, clearly, was not just the realistic question of what limits there may be to the ability of American power to dictate outcomes in various regional struggles; nor was it just the legitimate question of how well the American military and political systems had performed in the conduct of war in Vietnam. We had lost, and the fact of defeat had dealt a blow to the whole grandiose but fragile image we have built up about ourselves as a chosen people. God was not on our side. Fortune did not smile on us. We felt rejected. And we lapsed into that depression that comes from reexperiencing such rejection.

In a few years, in the United States, the compensatory structures were built back up. With the help of a further humiliation in the prolonged (and overblown) hostage crisis in Iran, the depression from narcissistic injury was converted to rage. A new group of leaders was voted into power, promising that America would "stand tall" again, and showing eagerness to find places where our national power could be affirmed, our national honor vindicated. In tiny Grenada, overwhelming American power forced Fortune to smile on us again. We were back from defeat ready to fight. The age of *Coming Home*, about a crippled Viet vet in a wheelchair, had passed. The age of *Rambo* had begun.

The age of Rambo is an age of preoccupation with winning. For the narcissistically injured warrior, all of life's diverse panoply of meanings is

---

*It must be conceded that even in realistic terms, defense of national honor can be important. If a nation's commitments lose their credibility, then others will be more likely to challenge them in the future. In the case of Vietnam, however, it seems to me that this argument was used far beyond what was realistic: if a nation is willing to expend the years, the tens of thousands of lives, the tens or hundreds of billions of dollars that the United States did to prop up its South Vietnamese allies, that would seem a sufficient proof of commitment. Taking the attitude that one must win at any cost seems to go far beyond establishing credibility.

reduced to the single spectrum of winning and losing. Winning can be the "only thing" only when the defense of narcissism squeezes out all other concerns. This perspective illuminates the conceptual failings of the cold warriors into whose hands we once again placed our relations with the rest of the world. As was often observed, our leaders in this age of Rambo saw all the world's events in the very narrow terms of the East-West struggle. Whenever an oppressed people rose up to struggle against their oppressor, these cold warriors only asked: are they for us or for them?—i.e., how can this situation be played to advance *us* in our efforts to win against our competitors?

The usual interpretation of this reduction of a complex world to a single win-lose contest is that it reveals an extraordinary blindness to complexity and insensitivity to the aspirations of others with lives of their own to lead. That is true, but we will understand this narrowness and callousness better if we recognize that it displays on the macrocosm of the world the distortions practiced first in the microcosm of the self. The indifference to those human concerns irrelevant to the Big Contest is but a magnification of the warrior's neglect of all his own other needs apart from his need to triumph. The reduction of the world is first an impoverishment of the world within. Thus can the warrior's narcissistic insistence that Fortune smile upon him in the specific arena of winning and losing inflict on the whole world a great misfortune.

Winning and Manhood

All good fortune and misfortune are experienced as narcissistically relevant judgments upon one's worth. In the eyes of the people of ancient China, even earthquakes, floods, and droughts could be read as signs that their Emperor had lost his Mandate from Heaven. Our elected officials too gain and lose support according to whether crops have thrived or failed during their incumbency.* All of life functions as a test of whether the cosmic order approves of our individual or collective being.

---

*A recent remark by a television commentator gives some indication of the intuitive belief that some leaders are blessed by fortune while others are, in the Yiddish phrase, *schlimazels*. In the wake of the capture by American jets of the Egyptian plane carrying the hijackers from the *Achille Lauro*, the commentator said that if Carter had been President, the U.S. jets would probably have crashed into the Mediterranean.

But the battle renders a judgment of a particularly important kind. This is because it is an enactment of a dimension of our experience that is particularly crucial to the development of our narcissism. It is a test of power, and it is in interactions where we are critically lacking in power that we suffer most grievous narcissistic injuries. As individuals, when we are children, we may suffer abuse and violence from beings five times our size, as did Hitler and Stalin at the hands of their fathers. And the experience of humankind at the intersocietal level, as the parable of the tribes shows, has been to suffer a similar fate, as smaller and weaker societies have been dominated and destroyed by their more powerful neighbors. Experience has therefore taught us to associate being weak with suffering narcissistic injury. To be a winner in battle is to prove that one has escaped that condition; victory thus implies that one's compensatory narcissism is safe.

In the world of scarcity, there are roles to be apportioned. And the battle will answer the question, "Which role is mine?" Am I a winner or loser? Am I on top, standing tall? Or am I the one on the bottom, lying hurt and prostrate? As that imagery suggests, we return here to the issues of manhood encountered in chapter 1, "Damaged in the Male."

For reasons given in that earlier discussion, the narcissistic connection with power—although relevant for all people—is particularly strong for men. For the genesis of life, God created us male and female. The disruption of the natural order of human life by the problem of power perverts our energies and establishes as essential a new, perverted dichotomy: between the powerful and the powerless, the victor and the victim. The narcissistic struggles among men push the male-female bond to the side, as males, injured by the destructive use of male power, may become disabled from participating open-heartedly in the connection between male and female.

Later in part 2, we will explore the central meaning—to the struggle among the males—of women and the feminine.* Our present concern is how, in the struggle for power, manhood comes to be defined in terms of winning against other men. Because the problem of power has warped human relationships, men turn to the battle to test their status: the question, "Am I a winner or a loser?" can be translated, "Am I a man or am I unmanned?"

If, in emotional terms, these are the options, the sense of scarcity strikes a vital area. This will exacerbate the relationships among warrior

---

*See "By Possession Possessed" (p. 163).

powers. Which of us is truly the man? If the antagonists experience manhood as something they cannot both enjoy, then the stakes of conflict will be high indeed.

At a happy moment in his misadventure in Vietnam, President Johnson declared triumphantly, "We not only screwed Ho Chi Minh, we cut his pecker off."[44] Later, when he could not disengage from an effort whose futility was increasingly evident, the sexual dimension of the meaning of such disengagement was intuited by the protest movement with its numerous jokes about LBJ "withdrawing." For LBJ to withdraw would have been to concede that Ho Chi Minh had cut his pecker out of Indochina. Johnson's successor, having committed the error of making the war his own, was likewise caught in the trap of attaching enormous emotional stakes to the issue. We could not disengage from Vietnam, Richard Nixon explained, or the United States would appear to be a "pitiful, helpless giant." We have a big one, in other words, but we can't do anything with it. This great nation would appear impotent.

There is a joke I've heard in Washington. The Soviet government places an order through the U.S. government for hundreds of cases of twelve-inch prophylactics. The Americans are stunned and frightened. What to do? Such a size isn't available. Not wanting to admit this—i.e., to admit what this would imply—the Americans make up a special batch and send them over to the Soviet Union. Marking the case—"Short."

In this joke, we see the situation only from the American side: the Americans do not want to be seen as the lesser men. The question of what stands behind the Soviet decision to place the order does not arise. This illustrates, I believe, the underlying emotional condition of the real actors in their real-world competition. Each actor secretly, and probably unconsciously, fears seeming to be no man at all in relation to his antagonist. The fear is that his is bigger than mine, and (like LBJ's Ho Chi Minh) I will get screwed and castrated. *

On the American side, I have seen some sign of this. At the end of 1979, I met with a member of President Carter's National Security Council staff. On his desk were scale models of the principal U.S. and Soviet ballistic missiles. One could not help but be impressed with one salient observable fact: the Soviet missiles were much *bigger* than the American. That seemed to be the point of the display. Never mind that

---

*It was Nietzsche who said that envy and jealousy are "the private parts of the human psyche."[45]

U.S. missiles were built smaller by our deliberate choice, and that the smaller size was made possible by American superiority in the technology of rocket fuels. This disparity of size was emotionally significant, and I have heard it used in high places to bolster a sense of urgency to redress presumed imbalances so that an American president would be able to "stand up" to the Russians.

This also was the time during which the idea of the presumed "window of vulnerability" was gaining currency.* This idea expressed the fear that a Soviet first strike could disable the United States from making a credible retaliatory strike. The technical issues were far from simple. Having made a considerable effort to study these scenarios of a Soviet first strike or of Soviet nuclear blackmail, however, I concluded that they are quite implausible. (Just one of the reasons for this is that even if our land-based missiles could be taken out in a first strike, with the thousands of warheads still available on our submarines, our capacity to destroy the Soviet Union would not be less in any meaningful sense from what it was before their first strike.) Nonetheless, the anxiety about being rendered impotent seems to have been real. And perhaps a part of it was illustrated by the model missiles on the NSC man's desk: with their bigger missiles, the Soviets could cut our pecker off.

Who is the bigger? Those who try to understand the anxieties in the U.S.-Soviet struggle frequently use an image of size. "The Russians aren't ten feet tall," it is frequently said. And conversely, those who work with the Soviets report that the Soviets need to be assured that the Americans are not ten feet tall. Secretly, perhaps unconsciously, each fears that the other is more potent than it can ever be. Trauma having fixed in our minds an image of ourselves as small and weak, we tend to fear that our antagonist is out of our league: ten feet tall, and needing twelve-inch prophylactics.

The prophylactic joke also illustrates our way of coping with these fears. By marking the cases "Short," we cover up or deny our true sense of ourselves. (The Soviets who placed the order may be presumed to have done the same.) In the joke, it is a conscious decision to deceive. In reality, the decision—the denial—is at an unconscious level. Out of weakness, we pretend strength. Out of a sense of smallness, we try to magnify ourselves. Outside the realm of jokes, the equivalent of ordering twelve-inch prophylactics and of sending them marked "Short" is the nuclear arms race. Out of a sense of a probably unrealistic

---

*Is this some opening through which the enemy can successfully screw us?

"window of vulnerability," the United States has placed missiles in Europe that are scant minutes from Moscow, has constructed missiles that can threaten Soviet silos, and has begun work on a defensive system the achievement of whose stated purpose would render Soviet missiles impotent.

It may seem incredible, and it is certainly frightening, that the survival of our entire species and of our marvelous planet could depend upon such human-scale fears as the need to protect and assert one's manhood. But whatever the scale of our weapons' power, we remain but human creatures measurable in mere feet and inches, and prone to feelings that go with our scale. Even "nuclear giants" are led and controlled by mere men, and men unsure of being even that.

When JFK was to go to Vienna in 1961 to meet Khrushchev, Averell Harriman advised him how to conduct himself. "Don't try to test his strength and his mettle. First of all, he knows your wife is far more beautiful than his, and he has certain kinds of jealousy; you are young and handsome . . ."[46] But Kennedy did just the opposite, says Garry Wills, "because he felt that he had to show that he was *not* a weak, young, inexperienced president. Khrushchev led him by the nose all during the week and Kennedy was simply on the ropes at the end of the meeting and left, coming home completely dejected." Cooper, relying on David Halberstam, goes on to relate the consequences: "He then made the decision . . . to change the involvement in Vietnam from merely advisors to combat orientation. He had to find someplace to show, to prove to Khrushchev, that he wasn't what Khrushchev thought he was."[47] Kennedy made a test of strength out of Vietnam, a move that was to debilitate the United States for a generation.

This story is an excellent illustration of a major theme of this work: that it is out of a sense of weakness and vulnerability that the preoccupation with showing strength arises, which leads to still further weakness and vulnerability.

The trail of consequences from the test of manhood between Kennedy and Khrushchev unfortunately leads further. From Kennedy's humiliation in Vienna in 1961 the path leads to the Cuban missile crisis in 1962. Here, as we saw earlier, the humiliation went the other way: Kennedy "rubbed Khrushchev's nose in the dirt." And we can recall Wills's verdict on Kennedy's taking the world, during this crisis, closer to the brink than it has ever been: "Macho appearance, not true security, was the motive for Kennedy's act."[48]

But there is still more, for among the fruits of this deadly game of manliness and unmanning were those big scary missiles modeled on the

NSC man's desk almost two decades later. Those who study Soviet behavior say it was their humiliation in the Cuban missile crisis that led the Soviets to inaugurate their massive buildup. Never again would they allow themselves to be caught short in a military showdown. Kennedy had his triumph, as the Soviets were compelled to retreat with but their tail between their legs. By the 1970s, those big missiles for the lack of which the Soviets had felt humiliated were pointing menacingly at the United States.

The Honor of the Warrior

The cleaving of the world into winners and losers is thus, at one level, a division between the man and the unmanned. There is the one who "stands tall," and the one who lies prostrate. The proud and the humiliated. The one who is best can issue insults, and one who is bested must absorb them. No man of honor accepts insults lying down, and this refusal to accept insult is at the heart of that central image of manhood, the warrior. Equally central to the energy of the warrior is the sense of already having absorbed an insult that must be avenged.

This is neatly represented in the ceremonial dubbing of the knight by his king. The dubbing was said to be the last blow the warrior would receive without returning it.[49] It is, fittingly, this unavenged blow that readies the warrior for his role. Henceforth, he will defend his honor with violence against any insults. Yet, as the ceremony symbolizes, this defensive posture with respect to honor derives from the experience of having already been dishonored. It is not from the experience of being treated with respect that the issue of keeping one's honor unstained becomes for men a life-and-death struggle.

Already aggrieved, the warrior is eager for a chance to redress his grievance. He is looking, that is, for a fight. The burden of narcissistic injury is worn as a chip on the knighted shoulder.

The figure of Rambo is instructive here. Rambo is a mythic symbol of the sense of honor of the warrior spirit of the American nation recovering from defeat in Vietnam. In the first Rambo film, the action begins as Rambo—a returned Vietnam veteran—is railroaded out of a small American town by a domineering sheriff who regards him as a punk and who thinks his presence degrades the town. The crucial decision point for Rambo occurs after he is let out of the sheriff's car on the far side of a bridge outside the town: should he keep going away from a town he was just passing through anyway, or should he go back to the town? Seen in terms of Rambo's original intentions, there is no reason he should go back: why go where you aren't wanted and don't want to be? But Rambo is the quintessential man of honor, which is to say that narcissistic injury is at the heart of his karma. The issue, therefore, has little to do with the question of where he wants to be. Rather, the question is: should he accept the insult unjustly inflicted on him by the sheriff and walk away, or should he turn back to assert his honor? As the embodiment of an American humiliation, this American symbol cannot swallow another insult. So, he crosses the fateful bridge. And as the embodiment of the compensatory American narcissism—Rambo, it turns out, is not just a Viet vet, he is also a Congressional Medal of Honor winner, "the best there is"—Rambo has his sweet revenge. By the time the film is over, Rambo, quite scrupulously following his code of honor, has stood over the fallen sheriff and laid waste the sheriff's town.

The name of this first Rambo film, notably, is *First Blood*. The phrase is used once in the film, when the question of Rambo's surrendering is raised by his former Green Beret commander: "They drew first blood," says Rambo in refusing to give up the fight, "not me." It is this sense that *they* started it, while *we* are the aggrieved party that makes the action so gratifying for the audience. Feeling wronged ourselves, we are glad to identify with a figure who is innocent of the breach of the peace, and who gets the revenge we crave. So long as they drew first blood, and our hero follows the code of honor, we can have our blood and our innocence too.

But this sense of "first blood" also shows why the peace is so hard to preserve. If it is part of the warrior spirit to have been "dubbed" by some blow unreturned, then all the actors are likely to feel that it is "they" who drew first blood. And thus indeed we find it in the world of warriors and warrior nations. Whatever the scenario of conflict, each party pronounces itself the aggrieved one. It is merely defending its honor. The Argentines regarded it as an affront to their honor that islands so close to them would belong to a distant power, so they seized them. This the British took as a slap in the lion's face, so they sent the fleet. To the Argentines, this was yet another outrage. No one is ever guilty of aggression, only of retaliation. The Israelis and Palestinians exchange acts of violence, each only avenging the insults and injuries inflicted by the other. The Greeks and Greek Cypriots consider the Turks guilty of unpardonable aggression in seizing a portion of that Mediterranean island, forgetting that it was a Greek effort in 1974 to annex the whole of Cyprus—disregarding the rights of the Turkish

Cypriot minority—that overturned the old status quo and provoked the Turkish invasion.*

At times, one is tempted to regard the universal claims to being the aggrieved party as disingenuous and hypocritical. But the psychology of narcissistic injury and its role in the warrior's sense of honor suggest that the protestations are sincere. The problem is that everyone can validly say of the interactions between himself and the world, "They drew first blood, not me." Thus dubbed, we come into our interactions already aggrieved, and see even our aggressions as but revenge.

The scarcity of honor is a direct correlate of the ubiquity of narcissistic injury, of the blow unreturned. Everyone feels he is owed one, so there is not enough to go around.

Because each actor has suffered narcissistic injury, everyone has a chip on his shoulder. Everyone also is eager to be relieved of this burden. How satisfying it is to impose the humiliation on someone else. "I demand satisfaction," says the warrior as he challenges the one who has insulted him to a duel. And with those words, he slaps the face of the offender with his doffed glove, thereby returning the insult. The challenger knows that no man of honor will let this slap go unavenged, and so he will have the satisfaction of combat to avenge himself. But in a sense, he already has his satisfaction, for he has passed the insult back.

The way of the warrior of honor thus makes the cycling of humiliations into a game of Old Maid, where the burden is passed around the system but never removed. In such a world of scarcity, it is not possible for everyone to have a hand with which he can be at peace. Whoever has the fateful card that insults or engenders rage must attempt to hand it on to someone else. And so the system can have no peace. Where a social order is rent with ceaseless feud or vendetta, there you will find that the essence of virtue for a man is the preservation of honor.†

---

*In October 1985, the United States and Egypt felt mutually aggrieved at each other. The Americans were outraged at the willingness of the Egyptians to allow the hijackers of the *Achille Lauro* to go free even after it was discovered that they had murdered an innocent American, and outraged also at the lies the Egyptian president apparently told about having unfortunately let them go before the murder was discovered. Having uncovered the lie, the United States acted in defense of its honor and forced down the Egyptian plane carrying the hijackers. This act of "piracy" was humiliating to the Egyptians, an affront to their national honor. One Egyptian official referred derisively to the difficulties of dealing with Ronald Rambo.

†In his study of feud, Jacob Black-Michaud makes explicit the connection between the strife and the sense of scarcity. Feud can materialize, he says, only where social life is characterized by "total scarcity." This he summarized as "the moral, institutional and

The interaction among honorable warriors thus escalates the problem of narcissistic rage above the level of Snow White. It was Snow White's existence alone that enraged the queen. But the aggrieved warriors' shared need to deal the last blow keeps ever fresh the sting of narcissistic injury and the rage for vengeance. In the confrontation of men of honor, the sense of scarcity is aggravated by a direct contest with an identifiable competitor.

The tragedy of one warrior spirit encountering another is delineated at the very outset of that great classic of warrior literature, the *Iliad*. Achilles feels insulted by Agamemnon's unjustly taking from him—the greatest of warriors—his prize of war. Agamemnon feels insulted that Achilles does not show sufficient deference to him—the most powerful of the Greeks. The very qualities that make each suited for war disable them from making peace with each other. The ensuing tragedy of death and grief and revenge unfolds from this "confrontation of each man with the other's pride, before which neither yields."[51] Like Rambo, each warrior feels he has already yielded too much. His narcissism demands satisfaction, and his pursuit of this satisfaction yields destruction.

Narcissism makes a deadly mix with the sense of scarcity. Narcissism, of course, creates a kind of scarcity: not all can be the best. Then, if what we have we must take from others, caring for the self *means* inflicting narcissistic injury on others. And so the two feed each other, and feed also the flames of conflict. Agamemnon takes Achilles' prize because he has been compelled by circumstance to surrender his own. Never mind that it is Agamemnon himself, in his own hubris, who has created that circumstance. Narcissistically assuming that he is owed one, he makes good his loss by taking from another. But the other is also a man of honor: thus, for his loss also, others must pay. As a result, everyone loses, heavily.

---

material premise of a certain type of society in which *everything* felt by the people themselves to be relevant to human life is regarded by those people as existing in absolutely inadequate quantities."[50] Black-Michaud believes this sense of total scarcity comes from circumstances in which material resources are objectively in insufficient supply. I would suggest that it is physical security that is objectively in scarce supply, that it is the cycling of the insult of violence and narcissistic injury that creates the more general sense of scarcity. A place where feud is rampant, according to this hypothesis, is more likely to be characterized by the lack of a political order that can provide protection than by the lack of material resources. The factual scarcity of power thus can combine with an exaggerated sense of scarcity, as argued at the outset of part 2, and create that sense of "total scarcity."

In a world ready to hurt us, we must be warriors to defend ourselves. But the narcissistic hurts that ready us to be warriors disable us from making peace.

The Mirror in Other Men's Eyes

The *Iliad* reveals another aspect of the drama of the warrior's pursuit of honor: it is played out publicly, before an audience. Each man digs himself into a public posture from which he cannot be *seen* to retreat. To retreat before the eyes of other men is to "lose face." "Face" is the part of us that is in front for the world to see. It is the way things look. Likewise, "humiliation" is a feeling of having been shamed in the eyes of others. This dimension of the role of audience is also central to the narcissistic struggle and to the warrior code.

It is in patterns that we discover clues about the forces at work in human affairs and in nature generally. All over the world, throughout history, there have been societies of a certain pattern. These societies are organized around the martial virtues, which are largely summed up by the concept of honor. The men are bound by loyalty to their group for the purpose of revenge, which is to say the defense of honor. In these societies, a man's sense of self-worth depends on his being seen by the other actors—both friends and enemies—as having his honor intact. Pierre Bordieux sums up this dimension common to societies in which honor is afforded high importance: "the being and truth about a person is identical with the being and truth that others acknowledge in him."[52]•

This dependence upon the mirror in other men's eyes can be seen wherever the spirit of the warrior is at work. The *Iliad* begins with the war already in its ninth year, and one reason it continues is that the attacking Achaeans fear the disgrace of leaving with nothing to *show* for their efforts. Their fear of what others will think of them goads them back into battle, and when anyone hangs back from the fray, this fear of shame— the losing side of the coin of honor, the one without "face"—is used to drive him back into the arena of death. Again and again, in the great

---

•Bertram Wyatt-Brown, in his description of the honor ethic in the American South, speaks similarly. One of its characteristics, he says, is that the "opinion of others [is] an indispensable part of personal identity and gauge of self-worth."[53]

What matters most is not so much what we *are*, as what others think us to be: so we label the prophylactics "Short," to become large in our adversaries' eyes.

and horrific battle scenes of that epic, the leaders move among them holding up to them the mirror of their allegedly dishonorable appearance:

> Argives [calls out Agamemnon], you arrow-fighters, have you no shame? Why are you simply standing there bewildered, like young deer who after they are tired from running through a great meadow stand there still, and there is no heart of courage within them? (Book IV, 242–45)

Likewise, we find in the Bhagavad Gita, when the hero, Arjuna, wishes not to fight, the god eggs him on, saying that he must fight or "men will forever speak of thy dishonour . . . The great warriors will think that thou hast abstained from battle because of fear and they who esteemed thee will think lightly of thee."[54]

This scene in the Bhagavad Gita is similar, in dramatic terms, to a recurrent theme in the American Western. The hero wishes to renounce violence. He has been a warrior and a winner, but he is weary of the killing and wants now to walk the way of peace. Perhaps the hero wears no gun, or perhaps he just refuses to allow himself to be goaded into a gunfight. But when other people, important to him, interpret his forbearance and love of peace as cowardice or weakness—as shameful—he is driven back into the ways of violence.* The movie *Shane* provides an

---

*This theme in the Western actually arises at a particular historical moment: during the first decades of the nuclear era. Notable examples, besides *Shane*, discussed here, include *High Noon* (where, admittedly, the hero never really entertains pacifism, but his new Quaker wife represents these values), and *The Fastest Gun Alive* (with Glenn Ford). In his study *The Six-Gun Society*, Will Wright identifies the hero's attempt to avoid involvement in the conflict against the villains as one of the typical motifs of the Western movie of the postwar era.

Perhaps the dawning of an age of weapons whose only reasonable use is the prevention of their ever being used created a dilemma for the American warrior. The virtues of the peaceful resolution of conflict were suddenly much greater, yet the age-old narcissistic code of honor defended by violence remained within us. Perhaps the realm of fantasy gave us an outlet for the ancient warrior energies that in the real world needed to be inhibited as never before: paying lip service to the desire for peace, the movies affirm the virtues of the warrior. Our culture continues to wrestle with this issue, and apparently continues to find no satisfactory substitute for the gratification of winning through violence and the restitution of honor. In the 1980s, *The Karate Kid* films play around with the repudiation of the violent way of the honorable warrior in favor of other values. But at the end, the films give us our satisfying humiliation of our bloodied foe. Likewise, the final film of the *Star Wars* Saga, *The Return of the Jedi*, flirts with the idea of an alternative, only to return to the tried and true. Luke Skywalker confronts the trap that if he does nothing, the forces of the "Dark Side" will win, while if he yields to his own rage and fights back, the "Dark Side" will have won within him. Having dramatized this dilemma,

apt example. Our warrior hero is insulted in town by the cattle baron's gunslingers, but he swallows the insult. A group of farming families have become important to Shane, and because they are threatened by the cattle baron, the warrior virtues have become important to them. When it becomes clear that Shane's restraint in town has made them "think lightly" of him, he makes sure on his next trip into town that there is a replay of the previous incident, except this time he defends his honor manfully—and in full view of the farmers whose esteem he wishes to regain.

Such concern with the opinions of others is not, of course, confined to the world of epic and fantasy. The ancient Romans, according to the republican historian Sallust,[55] "were eager for praise and consumed with a burning passion for glory." And in our own times, at one of the most crucial and perilous moments, the fear of shame was uppermost in the minds of the most prominent Soviet warriors. Khrushchev reported that during the Cuban missile crisis, what his military advisers thought would be the biggest tragedy would be "that the Chinese or the Albanians would accuse us of appeasement or weakness."[56] Fortunately for us all, these warriors were advisers and not decision-makers.

This preoccupation with the mirror in other men's eyes points up an interesting paradox about the world of the narcissist. On the one hand, as was said in our original discussion of narcissism, the narcissist is focused upon himself. Others are real for him only as they relate to himself. Whatever "does not form part of the person or is not an object of his needs" (to quote Erich Fromm again) is but shadow. On the other hand, while others exist only in terms of the self, the self is only what others think it is. In the warrior's ethic of honor, which I am treating as a structure for coping with the danger of narcissistic injury and as an expression of narcissism, the reality of the self is what the mirror says it is.

What is the meaning of this paradox? If these are both aspects of the same phenomenon, how are we to reconcile the image of Narcissus longing for himself by the pool, and the idea that, as Pierre Bordieux says of the honor ethic, the relationship one has with others takes precedence over one's relationship with oneself?

---

however, the film despairs of finding any satisfactory solution other than total victory for our warrior, and the complete destruction of the enemy. In an age of nuclear weapons, perhaps it is time for the imagination to enact other paths: if we cannot even *imagine* any other outcome being acceptable to us, we surely will not be able to enact it in the real world.

In narcissism, which is a sign of distress in the system of human relationship, both the sense of self and the sense of connection are impaired. The sense of self is impaired because the world from which a secure sense of self must be derived is too hostile a place. And for the same reason—the failure of others to meet one's needs with sufficient dependability—relationship to others is also impaired. The two structures thus lean precariously on each other, like a house of cards.

Our paradox grows out of the paradox at the heart of narcissism. The narcissist may be turned toward the self, but he is also running away from himself. On one level, he meets his need for love by appreciating his inflated image of himself; on the other, he must turn his back on that painful place in himself where he has absorbed narcissistic injury. As we see throughout this book, it is the avoidance of some unbearably painful part of our experience that drives the whole drama.

We recall why the narcissist needs the world to mirror his inflated image of himself: because he is always in danger of being overtaken by the contrary, painful image of himself that he bears within. The narcissist needs help from the outside world in holding off this painful experience. That is why that particular kind of narcissist we call the man of honor is so concerned to appear honorable in the eyes of other men. Preserving an image of himself is his way of avoiding unbearable pain. Thus, emotionally, the defense of honor is a matter of life and death.

Death and Worse Fates

This brings us to another paradox in the world of the warrior, concerning the value of life and death: (1) On the one hand, surviving is a form of winning and the warrior wants to be a winner; (2) on the other hand, the pain of narcissistic injury is itself a form of death, and the honorable warrior may choose actual death to avoid the death of his inflated self-image.

1. SURVIVING AS WINNING

Ernest Becker provides a vividly grisly image of the survivor:

> [L]ife on this planet is a gory spectacle, a science fiction nightmare in which digestive tracts fitted with teeth at one end are tearing away at whatever flesh they can reach, and at the other are piling up the fuming waste excrement, as they move along in search

of more flesh . . . [E]ach organism raises its head over a field of corpses, smiles into the sun and declares life good.[57]

It is a Darwinian view of life, in that nineteenth-century sense that was so useful to the imperialists and capitalist-individualists of the Western powers. Life is built upon death; success upon failure. The flesh of the losers forms the substance of the winners. It is kill or be killed, and to say that life is good is to say that it is good to be a killer. Such a love of life is, paradoxically, reminiscent of Fromm's necrophile, the lover of death, for whom the two sexes are the killers who are beloved and the killed who are despised.

In a world of scarcity, to love life may seem to require a love of death. If life and death are seen as a zero-sum game—the way the wins and losses must be balanced in the National Football League—then it follows that one's own life requires that the corpses of others be strewn around. Annihilate or be annihilated, as the Bolsheviks saw it.[58] And now in the nuclear age, that same sense of scarcity helps inflame the arms race. "As if their more thorough annihilation would increase our security," I wrote in the prologue. But now we can see that a sense of the intimate connection of life and death in a world of scarcity might make just such a connection between the vaporization of the Soviets and the survival of Americans (or vice versa) feel valid, even if mutual survival or mutual destruction are the real alternatives.

The world of scarcity is one where power is the essence of human relationships. At those loci where the struggle for power reigns, there winning will be everything, and winning will mean surviving, and surviving will mean the annihilation of others. One such locus is the kingship. In At the Dawn of Tyranny, Eli Sagan describes the process by which the successor to a deceased king was chosen in some of the traditional kingdoms of Africa. Of the contending sons of the previous king, one would become the new king when he had eliminated all his rivals. This process of elimination—one thinks of the fuming excrement at the other end from the biting teeth—was apparently utilized not only for want of an institutionalized procedure. It was seen to have virtues: "Only he who had killed his brothers in the worst kind of guerrilla warfare was worthy to lead the country."[59] Into the position of kingship, therefore, rose the winner, the chosen, one whose demonstrated prowess in the art of survival has made him an attractive symbol for personifying the country as a whole.

We want a survivor as king because the king represents us against anarchy, and anarchy threatens us with annihilation. The king faces anarchy in two directions. First, within the country, he represents the Hobbesean solution to the interminable predations of all upon all. In those African kingdoms, the interim period between rulers is, as described by Rev. John Roscoe, truly a Hobbesean state, where "anarchy reigned, people tried to rob each other, and only chiefs with a strong force were safe, even the smaller chiefs being in danger from stronger chiefs, who did as they liked during the short interregnum."[60] Second, the king represents the country in relation to all the other sovereign states, i.e., in that system where "the state of nature" and its ceaseless strife has persisted since the dawn of civilization. In this state of nature, power is life and we will regard as the chosen one, in whom to invest our sovereign power, the one who has demonstrated the power to kill and survive.*

But to choose such a chosen one is to choose death as well as life. For the king who emerges on top of such a pile of corpses is not just a representative of the whole but is also an individual human being with his own selfish passions. And, given what it takes to get where he is, those passions are not apt to be pleasant. Elias Canetti has written of the hatred—"common to all despots"—of other survivors. To illustrate, he tells the story of Muhammad Tuglak, the sultan of Delhi. This sultan:

> had various schemes even more grandiose than those of Napoleon and Alexander. Among them was the conquest of China from across the Himalayas. An army of 100,000 horsemen was collected, which set out in the year 1337. Of this whole army, all but ten men perished cruelly in the mountains. These ten returned to Delhi with the news of the disaster and there, at the command of the Sultan, all were executed.[61]

Despots, says Canetti, "regard survival as their prerogative."

Just as power is necessary, it is necessary that those in power understand the realities of scarcity. But just as there is more to human life than power, so are we endangered by an excess of the sense of scarcity. This danger is manifest wherever the process by which power is gained tends to favor those who see their survival as dependent upon the annihilation of others. The scarcity mentality of these "survivors" is further reinforced by their experience of gaining ascendancy by wading

---

*The selective process of our democratic presidential campaigns is less bloody, but may have a kindred symbolic meaning. (See the discussion of these in chapter 2, "The Demand for Invulnerability.")

through the blood of their brothers. The pictures, relayed to us by European explorers, of kings in Africa or Polynesia surrounded by decorative skulls in mounds—kings who drank from goblets made of the brain cases of their victims—disclose to us something about the jealous love of survival and about the worship of power that derives therefrom. It is not just about the preservation of life, but about the manufacture of death as well. We must bear this in mind as we create systems capable of mass destruction to rule over our security.

2. Loving Honor More

The worshiper of power who pursues his own survival at any cost is one kind of warrior. The man of honor is another. The sultan who executes the straggling survivors operates outside the realm of morality. The knight follows a code of honor. The survivor practices a form of the amorality of might makes right. The survivor operates by the equation: might is the only virtue because might protects one's life, and one's life is the only good. The code of honor, by contrast, places other values higher than life.

These represent the two faces of war. On the one side is the grisly spectacle of brutality, of the slaughter of innocents, of living fetuses ripped out of the bayonetted bellies of their mothers, of unspeakable barbarities. This is war as ugly savagery, of the worst of our demons run rampant, of all order overthrown. On the other side is war as a noble enterprise, as a ritual dance, of knights charging each other at an agreed signal, of duelers marching the prescribed distance in step before turning to fire. It is a game played by rules, a game for noble and heroic men.

But in this noble game, blood flows nonetheless. The code that serves so well for the preservation of honor can be profligate in its expenditure of human life. Indeed, despite its exhibiting a higher morality than the purely bestial aspect of war, it may be war's more noble face that poses the greater danger to us. No, not despite its nobility, but rather because of it. For war's ugly face is so repugnant that we know—most of us—to slam the door in its face. But when war visits us with the inspiring visage of the hero, we are charmed and invite him in.

We ought now to look more closely at that face of the warrior of honor.

The code of honor makes the preservation of honor an absolute value. Wherever men live by such a code, men will be ready to die by that code. Death is fine as long as that death is honorable. A life without honor is a fate worse than death. "Mine honor is my life," says

Shakespeare's Richard II. This weighing of the balance between honor and life, and finding honor the weightier, is why honor is so often the theme of tragedies. In the plays of honor and revenge, enacted on the stages of premodern Europe, we see dramatized the costs of preserving the warrior's honor.

"Surely to a man of spirit," spoke Pericles to his fellow Athenians in praise of their fellow warriors, "the degradation of cowardice must be immeasurably more grievous than the unfelt death which strikes him in the midst of his strength and patriotism."[62] These words, preserved for over two millennia as among the most cherished in the history of the oratory of our civilization, were spoken while Athens was still in its glory. Within a generation, however, a generation plagued by chronic war, the glorious flower of Athens lay crushed in the dust. The men of spirit had avoided the degradation of cowardice, and in the process brought about the destruction of the city they ostensibly fought to protect.

For the warrior of honor, the possibility of losing his honor is too terrible to contemplate. "Dishonour is worse than death," says that god in the Bhagavad Gita whom we quoted earlier as shaming Arjuna back into battle. In the honor-ruled, feud-ridden society of Albania, a monk tried to deter an Albanian bent upon revenge. His act of vengeance, said the monk, would condemn him to hell. "I would rather clean my honor," replied the man of honor, "and go to hell."[63] And so honor is served, and damn the rest.

What is going on with this single-minded devotion to honor?

This willingness to put other values ahead of one's life reveals one of the virtues of the warrior. But it manifests his madness as well.

As protector, the warrior is structured to be prepared for self-sacrifice. The male baboons who move forward from their troop to confront the leopard also place something higher than their own individual safety and survival. Likewise, human societies have need of warriors prepared to sacrifice their lives for the sake of something larger than themselves. The code of honor that emerges in such chronically threatened groups can be understood as a means of structuring the motivation of their males so that they will willingly make the needed sacrifice.

But, as we have seen before, adaptation combines with excess. The pattern of chronic injury that turns men into warriors also makes them narcissists. Thus it is that the code of honor that springs up in response to unceasing threat protects not only the endangered social group but the warrior's own embattled narcissism. The deeper the injury, the more likely it is that the code that was to make the warrior useful will make him dangerous instead. The preservation of honor and the preservation of society may conflict, and if the narcissistic element is predominant, the warrior may say: I would rather cleanse my honor and let the world go to hell.

Better dead than red, our cold warriors have said. Thus have heroes always chosen. Better to die than to bow before idols, better that one's head roll in the dust than that one's knee bend before false gods. Better to die a free man than to live a slave; better to die with honor than to live in shame. In the nuclear age, more than ever before, it is important to understand why these choices are so appealing, so appealing that those with the resolve to choose thus are enshrined as our heroes.

The choice of honor over life is dictated by narcissism. The narcissist, we saw, is identified with his ideal image of himself. Honor represents this ideal self. "If I lose mine honor," says Shakespeare's Antony, "I lose myself." This part of myself I regard as all that I am. The narcissist will not accept his self as a whole; he will not even confront it. Such a confrontation would threaten him with overwhelming pain. He would experience the collapse of the fiction of the ideal self as a kind of death. Opening up to the wounded and devalued parts of the self would be a hell. This death, this hell, we know from experience. The real death that lies at the end of life, and the hell of which the priest speaks, are but hypothetical abstractions. Dangers we can only imagine can weigh little against the burdens of our actual traumatic experience. Better, therefore, the real but only imagined death of the body than the symbolic death of which we have excruciating intimations.

Heroes are those who affirm for the rest of us that the fragile ideal of ourselves **can** be preserved. They die but their honor lives. Their ideal of themselves thus survives—as honorable warriors, as good Christians or Jews or Muslims, as freedom-loving patriots. Heroes are immortals: their death becomes unreal, for they live on in our hearts as ideas. (At the end of many American movies about World War II, we are shown again the animated faces of the heroes we have just seen die in battle; our final image of them is as living men.) To die a hero is not to die. *

---

*Sometimes, the belief that a hero's death confers immortality is quite explicit. The Ayatollah Khomeini, for example, speaks in words entirely recognizable to the warrior of honor: "[O]ur nation is no longer ready to submit to humiliation and abjection; it prefers a bloody death to a life of shame. We are ready to be killed and we have made a covenant with God to follow the path of our leader, the Lord of Martyrdom."[64] To the warrior's preference for death with honor to life with shame, however, Khomeini's religion adds the assurance that those who die in battle in the service of God's cause will go straight to heaven. This belief has certainly helped to prolong and make bloodier the brutal war between Iran and Iraq.

This suggests why, for the narcissist, the choice of death is not so hard. Not only is the alternative, for him, a painful symbolic death of his fragile identity. But for him especially is an honorable death liable to seem no death at all. For one who identifies only with his ideal self, the drama of life has been confined to a particular, narrow form: he has lived as his own hero. Much of himself he has already consigned to oblivion, allowing only a heroic fiction to embody his life. Thus, to die but live on as an ideal in the imagination may seem to the narcissist but a continuation of life as he has known it.

Those who study suicide report that many who attempt it believe unconsciously that somehow after their death they will be present to enjoy the drama they have created among those they leave behind. Similarly, the narcissist hero can find it easy to believe, as he goes to his death before an imagined audience, that his death will mean not oblivion but a life that, in a symbolic and essential way, is continuous with his life before.

Thus it is that the creature with thermonuclear weapons may threaten the survival of our planet less with his blatantly murderous passions than with his aspirations to an unsullied honor. For our species, the true dishonor, the mortal shame, would lie in our self-destruction. This "shame" of our species—to use as a metaphor the terms that the honor code applies to a sexually sullied woman—is less likely to come to pass because of our impulse to ravage each other than because of our inclination to seduce ourselves.

At the time of the Cuban missile crisis, it will be recalled, Khrushchev heard the counsel of his military advisers, those for whom the biggest tragedy would be if the Chinese or the Albanians thought them weak. Fortunately, at least to judge from his own account, Khrushchev did not lose touch with the more genuine life-and-death issues at stake.

> So I said to myself, "To hell with these maniacs . . ." What good would it have done me in the last hour of my life to know that though our great nation and the United States were in complete ruins, the national honor of the Soviet Union was intact?[65]

8

RUNNING THE SHOW: THE PARANOID ECONOMY OF THE WILL

I. THE NEED TO CONTROL

Winning, as we have seen, has many dimensions. We began with the need *to be invulnerable*, which manifests in the worship of strength. In a world of scarcity, the quest for security means winning over others. For the narcissist, this means first *the need to be the best*: the superiority of his being must stand clearly mirrored by the world around him. In a system beset by chronic strife, contenders for superiority do not just stand next to each other, like entrants in a beauty contest: they compete directly in battle. The quest for superiority creates, under those conditions, *the need to prevail*. The warrior of honor must be on top. If that should prove impossible, at least he cannot allow anyone else to be on top of him. He will not take insults lying down.

Now we enter another dimension of winning. The quest for superiority is a narcissistic issue, having to do with the image of the self. For the narcissist, the ability to defend that image is a vital component of security. But in this dangerous world, we have more to defend than our image of ourselves. Our quest for security requires us to have sufficient control over our environment to prevent our being injured by forces hostile to us. To win, therefore, means not only to display superiority but to achieve dominance: things must go my way. Beyond the requirements of narcissism, therefore, we want to win because of *the need to control.*

This, indeed, is the essence of power. In *The Parable of the Tribes,* I have defined power as the ability to achieve one's will against the will of another. The struggle for power is thus a drama to determine whose will shall triumph. And much of the excess in this struggle that afflicts civilization derives from a sense of the absolute necessity of absolute control. An excessive need to control fuels the war system, since surrender of the other rather than mutual accommodation is seen as necessary for one's own peace of mind. This same excessive need engenders the ancient plague of tyranny, which has culminated in our time in the totalitarian state.

Part of this excess derives from an exaggerated sense of the scarcity of control: there is so little to go around that I must have it all. Part is from an exaggerated sense of being threatened by anything one does not control: whatever I do not control will try to kill me. These are the elements of the paranoid economy of the will.

As with the pathologies of narcissism, these pathologies of the will point to the locus of traumatic injury. As we crave superiority because we have been treated like dirt, we insist on total control when we have been at the mercy of the merciless will of another. Of course the two—being treated as nothing, and being injured by the dominance of another—tend to go together. The narcissistic quest and the paranoid economy of the will, having common parentage, are as sister and brother: the close kinship between the need to be "on top" and the insistence on "running the show" will be explored later in this chapter.

But first let us explore the genesis and the consequences of the pathologies of the will.

The Annihilation of the Will

The traumas of victimization occur, again as with narcissism, on both the macro levels of history and the micro levels of individual development within the family. The inevitable reign of power in the evolution of civilization has meant the devastation and submission of the weak. We have spoken earlier—in "Damaged in the Male" (p. 35)—of how ubiquitous among civilized societies has been the experience of coming under the conqueror's cruel boot. Whole peoples have been compelled to swallow the poison of submitting to the will of their enemies. This poison then spills out into the family.

Anarchy dictates that a chronic contest of wills afflicts the whole system of civilization. The people wounded in this contest make wounded parents. Unable to exercise their right as human beings to a say in their destiny, adults may compensate by being tyrants with their children. What is strangled in the macrocosm pours forth with a fury in the microcosm of the home. Thus is the disease spread from generation to generation, from chicken to egg and back again: the lesson is taught that relations among wills are a matter not of give and take but of all or nothing.

The tyrannization and terrorization of children has left behind, in addition to scars, some literature of its rationalization. Consider German culture. Two centuries before history's greatest nightmare erupted under the banner of "The Triumph of the Will," pedagogues were extolling the rectitude of inflicting upon the will those injuries that create tyrants. In his "Essay on the Education and Instruction of Children" in 1748, J. Sultzer was advising that although "It is quite natural for the child's soul to want to have a will of its own . . . willfulness must be driven out in a methodical manner . . . If one gives in to their willfulness once, the second time it will be more pronounced and more difficult to drive out."[1] Kill the will, that is the only way to have the right kind of child. (Similarly, Howard Stein notes that children growing up in the cowboy subculture that breeds much of American militarism are required to show "only perfect willlessness" in relation to their parents and to God.)[2]

The dominance of the parent should be complete and unquestioned. Again, Sultzer: "The blows you administer should not be merely playful ones but should convince him that you are his master." The growing human being is taught through fear and injury to submit; tyrannical rule teaches him that the exercise of the will is a scarce commodity. Human relations, the child learns, can take two forms: war, or the unwilling submission of one person to another. These are the choices confronting the gods under Zeus, as depicted in the warrior epic, the *Iliad*. Confronted by Zeus's fiat and threats of retaliation for disobedience, the gods can "revolt and be punished, or repress anger and submit."[3]

War or tyranny. These are the two alternative conditions to which the process described by the parable of the tribes has condemned civilized peoples. Either there is anarchy with its war of all against all, or that war leads to government established and maintained by force. (Those of us who have known more benign forms of order are a very fortunate minority.) Traumatic historical experience having impressed upon civilized people these cruel alternatives, parents have construed the order of the family in similar terms. To those who cannot imagine order except in the form of tyranny, any exercise of independence of will by the child will seem to be a redeclaration of anarchy's state of war. Another learned German pedagogue, J. G. Krueger, wrote in 1752 that any disobedience by a child "amounts to a declaration of war against you. Your son is trying to usurp your authority, and you are justified in answering force with force in order to assure his respect, without which you will be unable to train him."[4]

Obedience is *the* virtue for a child. One German raised in the late nineteenth century reported of his upbringing:

> It was constantly impressed upon me in forceful terms that I must obey promptly the wishes and commands of my parents, teachers, and priests, and indeed of all grown-up people, including servants, and that nothing must distract me from this duty. Whatever they said was always right. These basic principles by which I was brought up became second nature to me.[5]

The name of this child was Hermann Hoess, who would grow up to be the commandant of Auschwitz. Germany was not unique in compelling the complete subservience of children to the authority and power of the parent, however. The Russian historian Kostomarov has written that in his country in the seventeenth century, "between parents and children reigned a spirit of slavery, covered by the cloak of holy, patriarchal relations . . . [T]he obedience of children was more that of a slave than a child, and parental power turned into blind despotism, lacking any moral force."[6] The imbalance of power, combined with the parents' insistence on total domination, assures that the warfare between the generations will be speedily resolved into tyranny. The child is reduced to a slave, who is entitled to no will of his own.

The virtue of obedience may bring the reward of appeasing the wrath of the tyrant, but at what a cost! The annihilation of the will is a form of murder. The child as obedient slave is denied the respect to which he is entitled as a separate being, with needs and feelings of his own. Those needs and feelings, which could direct his independent will, are regarded by the power system in which he is molded as the subversive forces of the enemy. What belongs to the child's own being is therefore squeezed out, to assure the child's complete submission to outside domination. J. Sultzer, in his "wisdom," recommends:

> Everything must follow the rules of orderliness. Food and drink, clothing, sleep, and indeed the child's entire little household must

be orderly and must never be altered in the least to accommodate their willfulness or whims so that they may learn in earliest childhood to submit strictly to the rule of orderliness.[7]•

The parental impulse to tyrannize and brutalize children doubtless comes blindly from the depth of the parents' own pain and fear and rage. But, like most of the crimes we commit, the abuse of children is transformed by rationalization into virtue. Only if the will is annihilated will the child learn the upright path of duty. Only by brute force can the child learn the necessary respect for parental authority. What is done out of inner compulsion is thus represented as required by objective necessity.

As the need is rationalized, so are the costs minimized. Sultzer, for example, assures parents that it is fine to brutalize the tiniest of children. Clearly, just in terms of the strategy of warfare, it makes sense to strike while the balance of forces is most advantageous to one's own side. This realpolitik approach is conveyed, for example, in the advice of the fifteenth-century Russian Domostroi on how to break the autonomy of a son: "Do not give him his will in his youth, but crush his ribs while he is not yet grown, or else he will harden and cease to obey you, and then there will be grief and vexation for your soul . . ."[9]

But Sultzer does not rest content with the obvious strategic advantages of a preemptive strike against the defenseless. He wishes to convince parents that their brutality does no harm: "Over the years children forget everything that happened to them in early childhood. If their wills can be broken at this time, they will never remember afterwards that they had a will, and for this very reason the severity that is required will not have any serious consequences."[10] We know now how fallacious is that psychology. The earliest years are the most formative: whether remembered or not, the experiences of childhood strongly shape the personality for a lifetime. Indeed, it may be the experiences that leave the deepest and most damaging wounds that are most likely to be forgotten, since the suppression of memory is one of the ways of coping with the overwhelming pain and terror of traumatic

---

•The child is squeezed out, obliterated by the parent and the parent's will. Steele and Pollock describe an effort to interview an abused child: "Her mother would 'take over,' answer questions directed to the daughter, tell the daughter what to answer, indicate in many ways what she expected the daughter to do, and either overtly or implicity criticize and belittle her, all without paying attention to what the daughter was thinking, feeling or trying to do."[8]

experience. Thus does Sultzer's pedagogy perpetuate the blindness of the compulsion that drives the cycle of violence.

No "serious consequences" from the annihilation of the will, says Sultzer. The child will forget he ever had a will. The purpose of this chapter is to explore the profoundly serious consequences for civilization of the traumatic experience of impotence before the conquering will of another. The will may bend to submission, the child may forget he has one, but the will does not disappear. To be our own human being is part of our birthright from nature, and to war on that nature is not the road to true peace. As Horace said, "If you drive nature out with a pitchfork, she will soon find a way back."[11] Submission to duty may have become "second nature" to Hermann Hoess, as he says, but look what happened to his first nature. Even as he fitted himself as a dutiful part of a tyrannical regime, he himself also *willed* the most brutal dehumanization and annihilation of others. Here is nature, thwarted, coming back with a pitchfork of its own: the will, driven underground, reappears in satanic form.

"Among the leaders of the Third Reich," writes Alice Miller, "I have not been able to find a single one who did not have a strict and rigid upbringing."[12]

The Denial of Powerlessness

In the beginning, there is the terror of being impotent in the hands of a hostile power. Again, this terror can be felt in the abusive environment of an individual's childhood or amid the cruel currents of a people's history.

The terror of impotence—strong words, but apt. The child's feeling of impotence is the natural offspring of the parent's insistence on total control. The socialization process that molds the character typical of the American West, Howard Stein discovered from both male and female informants, produced a "feeling of parental power and control over their lives [that] was both overwhelming and total."[13] As Sultzer said, everything must follow the regime of the parents, and thus the child is compelled to accept his impotence.

Such impotence implies terror, for tyranny implies the profoundest hostility toward the child. As in our earlier discussion of narcissistic injury, the annihilation of the will of the child is an act of war on what the child is by nature. Tyranny, by virtue of the distrust it implies of the impulses it suppresses by force, can never be benign. Thus, we should not be surprised that those informants of Stein's who felt their parents' power over them to be total expressed also "the fear of being destroyed by [their parents'] power."

In the nightmare of such childhood, and in the nightmare of history, there has been no escape from this terrifying condition of impotence. But we are simply too weak to stay face to face with terror. Where a terrifying reality cannot be changed, the escape from terror requires an escape from reality. Thus, people create fictions that deny their impotence and helplessness at the hands of hostile and unpredictable powers. *

Helplessness being the worst fate, better that we should be the masters of our fate, even if that means finding the causes of our undoing within ourselves. This abhorrence of helplessness is illustrated by several kinds of fiction at the macro level of nations and ideology.

One of these is exemplified by the Israelites' relationship with their God, as described by Jacobson. The people of Israel were compelled to cope with their chronic subjugation to the nations surrounding them. As it was unendurable to think of themselves as the helpless victims of others, they chose to interpret their fate as an expression of the attitude of God Almighty, an attitude which was in turn the consequence of their own behavior. "Outwardly, the Israelites may have appeared to be a defeated people . . . Yet their actions, and their attitudes, alone were all that mattered ultimately."[14] In part, such an interpretation may reflect the natural tendency of the "ethical animal" to interpret all fate as an expression of parental judgment of one's worth. But in part also it expresses the *wish* to believe that one has the power to control one's destiny.†

This insistence on being the master of one's destiny takes a more pernicious form in some of the fictions created by paranoid political movements. For people in the terrified state of mind that gives rise to such movements, national disasters always require uncovering some national betrayal. God forbid that we should be simply powerless to prevent what we feared. Thus, the Nazis' paranoid movement grew out of the same climate as that which gave rise to the "stab in the back"

---

*In part 3, "Boundaries," we will also see that the converse is true: to escape the confrontation with their own moral natures, people will create fictions that deny their moral responsibility for the evils in which they participate.

†Dan Jacobson makes another interesting interpretation of biblical history that connects with the need for control. The idea of the covenant between God and His chosen people, says Jacobson, served as a protection against unpredictability. "[I]n lashing themselves down with the covenant, and to all its accompanying laws, they hoped to lash down Yahweh too. Quid pro quo."[15]

fiction that was created to explain the German defeat in World War I. "Germans were totally unprepared for the sudden news of defeat in 1918. Patriots spread the story that the army had never really been defeated in the field. Rather, like Wagner's Siegfried, the Fatherland had been betrayed and given a stab in the back (*Dolchstoss*)."[16] Similarly, in the United States in the period of the paranoid fears that characterized the early 1950s, the question was raised, "Who lost China?" As if China had ever been ours to lose! Better to imagine that our losses come from a perversion of *our* power—i.e., from traitors among us—than from the limits to our power.

They can have no power over us. We are reminded here of the Star Wars fiction discussed in Chapter 4, "The Wages of Denial." It *cannot* be true that our survival depends upon powers alien to us. Those who have been traumatized as victims cannot bear to acknowledge again that the will of another can govern their fate. It is we who are in control.

This leads to that central fiction in the denial of helplessness: the identification with the aggressor. "If I am the object I fear, then I need not be afraid." The reality of being the victim is too terrifying, so by the magic of fantasy I will become the victimizer. The fiction of identification with the aggressor grows out of the traumas of individuals and of whole peoples, at both levels serving to perpetuate the cycling of brutality as today's sufferer becomes the agent of tomorrow's suffering.*

When I identify with the aggressor, with the one whose will reigns, I am in the first place denying my actual identity as the helpless victim: That is not me. Eli Sagan describes the use of the mock king as a figure associated with the cruel African kingships. The Ankolean mock king, says Sagan, was called *ekyibumbe*, one of whose meanings was "a small infant, left to the mercy of its mother."[18] The mock king was a figure created to be murdered. Here is what Sagan says of the meaning of this murder:

---

*The best defense, one might say, is a good offense. A wonderful illustration of the defensive identification with the aggressor is cited by M. Scott Peck:

> The builders of the medieval cathedrals placed upon their buttresses the figures of gargoyles—themselves symbols of evil—in order to ward off the spirits of greater evil. Thus children may become evil in order to defend themselves against the onslaughts of parents who are evil. It is possible, therefore, to think of human evil—or some of it—as a kind of psychological gargoylism.[17]

The grotesque face of civilization—shaped by our terrifying history—can itself be seen as a kind of gargoyle.

> The new king, having killed his brothers in the war of succes-
> sion, kills the *ekyibumbe*, symbolically announcing: We are not
> small, toothless, helpless infants; we are strong, powerful killers,
> omnipotent kings. Thereby they killed within themselves doubts of
> their own pretensions. So pervasive were these doubts, it seems,
> that, at least in Bunyoro, the rite had to be renewed yearly.[19]

For me to be the object I feared, I must kill off my real underlying
experience of myself as a helpless victim.

But reality has a way of growing back up through the fabric of the
fictions we create. As Freud says, the repressed returns. The helpless
infant needs to be killed regularly, because he will not stay dead.

In his terror, the battered son wishes himself into the role of the
terrifying father, but the reign of the wish is incomplete. Because it is a
denial of reality, the identification with the aggressor leads to endless
confusions on the fundamental issue, "Who's who?" Who is powerful and
who is weak? Who's the aggressor, and who's the victim? Who's the one
who makes war out of the issue of will? The father of a nine-month-old
boy whose skull he has split said: "He thinks he's the boss—all the time
trying to run things—but I showed him who's in charge around here."[20]
To Lloyd deMause, this is an example of "reversal"—where the parent
perceives the child as being in the role of the parent—which, he says,
underlies much of the battering of children. (One recalls J. G. Krueger's
statement that any disobedience in the child is a "declaration of war"
against the parent.)

At one level, one might say that—in reversal—the parent wants to
reenact the trauma of his own childhood, where he was the victim of
the tyranny of the parental will, in order to succeed at last in being the
boss. And his own child is a satisfying substitute for the parent of old,
since the balance of power so favors the now grown-up avenger. But the
reversal of roles here is more than simply a choice of a winnable battle
of wills. It is also a reflection of the confusions around one's own
identity to which the repression of one's true sense of self gives rise. The
reversal described by deMause, in other words, is a fiction that is the
son of that earlier fiction, the identification with the aggressor.* Both
these levels of analysis of what underlies reversal help explain how
battered children grow up to batter their own children.

---

*These confusions of identity—in whom is the helplessness? who possesses the
unchallengeable will?—are also entwined with the issue of "boundaries," which is the
subject of part 3.

This also helps explain why the tyrant is so excessive in the exercise of his power, in the imposition of his will. The magic of the identification with the aggressor—like the other forms of the denial of weakness and vulnerability explored in this book—does not bring true security. Just as the mock king, the helpless infant, keeps arising again needing to be killed off, so does the terrifying figure of the omnipotent persecutor remain lurking in the shadows. The certainty that one is, oneself, the possessor of the power is most precarious. Ever-present is the possibility that the fiction will crumble, and the real persecutor will return, that the old drama of annihilation will be played out in the old roles.

Consider Hitler. At one level, he has become the aggressor, and he celebrates the absolute victory of his absolute will. "*He*, like his father before him, was now the dictator, the only one who had anything to say. It was the place of all the others to be silent and obey."[21] But then there are the Jews, an omnipresent threat to destroy everything that is good, that is ours. Like the nine-month-old child whose father split open his skull, the Jews make a handy target because they are vulnerable. But also like the infant, the Jews are *seen* as a genuine threat to the triumph of one's own will. The terror is real, even if not objectively realistic. The sense of overwhelming threat is genuine, even if its expression deals in fictions. It is no wonder that the worldview of the threatened tyrant is filled with contradictions—e.g., that the Jews are at once so clever and powerful to threaten to take over the world, and so inferior and subhuman as to be vermin who warrant extermination—for the tyrant's own identity is founded upon a contradiction of reality.

The tyrant fears even the smallest challenges to his will because his solution to his having been tyrannized was no real solution. He cannot even be sure that his own will is his own, since he has assumed the identity of another. Having abandoned himself to escape the reality of his victimization by a tyrannical and hostile will, the tyrant will see every challenge to his will as dragging him back to that scene of dread where his emotional business remains unfinished.

The Compensatory Need for the Imposition of the Will

An Auschwitz, therefore, plays a crucial role in keeping intact the fragile fiction: As long as I persecute, it must be I who am the persecutor. As long as you are the victim, I am not.

Here is another, most malignant manifestation of the sense of scarcity. Earlier we discussed the game of Old Maid played by men of honor who pass the humiliation around. In the paranoid mentality of the tyrant, too, there are certain cards that must be in someone's hand. Someone must be the helpless victim; another gets to be the powerful man of iron will. If I can make another suffer against his will, then I needn't fear that I will hold the victim's card. Cruelty is "a defense mechanism used by the ego to ward off the threat of annihilation."[22] (Horst-Eberhard Richter and Alice Miller were quoted earlier, saying that making others suffer is a way of warding off one's own feeling of suffering.) Your suffering replaces mine. Human sacrifice, says Eli Sagan, is used by its practitioners to ward off their own fears of being destroyed. If I control death, I will not be its victim.

The logic of scarcity tells me I am safer when I see the Angel of Death sate his appetite on the flesh of another. Through identification with the aggressor, I can get the further assurance: *I am the Angel of Death.*

Thus the fictions that give temporary relief to the traumatic terror of impotence do so at the cost of perpetuating the cycling of trauma. The tyrant's need to exercise his will is marked by that stamp of excess that always accompanies the denial of reality.

War and slavery. Those are the only possibilities understood by those traumatized by the war waged by a great power upon their will. There is no envisioning an order blessed by both peace and harmony; no sense of cooperation that is willing. Bronco-busting in the American cowboy culture is described in these terms in *Rodeo: An Anthropologist Looks at the Wild and the Tame*:

> "Bronco-busting," the taming and training of wild horses to be used for riding, was as brutal as any activity involving man and beast; commonly termed "breaking," the aim was to conquer the horse physically and in spirit. Typically, there was no gradual gentling and training with an intent to establish mutual confidence between man and animal. Rather, full-grown horses were abruptly roped, thrown, saddled and bridled, and usually beaten into submission by "rough riders" whose aim was to "break the pony's heart on the first riding." . . . The object was to quickly impress upon the bronco the notion of human supremacy, so that it would leave a lasting impression. The absolute right to instill fear and inflict pain in order to establish man's mastery was unquestioned.[23]

It is understandable that this right would not be questioned in a culture whose members shared the need to quell their own fears and assuage their own pains by imposing their will on others by coercive force. Whence comes this shared need? We already know. Howard Stein says of that passage on bronco-busting that "With but little change, one could substitute 'child' for 'horse' . . . and come out with a remarkably widely generalizable description of parent-child relations and the child-rearing philosophy that underlies it."[24] The bronco-busters had themselves been busted.

When submission is unwilling, the battle of the wills continues. Had the spirit of the horse's rider been treated with more gentleness, he would be more inclined to "gentle" the horse instead of breaking him. But as no one ever made peace with him, all he knows is the way of war. He seeks it out, provokes it, wanting only that this time it will end with the *other's* spirit broken by *his* will.

But as the bronco-busters' perpetuation of the cruelty shows, the "peace" that is made by busting brings no peace. The excessive imposition of the will is a declaration of war, and it creates its opposition. The tyrant creates the rebel, the bronco-buster creates the bucking bronco. Slaves they create too, when they break their victim's spirit. But even slaves are often rebels of a sort: the obedient serf may brutalize his wife and children. The Reign of Terror lurks behind the glory of the Sun King's absolute rule. Slavery but drives the war underground.

What is suppressed excessively becomes wild. This is nature coming back with a pitchfork of her own. And the wildness then is used to justify the restraint. Thus tyrannical rule (e.g., in South Africa) often makes violence the only way of expressing an opposing will, and then uses the violence as a justification for continued tyranny. The tyrant creates a world that presents to him the only options he understands: coerced submission or violent revolt. "If you don't break [the child]," says an Oklahoma woman, "it will run wild."[25]

By stunting the growth of a healthy and independent will on the part of the governed, repressive regimes can rationalize their perpetuation. An example of this is the rationalization for the swaddling of infants that was the traditional practice in Russia. Aside from the practical reasons of keeping the child warm and making it into a bundle easy to carry the Russians would say, "[H]ow could one otherwise keep him from scratching and harming himself with the sight of his own hands?"[26] To the Russians, the need for complete suppression of the child's movements was self-evident because of the child's inability adequately to control himself. But Erik Erikson sees how the regime of swaddling created the conditions for its own justification.

> Now it is probably true that a swaddled baby, especially when just unswaddled, has not sufficient mastery over his own movements to keep from scratching and hitting himself. The further assumption that *therefore* he has to be swaddled again is a favorite

trick of cultural rationalization . . . You must swaddle the infant to
protect him against himself; this causes violent vasomotor needs in
him; he must remain emotionally swaddled in order not to fall
victim to wild emotion.

What is caged becomes too wild to let out. Thus, the cage makes
itself necessary. You must be bound by my will, for your will is too wild
to be trusted. The binding of the swaddling clothes, like J. Sultzer's
regime of total orderliness, is a cage that wars upon the will of the child.
Movement is the most elemental expression of the will, but the child is
told: you are bound by my will. Submission is forced. In part, the spirit
is broken: the bronco-busted child takes the bit in his mouth, obeys the
commands, goes only where bidden. Order is achieved. But underground, where the will has retreated, it has taken a menacing form: in
Erikson's language, the needs grow "violent," the emotions "wild."

On the surface, the child grows into an agent of the order. But the
appearance is deceiving, just as the nature of the order itself is not what
it seems. Sultzer's tyranny speaks of order and rectitude, but those are
masks for the waging of war. (Tyranny is not an end to the war of all
against all, but merely one of its forms.) Just so, the child who grows
into an upright upholder of the tyrannical order is wearing a mask to
obscure the expression of a will made wild.* With this wild will,
emerging at last from underground, he splits the skull of his defenseless
child—to establish, he says, the proper standing of authority. The
infant no longer thinks he is the boss, says the crazed will of the
once-wounded, onetime child. "You break [the child's] will to give it
character."[28] Yes, character of a sort.

Thus does the pathology of the will perpetuate itself. From generation to generation, the war of wills is handed down. Those who
have been denied the gift of mutuality—of respect, of compromise,
of accommodation—do not have it themselves to give. Each generation growing up as war captives feels compelled itself to find captives
whose submission they can compel. The way of war cannot make
peace.

---

*In the undressing room next to the crematorium at Treblinka, the Nazis placed a sign
expressing the proper German values of "*Rein ist fein*" ("Clean is fine"), to help them go
about their dirty business of mass slaughter.[27] Papa Eicke, in his concentration camp,
promised his victims to make their dying "tasty," as if his cruelties were "For Your Own
Good," as Alice Miller entitles her book on the poisonous pedagogy. The cycle of poison
masks everything as its opposite—hate as love, injury as help, the dirty as the clean. It is
war and chaos waged in the name of peace and order.

Shalom means knitting together, but trauma drives apart. The problem lies in what has been split off and driven underground: the will gone wild, the terror denied. To make peace with a tyrant, we must wear a mask and bury part of ourselves. And what is pushed down becomes demonized. To endure a fear that is unendurable, we must flee the reality of our experience into a fiction that we are more powerful and invulnerable than we are. And what we run away from becomes a pursuer. Thus, under attack from an angry will and an unacknowledged terror, we ourselves become the attackers. Not having made peace with what we are and what we experience, we cannot be at peace with the world. Until we find a way to knit ourselves together, we will be makers not of shalom but of war.

The Paranoid Economy of the Will

The intersocietal system has been an arena for the chronic contest of wills. In the words that Thucydides put into the mouths of his imperialistic Athenians, "Of the gods we believe, and of men we know, that by a necessary law of their nature they rule wherever they can."[29] Thus, history presents us with a seething landscape of wars and empire-building. Virtually every sovereign entity we see today was melded by war, as one sovereign actor has forced others to submit to the dominion of its will. The inexorable process of consolidation by force has found no stopping place. However big they are, neighbors in the arena of anarchy have seen each other as rivals, and rivalry has been a prelude to war and the further expansion of the empire of the victorious will. This pattern is one we can only hope can be broken, as we see now two wills colliding, each the expression of a continent-sized empire and each backed by weapons of mass destruction.

Realism and excess again operate together to accentuate the anguish of civilization. Anarchy does enshrine power as the key to survival. There is thus a degree of realism in Machiavelli's belief that states that lose their appetite for the extension of their rule are doomed to be destroyed by others hungrier for power. But realism by itself does not explain the intensity of the lust for dominion displayed in human history. Not just threat but a *distorted sense of threat* has fed that lust. And what has distorted our understanding of the threats we face has been the traumatic experience of being the powerless victim.

We have looked at that trauma in the system of the family, where the pathologies of the will cycle down through time from the victimizer to the victim who, in turn, becomes a victimizer. A similar process can operate among societies, as in the rise of Rome as conqueror of the world: it was out of a traumatic time of being conquered and nearly destroyed that the Romans emerged with the militant and domineering spirit that drove them to be master of all those around them. In large measure, however, the intersocietal system can be regarded as a group of peers, all of whom have had battered childhoods and who are compelled to live within reach of one another. Because the intersocietal system has been for millennia an arena for continuous brutalization and persecution, virtually all nations are to some degree afflicted with the pathologies of the will we have discussed. A struggle for power made inevitable by the conditions of anarchy is thus rendered ferocious by the "paranoid economy of the will" learned in the jaws of trauma.

All or none. That is what brutal victimization teaches: either I have complete control, or I am helpless. The only roles that are understood are those of victim and victimizer. Give and take is foreign to the worldview taught by such trauma. To the extent that nations embody this worldview—which to some extent they do*—the possession of will and autonomy is rendered a highly precious, excruciatingly scarce commodity.

If autonomy is an "all or nothing" affair, the mutual respect of a meeting of equals is impossible. To the paranoid, says W. W. Meissner, "The independence of other individuals is extremely threatening."[30] It is threatening because your power implies my powerlessness. And also because traumatic experience has taught me that others' power is hostile power, to be used for my destruction. "Any power which others possess, even if it is merely the power of self-possession and personal initiative and independence, tends to be distorted [by the paranoid] into a hostile and destructive power which is interpreted as intending the subjugation and humiliation of the self."[31] In his terror and confusion, the paranoid regards any expression of autonomy by another as an attack, and "he cannot rest until he has blotted out the . . . offender . . ."[32] Your autonomous act is "a declaration of war," requiring that I show you who's boss. There is room for only one will, and that's mine!

This makes it clear why, if the traumas of history have generated a stream of paranoia in civilized consciousness, peace would be so difficult

---

*Only rarely do such *extreme* views dominate the outlook of the actors on the world stage. But such views are a component of those actors' psychology, a voice in the back of the mind. And, as the influence of that voice contributes significantly to the problems in human affairs, it is worthwhile for us to attend to its most blatant expressions, so that we learn to discern its message and its destructive effects.

for civilized peoples to achieve. Our societies confront one another as sovereign entities. Autonomy is the essence of sovereignty, and the autonomy of others is precisely what terrifies the paranoid. Inevitably, power is scarce. But the economy of "all or none" makes it much scarcer. It is as if people on a lifeboat all looked at their supplies through the wrong end of a telescope and erroneously concluded that there was enough to keep only one of them alive. A sane bystander would find strange and unnecessary the efforts of each to throw all the others overboard.

Trauma cripples the ability to see things in a balanced way. The insistence on total power derives from the fear of utter impotence. Just as the identification with the aggressor produced the confusions over whether one is the powerful or the weak one, a similar polarization of possibilities derives from the paranoid economy of the will. Meissner describes the paranoid as fluctuating between a denial of the inner capacity of the self and a denial of the independent capacity of the other. Either case—the perception of the self as "a threatened and helpless" victim or as "a powerful, evil, and dangerously destructive monster"—"reflects a distortion of autonomy."[33]

A distortion, yes, but our paranoia does indeed make us dangerous and destructive. Yet we can see once again how the exercise of our power is so often an expression not of real strength but of weakness, not of our confidence as much as of our terror. The psychoanalyst Anthony Storr writes:

> I think that the tendency of human beings, unlike other animals, to pursue their enemies to the death and to treat them with cruelty is intimately associated with paranoid projection. One of the features of a full-blown paranoid delusional system is the conviction that the persecutors have magical powers against which the subject is relatively helpless.[34]

It is because we are haunted by the terror of being at the mercy of powers much greater than ourselves that we traumatized humans have so often been merciless. It is because we fear that we will be destroyed by forces beyond our control that we crave the possession of complete control of our world.

The paranoid economy of the will is an important part of the specter of destruction that haunts our planet today. The Cold War grew directly out of the trauma of World War II. From the Nazis' destructive drive toward world dominion, the two surviving great powers learned and overlearned their lessons (lessons already ingrained in their beings from previous history).

The Soviets overlearned the indispensability of maintaining dominion over everything around them. The nations of Eastern Europe have
therefore been vassals in the Soviet empire for more than forty years.
What we don't control will become the avenue for invading us. As was
said earlier, the Soviets could not grasp the idea of governments in
Eastern Europe that were at once friendly to the Soviet Union and
independent. As Meissner said of the paranoid, the independence of
others is threatening; the autonomy of others is assumed to imply powers
hostile to oneself. One thinks of the apocryphal Texas rancher who
didn't need to control much, just his own domain and everything that
adjoined it. The need for domination that goes with a paranoid worldview
knows no limits: whatever is beyond the boundaries of empire must be
brought safely within them. The existence of an independent other
raises traumatic memories and insecurities. Lenin said, "As an ultimate
objective peace simply means Communist world control."[35] Our complete domination is the only alternative to war.

But even this route brings no true peace. The Soviet insistence on
domination, like other forms of tyranny, creates its own insecurity. As
Hungary in 1956, Czechoslovakia in 1968, and Poland in 1981 all
demonstrate, only the brutal force of the Soviet will holds its "allies" in
line. In Western Europe, meanwhile, a less anxious United States
granted real autonomy to its allies, and consequently need not worry in
which direction they will shoot if war were ever to break out in Europe.
The order created by the paranoid economy of the will is like riding
on the back of a tiger. What is driven underground—the suppressed
will of the tyrannized—becomes wild and dangerous. The ruler on top
cannot afford to get off, lest he be devoured; but neither can he stay
atop forever. The Soviet empire may prove to be such a tiger. In South
Africa, the whites riding upon the black majority are another currently
most precarious instance. And in Central America, which the United
States regards as its own sphere of influence, another tiger* has become
visible: the tight grip of right-wing dictators, which U.S. governments
have believed secured American interests, creates the very forces that
threaten those interests.

It is not, however, in its insistence on a sphere of influence that the
United States most clearly displays the pathologies of the will that have

---

*As this work goes to press, the restiveness of Soviet Armenians gives a glimpse of the
"tiger" of nationalistic upheaval the Kremlin may be riding as a result of the brutal
coercion of peoples with which the Soviet "Union" itself was put together.

rippled from World War II's traumatic impact. If the Russians overlearned the need for complete control, the Americans overlearned the need for resolute will. This was "the lesson of Munich." Any sign of weakness of will only encourages would-be aggressors. Every confrontation, therefore, is seen as the hinge of history; every point of contact a potential chink in the armor. Every interaction requires above all the proof that one demonstrate that iron resolve that the West failed to display in Munich in 1938.

A chief characteristic of traumatic learning, I have stressed here, is its excessiveness. Everything looks like what inflicted the trauma. (I remember that, for a few days after I lacerated my eye on a TV antenna, anything that stuck out toward my face made me shy away.) It has often been observed how the "lesson of Munich" was overapplied by a whole generation of American policy-makers. Ho Chi Minh was explicitly likened to Hitler, and it was assumed that the way to deal with the threat he was believed to pose was to show that we meant business. At the time of the Cuban missile crisis, President Kennedy believed that Khruschchev had placed the missiles in Cuba for the purpose of demonstrating the lack of U.S. will—a belief for which there is "not a shred of evidence."[36] To thwart this nonexistent intention of a foreign power, Kennedy displayed will aplenty. To avoid the mistake that had helped start World War II, JFK came perilously close to bringing on World War III.

Just as the Soviets create a brittle and insecure dominion by virtue of their insistence on complete control, so has the United States tended to undermine its national will by its obsessive insistence on demonstrating it. "There is more than a little irony," Richard Ned Lebow writes, "in the fact that decades of zealous American efforts to safeguard credibility have done more than anything else to undermine it."[37] Following the path of excess resolve led, by the mid-1970s, to an erosion of national will that still might inhibit even a necessary use of American power. An overwillingness to impose American will on regional struggles all over the world has diminished rather than extended the nation's influence in the world.

Nonetheless, in the Reagan administration, the Cold War mentality, reflecting these pathologies of the will, again has dominated the American approach to the world. In our discussion of winning, we mentioned the tendency of our cold warriors to see all world events narrowly in terms of the East-West struggles, ignoring the many and diverse aspirations of the world's peoples. This problem of perception relates also to the paranoid economy of the will. The parnoid, writes Meissner, "cannot recognize an opponent as somehow an independent focus of initiative, which happens to be at cross-purposes to his own."[38] Herein perhaps lies a good deal of the failure of American warriors to understand the strivings of various oppressed peoples around the world. If their purposes seem to cross ours, they must be our enemies. We must pit our will and our power against theirs, bend them to our purpose. It is an approach to others' strivings that inevitably makes one embattled across the map. Perhaps the nationalist strivings of the Viet Minh, and those of the Sandinistas in Nicaragua, would inevitably run counter to U.S. interests. But one thing is clear: our failure to understand their aspirations magnified, if it did not create, a serious conflict of interests.

Although it is less rigid than the Soviet empire, there has nonetheless been an American empire of the will. An anxious mistrust of the world has driven this empire and has imposed an unnecessarily heavy burden of conflict and intervention. Realism has no doubt required some of this. But an element of excess has been added.

Those who began World War II to see their will triumph failed. But the pathologies of the will of which they were carriers did triumph in spreading through the whole of the postwar world.

"Peaceful coexistence." This, we have understood, is what is required of superpowers in an age of nuclear weapons. But peaceful coexistence is precisely what the paranoid mentality is incapable of achieving. The paranoid, we have seen, cannot comfortably coexist with other centers of independent will and power. The superpower relationship, clearly, is an encounter that engenders mutual paranoia. We two nations have emerged from the terrors of history only to confront each other with weapons that epitomize the victim's trauma: we both are held hostage to the will of the other. To the extent that we look at the threat from the other through the lens of our paranoia—and there are clearly powerful elements in each country that do—we magnify that threat. By themselves, our weapons will not destroy us. But if to our technology we allow ourselves to add the paranoid passions of panic and rage at the power of another, the mixture could prove catastrophically combustible. It is a profound spiritual challenge, under these conditions of a balance of terror, to find in ourselves the peace of mind to let go of the paranoid economy of the will. We cannot survive with an "all or nothing" approach to power. To the paranoid, in the grip of scarcity, there is not room on this planet for another great power. If we are to survive, we need to find that more secure state of mind where it becomes evident that there is room for all to live, for each to follow his own spirit in his own domain.

Afterword: The Narcissism-Paranoia Connection

The paranoid needs to "run the show." The narcissist needs to "be on top." These two scarcity-creating mentalities, considered separately here, are in many ways different dimensions of the same underlying psychological world.

The signs of this kinship are already evident. Both emerge out of traumatic injury. The same assaults from the outside world that create the paranoid need for control are also absorbed as narcissistic injuries engendering the need for compensatory narcissistic self-inflation. Thus Meissner writes, "All of our [paranoid] patients are victims of injured narcissism . . . [T]he workings of the paranoid process in each . . . can be seen quite directly as a manifestation of this narcissistic conflict and torment."[39] Conversely, the maintenance of the narcissist's identification with his perfect self can be maintained only by the utilization of the paranoid's projective mechanisms. In the pathological narcissist, says Otto Kernberg, "the remnants of the unacceptable self-images are repressed and projected onto external objects."[40]* Both narcissism and paranoia entail confusions of identification with which they deal similarly. Violation from the outside produces efforts at the same time to refurbish the damaged self and to gain the control necessary to prevent any repeated onslaught.

Just as both arise from the trauma of injury, so do both reveal a damaged capacity for relationship. The narcissist relegates others to a shadowy, less than real existence: people are real only to the extent that they connect with his own narcissistic needs.** Similarly, as we have just discussed, the paranoid cannot recognize others as autonomous actors with needs and purposes of their own. The scars of past injury cause, in both, a breakdown of mutuality into solipsism defended by rage.

And of course, all these shared characteristics reinforce the world of scarcity. The division of roles required by the defensive fictions of narcissism and paranoia generate a scarcity of goodness and power. A further scarcity of autonomy and respectability are implied by the isolation that comes with the breakdown of relationship.

What we have been exploring, therefore, may not be two separate islands of the consciousness of the injured warrior, but two aspects of the same territory.

---

*On the use of projection, much more will be said in part 3, "Boundaries."
**Cf. "Narcissism and the Crippled Capacity for Relationship" (p. 101)

II. BY POSSESSION POSSESSED

We are exploring the empire of the will. Out of the anxieties induced by an injurious world, the warrior develops a need to control. Bound up with that need is the idea of possession. To control is not just to command but to have and to hold. In a world fraught with danger and ruled by scarcity, the warrior feels impelled to guard jealously what is his.

Dominion is possession. The idea of possession warrants a special focus here. For the need to possess lies close to the core of the problem of war. And exploring that need can take us close to the heart of human fear.

For the warrior, there are two principal arenas of life. There is the arena of fighting, and there is what is being fought over. The first is the world of armor and weapons, of the hard surfaces and cutting edges. The second is the world of the delicate, of the soft and precious. A man's honor is part of that inner sanctum of the delicate: Cyrano, on the verge of death, refers to his honor as his "unsullied plume," a feather, the very antithesis of armor, or of that steely sword he wielded so expertly. This delicate, unsullied plume is what a man has that he cannot allow another man to take away from him.

There is another way this dichotomy is represented, this dichotomy between the fighting and the fought over, the outer and the inner, the hard and the soft: it is a split between the male and the female. Men fight, and what they fight over is women.

Sexual Possessiveness

In the first place, men's honor traditionally is intimately connected with the defense of their womenfolk against other men. "Nothing," says Bertram Wyatt-Brown, "could arouse such fury in traditional societies as an insult hurled against a woman of a man's household, most especially his mother."[41] The man of honor must keep his women, like his delicate plume, unsullied. Insults against the women arouse fury, but the real threat to the purity of women comes not from words but from intimate sexual contact. Sexual possessiveness is the pulsating heart of honor.*

---

*The core of the honor of an Arab (his *sharaf*), it has been said, "is clearly the protection of one's female relatives."[42]

We may think again of that quintessential expression of the warrior spirit, the *Iliad*. The centrality of sexual possessiveness to the warrior's pride and to the occasion for violence is demonstrated and underscored here. The scene opens on the Trojan War, a conflict provoked by one man's theft of another man's wife. Beautiful Helen, wife of Menelaos of the royal House of Atreus, is stolen by Paris, son of Priam, king of Troy. Because of this fundamental affront to the core value of sexual possession, whole armies clash and, for ten years, blood is shed upon the plains of Troy. The honor of the Achaians cannot acquiesce in the Trojan's violation of the claim of one of their principal kings to his woman. The face that launched a thousand ships was not just Helen's, but also the "face" that Menelaos and his kin would lose, should the Trojans get away with their rape of Helen. At one point, when there is a chance that the Achaians would retreat from Troy to put an end to the war, the goddess Hera comments to Athena that such a retreat would leave Helen for the Trojans "to glory over." This glory of the violators, the counterpart of the shame of the men violated, cannot be countenanced, and so these anti-Trojan goddesses conspire to assure that peace does not break out.

But if the Trojan war sets the stage for the *Iliad*, it is the confrontation between Agamemnon and Achilles that sets the epic's drama in motion. And while that confrontation is over honor and status and power, the medium of its enactment is, again, the woman as a cherished object of possession. "Fair Briseis," Achilles' prize of war, is unjustly taken from him by Agamemnon. This wound is intolerable to the great warrior. And just as the violation of Menelaos' sexual possession drives him and his allies to war and the vengeful shedding of blood, the violation of Achilles' rightful possession of this girl provokes Achilles to withhold himself from the battle, also with the result that much blood is shed, ultimately including that of Achilles' beloved companion, Patroclus. Eventually, Achilles returns to the battle, because his rage against Agamemnon is overshadowed by his desire for revenge upon the slayer of Patroklos, the Trojan Hector. But even then, his return to the fight is preceded by Agamemnon's restoration to him of the fair Briseis, along with an official declaration that he, Agamemnon, has not lain with the girl. The cherished object is returned, intact.

Intact: this is the word (e.g., *intatta* in Italian) to describe a virgin. And of course there is little that more clearly shows how essential sexual possessiveness is to honor societies than the premium they place on the virginity of a man's bride. A bride who is not a virgin is damaged goods, and can be returned to her people with all marriage agreements canceled. She must be all mine! Mine alone! Otherwise, she is without value.

A woman who is shamed brings dishonor upon her menfolk. In this system of emotional meanings, the "shame" of a woman reflects less on her will and character as a *moral agent* than upon her objective properties as an *object*. In some societies where honor is paramount, even a woman who is raped is ruined, and her menfolk are obliged to kill her. This is not punishment of a person for her wrongdoing, but an act of disposal of goods that are irreparably damaged. Like throwing out the shards of some precious porcelain vase that has been shattered.* (Even in our society, sometimes the husband or father of a woman who has been raped turns away from the victim, repelled by the "impurity" she has incurred by being wrongfully touched. In the realm of his own emotional experience, such a man feels himself to be the victim.) Thus did Moses command the Israelites, after their conquest of the Midianites: "Now therefore kill every male among the little ones, and kill every woman that hath known man by lying with him. But all the women children, that have not known a man by lying with him, keep alive for yourselves."[44]

That some *other* man has touched our women is intolerable, the most emotionally charged of injuries. We must protect the purity of our women: the image of the violation of "our" women's purity by "them" has been central to the violence of white men against black men in the honor society of the American South. And wherever we are to be mobilized to fight "them," the image of such violation is conjured up, as for example in the World War I posters of the Hun committing atrocities against women. As the knight rescued damsels in distress from the hands of the evil-doer, the modern soldiers feel themselves to be fighting in defense of their wives and daughters.[45]

This sexual dimension of intergroup conflicts is taken one more crucial step by Franco Fornari: in fighting to defend our country, we are protecting the motherland from invasion.[46] The country, symbolically, is the mother. Again, those who fight are men, and that which is fought over is female. The Russians in World War II, it has been said, had little heart to fight to defend the "Father of all Russians," Stalin; but to resist

---

*Raphael Patai reports: "From the southern end of the Arab world comes the report that during the Mahdist uprising, some Sudanese Arabs 'killed their wives and daughters for fear that they would be attacked by soldiers from the Khalifa's army who were considered as slaves.' "[43]

the penetration of Mother Russia by the Nazis they were fierce indeed. In the imagery of warfare, the invasion of the motherland "is metaphorically described as rape."[47]*

The warrior as defender protects the feminine at the core—the home and the homeland. But the warrior has also the role of violator. The sacred female possessions of the *other* men are objects upon which vengeful passions can be directed. In the *Iliad*, shortly after the anti-Trojan goddesses are alarmed at the prospect of the Trojans glorying over Helen, the Achaians press onward to restore their honor. This restoration requires revenge, which includes returning the insult. "Let no man," exhorts Nester, the wise in council, "be urgent to take the way homeward until after he has lain in bed with the wife of a Trojan to avenge Helen's longing and her lamentations." And of course, however much the threat to white womanhood from the blacks (slaves and then freemen) of the American South was but an anxious fantasy of the southern men of honor, those men frequently violated black women. The mixture of the races owed little to assaults by black men on the purity of white women. The other side of sexual possessiveness as a core value for the warrior to protect, the successful violation of other men's sacred domain of the female, serves as a triumphal proof of manhood.†

There is an expression in our language that says that when a man and a woman have sexual intercourse, the man "possesses" the woman. And we can see that in certain cultures, sexual intimacy is associated with the most fierce feelings of possessiveness. To what extent are such feelings a natural part of a healthy sexual relationship between a man and a woman? While the answer to this intriguing

---

*Fornari's psychoanalytic insights into these meanings give a partial glimpse into why it is so difficult for our nuclear warriors to follow the implications of their new weapons toward the necessary disarmament:

> "Although St. George's sword is now an H sword, the prospect of no longer being able to exhibit our sword-potency to the dragon arouses in us anxieties of impotence. Since no longer to have a weapon (which is unconsciously sensed as a sexual symbol) arouses in us the fantastic fear that our mother-country is at the mercy of anyone, that she may be possessed by anyone, the disarmament fantasy arouses in us the anxiety that we shall cause our mother to become a prostitute and that we ourselves shall be made cuckolds of.[48]"

†*"Que chingon!"* is a phrase quoted in a recent discussion of the Latin culture of contemporary Mexico. "Literally 'What a rapist,' the expression really means 'What a man!' "[49]

question is far from clear, there does seem to be a connection between the high valuation of sexual fidelity (the granting, particularly by the woman, of exclusive sexual possession) and cultural bellicosity. James Prescott, for example, has found that the cultures that value monogamy tend also to "emphasize military glory and [to] worship aggressive gods."[50]

It is clear, at any rate, that for men of honor, for warriors, their possessiveness toward the cherished female (mother-wife-daughter-motherland) is a focus of profound emotional energy. For the men in Arab society, says the Algerian writer Mouloud Feraoun, "their honor was buried in the vagina as if it were a treasure more precious than life."[51] What, we must ask, is the meaning of this proximity of sexual possessiveness to the core dynamics of honor and war?

In part, this insistence on an exclusive sexual domain is an expression of what we have been exploring throughout this chapter: the emotional economy of scarcity. If there is not enough of the world's goodies to go around, then one's core relationships will naturally be jealously guarded. Honor, which we have repeatedly seen to be connected with scarcity, is akin also to jealousy: the Greek word for honor, *philotimia*, also means "jealousy," and the corresponding adjective *philotimos* means "jealous."[52] Whatever you have means less for me. Consequently, if anyone else enjoys the pleasures of intimacy with my cherished female possession, there must necessarily be a corresponding diminution of what is available for me. There is an amusing story by Boccaccio in which an older man brings his younger wife to court for her adulterous relations. She argues that she has never turned her husband down: the supply, she suggests in other terms, exceeds the demand; hence, there being no scarcity, there can be no injury. The court is persuaded by her argument. Part of the humor of the story is that her logic, triumphant in the tale, is utterly foreign to the society of men of honor. Scarcity is an a priori emotional assumption in such a world.

But I think the very irrelevance to a man of honor of the agrument in the Boccaccio story requires us to look further: the idea of emotional scarcity is not sufficient to illuminate the meaning of sexual possessiveness among men inhabiting a violent world. We need to look deeper into what the women mean to the men.

With something so fundamental to life as the relations between the sexes, no single approach can exhaust the dimensions of meaning. Sexual intimacy is the means by which the genetic heritage is passed along, and with this big Darwinian pay-off at stake, sociobiological

explanations of sexual possessiveness are quite plausible.* Sexual possessiveness is not confined to human societies—consider the ferocious
defense of his harem by the elephant seal—for if the male's biological
purpose is to pass along his own genes, nature will likely equip him with
a motivational structure to assure that he does not expend his energy
sustaining the offspring of another.

In many different kinds of human societies, marriage bonds are also
an essential means of regulating relations among kinship groups. Therefore,
biological explanations of the scrupulosity surrounding sexual connec-
tions can easily be supplemented by anthropological explanations involving such purely cultural factors as the need to maintain the harmony
of political networks. But the swirl of violence around sexual possessiveness is not a universal among human societies, so that the problem is
not solved by reference either to Darwinian rewards or to kinship
networks.

It appears that the emotional meaning of the female has a particular
coloration for men when they live in a world beset by strife. The sense
of scarcity, it will be recalled, grows out of injury. And I think the
meaning of sexual possessiveness is most profoundly to be illuminated
when it is seen in the context of a world that subjects its males to the
chronic threat of injury.

The warrior begins, as do all mammals, as a fetus growing within the
body of a female. This is Eden, a place of safety and abundance. When
the baby is born, the mother's role in suckling the infant reinforces the
association of the female with softness and comfort. As the growing
human being must gradually find his way in a world of violence and
conflict, paradise is lost. But the feminine has been established as a safe
harbor.

The socialization of the male growing up in a warrior society accentu-
ates the dichotomy between the male and the female. We saw this in
chapter 1, "Damaged in the Male." The growing male is required to
renounce all weakness and vulnerability. His natural human softness is
denied as he assumes a protective mantle of hard character armor. Harsh
preparation for a harsh world of conflict requires the boys to renounce
the world of comfort, and that usually entails a kind of renunciation of

---

*"[I]nsofar as the main value of a woman from the point of view of the group," writes
Patai of Bedouin society, "is her capacity as potential or actual mother of male group
members, if she commits a transgression which makes her unfit for this supreme task of
womanhood, she seals her own fate: she must die."[53]

the mother.* To establish the male identity, the original identification with the nurturing mother must be denied. Henceforth, a whole category of his being will be renounced by the budding warrior out of fear of being shamed by the fathers for being like a woman, effeminate. ("Sure, Andrew, why don't you wear lace gloves.") A "mama's boy" is one who has failed to make the transition to manhood, failed to make the demanded break with the soft world of the mother. Earlier it was said that boys are taught to "relinquish their suffering to the female," but it is not suffering alone that, in warrior societies, is so assigned in the exaggerated division of human labor between the sexes. Taking up his armor requires the male to leave behind much of his humanity: "hardened for his future life."

The female thus represents not only the paradise that has been lost, but also a part of the warrior that has been lost in the creation of armored strength. But, of course, although renounced it is still there: the warrior is still a human being with a soft core of flesh and blood. The pain of injury in harsh socialization has compelled the male to deny some of the most human, and thus also the most cherished and sacred, parts of his being. But since the female embodies these parts, it is through her that he retains access to them.

The woman embodies, for the warrior, the core of life. The warrior lives on the outside, where the fighting takes place. (Like the Trojan warriors, who make war on the plains beyond the city walls, while their women and children remain protected within the fortress.) The warrior's domain is the hard exterior, the case of armor, the erected fortifications, surrounding the domain of flesh-and-blood living that has been assigned to the female. She is the part of the world that is being fought for: she is the interior, the living energies that the lifeless armor protects,† the place of comfort where no armor is needed.‡ It is with

---

*In the socialization of the Arab boy, the change from the world of the women to the men's world is especially harsh. The main task of the woman who takes care of the boy was "to make him happy, to give him what he wanted, to care for him, to fulfill his whims and wishes." In the men's world, his "wishes are disregarded more often than not." Maturing into a new status, the boy must learn "the bitter taste of the father's heavy hand, the rod, the strap, and, at least among the most tradition-bound Bedouin tribes, the saber and the dagger," which, as was said earlier, are used to harden him for his future life.[54]

†For more on the imagery of the form of fear, see pp. 3–4 in the prologue.

‡"No wonder that in the early period of the Arab boy's transition into the men's world, and until such time as he learns that it is shameful to do so, the boy runs back from the father's discipline to the mother's arms, in which he finds comfort, love, indulgence, reassurance."[55]

her that the warrior has a chance to embrace the life that grim necessity in a hostile world has forced him to deny within himself.

It becomes clearer why the warrior would be willing to fight to protect a female pregnant with so much meaning. And perhaps we get a glimpse too into why the intrusion of any other male into his female domain is so intolerable. It is the hostility rampant in the interactions of bellicose male forces—it is, in other words, the problem of war and the struggle for power—that has compelled the male to erect this structure of male armor and female life. The female within the fortifications is an externalized representation of the parts of himself that the warrior must at all costs not expose to other men. There are parts of himself that the warrior wants to prevent other men from *seeing*, just as in the warrior societies of the Arabs, the female must wear a *chaddor*, a veil, to prevent her being seen by men outside the intimate family. Likewise, it is essential that she not be *touched*, for she embodies what lies vulnerable within the armor, the palpitating soft flesh, protected from the swords of other men.

Again, therefore, at the core of the matter we find the experience of the world as a hostile place. Just as the need to *control* everything reflects a dread that any other locus of will will seek to encompass one's destruction, so also with sexual possessiveness: the man's insistence on exclusive ownership of the female reflects the intense fear that the male energy of the "other" will wreak havoc in one's interior life if it is allowed into the core. The fragile construct of the defense of one's most vital being will collapse if penetrated; the defenses must at the core level of intimate contact remain intact. One's sacred female inner sanctum must remain one's own inviolate preserve. That place to which all vulnerability has been consigned must be entirely one's own, possessed beyond the possibility of trespass.

Possessiveness versus Life

Sexual possessiveness is but the prototype of the warrior's characteristic way of dealing with the world. The warrior's relationship with the female, his most prized possession, epitomizes his "object relationships." Earlier we encountered the idea that the way a person regards the world as a whole tends to be a projection of his relationship with that primal object, his mother. From the core experience out to the periphery. To the infant, the mother *is* the world. To the warrior, the land he protects is the mother-land. To the man of honor, the female is the core possession which he alone can own. So also with the others of this world's goods.

The warrior, thus, acts as the protector of dominion. He is the drawer of boundaries: this within the boundary is ours. With the progress of civilization, the notion that we human beings belonged to the earth has been replaced by the notion that the land and all the creatures upon it are under the dominion of a sovereign human power. Each of our warrior nations is possessive about its domain, and cannot rest as long as some other power holds even one inch of its "sacred soil." Border disputes can rankle indefinitely. Our proper domain must remain intact, our control must be complete. The Falklands must remain British; a non-Islamic enclave in Palestine cannot be tolerated; Taiwan must be acknowledged an integral part of the Chinese empire. Boccaccian logic notwithstanding, unfettered Arab access to holy Jerusalem is not enough: it must be under Arab sovereignty. It is *ours*.

Again, the role of protector is one side of the warrior's coin; the other is the violator. Protector within his boundaries, violator outside. Just as the "man" is a *chingon*, a rapist, so is he a plunderer. The bloody chronicles of the ancient world show the warrior lusting after the spoils of war, the treasure that can be seized. In the *Iliad*, the victory in hand-to-hand combat has two stages: killing the opponent, then stripping his armor for one's own display and enrichment. In much of warfare, the taking of the valued property of the opponent has included taking his head (or cutting away the most physical emblem of manhood) as a prize. The headhunter, says Eli Sagan, by preserving a permanent trophy of his opponent's power, can build a "capital stock" of that power.[56] The warrior seizes for his own possession the sacred goods of other men: his women, his treasure, and, in imperialistic warfare, his lands and liberty. You are now possessed by me, and what was yours now swells the domain under my control.

All the factors considered in this chapter combine to make possession—ownership and control—the way the man of war relates to the goods of this world. In a world ruled by scarcity, each power asserts its exclusive claim upon everything its power enables it to possess. This is the spirit that characterizes much of the interaction among our warrior nations—one of possessiveness rather than sharing, of exclusivity rather than mutuality. In an anarchic world, an orientation toward dominion is, to a degree, a requirement for survival. Such inescapable realities combine with the pathological excesses of our injured psyches to infuse such a spirit within us.

Whatever the reasons, we are by possessiveness possessed. And whatever the cause, the effect is an impoverishment of the human condition. An old folktale related by Lewis Hyde conveys the costs of our possessive spirit:

Once a man and his wife were sitting outside the front door with a roast chicken before them which they were going to eat between them. Then the man saw his old father coming along and quickly took the chicken and hid it, for he begrudged him any of it. The old man came, had a drink, and went away. Now the son was about to put the roast chicken back on the table, but when he reached for it, it had turned into a big toad that jumped in his face and stayed there and didn't go away again. And if anybody tried to take it away, it would give them a poisonous look, as if about to jump in their faces, so that no one dared to touch it. And the ungrateful son had to feed the toad every day, otherwise it would eat part of his face. And thus he went ceaselessly hither and yon about the world.[57]

For us, the ungrateful sons of the earth, the toads on our faces are the military establishments of modern civilized societies. These apparatuses represent our collective attitude toward one another, of protecting our possessions from one another. And as the spirit that gives rise to our militarism disfigures the face of our humanity, so also do these enormous systems of destructive power eat away at the flesh of our societies.

It has long been among the spiritual insights of mankind that there are ways of holding onto the goods of this world that takes the goodness out of them. Possessiveness is a misguided approach to relationship because it comes from a spiritual condition antagonistic to true fulfillment. It is not because possessiveness is not "nice," but because it reflects a fundamental misapprehension of *the way life is*. As with our earlier discussion of scarcity and Spinoza's remarks about true blessedness, the fundamental issue is less moral evil than spiritual ignorance.

Our cultural heritage provides many images to illustrate the fundamental ignorance that imbues the spirit of possessiveness.

The myth of Midas, for example, shows that his understanding of wealth is desperately impoverished. Granted one wish, he asks that everything he touches would turn to gold. His ignorance of the true nature of life is mortally dangerous: food he brings to his mouth turns to metal before he can eat it; his beloved daughter is transformed into a golden statue at his touch. Life is a flow. The food passes in and out, leaving only the continuation of life's processes as its legacy—and even this can no more be possessed than can the flow of time. Relationship fulfills through the continuous exchange of love, not through the transformation of the other into a cherished *object*.

The mythical figure of Midas was not particularly warlike, but his tale helps illuminate the spiritual ignorance of the warrior whose possessiveness we have described. The man of honor's possession of his cherished female reveals a kind of Midas touch: the possibilities of genuine relationship are forfeited, killed by the transmutation of a living human being into a mere object. An image of this is found in the grotesque chastity belts employed by the medieval man of war to safeguard his treasure of flesh and blood during his absence. The flesh-and-blood channel of life's expression is turned into a mere thing, like so much lifeless gold, to be locked away. This way of clinging to the world's goods reflects an anxiety, a constriction of the spirit, that kills love and the rest of life's flows.

The desperation to have, to hold, to build a permanent empire is an effort to deny what we are: mortal creatures through whom life courses but for a while. We are the channels of life's sacred empire, but unable to accept our place in the flow we would become instead the emperors. Tolstoy's story "How Much Land Does a Man Need" shows the deadly results of a man's misguided use of a boon. Again, a blessing is turned into a curse. In the story, a man is told that he can possess all the land he can mark off on foot in a single day. Possessed by greed, the man runs feverishly for the entire day; to lay claim to as much of the earth as he possibly can. He so overextends himself that at the end he collapses and dies of exhaustion. His portion of the earth: the six feet under which his dead body is buried.

That wishes and boons so often prove dangerous in stories is an expression of the insight that our will, if it is directed by spiritual ignorance, is our own greatest enemy. Be careful what you wish for—a warning sounded by many fairy tales, and underscored as well by the destructiveness that has accompanied the growth of human powers. Tolstoy's landgrabber finds not empire but death. In his misguided effort to possess the earth he loses the greatest gift, life, and thus hastens the ultimate destiny of all creatures—the earth's repossession of his mortal body.

Possessiveness, based on misunderstanding of the nature of life, acts as an agent of death. Erich Fromm's necrophilious person "can relate to an object—a flower or a person—only if he possesses it." Possession is a function of the love of control, but "in the fact of controlling [the necrophile] kills life."[58] John Fowles's The Collector comes to mind, a tale in which a man who is a butterfly collector reaches out to a woman with his own way of loving: he kidnaps her and tries to build a relationship with her based on his possession of her. In the end, however, her spirit cannot survive such imprisonment, and like the butterflies she becomes but one more dead object. As an image of the deadly implications of possessiveness, Fromm uses the story of Solomon's judgment in the case of the disputed baby.* The woman whose claim is wrongful "would rather have a properly divided child than lose a living one."[59] (Here, of course, possessiveness works together with its sister, spite: what I cannot possess, I can at least deny to you.)

In the absence of a wise Solomon reigning above them, the nations of the earth are hard-pressed to escape that spiritual trap of possessiveness. After all, in the absence of Solomon's final intervention, the Solomonian choice that arose out of the struggle for the child—yield the baby or have it torn in half—would have resulted in the true mother's giving the baby over to the false and necrophilious one. And indeed, the parable of the tribes says that in the course of social evolution this is what has occurred: in the ongoing struggle over the lands of the earth, it has been those possessed by the spirit of possessiveness—the greedy, the empire-builders, the worshipers of power—who have prevailed. Those whose hearts are most attuned to the true nature of life, like the true mother in Solomon's tale, simply do not have the heart to do what the achievement of dominion demands. Under these tragic yet unavoidable circumstances, it seems that the best we can hope for is that some who of necessity employ the spirit of possessiveness in their arsenals do so with restraint and with regret.

Yet certainly, as the age-old struggle for power has reached the point where two powers with the capacity to destroy the earth confront each other, we must hope for more than that. For we could now indeed enact that first Solomonian judgment with no trick in it to make possible the second, wise one: we could indeed tear the baby in half, with no power above us to declare the combatants unfit to care for life's cherished gift and to hand it over to the care of another.

What we must hope for is that we as a species will place as ruler over us a truer understanding of our place in the scheme of life. *Life is a gift.* It is something we get for nothing. And it is a gift in yet another way. In his wise book *The Gift*, Lewis Hyde has studied the image of the gift as used in the world's folktales. In the stories, Hyde finds, "the person

---

*Two women have newborn babies. In the night, one infant dies, and its mother steals the other's living baby. The two women bring to Solomon their quarrel over whose baby it is. To render judgment, Solomon gives first a judgment by which he shall learn the truth: the baby, he decrees, will be cut in half, with each woman getting half. One woman, the true mother, chooses to surrender the baby to the other rather than let this judgment be carried out. From this willingness, Solomon knows who the true mother is, and awards the baby—whole—to her.

who tries to hold onto a gift usually dies."[60] The passing along of the blessing is essential to the preservation of its blessed quality. "The gift must always move."[61] As with material objects, so also with the gift of life. In many tribes around the world, networks of gift exchange are an important medium for maintaining the social body, like the circulation of blood; and in them, too, Hyde finds, the gift must always move. Life itself is also a flow. It resides with us awhile, and then it moves along. As the saying goes, you can't take it with you.

Oh, but we try! Much of civilization stands as a monument of those misguided efforts: the pyramids on which were expended the lives of countless slaves, that the man of power might travel to the next world in the fashion to which he had been all too accustomed; the empires by which the wielder of the sword would make the systems of life subservient to his will; the systems of corporate power that amass wealth far beyond the rational needs of their owners, who possess still but one mouth to feed, one body to clothe. Unable to accept what we are—channels for the gift of life to flow through—we attempt to transform into permanent coagulation the stuff of life that can exist only in process.

The gift must always move, and he who clings to it possessively brings death upon himself.

Beyond Possessiveness

The spiritual importance of relinquishing possession is an ancient insight. The monastic life embodies the belief that the path to God is best traversed unencumbered by possessions. "Sell what thou hast and give to the poor if thou wouldst follow me." The monks in the desert, reducing life to its essentials, seek the way of harmony. It is not without significance that the foremost man of peace in our times, Gandhi, practiced such material simplicity.

As with material possession, so with sexual. In part, the celibacy of Christian (and some other) monks is evidence of a failure of their spiritual path to achieve peace with the body, an inability to incorporate the whole human being within the compass of spiritual harmony. But in part also the practice of celibacy expresses the spiritual understanding that it is important to learn not to hold on. The spiritually enlightened person relinquishes possessiveness of all kinds. Where the warrior builds a personal empire of material and familial property, the monk eschews both.

The example of the monk helps signal the spiritual necessity of overcoming possessiveness, but there are limits to the usefulness of the monk's solution to the problem. The monk escapes from the problem of possessiveness by renouncing the relationships in which he might be possessive. The problem, however, resides not in the *objects* of possession, but in the *spirit* of possessiveness with which one clings to the objects. The renunciation of connection with the world is one way to avoid the pathologies of our way of connecting, but it is an extreme solution. It is perhaps a still greater challenge, and a higher level of spiritual achievement, to find a way to remain in full relationship with the world without infusing that relationship with the spirit of possessiveness. Instead of letting go of the world, let go of the part of oneself that needs to incorporate the world into an empire of the self.

The problems of our world are not going to be solved by our abandonment of the world. The way of the monk, it seems to me, emerges as a reaction against the tendency of the man of war, and as the one is extreme in one way, the other goes to the opposite extreme. The monk rejects this world, which is corrupted by the warrior's spirit, saying that our true life is in another realm altogether. But I believe that it is to this world we are born, and in relation to this world that our true fulfillment and true calling are to be found. The warrior is insufficiently cognizant of the problem: What does it profit a man if he gains the world but loses his soul? But the monk does not meet the challenge: how does it profit the world if men, to keep pure their souls, abandon the world to the ravages of wolves? A spiritual leader tells us to render unto Caesar what is Caesar's, and to render unto God what is God's. But the problem is, when Caesar stakes out his claim he seizes part of the realm of God.

There are important reasons, therefore, why we must find a way to stay engaged with the world that is the arena of the warrior, but to be able to bring to it the monk's capacity to let go of the impulse to build empire.

Not insignificantly, what little I know of such a way of being grew out of my one experience of war.

This war was a private war, in which no blood flowed. But it was war nonetheless, and painful. I found myself the recipient of continuous abuse, the object of another person's ongoing irrational rage. It was for me as traumatic an experience as I have had. As traumas do, it injured me. But as traumas also sometimes do, it broke open my structures sufficiently to allow a liberating new way of being to emerge.

As the world sows in us, so does the world reap from us. In this private war that was waged on me, I had plenty of experience of how this works: as I received poisonous treatment, I felt poisoned, and my impulse was to project it back out into the world in retaliation. But out of my pain I also found at times a way of letting go of the poison, of ceasing to be a channel of the bitterness. In the midst of my state of siege, I found a territory of greater freedom than I had ever known.

As I oscillated between the two states, I gained some sense of what opened the doors to this freedom. It included a letting go of a sense of my life as an empire, a structure I built to assure the meeting of my needs. Wherever I was attached to this empire, I felt vulnerable to attack and enraged by threat. But when I could let go, and let my sense of self fall back upon some irreducible core that simply *is*, simply flows, I felt beyond threat. It is not, for me, an easy spiritual condition to maintain. But its possibility taught me a good deal.

In this state, I could still act as a protector as I needed to, but I *knew peace even in the midst of war*. And the poisonous passions of war that flowed into me neither remained within nor were projected back into the world.

This experience reminds me of something I came across in a book of Zen thoughts, and gives me some fuller understanding of it:

> A monk asked Lung-ya, "What did old masters attain when they entered the ultimate stage?" "They were like burglars sneaking into a vacant house," came the reply.
>
> To which the commentary is given by Nyogen: "This monk probably thought masters have something others do not have, whereas they have nothing others have."[62]

What characterizes the enlightened is not what they have gained but what they have relinquished.

9

THE SEARCH FOR
A WORLD
BEYOND SCARCITY

The Losing Battle of Winning

I n most conventional views of morality, the wrong path is simply the forbidden way. If it were not against the rules, it would be positively attractive, strewn as it is with forbidden fruit. One even gets the impression that its very desirability is what makes it wrong. And succumbing to temptation is the essence of wrongdoing.

There is, however, another strain of thinking about the right and wrong path for human beings to take. Here, what is wrong is wrong because it does not get one where one really wants to go. At each fork in the road, the wrong way is the one that does not lead toward one's true goal. The Platonic notion that evil is a branch of ignorance is an example of this view of morality. The essense of wrongdoing is a misapprehension of the way reality is laid out.

This latter view, I believe, contains the more fundamental wisdom. At the heart of it is the spiritual insight that the human task is to understand the cosmic order of which we are part, and to align ourselves with it. Taoism expresses this idea, as do other mystical traditions. True strength comes from such alignment, and true progress toward one's goals is possible only when one travels with the current. One's own good is in harmony with the good of the surrounding order. Conversely, what the evildoer does is wrong because it is contrary to the way things go. But not just wrong in some moral sense; wrong also because it is futile. He who fights the current will be washed up. The gravity of his error is that he makes the search for his fulfillment an uphill fight.

So it is with the striving for winning that we have explored here in its several dimensions. One can, it is true, condemn the winners for the injuries they cause others in the pursuit of their own gratification. But the more fundamental insight is the recognition that "winning" is a losing battle.

Consider the struggle for *narcissistic* gratification. The goal of the narcissist is, in one sense, a fundamental part of the human task: to bring the self into connection with positive value. However, because of the injuries he has suffered in his connection to the world around him, the narcissist adopts an uphill path toward that fundamental goal. The narcissistic goods he seeks to preserve are always "highly vulnerable and fragile and open to attack," writes W. W. Meissner.[1] And Gregory Rochlin says of the narcissistic image, "It seems to have a fundamental instability. Time and circumstances are its adversaries."[2] Narcissism, he says, "has no allies. It has only enemies."

These are the signs of a path running against the order of things. Progress along it is difficult to maintain. The natural flow runs against it. The narcissist's way of seeking to connect with goodness not only sets him against other people in a struggle for the ostensibly scarce supply of value. His battle is also *self*-defeating. He adopts as his goal a kind of isolation of the self that precludes his reaching his true goal. In this, he makes the spiritual error of fighting against his true place as a part of a greater order.

What man really wants, writes Ken Wilbur, in a passage that seems to illuminate the losing battle of narcissism, is "real transcendance," but he seeks it in ways that prevent his attaining it. "He substitutes his ego for Atman [the great order of the whole]."

> Then, instead of finding timeless wholeness, he merely substitutes the wish to live forever; instead of being one with the cosmos, he substitutes the desire to possess the cosmos; instead of being one with God, he tries himself to play God.[3]

Part of this playing God is the effort to dominate the world by the imposition of one's own, almighty *will*. As with the pursuit of narcissism, so with the fixation on domination: the effort to run the show is also self-defeating. Like the narcissist, he who seeks to impose his tyrannical will also has lost sight of his place in the order of things. The tyrant

forgets that others are human beings like himself, with the same fundamental needs. Granting only to himself such basic needs as the need for
autonomy and respect, in his spiritual ignorance the tyrant makes war
upon the order of things. Such a war can only be a losing battle.

The tyrant might also be seen as seeking a fundamental human value:
assent from others on an arrangement that safeguards what he values.
To gain that assent, however, he knows only how to employ threat and
force. In the way he seeks to gain his ends, the tyrant, like the narcissist,
manifests the scars of his own traumatic learning: pain and fear have
taught that power, not mutality, is the essence of relationship. The way
of injury only perpetuates itself, for the coercive methods of the tyrant
can only work partially while at the same time *creating* the very resistance the tyrant fears.

Consider this story, concerning approaches to child rearing, told by
Rudolf Dreikurs:

> Five-year-old Jimmy was driving Mother crazy. She said so to
> him and to others in front of him. Mother fought with him about
> one thing or another all the time. Jimmy simply would not mind,
> no matter what. And when Mother resorted to spanking, it only
> helped for a short moment, if at all. Today, for instance, Jimmy is
> not regular with his bowel movements, and Mother had been trying
> to train him for years. This morning she sent him to the bathroom
> after breakfast, but he came back and said that he couldn't go now.
> She let him go out to play and went on with her work. About
> noon, while putting some clothes away in the closet, she noticed a
> fecal odor. She investigated and found that Jimmy had had his stool
> in his Daddy's hat! She raced out, found him, brought him in,
> confronted him with the hat, and whipped him hard. He wet his
> pants immediately, but she figured that was because of the whip-
> ping. However, Jimmy wet his pants the rest of the day, and wet
> his bed that night.

About this Dreikurs says: "Mother has been concerned about Jimmy's
bowel movements from the time he was an infant. She indicates, 'You
will move your bowels when I say so.' Jimmy's action says, 'I will have
my own movements where and when I please.' "[4] An excessive need to
impose one's will needlessly engenders a battle of wills.

The belief that matters can be settled only by threat or by force
means that there can be no settlement at all. At the core of the futility
of the coercive approach is a failure to acknowledge the reality of the
other and the real needs of the other. To the paranoid, as Meissner said,
"The independence of the other is extremely threatening."[5] There is

always the temptation to deny, as well as to attempt to destroy, what is seen as threatening. Thus, in the paranoid realm of international relations, there is an excessive belief in the efficacy of coercion. Like Jimmy's mother, nations resort again and again to coercion to "teach them a lesson." And, like Jimmy's mother, nations seem again and again to be surprised at the recalcitrance of those they are trying to teach.

The coercive approach seems entirely rational: show them that the cost of not acting as we would like is too high, and they will get in line. To some extent it works, of course, but there are limits to its rationality that derive from blind spots in its understanding of the "reasons" for human action. Franco Fornari describes the American approach to Vietnam in the 1960s in such terms: "a practice of dissuasion of the aggressors through successive, aggressive/punitive interventions which increase in violence until the aggressors no longer find it 'convenient' to attack and, consequently, desist from further aggression."[6] This approach, he says, "would be valid only if applied to a dispute between two individuals or two groups whose actions would be governed only by concrete utility." What is ignored in the ostensibly rational calculus of such utility is how coercion dramatically changes its object's sense of what is at stake. Suddenly, in addition to whatever else was involved, the highly charged issues of autonomy and self-respect are added: will I allow the hostile power of another to control me, will I bow down before his will?* The threat can backfire: instead of deterring, it can provoke.

The paranoid insistence upon control creates the very hostility and rebellion it fears. The Vietnamese did not back down in response to the application of Secretary of Defense McNamara's doctrine; nor did they learn the lesson the Chinese went in to teach them in 1979. Similarly with the cycle of pedagogic retaliations in the Middle East, and the now-escalating cycle of repression and terror in South Africa: each side draws the opposite lesson from the one its adversary is trying to teach. Each side uses force to impress upon the other that it is a force that must be reckoned with, but its adversary instead concludes that the dastardly

---

*John C. Calhoun articulated the warrior's contempt for such a rational calculus of utility, to the neglect of the warrior's sense of honor, when he responded in 1811 to economic, cost-benefit arguments against fighting the British: "Sir, I enter here my solemn protest against this low and 'calculating avarice' entering this hall of legislation . . . [Peace with submission is] only fit for shops and countinghouses. . . . [The nation] is never safe but under the shield of honor."[7]

attacks prove their perpetrator too irredeemably evil to deal with. Each side intends its threat to bend the will of the other toward its own will, but its adversary responds by stiffening its resolve not to yield. After the misjudgment of the other's "reasons" leads to irrational policies, the misinterpretation of the other's "surprising" unyieldingness serves to reaffirm those ineffective policies: the other's recalcitrance confirms that he is so unreasonable and beyond the pale of humane interactions that the only language he could possibly understand is force.

Thus, the failure to acknowledge the humanity of one's adversary tends to be out of the reach of correction, but only to perpetuate itself and the consequent cycle of violence.

This is not to say that coercion is always ineffective. The fear of injury often does inhibit people. But especially in the interactions of people for whom autonomy is of the utmost importance—which tends especially to characterize the actors in the paranoia-inducing realm where sovereign entities interact—it can very easily backfire.

One of the interesting questions raised by this pattern of futile coercion is why is it that each *expects* the other to respond to threat in the opposite manner from the way he himself responds? When the United States perceived itself to be at a disadvantage to the Soviets in strategic weapons in the early 1980s, some American hawks were adamant that we should not negotiate arms agreements from a position of weakness. Their solution, however, was to gain a degree of superiority that would "force the Soviets" to the bargaining table. In other words, they expected the circumstance that would keep *us away from the table* to compel *them* to negotiate. Again and again, the same people who are most determined not to be intimidated by threats are the ones who believe most fervently in the efficacy of threats to intimidate others.

This contradiction is a matter to be explored further in part 3, "Boundaries." For now, suffice it to say that it is another manifestation of the inability of people who are scarred in relationships to recognize that others are people like themselves. Those for whom the triumph of their will is of paramount importance have difficulty acknowledging the need of others to have some autonomy and will of their own.

Another question raised by the blindness that seems to underlie much of the use of coercion in the world is this: if what is ostensibly intended to inhibit often serves instead to provoke, what does that say about the balancing act we call nuclear deterrence?

The futility of the pursuit of narcissistic gains, and of the pursuit of a world that bows to one's unchallenged will, are both elements of the world of scarcity, the world of "winning." In these approaches, one can win only if others can be made to lose. In our culture these days, however, there is a growing current of ideology that challenges this approach to the world.

Some of this current is expressed in popular culture. Just as "I'm okay, you're okay" expressed an alternative to the "I'm okay, you're not okay" approach of narcissism, now there is widespread talk of replacing the "win-lose" approach of the warrior. Lee Iacocca, a new hero of the American success ethic, appears in the mass media[8] saying that in his experience the only deals that really have worked are where the other guy has felt that he won too. And there is a proliferation of books on negotiation and mediation that points to the possibilities of achieving mutually satisfactory resolutions of problems that might previously have been perceived as zero-sum conflicts. As articulated in popular culture, these ideas can suffer from oversimplification, reflecting in part a desire to wish away the genuinely problematic aspects of conflicting interests. There is nonetheless a very serious and promising impetus from these cultural currents.

One very intriguing and intellectually clear exploration of the possibilities of transcending the losing battle of winning is Robert Axelrod's *The Evolution of Cooperation*. This book attempts to elucidate the circumstances in which patterns of cooperation can arise despite the existence of potentially divisive competing interests and the absence of an overarching Hobbesean ruler to hold the competitors in check.

Axelrod's study derives from a contest that was conducted to see who could formulate the most successful policy for playing a version of the Prisoner's Dilemma. This is a situation where if both cooperate, both will win, and if both act noncooperatively both will lose. But the biggest gain and the biggest loss occur when one player does not make the cooperative move while the other does. Using a computer to run the tournament, Axelrod had each policy that entered the contest play a series against every other policy to see which would end up with the largest net winnings.

To make a long story short, the striking finding was that it was a nice guy that finished first. "Niceness," in Axelrod's lexicon, means that the player is never the first to "defect," i.e., to make the uncooperative move. The winning entry was not so nice that he invariably cooperated: on the contrary, he reliably retaliated when the other player defected. But he was forgiving, and would return to cooperation as soon as the other did. The winner was named: TIT FOR TAT.

Some of my early exposure to Axelrod's work was from people who have seized hold of it to support their wish to believe that competitiveness and conflict are inevitably losing strategies. From these presentations, it seemed to me that Axelrod's findings might challenge the thrust of the parable of the tribes. According to that theory, nice guys get finished first: the struggle for power in social evolution has often favored the aggressive and the ruthless, who could eliminate their weaker or more pacific neighbors. Social evolution, says the parable of the tribes, has *selected for the ways of power*. But a close look at Axelrod's articulation of his findings disclosed that there was no contradiction. Axelrod clearly understood that the success of cooperation and the consequent *selection for cooperative policies depended on how the game was structured.*

For "niceness" to pay off, the players must have a future together. The shorter the time frame of their interaction, the more the immediate payoffs of the "win-lose" of a successful defection will outweigh the long-term mutual benefits of joint cooperation. An example shows clearly the difference in the two kinds of games, the one-shot versus the ongoing.

As an illustration of the real-world operation of the principles uncovered by his computer tournament, Axelrod adduces the example of trench warfare in World War I. Because the war was mired in stalemate, the same groups of enemy soldiers often faced each other across a no-man's land for extended periods of time. Being enemies at war, these soldiers seemed to have an ample incentive to snipe at one another from their trenches. The problem with that is that the other side could also pick off those men on one's own side who raised their heads. The protracted nature of their interactions, therefore, made manifest the common interest of both groups of soldiers to refrain from killing each other. As Axelrod demonstrates, not only was this common interest visible to the men but, without explicit agreement, the two sides worked out ways of colluding to spare each other. Communicating with each other through episodes of killing and retaliation and of firing deliberately over each other's heads, the two sides arrived at various charades of appearing to fight to please their commanders while actually sparing each other. Only the determined efforts of the commanding officers to make such collusion impossible upset the impromptu cooperation that had evolved between the armies.

But not all "games" are structured that way. In this example of protracted trench warfare, as in the Prisoner's Dilemma as designed by Axelrod, the worst possible outcome of each play is nonlethal damage. A sniper may kill an enemy soldier, but the units of interaction here are the *groups* of soldiers as a whole, which can survive the death of particular individuals. A contrasting example is the one-on-one gunfight à la the Western movie. Here, if one cooperates (does not draw) while the other defects (draws and fires), the cooperator has played his last game and the street belongs to the defector.

The parable of the tribes calls attention to some crucial ways in which the game of intersocietal relations has been like the shoot-out in the old Western in which losing in the short run means being excluded from the long run. When a defeated society can be annihilated (e.g., Carthage by Rome, the aborigines in Australia by the European colonists) or subjugated (the various groups absorbed by the Chinese empire of two and three thousand years ago, the various non-Russian nationalities now absorbed into the Soviet empire, and the Indian tribes of North America), defeat can be more or less final, and the immediate rewards of not being "nice" can remain undiminished by eventual retaliation. The ability to eliminate other players from long-term play makes niceness less advantageous and ruthlessness less costly. The evolution of civilization, therefore, has not yet emulated Axelrod's tournament.

Of course, not all interactions in the intersocietal system are conclusive duels to the death, and therefore a degree of "niceness" has also been selected for in the actors, moderating their ruthlessness. Major nation-states may have to deal with one another over prolonged periods involving many plays, and therefore in their dealings with one another they learn the value of being nice. This is reflected in the manners of diplomacy and in the willingness of nations to honor treaty commitments. The increasing interdependence of the world, meaning as it does that nations must deal with one another with increasing frequency about more and more issues that do not get resolved by shoot-outs, may be increasing the value of niceness in the intersocietal system.

It is the advent of nuclear weapons, however, that most dramatically changes the game in the intersocietal system. Nuclear war between the superpowers most emphatically is not like the game that Axelrod's computer simulated, for a major defection (an all-out first strike, for example) would cost its victim all its chips, not just a small portion. Fortunately, this situation contains the equivalent of protracted play to make niceness the best policy. Deterrence theory says that niceness is rewarded as long as it is clear that the side that is struck first will still have the capacity to give a massive TIT in retaliation for the other's TAT. That theory has therefore focused on the survivability of the retaliatory capacity. As long as that capacity is secure, a not-nice interaction pattern does not have to be long-lasting to be mutually catastrophic. To the extent that even the user of nuclear weapons is punished directly by the destruction of the global environment, the value of niceness is reinforced. Between the capacity of even a destroyed adversary to inflict devastating retaliation, and the possibility that even one's own weapons will undermine one's environment, nuclear weapons turn the win-lose outcome to which warriors could previously aspire into a lose-lose result. So let's be nice.

As the movie *War Games* articulated it recently for the popular culture, where nuclear war between the superpowers is concerned the only way to win is not to play.

Axelrod's simulation does not, and does not pretend to, answer the question about the value of the win-lose approach for *all* potentially competitive situations. But, I would argue, the situation to which it does apply—the long-term interaction with mutual ability to hurt or to help—is not just a peripheral case. *It describes the essence of evolving living systems.* Humankind may, in the short run, develop different kinds of games with different kinds of payoffs: the parable of the tribes describes one such game. But the evolution of the biosphere suggests that if our species is going to make it into the long run, we will have to restructure our games. Those that provide immediate gains on a win-lose basis will have to be discarded in favor of, or transformed into, those that foster the long-term win-win benefits of mutual cooperation.

That winning is a losing battle is something the Social Darwinists did not grasp, but it does not contradict the parable of the tribes. The imperialists who saw their predations as emulations of the way of nature misconstrued the way of nature and were blind to the bitter harvest their descendants would reap from what they sowed. The parable of the tribes shares with Social Darwinism the view that the struggle for power has shaped civilization, but does not share Social Darwinism's sanguine view about the viability of the survivors of that bloody process. Its analysis culminates in the notion of "the death of the unnatural," the idea that the winners in this scarcity-oriented competitive process contain the seeds of their own destruction.

After ten thousand years of escalating struggle driving our social evolution, we have reached the point where either we end the struggle or it will end us. The win-lose interactions among societies must be transformed.

So also the way our species interacts with the natural order must change. Our present approach is characterized by take without give, by exploitative use premised on scarcity rather than on the synergistic cooperation that produces abundance. About the dangers of our current pattern of interaction with nature, Gregory Bateson said that *no creature can win against its environment for long.* Similarly, when Axelrod extended his computer-simulated interaction across hundreds of generations of play, the lesson emerged that "not being nice looked promising at first, but in the long run it can destroy the very environment it needs for its own success."[9]

In the science of ecology it is said that if a parasite kills its host, you know that the relationship is of recent origin. Over a long period of time, a virus had evolved a benign relationship with the oriental chestnut tree. When that virus came to the New World, however, aboard transplanted oriental chestnut trees, it virtually wiped out the American chestnut of the North American forests. For the virus to have a niche on this continent, its relationship with the trees here would have to be different from that. In Axelrod's contest, a program named HARRINGTON, which was not nice, had immediate success. But:

> By the two hundredth generation or so, things began to take a noticeable turn. Less successful programs were becoming extinct, which means that there were fewer and fewer prey for HARRINGTON to exploit. Soon HARRINGTON could not keep up with the successful nice rules, and by the one thousandth generation, HARRINGTON was as extinct as the exploitable rules on which it preyed.[10]

Not understanding his place in the order of things—i.e., not understanding the mutuality and interdependence characteristic of living systems—HARRINGTON pursues a win-lose policy and becomes himself a loser.

Strategies based on scarcity are strategies only for short-term survival. We have seen throughout part 2 that the sense of scarcity not only reflects conditions of scarcity but also creates them. Thus HARRINGTON, seeking to win at the expense of others, eliminates those others and eats itself out of house and home. In the long-term evolution of a system, the HARRINGTON'S either change or disappear.

Thus in the living systems that evolved over four billion years, and out of which civilization emerged, what we find are patterns of synergistic interaction that produce abundance. Even struggles like that of the trees evolving in adaptation to a virus are parts of larger patterns of interaction that create the abundance that allows all the parts of the system to survive perpetually. When the wolf kills the lamb, far from injuring lambkind he contributes to the pattern of survival of the prey species even while keeping himself alive. Without predation, the sheep will overgraze the land, the soil will be eroded, and the basis for the perpetuation of the sheep will be undermined.

All the goods of life cycle endlessly like the gift that must move: nothing is lost. The excrement of one is the food of another; matter and energy recycle endlessly. Just as the premise of scarcity is the way of death, *the way of sustainable life is intertwined with abundance.*

Out of the long-term evolution of Axelrod's system emerges triumphant the nice player, TIT FOR TAT. But what kind of "winning" does TIT FOR TAT's triumph represent? "On average, [TIT FOR TAT] did better than any other rule with the other strategies in the tournament. Yet TIT FOR TAT never once scored better in a game than the other player! In fact, it can't!"[11] (It can't, because its policy prevents it from ever exploiting the other player more than the other has exploited it, and that is the only way one player can outscore its immediate playmate.) Even as TIT FOR TAT fattens itself, it feeds its fellow players. While HARRINGTON eats itself out of house and home and into oblivion, TIT FOR TAT feeds its feeders, thus providing for its own sustainable success. Life can be perpetuated only by players who embody the principles of mutuality, while those who understand winning only in zero-sum terms are carriers of death.

HARRINGTON and TIT FOR TAT bring to mind another fairy tale Lewis Hyde relates in his exploration of the gift. One after another, each of three sisters goes forth to seek her fortune. Their mother bakes for each a loaf of bread and asks, "Which wouldst thou like best, a little bit and my blessing or the big bit and my curse?" The first two choose the big bit of bread with their mother's curse. On their adventures, each of these is asked by a mother bird for a bit of bread for herself and her brood. These first two sisters refuse her, saying, "I have not much for myself." These sisters eat all their bread themselves, yet remain hungry. They each proceed to undertake a task, at which they fail, bringing about their own deaths. Finally, the third sister goes forth. She chooses the little bit of bread and her mother's blessing. When she encounters the mother bird and her little ones, she gives freely of her little bit of bread and, somehow, all are satisfied. The youngest sister then proceeds to the task at which her sisters had failed. Not only does she succeed, but she manages even to restore her sisters to life.

Here are contrasted the ways of scarcity and abundance. Those who are fixated on scarcity will choose the big piece, even at the cost of their mother's curse. Feeling there is not enough, they will not share. Yet their hunger is not sated, and their way leads to death. This is the way of the HARRINGTONS of the world. The third sister, like TIT FOR TAT, sees that cooperation and mutuality are the way of life. Embracing the abundance of the gift of life, which is the blessing given by the mother, she knows that giving and receiving are intertwined. Even the small bit with the blessing gives abundance enough for all. So great is the abundance of the path that has been blessed that she can even redeem her sisters.

We as a species have emerged from the house of our mother, the living system of the earth, and have gone off to seek our fortune. Our path thus far—as civilized societies—is largely that of the two elder sisters, the path of scarcity, of seeking for ourselves at the expense of others, and at the cost of a curse in our relationship with the living systems around us. This is the path described by the parable of the tribes. If we are to survive, we must enter into a next phase: off on our own, but embodying the blessing of the way of life given us by our mother. At the end of the first chapter of *The Parable of the Tribes*, I wrote: "If we are lucky, the evolution of civilization to this point may prove to have been a transitional period in the history of life. It may be a period of anarchy and destruction between two eras of synergistic order."[12] To which it may be added, it may be a period of scarcity between two eras of abundance. We may give up the losing battle of winning before we ourselves are irretrievably lost, and find the way by which life's blessings are truly won.

Loaves and Fishes

There is no denying the reality of scarcity. But this is only part of reality. The world of scarcity is a layer superimposed upon the more fundamental truth of abundance, just as the reality of the wolf's drinking the lifeblood of the lamb is subsumed within the larger truth that, with the gift of the sun's energy, life for the wolves and the sheep and all the parts of the biosphere can be preserved forever by their synergistic interactions. In the living systems that demonstrate the sustainability of abundant life, the undeniable fact of competition is part of the pattern of cooperation. In civilization, by contrast, the overarching fundamental harmony has yet to be established. We have indeed trapped ourselves in a world of scarcity, a world where too often the gains of one are the losses of another. It is a world where the sums of many of the games are less than zero. That is why our civilization is haunted by the specter of death.

In the condition of overarching anarchy where the Hobbesean war of all against all obtains, we need to be warriors. Where scarcity has slipped out of its natural niche in the order of things, we must of necessity increase our ability to protect our interests. Nonetheless, even while we are compelled to keep ourselves fitted for war, our aspiration must always be toward the building of a more fundamental peace. Otherwise, the scarcity-creating mentality of civilization's struggles will ultimately strangle all our interests. To survive as nations, we must be warriors; to survive as a species, we must transcend and transform the system of war.

This dual task is well illustrated by some emblems of peace.

The first emblem is TIT FOR TAT, just described. TIT FOR TAT shows us that winning is not at all the same as defeating the other player. TIT FOR TAT shows its openness to peace by its policy of *never starting a fight*, and by its continuous readiness to *forgive past sins and stop the fight*. At the same time, however, it should be noted that TIT FOR TAT is no pacifist. In Axelrod's game, those who will not retaliate do not survive. TIT FOR TAT is a warrior,* but one immune from excess. Protecting itself from those who are not "nice," this noble warrior can help over the generations to build a world where "niceness" thrives, a world of peace, a world safe perhaps even for those who are not warriors.

Another emblem of peace is the Round Table constructed by the legendary King Arthur for his knights. If TIT FOR TAT provides an answer for the scarcity orientation of "winners," the Round Table offers an alternative vision to that of the scarcity-creating narcissist.

Wishing to bring peace to a kingdom rife with strife, King Arthur seeks to forge a new order at Camelot. To do so, he must find a way to bring together the belligerent warriors with their prickly pride. How can they all sit down together without the narcissistic struggle to be the favored, the chosen, shattering the peace of the realm? The Round Table is part of the solution, for it has no head. At a round table, each sits at the point that, from his perspective, is the head. This, too, is a world of warriors, but a world also where peace (albeit a precarious and tempo-

---

*Indeed, TIT FOR TAT could be used to justify a variety of policies considered hawkish in our policy debates. Examples from the present situation could include a military strike against Libya in retaliation for Libya's involvement in terrorist attacks, and measured violations of the SALT II agreement in response to Soviet violations. (Both these policies *might* indeed contribute to the establishment of a more cooperative world order.) In the real world, however, it is not always easy to establish the original "defection"—did the Libyans really play a role, are the Soviets really violating the treaty?—or to know what magnitude of retaliation is appropriate. And given the warrior's tendency always to think it is *they* who drew first blood, the example of TIT FOR TAT, rather clear in Axelrod's game, provides a guide of but limited clarity.

rary peace) gains ascendancy. The establishment of an order sensitive to the needs of each to be treated with respect is what makes peace possible.

We recall the case of Cain and Abel. The fratricide came *after* God's rejection of one of the brothers. "In order to achieve the brotherhood of man on earth," I wrote in chapter 7, "we will have to have a vision of a cosmic order in which all are accepted." Arthur's Round Table is a mandala of such a vision.

The circle appears here as the shape of peace and abundance. This is true also in the harmony of the ecological order, in which abundance is created by the endless cycling of the world's finite goods. With the Round Table, the circle fosters peace because it replicates the psychological reality of the human world, in which each feels special, sitting at the head of his own banquet.

A final image is the biblical story of the loaves and the fishes. In this story, a multitude of thousands has gathered to hear Jesus. His disciples wonder how these people can possibly be fed, since all they have to give them is seven loaves of bread and a few small fishes. Yet, when Jesus fed the four thousand people from this meager stock, there was enough for all.[13]

It would be superficial to see this story as only a wish-fulfillment tale of miraculous powers employed by an object of worship. Like the story of the little bit of bread and the mother's blessing, the story of the loaves and the fishes conveys that abundance comes from the right spirit. The Prince of Peace, who said that the cycle of strife can be broken by turning the other cheek—thus relinquishing the warrior's sense that an insult unreturned makes one a loser—is again addressing the scarcity mentality of the warrior spirit by showing that in the kingdom of heaven, which is there for all to enter, there is enough to go around.

The story of the loaves and the fishes is, indeed, a fitting reversal of what the scarcity mentality creates. As we have seen repeatedly in part 2, the warrior in his excess makes scarce the spiritual goods of which there could easily be abundance: identity, respect, and, to a lesser degree, autonomy are among such goods.[14] Where wars can arise from treating the immaterial as if it were scarce like the material, Jesus here renders the material abundant like the goods of the spirit. The excesses of the spirit of scarcity are here countered by an excessive assertion of the spirit of abundance.

Religious truths, it seems, are often stated hyperbolically. We cannot escape the reality of scarcity; nor, in the world as it is and is likely to be in our foreseeable future, can we afford altogether to throw away the sword. (Of our three emblems, the loaves and the fishes is the only one that does not represent the warrior and acknowledge the necessity of his way.) Visions of loaves and fishes and of lions lying down with lambs are both true and false. False in their denial of part of the inescapable truth of our world, but also true in their confounding our deadly assumptions—assumptions that there are no powers accessible to us for transforming this world, that a different kind of world could never be.

Perhaps it is not possible for thousands to feast on a handful of food, but there are other hungers that can be met with abundance if only our hearts know the kingdom of heaven. In the same way much of war is the offspring of false scarcity, so can the way of peace be cleared by drawing upon true abundance. Look at the great historic gesture by Anwar Sadat. In 1977, the Egyptian president went to Jerusalem and spoke to his nation's enemies, the Israelis. After a generation of unceasing rejection and denial, Sadat spoke to them as fellow human beings. He recognized them as neighbors. Such *recognition* is one of those essential commodities that behave like the loaves and the fishes: one can bestow it and have one's own stores left undiminished. Sadat gave the Israelis a precious gift, but he "gave away" nothing. His gesture made possible the restoration to Egypt of the Sinai. It opened a little the door to peace.

Another example of giving the priceless gift that costs nothing comes from the relations between the Israelis and the Palestinians who live under their rule. Richard Sennett spoke with a Palestinian who had litigated in Israeli courts for certain rights for his people. In going to court, the Palestinian had disregarded pressures from other Palestinians who wished to withhold such implicit recognition of Israeli law. Why had he done it? Sennett asked.

> He avoided the question, but for the first time a look of fire came into his face. "Do you know that when we won in the courts, Mayor Kollek [of Jerusalem] came here with a delegation; yes, this delegation formally called upon us here at the office to offer congratulations; that meant something." . . . A delegation: the symbol of courtesy, of recognition, of respect.[15]

Here are gifts that cost us nothing. The status as valuable human beings, worthy of respect, only *seems* to be a scarce commodity. But that is an illusion, an illusion that grows out of the illusions we cultivate about ourselves: afraid to recognize and embrace all of ourselves, we project into the world the cleavage between the accepted and the rejected. When we enter the kingdom of heaven, where the abundance of love makes true acceptance of ourselves possible, we discover that there is a feast to be had, that even our little bit of bread can feed the others and leave plenty for ourselves.

In this world of abundance, where feeding and being fed merge, we become parts of a whole knitted together in the way of shalom.

PART 3

Boundaries:
The Dirty Business of
Cleaning House

10

INTRODUCTION: BOUNDARIES AND THE PSYCHE

The Genesis of the Need for Boundary

I f we look at life's peak experiences, it is the disappearance rather than the creation of boundaries that seems more saliently to characterize them. The mystics' vision is of an ineffably wonderful Oneness. The feeling of falling in love entails the falling away of the sense of boundary that separates two people. Love brings a blurring of boundaries. And at the core of our understanding of the sacred seems to be a realization of the profound interconnectedness of all things.

So deep and positive are these experiences of union that one might say that our natures are evolved to strive for the overcoming of boundaries. But that is only part of the picture. The other part is our devotion to constructing them. We have this twofold policy because of a dichotomy in our experience: a dichotomy between good and evil.

The raptures of union are filled with a sense of the goodness of that with which we merge. The mystic reports an experience that not only are all things One, but that they are indescribably beautiful and good. When lovers become one, the image of the beloved too is suffused with goodness. If the world were so ordered that good experience was always the reward for our openness, we might well live in this state of mystical union, merged with one another and with the cosmos.

But life brings pain and injury as well. Because we suffer evil, we erect boundaries. The boundary is our fundamental defense. Keep out! We want to have what is good and pleasurable within our domain, and we want to protect ourselves from what is evil and painful. The basic cleavage effected by boundaries—between the inside and the outside—is thus a way of dividing good and evil: we construct a microcosm for ourselves to live in that consists of all that is good and desirable, while banishing to the outside all that is evil and unwanted.

We may look at ourselves, therefore, as systems that can be more or less open or closed, depending on how great is our need to defend ourselves against evil. The more the world offers us love and nurturance, the more readily we open ourselves to floating freely into it. The more injurious is the world, the more impenetrable the boundary by which we seal ourselves off from it. *

We have looked at this sealing off before, in our discussion of narcissism. Injurious relationship causes narcissistic injury, and the narcissist seals himself off from the world. The core problem is the bad relationship. One can look at the injury in terms of narcissism, or in terms of boundaries, but they are both dimensions of the same system of defense. The cleavage of the world into inside and outside is entwined with the narcissist's efforts to protect and restore the injured self. "Freud describes the earliest stage of narcissism as attributing all that is *pleasurable and benign* to oneself and projecting onto the external world all that is *disagreeable, uncomfortable, tension-producing, and hostile.*"[1]

Just as we merge with the world from a sense of the possibility of good relationship, our defensive separation from the world is a function of our fears learned in injurious relationship. Injury in relationship drives the narcissist to seek invulnerability and isolation. But the reality is that we are vulnerable, that we are interconnected, that we are in relationship. The injuries the narcissist has suffered have brought pain and evil into the self, but to escape this damaged sense of self, the narcissist desperately seeks to equate the "inside" with goodness. At its root, therefore, the "boundaries project" of the narcissist is an effort to deny reality, and it is futile.

---

*This is not to deny the positive value of individuation. Awareness of oneself as a separate being is a positive and natural part of the process of maturation. I confess to being uncertain about the distinction between individuation and the defensive drawing of boundaries. But my intuition says that not only are they different in nature, but perhaps individuation also helps provide the foundation on which the dissolution of boundaries in love and in mystical experience can be achieved.

But there is an experiential validity to the sense that the evil is not of the self but of the outside world. This becomes clear from an analysis of that other pathological dimension of our drive to construct boundaries: the paranoid process.

Boundaries are essential to paranoia, which is a confusion about, and an obsession with, what is inside and what is outside. Like narcissism (to which, as we saw in part 2, it is connected), paranoia is the child of injurious relationship. The more violative the relationship, the less able we are to assimilate it into the self. The greater the experience of evil, the less can the experience be digested.

W. W. Meissner, in his analysis of paranoia, speaks of "introjects." These introjects are embodiments of a core relationship which is "overloaded with intense ambivalent affect."[2] Where love is not overly admixed with hate, the relationship can be integrated into the self. But the burden of receiving intense injury where love was needed brings into the self something indigestible. Unassimilated, it is experienced as being "other," as if it were autonomous and separate from the self. "Thus our patients acquire a presence within the inner world of their experience of themselves which is quasi-autonomous and which is the bearer of a burden of painful, anxiety-producing, and self-depreciating affects."[3] The introject is described as if it were a foreign body embedded within.

It is these introjects that the paranoid is likely to project out, over the boundary, back to the Outside. "The more primitive the level of organization . . . the more susceptible are introjects to subsequent projection."[4] The process of projection, by which what is inside is experienced as being external, reflects something valid about the experience. First, that the introject was thrust into one from a hostile world. (As Henry Dicks writes in his study of Nazi SS men, projection is a product of the experience of "a frustrating, hate-evoking act by the love-object."[5]) Second, that what is projected was too frightening and painful to have been organized into the self as a whole, so it always has seemed "other."

Thus, the more frightening the world, the more need we have of boundaries. Oneness being impossible, or experienced as entailing the threat of our annihilation, we build walls so that we can consign all that frightens us to the other side. Again, quoting Dicks: "The object that should have been good and soothing has turned wicked, poisonous. So the infant's automatic defense against this hate- and fear-laden experience is to split it off . . ."[6]

Housecleaning in the Psyche

It is, of course, an issue of war and peace. We would all like to live in peace, but if the world makes war upon us we can know no peace.

As before, we are investigating the cycling of war. First, the world makes war upon the psyche of growing human beings. Then this war is brought within, as the world's hostility is internalized. Then, in the search for internal peace, the person projects back into the world some of the warring elements, choosing the perils of having an external enemy over the torments of tearing himself apart.

Traumatic experience teaches us that the world is composed of warring elements: complete peace is thus impossible. We seek, therefore, the best peace we can find—a delimited peace within our boundaries. If there must be war, let it rage across the boundary. By a kind of psychic housecleaning called projection, we achieve a less agonizing war.

Again I speak of "we," as if paranoia were a human universal. Projective defenses are most blatantly practiced by people whose socialization has warred most intensely against their natures. But "low-intensity warfare" within the psyche is a general—and perhaps universal—human problem. And, I believe, the more extreme examples of projection serve to illustrate something about ourselves: how human beings generally make use of boundaries.

To achieve relief from internal warfare, we seek to banish part of ourselves. But which part should be thrown over the wall into the Outside? When the world makes war upon our natural being, the enemy comes within in the form of a persecutory introject. It is this introject that we experience as evil and project back out—in the beginning.

Yet, the forces of persecution remain entrenched in the world that surrounds us and upon which we depend. To identify with our natural selves and declare as the enemy the forces that condemn us is to wage a most perilous war. Ultimately, therefore, we identify with the persecutor and adopt his point of view. Eventually, we are taken over by the enemy, allowing his commandments to define good and evil. In the end, therefore, it is a part of our natural core that we learn to regard as evil and that we project out beyond the boundary.

Civilized societies, making war upon our "evil" natures, teach us how evil is to be dealt with: by war. With commandment and impulse both within us, we are compelled to be participants in this war between "good" and "evil." Aligning ourselves with the forces of "goodness" that have condemned and persecuted us, we create external enemies to condemn and persecute. Thus are all our dichotomies in the optimal order: inside are goodness and peace, while war and evil are swept into the outside world.

Those onto whom we project what we cannot acknowledge in ourselves—they are our enemies. From the history of persecution come some striking illustrations of what it is that is forbidden, and thus projected. Let us look at a few.

We come into this world needy creatures. Each human infant clings to his mother hoping to suck from her the sustenance on which his life depends. The Anglo-Saxon culture of early America, however, made war against such *dependency*. Those reared in a culture that demanded tough autonomy, and condemned as evil the natural dependency of the human child, could rediscover their dependency on the outside. Michael Rogin, in his work *Fathers and Children: Andrew Jackson and the Subjugation of the American Indian,* describes how this projective process worked: In the fantasy of the whites, the Indians were seen as remaining "in the earliest period of childhood, unseparated from 'the exuberant bosom of the common mother.' "[7] Projecting onto the Indians their own, denied dependency, as well as their rage from the war that had been waged upon that dependency, the whites made war upon the Indians. In the name of civilization, the whites ripped the Indian from "the common mother," the bosom of nature.

Another forbidden dimension is *sexuality*. The enemy is often depicted as a rapist. In the United States, the radical right in the 1950s saw rock and roll—which they condemned as provoking animal lusts—as part of a communist conspiracy, entirely contrary to the evidence that communists themselves are often quite in the grip of ascetic and puritanical moral constraints. In *Killers of the Dream*, Lilian Smith describes how white males in the South used projection to alleviate their guilt about their sexual exploitation of black women. The greater their sense of guilt, the more intense became the fantasy that black males were after white women, and the more heinous such a crime became in the eyes of white men. Finally, the process culminated in "the symbolic killing of a black male who, according to this paranoid fantasy, has 'raped' a 'sacred' white woman. It is a complete acting out of the white man's internal guilt and his hatred of the colored man and the white woman."[8]

And then there is *aggression*. Central to Franco Fornari's psychoanalytic explanation of war is the "paranoid elaboration of mourning." According to this idea, the death of a loved one evokes not only grief but also guilt. For the loved one not only was loved but also had been the object of fantasied attacks. (The more intense the ambivalence in the relationship, presumably, the more intense the death wish directed against the love object will be—and we have already seen that intense ambivalence in the core relationship is associated with the genesis of projection.) Under these conditions, the loss becomes the occasion for the projection of one's aggressive impulses and of the guilt that goes with them. "The experience of mourning then becomes not sorrow for the death of the loved person, but the killing of the enemy who is falsely thought to be the destroyer of the loved object."[9] (Fornari alludes to "the story of Kwoiam, one of the cult heroes in the Torres Straits, who exacted blood vengeance for the death of his mother, whom he himself had killed."[10]*

The harsher the warfare between the social environment and the developing psyche, the harsher the internalized conscience. And the harsher the judgments of conscience, the greater the need to find the object of those judgments outside the self. Thus Hitler, writes Robert Waite, was haunted by feelings of unworthiness and filthiness, because of which 6 million Jews onto whom he had projected those harsh judgments were sacrificed. Stalin was likewise pursued by an inner voice of condemnation and, according to Tucker, was consequently "under inner pressure to impute his own mistakes and failings to others and then to visit upon them the self-accusations and self-punitive feelings that these mistakes and failings caused in him."[12]

The voice of *blame* is a constant undertone, so someone else must be blamed. To salvage his narcissism,[13] Hitler "accused his teachers and his father of being the cause of his failure . . ." writes Erich Fromm. Nothing is my fault, it is always their fault. As Europe was about to plunge into the abyss in 1914, Kaiser Wilhelm sent out—over the boundary—all blame for the impending catastrophe. "The responsibility for the disaster which is now threatening the whole civilized world," Wilhelm wrote to the Russian Czar, "will not be laid at my door. In this moment it still lies in your power to avert it."[14] War breaks out, but all the combatants are blameless.†

There is the smell of evil in the air, so someone must be found to embody it. By psychic housecleaning, our forbidden impulses and the guilt that goes with them are projected out over the boundary.

---

*Also pertinent to aggression is the wildness discussed in part 2, in the context of the rodeo: "in the rodeo," writes Howard Stein of the cowboys, "they seek to subdue the[ir] externalized wildness personified by the horse or the bull . . ."[11]

†A headline in USA Today, in the unhappy aftermath of the superpower nonsummit in Iceland in 1986: "Reagan, Gorbachev: All Your Fault."[15]

To maintain peace within, we make war without. So painful is the burden of the sense of our own evil that we would rather spill another's blood than tear ourselves apart.

As the first part of this book documents our insistence that "We are not weak," what underlies our love of boundaries is the assertion, "We are not evil."

11

PASSIONS AT THE LEVEL OF PSYCHE AND SOCIETY

The Puzzle of Bloody Altruism

T his concept of boundaries can help us solve a puzzle about the sources of human destructiveness.

Thus far in this work, the picture that has emerged is of a wounded human being embattled against the world. Injuries engender the defensive structures of narcissism and paranoia, and these structures separate each person from his fellows and turn him against them in a struggle for the sense of value and control that he believes to be both in scarce supply and essential to his security. The sense of scarcity combined with the disturbance of interpersonal bonds thus renders the realm of interpersonal relationships an arena where self-centered actors wreak destruction upon one another. The problem of human destructiveness, therefore, appears to be a function of the selfishness, as well as the weakness and insecurity, of the human actors.

An interesting challenge to such a perspective comes from one of the most ingenious thinkers of our time, Arthur Koestler. In several works, Koestler has propounded a thesis that rejects "the dusty answer that all evil stems from the selfish, aggressive tendencies of human nature." Looking at history, he finds selfishly motivated violence negligible compared with the blood shed out of "unselfish devotion to one's tribe, nation, church or leader."[1] It is our capacity for altruism, says

Koestler, not our selfish impulses, that has contributed most to human destructiveness.

What are we to think of this idea? Were those who "lost themselves" in the throngs in the square at Nuremberg—hailing the victories for which they were ready to fight and die—in the grip of altruistic passions? Are those who are ready to be martyred in the service of Khomeini's revolution in Iran showing a selflessness that contrasts with the patterns of defensively motivated aggression we have been discussing? Is Koestler right in characterizing the corpses strewn upon the battlefields of history as "homicide [committed] for unselfish reasons"?

It is true that the individual—in his loyalty to his "tribe," in his willingness for self-sacrifice—shows a devotion to something larger than himself. But we have to look more closely at the psychology of the relationship between the individual and the group, and at the dynamics at work within the group. Otherwise, we will be unable to explain why it is that this "something larger than ourselves" deals with the larger world surrounding it in the ways that it does. Koestler's "altruism" hypothesis is unable to explain why all this "unselfish" energy so often is unleashed in the cause of murderous destruction.

To understand the problem of war, we need to solve the puzzle of "bloody altruism": of why the "unselfish devotion" of individuals to their collectivity results in so much carnage. Using the concept of boundaries we have been exploring, I will show that Koestler has been deceived by the superficial appearance of selflessness, and that, beneath the surface, selfish passions are running the show.

The Collective Dimension: "Us" and "Them"

When we discuss the problem of war and peace, we are discussing interactions not of individual human beings but of large-scale collective entities. Thus far in this work, for the most part I have ignored the distinction between these levels: asking questions about war, I have given answers in terms of individual psychodynamics. Even without Koestler's challenge, it would have been necessary eventually to examine the legitimacy of making this leap between levels. But his assertion—that what fuels human destructiveness is individual altruism channeled into the large collectivity—makes this the opportune moment for such an examination.

To *assume* that the psychology of collective actions (e.g., war-making) can be explained in terms of the psychology of individuals (e.g., narcissism and paranoia) is to commit the *fallacy of composition*. We commit this fallacy "whenever we assume, without adequate reason, that we can speak about groups in the same way we can speak about their members . . ."[2] We may be able to make such a leap "but this cannot be assumed without evidence."[2]

I am entirely sensible of the dangers of this fallacy. Indeed, *The Parable of the Tribes* is, among other things, an attack upon such reasoning. It exposes the gap in the logic of those who believe that, because history is made by human beings choosing and acting, social evolution *must* be ruled by human choice, and civilization must reveal human nature writ large. The parable of the tribes says no, the whole is more than the sum of its parts; and, in particular, the unchosen context in which people are compelled to choose and act can warp the course of events, making the thrust of the whole unreflective of the nature of the parts.

Similarly, I recognize that there are dynamics in the relationships among nations that have no counterparts in the interactions among individuals. Many whom I have known in Washington, for example, have been struck by the way the decision-making structures of governments shape the decisions that are made. The operation of bureaucratic interests has, as far as I can see, no equivalent at the level of the individual psyche.

Nonetheless, the psychodynamics we have been exploring *are* among the forces central to the problem of war and peace. They are not the only factors, but they are crucial, and they are the ones this work is about.

Making the leap between individual and collective levels constitutes a fallacy only if the equivalence or correspondence is *assumed*. Where evidence and reasoning are adduced to build a bridge between the levels, there is no fallacy. And the materials to build that bridge are at hand.

NARCISSISM AND BOUNDARY-DRAWING

One meaningful analogy we discussed in part 2: the connection between narcissism in an individual and group narcissism. It bears reexamination here, because it is quite germane to the subject of boundaries.

Narcissism, we have seen, entails a kind of sealing off, and it develops when positive relationship fails. For the individual's development, the failure of relationship is typically in the family system. For societies, a similar failure of relationship in the intersocietal system brings about a similar result: a turning inward of narcissistic self-nurturance, with hostility directed outside the boundary. A system that inflicts injuries creates thick boundaries.

In this context, one might understand Menachem Begin's need, described by Leonard Fein, to isolate himself and Israel from the rest of the world. Fein quotes an Israeli diplomat, talking in the early 1980s about the way Begin was alienating Israel's friends. He has to do that, the diplomat said, "for the world makes no sense to him unless we stand entirely alone."[3] This need to be an outcast makes sense in the light of another observation Fein makes concerning Begin's relationship with the world: "His world is a mean and brutish place, where none can be trusted."[4] A nation surrounded by implacable enemies, led by a survivor of Nazi genocide, became a self-isolating, nationalistic, and aggressive state.

In this context also, one might cite the early autarky of the Soviet Union. A nation with a history of invasive traumas, and an abiding fear of the outside world, the Soviet Union attempted for years to seal its economy off from the rest of the world. Economic autarky appears akin to the narcissist's caring for himself. What cannot be trusted is not to be let in. While there are other factors involved in a phenomenon like Soviet isolation, the narcissistic pattern of responding to injury by retreating within the self is one important factor.

Narcissistic injury creates boundary, on the inside of which is invested all the positive energy of self-care and self-regard, and toward the outside of which is directed the aggressive energies of rage. These are the two faces of nationalism. And, as Eric Hoffer argues, nationalism too draws intense energy from injury: "It was Napoleon's humiliation of the Germans, particularly the Prussians, which drove Fichte and the German intellectuals to call on the German masses to unite into a mighty nation which would dominate Europe."[5] Gregory Rochlin points out this "remarkable similarity" between the psychology of narcissism at the individual and the group levels: when narcissism is injured, "Restitution is always demanded. And whether by a group or an individual, narcissism is redeemed through aggression."[6]

In certain important respects, therefore, the psychological dynamics of a human society can operate analogously to those of an individual human being. There is, in other words, a kind of "group mind" that has some characteristics in common with an individual mind.

But the relationship between individual and group narcissism has another dimension: the group can function as the channel or vehicle for the expression of its members' narcissistic aspirations. In the period leading up to World War I, for example, the injured narcissism of individuals fueled the narcissistic assertion of nations: "There was a great mass of uprooted proletariat and urbanized petty bourgeoisie, for whom national pride provided a status and fulfillment lacking in their drab everyday lives."[7] Similarly, as Henry Dicks found in his study of the Nazi SS, an identification with "group power" provided a channel for individuals suffering from feelings of injury and weakness to make grandiose assertions in the name of something connected with the self.[8] By the magic of identification, the narcissistic passion for self-aggrandisement can express itself as the "selfless devotion" of the nationalist.*

A battle that begins as one across the boundary between the person and the world around him can, therefore, be rewaged farther out, across the boundary between that person's society and the world beyond it.

Two ways of looking at this pushing out of boundaries come to mind. One, implied above, is that the group may be better equipped than the individual to assert its narcissistic aspirations successfully. The other point is this: that the infusion of one's aggressive and self-inflationary impulses into the group with which one identifies offers a more *socially approved outlet* for those feelings. As we will see momentarily, these two points are really just different perspectives on the same thing.

Our societies have limited tolerance for individual self-assertion and self-aggrandisement, but can harness those impulses for collective purposes. Denis de Rougement writes that "It is accepted that every form of pride, every form of vanity, and even the most stupid boastings are legitimate and honorable so long as they are attributed to the nation in which one has taken the trouble to get born. What nobody would dare to say of his *me*, he has the sacred duty of saying for his *us*."[10]

The image of boot camp, employed near the beginning of this work, is apropos in this context. To make a few good men, I wrote earlier, first treat them worse than dogs. The humiliation of the recruits as individuals readies them for pride as members of a larger entity. In proportion as the individual is compelled to renounce his pride and self-assertion *as an individual*, the more he is energized and encouraged to manifest those feelings as members of his "corps." This "corps" really is like a larger body; it is an expanded self beyond whose boundaries one can gain

---

*George Orwell observed: "The abiding purpose of every nationalist is to secure more power and more prestige, not for himself but for the nation or other unit in which he has chosen to sink his own individuality . . . As nearly as possible, no nationalist ever thinks, talks or writes about anything except the superiority of his own power unit."[9]

social approval for directing one's well-stocked reservoir of compensatory narcissistic pride and rage.

In this respect, the boot camp serves as a metaphor for the nationalistic society as a whole. As the drill sergeant humiliates the recruits and evokes the surge of compensatory energy, so in society as a whole the structure of power inflicts on its members the injuries that the collectivity can then harness as aggressive nationalism.* Just as the recruits in boot camp refrain from attacking the authority who is turning them into real "men," so in society as a whole the aggressive energy is redirected away from those in power who have injured us onto some people *on the other side of the collective boundary.*

Alexander and Margarete Mitscherlich, for example, speak of the murderous feelings that—since the Middle Ages—the severe rule by German fathers has produced in German sons. Despite the intensity of the aggressive impulses, they say, "no direct outburst against the fathers has ever occurred." External enemies, rather, have provided socially approved, guilt-avoiding outlets for the Germans. "The guilt engendered by one's murderous aggressivity can thus be allayed by the fact that the father, at whom the aggression is in fact aimed, is felt ultimately to be the object to whom one has dedicated oneself . . ."[12]

Not only the sons. Alice Miller writes of

> a woman who never happened to have any contact with a Jew up to the time she joined the *Bund Deutscher Maedel*, the female equivalent of the Hitler youth. She had been brought up very strictly. Her parents needed her to help out in the household after her siblings had left home. For this reason she was not allowed to prepare for a career even though she very much wanted to and even though she had the necessary qualifications. Much later she told me with what enthusiasm she had read about "the crimes of the Jews" in *Mein Kampf* and what a sense of relief it had given her to find out that it was permissible to hate someone so unequivocally. She had never been allowed to envy her siblings openly for being able to pursue their careers. But the Jewish banker to whom her uncle had to pay interest on a loan—*he* was an exploiter of her poor uncle, with whom she identified. She herself was actually being exploited by her parents and was envious of her siblings, but a well-behaved girl was not permitted to have these feelings.[13]

---

*"Men do not face enemy machine guns because they have been treated with kindness," says Sergeant Toomey in Neil Simon's *Biloxi Blues*. "They face them because they have a bayonet up their ass."[11]

The psychological term for this redirecting of aggression is *displacement*. And it helps show how the two reasons for using the group as a vehicle for one's narcissism—that the group is better able to assert its narcissism than the individual, and that the individual is unburdened by finding a socially approved outlet for his narcissism through the group—are really different aspects of the same thing. That same thing is the intrasocietal power structure. The society can assert itself more successfully because it is not as immediately constrained by powers outside itself as is the individual. And it is this same constraint that causes the individual to displace his aggression onto objects beyond his social boundary rather than to attack the actual objects of his rage. For such an attack would be an act of rebellion that, given the balance of power, would bring disaster to the rebel. The recruit will not successfully defy the sergeant.

But displacement also points out another element in the bridge between the individual and the collective levels. Not only does it help explain how the narcissistic, aggressive energies of individuals are channeled through the group, it helps show another significant parallel between the psychodynamics of the individual and those of the group. This one connects with our other major theme concerning the psychology of boundary-drawing: narcissism's friend, projection.

Peace Within, War Without

In our discussion of projection in the individual, we saw that the direct experience of the internal conflict is so agonizing that it is a relief to transform it instead into an external war. By means of projection, an image of one of the elements warring within the psyche can be cast beyond the boundaries of the self and reexperienced as a menacing force from the world beyond. Displacement helps show how an analogous process operates within the collectivity.

Boot camp can serve, as it turns out, not only as a microcosm of the nationalistic society, but also as an analogue of the developing psyche. The war that a harsh society wages upon the growing psyche implants a punitive introject, like a separate internal voice that condemns and represses natural impulses. Similarly, threats external to society induce it to create the boot camp environment, where the ruling powers (e.g., the drill sergeant) humiliate and repress the raw material (e.g., the recruits). In both the psyche and the boot camp, the internalized war is reexternalized because continuing it internally would be too painful and disruptive of the system. The evil object of rage is projected outward, beyond the boundaries of the system, where it can be attacked. By this means, the tenuous integrity of the system within the boundaries is strengthened. In the name of the Fatherland, the rage evoked by the Fathers can be directed outward against the external foe.

Looking at this "defense of the Fatherland" from the viewpoint of the sons, we can say that the rage has been *displaced*. But looking at the same thing from the standpoint of the social system as a whole, we may say that an image of part of the conflicted inner system has been *projected* beyond the boundaries. For a social system, displacement and projection are different dimensions of the same thing: what is displacement by the recruits entails projection by the army considered as a whole. *

The connection, through analogy, between boot camp and psychic development is based on the internalization and reexternalization of conflict. This is not to say, however, that the conflicts that tend to rend civilized society are necessarily simply an internalization of the Hobbesean war of all against all that obtains among societies. These conflicts can stem from sources that are purely internal to the society as well; for the unregulated play of power can create not only war, but also repressive and exploitative systems of governance. In this way, the etiology of projection in the social organism may not be wholly analogous to that in the individual psyche: while the human psyche by nature strives toward some wholeness, the human society has long since left the protective harmony of nature. The strife between oppressor and oppressed is not bound to be in the interests of the living society as a whole, helping it adapt to the world in which it finds itself. Injustice and tyranny, rather, are often like a disease in the social body.

While the drill sergeant creates enmity to energize recruits to meet the enemy, many tyrants create enemies to discharge the enmity that might otherwise legitimately be directed against themselves. It is a commonplace observation that regimes threatened from within will stir up a war to pull their countries together and to fortify their own power. It seems more than coincidence that the Argentine junta invaded the

---

*One might express the analogy in another way: what we call projection at the level of the psyche as a whole can also be regarded as displacement from the standpoint of the warring element that is not projected. For the fear and hate and rage that were previously directed against another part of the psyche can now be displaced onto the object of projection.

Falklands just days after massive rallies of protest in Buenos Aires against the regime's domestic policies. Perhaps such reasons, too, underlie Khomeini's determination to perpetuate his war against Iraq; the war helps Khomeini to manufacture a national solidarity that might otherwise dissolve into discontent.* And perhaps this is one more reason why it is an American administration like Reagan's—one that serves the wealthy to the neglect of the health of society as a whole—that inflamed a national preoccupation with external enemies. Focusing attention on external threats like the Soviet Union, and inflating the threat from minor evils like Qaddafi's Libya, helped the Reagan administration rally support despite exploitive domestic policies (such as tax relief directed at the rich, environmental policies serving corporate interests, etc.).

Whether the internal social conflict is adaptive, as in the socialization of boot camp, or a symptom of disease, as in the age-old exploitation of the many by the ruling few, a similar projective process serves to strengthen social harmony.

A society that sets its members at war with themselves and with one another will teach them to use projection—to throw whatever is too painful to perceive or confront within the boundaries over the walls around their social group. If individuals were to relieve their inner tensions by projecting just over the boundaries of the self, onto their immediate social environment, the level of social tension would escalate. Individuals, therefore, are socialized to "dump their garbage" outside the town walls. For similar reasons, those tensions generated in social relationships, especially if they are too intense to be resolved within society, will be dealt with, through projection, across social boundaries.

Intrapsychic and intrasocietal tensions tend to go together. For the same harsh social dynamics that set individuals at war against themselves are also apt to be the ones that engender strife among their constituent members and groups. For it is, in a sense, "tensions in social relationships" that are internalized as intrapsychic conflict, and it is people who are at war with themselves who find it most difficult to live at peace with their fellows. Societies with such dynamics thus have a double need for projection beyond the boundaries:

---

*Khomeini's focus on threats, write Zonis and Offer, "further legitimizes the need for *tawhid*, internal unity, and the steps, however ruthless, which must be taken to bring that unity about."[14]

to maintain peace within the individuals and among the groups that constitute society. *

Projection onto out-groups is not always beyond the boundaries of one's own sovereign entity, as in nationalism. Many other kinds of boundaries—of ethnocentrism, of clans or moieties—can serve the same purpose. The "external" enemy may, therefore, be a subgroup of one's own society—such as Negroes, Jews, Greeks, Turks, neighboring villages, etc. Projection assists thus not only the evil of intersocietal warfare but also the evils of bigotry and feud, of intolerance and exploitation.

To keep the peace, people need to find someone on whom they can discharge the passions of war. To protect what is cherished inside, something on the outside must be sacrificed.

In his provocative study of the phenomenon of human sacrifice, Rene Girrard investigates the search for the sacrificial victim. He notes that the list of victims chosen by various societies for human sacrifice appears quite heterogeneous. "It includes prisoners of war, slaves, small children, unmarried adolescents, and the handicapped; it ranges from the very dregs of society such as the Greek *pharmakos*, to the king himself."[16] But beneath this diversity, he asks, "Is it possible to detect a unifying factor in this disparate group? We notice at first glance beings who are either outside or on the fringes of society."[17] This choice of victims either external to or on the margins of society suggests to Girrard something about the essential function of sacrifice. Onto the victim, he writes, society is seeking to deflect "the violence that would otherwise be vented on its own members, the people it most desires to protect."[18]

---

*The same device that preserves internal peace also protects narcissism, both group and individual. A report from a former U.S. ambassador to Lebanon helps to illuminate how projection beyond social boundaries can serve this narcissistic purpose.

Above, we were discussing narcissistic rage and self-assertion. Still more fundamental to narcissism is the need to rid the self of undesirable attributes. And for the "psychic housecleaning" required by narcissism, projection is the indispensable tool. John Mack reports Ambassador Richard Parker's observations of the stereotyping that went on among villages in northern Lebanon: "In each instance village members attributed to the inhabitants of neighboring villages through insults and stereotypes precisely those qualities which they most disapproved in themselves or about which they had the greatest fear or felt most uncomfortable. Of their own towns little was said, but the members of neighboring towns were said to be full of fears, crazy, sexually promiscuous, homosexual, diseased, stupid, 'a cock of the dung hill,' dishonest, untrustworthy, or otherwise worthless and devalued . . . The externalizations Parker has described seem to play an important role in maintaining village stability and self-esteem."[15]

Now, the relationship between war and sacrifice is deep and complex. In Girrard's analysis, sacrifice appears as a means to avoid war within society: the victim serves as a lightning rod upon whom the violent passions can be discharged, leaving the main social structure intact. By the use of displacement, the violence that might have wounded the social body can be discharged onto a scapegoat. External war and sacrifice, then, can serve the same function. Both can be ways of displacing aggression that might otherwise tear society apart.

Either the "victim" or the "enemy" can serve as a scapegoat. The original scapegoat—the *pharmakos* Girrard refers to—was loaded with all the sins of the community (an enactment of projection) and driven out. The widespread use of the term *scapegoating* to cover a broad spectrum of violence against "outsiders" suggests how clearly this ancient ritual of cleansing displays the essence of the more ubiquitous phenomenon of projection and displacement. Thus the Jews at Treblinka were scapegoats for the German nation—a People Chosen for being differentiable from the Aryan mainstream of German society and yet close enough to stand just over the social wall, handy for loading off all the psychic refuse from within the community gates. Scapegoating the "out-group" allows the "in-group" to do social "housecleaning." In the words of *The True Nature of the U.S. Regime, the "Great Satan,"* a piece of political literature from Khomeini's Iran, "The world must know that all the miseries of the Iranian nation and other Muslim nations stem from foreigners, from America."[19]

When nations go to war, the "enemy" can serve as a scapegoat for each of the combatant societies. Whatever is unacceptable within can be conveniently discovered outside, and whatever is forbidden to express within the group can be directed with full social sanction against the external enemy. The first of those steps is projection, the second displacement. It is projection that explains a phenomenon that has been much noted in recent years: that throughout history and in one war after another, regardless of circumstances, the "image of the enemy" has tended to be remarkably similar.[20] And it is displacement that helps explain the cathartic function of war, the release that comes from the unfettered discharge of aggression.

The distortive processes of narcissism and projection thus operate in the collectivity much as they do in the individual. The division of the world into a good "us" to be cared for lovingly and a bad "them" to be hated and destroyed serves useful functions for a society that might otherwise be at war with itself.

Realism and Excess

It would not be fair, however, to look at this cleavage of the world solely in terms of psychopathology. For an embattled society, compelled to live in an anarchic system plagued by the war of all against all, the boundary between "us" and "them" must be attended to as part of a strategy for survival.

In the case of intersocietal conflict, the same boundary between inside and outside that projective defenses can use to divide good and evil also objectively divides two realms of essential importance: the realm of order from the realm of chaos. However flawed the domestic order may be by tyranny and injustice, that order is the closest thing its members have to a domain of peace. Preserving social cohesion, while it *can* be part of the strategy of exploitation by a tyrannical element, does provide that sanctuary from unrestrained anarchy for which, in the Hobbesean social contract, people would rationally give up a great deal.* Maintaining internal peace, even by the use of projective distortion across boundaries, is an important adaptive function.

But there is a still more pressing way that the problem of anarchy makes the cleavage of "us" and "them" socially adaptive: it is only if we can maintain a cohesive "us" that we can protect ourselves from the objective threats from out there in the anarchic intersocietal system.

It is not just that the use of boundaries creates the problem of war. The reverse is also especially true: the objectively inevitable problem of war makes boundaries crucial to survival. For every society, writes Jules Henry, it is necessary that its members' attitudes will help both to preserve those within its boundaries and to destroy its enemies. For the survival of society, he says, it is equally dangerous to cherish the enemy and to destroy the friend.[21] Group solidarity being necessary for survival in a world riven with strife, the boundary around the group differentiates whether violence serves or hinders group survival. Jacob Black-Michaud writes that *intra*-group killing "is the complete antithesis of social behavior, and brings confusion . . ." On the other hand, "*Inter*-group killing, or feud proper, demarcates, separates and confers order

---

*And, indeed, there is evidence that Hobbes was right: e.g., the formation of the feudal order of medieval Europe seems to have entailed a willing surrender of liberty by the weak to gain the protection of the strong.

upon social relations [making] it possible for a given number of individuals to think of themselves as constituting a 'society.' "[22]* Achieving clarity of demarcation, versus confusion, is valuable not just because people need boundaries but also because the boundaries are already there and of vital importance.

It is in this context that we should understand the moral double standard employed by societies governed by the concept of honor. Members of such societies, writes J. G. Peristiany, feel bound by no moral obligations "in terms of citizenship or common humanity"; such moral considerations, rather, apply only within the boundaries of one's own family or village or nation.[24] The deep connection between the sense of honor and the commitment to one's group is reflected in the language of the Arabs, for example, in which the same term, *asabiyya*, refers to both.[25]

At one level, the limiting of moral concern to one's own group might be connected with the narcissistic pattern that infuses the whole code of honor (as discussed in part 2). To the narcissist, only what is within is real, while the outside has a shadowy existence. Behavior toward an outsider, therefore, need not reflect the degree of concern and connectedness appropriate to an insider, who stands within the narcissistic aura. This confining of the scope of love to one's own group might thus be looked upon as a kind of pathology, subject to condemnation from a more enlightened moral perspective. The wise being in C. S. Lewis's *Out of the Silent Planet,* for example, sees humans as more dangerous for following the law of the "love of kindred," since while holding this law they break all the other moral laws. (Again, as in part 1, the "bent" *hnau* does more damage than the broken one.)

But, again, such psychological and moralistic criticisms neglect the level of objective political reality, the reality that shapes the honor code in the first place. Namely, the reality of the Hobbesean struggle in which those in one's group are allies and those outside are actual or potential foes. The double standard thus reflects the different significance with respect to one's own life and death of people on different sides of the boundary. Just as injury engenders narcissism, the state of war creates the moral cleavage between inside and outside. Anarchy—

---

*Illustrative of this is the example of the Bedouins, whom anthropologists have found eager to talk about their fighting in feuds but extremely reticent to talk about violence and killing within the group.[23]

the fragmentation of human actors—is a barrier to the universalization of morality. *

But as we find repeatedly in our explorations, we do not have to choose between an explanation based on a necessary adaptation and one based on pathology. Realism and excess are combined. Moreover, the realistic threats and the pathological excess feed each other. Anarchy's war of all against all does imbue boundaries with moral significance; but it is also true that creatures overwhelmed by the polarization of the elements of good and evil within them are driven to make war to find peace, to accentuate boundaries in order to feel whole.

Irreconcilability and the Denial of Internal Division

The more extreme the war within, the greater the need to enact it as an external war. Herein lies yet another analogue between the psychic and the social use of boundaries. The greater the polarization of the warring internal elements, the greater the likelihood of projection. The less chance there is of achieving internal reconciliation, the greater the need for the perpetuation of external conflict. In this, too, the dynamics of individual and society are similar.

We may recall here the concept of the introject, which played a key role in creating the need for psychic housecleaning. The introject is less integrated into the self because it is "overloaded with intense ambivalent affect." Ambivalence is inevitable in human relationships, but it rages most intensely in those who are least likely to experience and acknowledge that ambivalence. Studies of the authoritarian personality,[26] for example, have shown that people whose upbringing pits impulse against prohibition in irreconcilable conflict are likely to report their relationships with their parents in unambivalently positive terms; while others with less polarized intrapsychic elements are more likely to acknowledge their ambivalence.

---

*The great universal religions—such as Christianity and Islam—have broadened the universe of moral behavior, and by so doing have helped create a basis in human consciousness for overcoming the objective anarchy among human societies (as in the concept of Christendom, which mitigated the predations of feudal anarchy, and in pan-Islamic movements, which stress the brotherhood among Islamic nations). But even these religions, as we will discuss in part 4, have themselves been riven with boundaries between the true believers and the infidels.

All socialization entails some conflict, but it is the harshest kinds of socialization that compel us to enact our conflict over external boundaries. This perspective enables us to give greater focus to an assertion, made by Alexander and Margarete Mitscherlich, that "it is anger over the prohibitions of *our own* society which motivates our resentment against our private or collective enemies, rather than the objectionable characteristics of the latter."[27] This is true when the anger is so intense that reconciliation is impossible, when the prohibitions are undigestibly harsh. It is then that the introject lodges like a foreign body embedded in the self, that the intense ambivalence toward the agents of socialization is denied, and that therefore the war internal to the psyche must be enacted against an external, "foreign" enemy.

It is in the very denial of the divisions in the internal reality that we find the clue about the use of boundaries. Daniel Heradstveit, for example, studied opinion in the nations involved in the Arab-Israeli conflict. He found that those who saw their own society as all of one piece—those whose perceptions excluded the internal divisions of ambivalence and ambiguity—were likely to advocate uncompromising policies toward the other side in the intersocietal conflict; whereas those who perceived their own side in pluralistic terms were likely to be willing to compromise. As physicists can infer the existence and course of invisible particles from the trails left by other fragments departing the point of disintegration, so we can infer from the "unitary" perception of one's society—with its artificial simplicity and goodness—the projection of a missing element for psychic and social housecleaning. And from this housecleaning, in turn, we can infer a sense of irreconcilable conflict that necessitates an uncompromising stance against the external foe.

We all experience conflict within ourselves and with those closest to us. Only when we have experienced the conflicting elements as reconcilable can we envisage peace. If peace within—in the psyche or the society—is experienced as impossible, war without will actually seem desirable. Thus, while objective circumstances in the surrounding system make boundaries necessary, the denial of internal polarization can drive people to exaggerate the boundaries and to use external war for purely internal purposes. Where the domain of peace is most tenuous, there will the boundary between "us" and "them" be most energetically employed.

The Implosive Threat

The struggle against reality is always an uphill fight. What has been externalized will always threaten to come back in. Projection is like a rocket booster that ejects the unwanted element out beyond the atmosphere, but can never put it into a stable orbit. Thus, there is always the threat of an explosive reentry. Thus, while the true realist will guard his boundaries in a world where there are external threats, the paranoid who externalizes internal threats will guard his boundaries with excessive zeal.

Consider, for example, the shooting down of the KAL airliner 007 in 1983 by the Soviet Union. This shooting elicited a good deal of moral outrage in the West about the murder of innocents, but little understanding of the genuineness of the fear that this and similar Soviet actions demonstrate. To people with a more fluid sense of boundaries, a stray airliner may not appear a "realistic" threat, but to people whose whole defensive structure is founded upon a strict dichotomy between what is inside and what is outside, such an intrusion symbolizes a catastrophic breakdown of their defenses. A "monolithic" ("one stone," all of one piece) society such as the Soviet Union has been—with its one-party government, totalitarian controls, state ownership of economic enterprises, and suppression of potentially autonomous religious and ethnic centers of ideology—must engage in paranoid housecleaning to preserve the fiction of its internal unity. To those who employ the paranoid externalization of conflict, which depends upon a clear division between inside and outside, any penetration is a great threat.

To the extent that a society allows itself to be the arena for many diverse and contending interests—as does a pluralistic society like the United States—its sense of boundary will be less invested with excessive fear. Thus, the United States enjoys a long, unguarded border with its northern neighbor, and to the south has a border that is readily penetrated yearly by millions of poor people from Latin America seeking economic opportunity and/or political refuge.

Of course, the United States is not "all of a piece" in its attitude about tolerating this combination of division and fluidity. In the United States it is those same segments—e.g., the radical right—who are least able to tolerate American pluralism who are also most inclined to interpret all threats as penetrations from the outside, such as from Soviet communist conspiracies (or Jewish conspiracies) to corrupt American youth and to take over the country. A comical and highly revealing illustration of this way of thinking was the character of General Jack D. Ripper in the 1964 film *Dr. Strangelove*. General Ripper, who, incidentally, launches against the USSR the strategic nuclear bombing attack that brings about the destruction of the world, has at the center of his worldview the belief that the communists—the outside enemy, the Soviet Union—are penetrating the American people through the fluoridation of the drinking water. It is significant that the general reports that his insight into the threat to the "purity" of our "precious bodily fluids" occurs to him after the "act of love," an experience often characterized by a dissolution of boundaries. Having realized the threat to American society from the invasion of foreign substances, he proceeds to launch the nuclear attack on the Soviet Union, an attack that can be recalled only with the code letters OPE, derived from his reconfiguration of the key letters of the two phrases central to his paranoid system: "Purity of Essence" (keeping the foreign element out) and "Peace on Earth" (which can be achieved only if the foreign threat is destroyed).

If it is vital to the paranoid structure that the outside be kept out, it is no less vital that there *be* an outside. If there were nothing beyond the boundary, the interior would become the whole universe—and the paranoid's universe is at war. This imposes a paradox upon the paranoid warrior. The enemy must be destroyed, but the enemy must always be there. *

---

*As the superpowers now grope toward a possible transformation of their relationship toward a less bellicose posture, it is well to remember that such a change is not craved by everyone. Subtle evidence of this surfaced recently when presidential candidate Senator Robert Dole was interviewed on television. On "This Week With David Brinkley" (January 10, 1988), Senator Dole was asked whether he shared President Reagan's assessment that under Gorbachev the Soviet Union may be changing. Senator Dole said that he did not share that assessment. Then he went on to say something quite remarkable—remarkable for its content, but still more so for its tone. In a reassuring tone, he declared: "In the Dole administration, we will continue to believe that the Soviet Union is expansionist."

In a world where things change, why does a would-be president guarantee us that his image of the world will not change? It would be one thing to assure us that he will remain prepared for the worst, but it is quite another to rule out even the possibilty of a change for the better. The solution to this riddle lies in the Senator's understanding that there is a constituency out there for whom the "good" news of an end to enmity is really not welcome news at all. His reassuring tone tells it all. Senator Dole's face and voice were not saying, "I'm afraid the reality is still grim," but rather, "Don't worry, in the Dole administration we will still regard the Soviet Union as the enemy." An astute politician, Senator Dole can be presumed to be addressing a constituency he knows well. In his remark, therefore, Senator Dole is giving us to understand that there is a large number of Americans who would find reassuring a commitment not to reassess our

The paranoid's sense of external threat impels him to crave dominion without limit. As was said in chapter 8, there are no bounds to imperial ambitions in the paranoid economy of the will. In Nazi Germany, in the expanding Soviet Empire, and in the more militarist circles of the American foreign policy establishment, one discerns the implied craving for complete control of the world. But to the extent that the real source of the threat is internal—psychologically and socially—the fulfillment of that dream would prove a nightmare. With the possibility removed of enacting the conflict across the borders, the precarious internal structure would break down.

Fortunately for humankind, this particular experiment has never been conducted. But fortunately for my argument, a somewhat equivalent circumstance demonstrates its plausibility. The spread of European power in recent centuries imposed on various subject peoples a kind of pax imperialia. For some of these peoples, intergroup warfare had served a vital function in maintaining a paranoid structure. This unchosen peace compelled the people to face their internal war. Thus, Franco Fornari writes, "Deprived of war as a paranoid reaction to mourning, primitive peoples evolved depressive positions. The bellicose tribes of Oceania have been in a state of particularly depressed confusion ever since the Europeans imposed peace on them."[28] Depression of this sort is aggression against the self. In addition to such intrapsychic internalization of conflict, the removal of the external enemy can precipitate manifestations of intrasocietal strife. The abolition of war among the Kanachi tribes, for example, led the people to fear their own sorcerers, a phenomenon Fornari describes as the "reinternalization of the persecutory object into their own group."[29]

The threat of peace. Maybe this is why so many of those who show the way toward peace—Jesus, Gandhi, Martin Luther King, Jr., Sadat— have been violently eliminated. It is the external enemy, not the peacemaker, who is the savior. Thus, it is the peacemaker who becomes the enemy.

The turmoil within creates an excessive preoccupation with boundaries and injects into the realm of intersocietal relations a need for war against external enemies. War therefore reflects two kinds of defensive needs. And sometimes what is presented as an objective necessity for

---

image of the Soviet Union, or to abandon the hostility and competition that ensue from that image. I would guess that even as "the need for the enemy" is a factor in the American body politic, this factor may be a still more potent obstacle to peace within the Soviet power structure.

defense against external threat is generated by the need to safeguard one's subjective defenses against internal threats too frightening to face.* To repeat: It appears that we make war because otherwise we would have no peace.

Bloody Altruism Revisited

We are now in a position to see clearly the fallacy in Arthur Koestler's argument that most of the bloodshed in human history has been inspired by altruistic passions.

Koestler asserted that "homicide for unselfish reasons . . . is the dominant phenomenon in history."[31] He called attention to the predominance of homicide, for there is no mistaking the bloodiness of our collective history. But he called it "unselfish" because, in the clashing of our collectivities, individuals seem so ready to transform their "selves" into instruments of the "us" of which they are part.

To be sure, there is such a thing as altruism, and true unselfishness can be expressed in the arena of war. Love of country can be the motivation that makes a person willing to fight in its defense and, if necessary, to sacrifice himself. As a mother may altruistically put herself between her child and danger, so out of love may patriots cherish— more than their own lives—their larger social entity. As the protective role of the male baboons suggests (as noted in chapter 1, "Damaged in the Male"), this altruistic impulse may be presumed to be a fundamental element of our animal nature. (And looking forward to the future, this altruistic capacity will be required of our species if our powers are ever to become compatible with a humane and viable world civilization.)

---

*One might cite, in this context, deMause's analysis of the United States' behavior leading up to the Cuban missile crisis. According to his reconstruction of the chronology, the imagery current in the American national consciousness in the months before the international crisis indicated an internal crisis of a group-psychological nature. So, we looked for an external conflict to defuse the internal one. "As we moved into 1962, we were . . . badly in need of something to fight about, but with no active war around to get into, the media began to comment on the 'strange calm' the world seemed to be afflicted by . . . By the summer of 1962, we found the solution: Cuba. Long before we even suspected there might be missiles there, we began to use war-like language against Cuba, passing war resolutions, calling Cuba a 'cancer' on America, declaring a blockade of the island, terming Castro's existence and a 'Red Cuba' intolerable to us, and then sending U-2 planes over to see what we could discover. The actual finding of the missiles after all this fantasy came as a great emotional relief . . ."[30]

But conceding that altruism plays a role in our collective bellicosities is not to concede the essential validity of Koestler's thesis. From the outset, the question hung over Koestler's interpretation: if altruistic devotion is the essential human energy being fed into the process, why is it carnage that issues out the other end? Our foregoing discussion has suggested the solution to this puzzle. Koestler has been misled by appearances: the "unselfish devotion to one's tribe, nation, church or leader" is not as unselfish as Koestler suggests; among the passions of patriots altruism is but one, and likely a subordinate one.

This solution lies in seeing through the apparent willingness of the individual to make himself a tool of the larger power. Much of this willingness to be a tool of power derives from the individual's understanding that only through the larger entity can he safely discharge his own selfish passions of rage.

We can see this same mystery of apparent submission in one of the most troubling social-psychological findings of our times. I refer to Stanley Milgram's famous experiments, reported in his book *Obedience to Authority*. Milgram set up experiments in which the subjects were to administer—or so they thought—electric shocks to other apparent subjects each time these people failed at certain tasks given in the experiment. In fact, the subjects to be shocked were actually in collaboration with the experimenter, and the apparatus for administering the shocks was fake. But those to whom the "shocks" were administered were convincing in their performance of agony and terror and in their entreaties for mercy. And as the level of the "shocks" to be given escalated into levels marked with terms like "extremely dangerous," the subjects apparently truly believed that they were causing great pain and possible damage to other people.

The other actor in the experiment was the Authority, the experimenter under whose auspices this "research" was being carried out. His role was to tell the subject what to do and, when a subject hesitated, to invoke authority as the justification for administering ever-higher levels of electric shock: "The Experiment must go on!" No threats were used to coerce the subjects into cooperation.

The troubling finding of this experiment was that the great majority of subjects (American college students) were willing to obey commands of almost murderous proportion in an intimidating but noncoercive environment. A lesson seemed to be: It can happen here, "it" being the kind of atrocities seen earlier in this century, for which the plea of innocence so often was, "I was only following orders."

Milgram's experiments provoked a great deal of controversy concerning the propriety of subjecting unwitting experimental subjects to experiences potentially so traumatic in nature. But there is room, too, for controversy concerning the meaning of Milgram's findings.

Milgram himself saw the experiments as revealing the power of the tendency of people to subordinate themselves to authority. Even ordinary people without hostility, Milgram concluded, will act destructively if ordered to do so.[32] Milgram is taking here a Koestler-like position: what is real in the event is the visible subordination of the individual's will to a greater power. But what is neglected is the possibility that what makes this subordination alluring is a correspondence between what authority commands and what the "subordinated" will secretly craves.

This is the thrust of Florence Miale and Michael Selzer's critique of Milgram, in their book *The Nuremberg Mind*. Whereas Milgram asserts that aggressive tendencies "have hardly anything to do with the behavior observed in the experiment,"[33] Miale and Selzer find the data insufficient to support that conclusion. It is just as consistent with Milgram's facts, they say, that the command of the authority "released the aggressive drives of the so-called obedient subjects."[34] Whereas Milgram assumes that the weight of authority induced the subjects to suspend their own values and feelings, Miale and Selzer suggest that the authority served rather to tip the balance so that impulses usually constrained by fear* could be unleashed. "The effect of the authority's command, then, is not to say, in effect, 'Be violent *despite* yourself; let me do the judging for you,' but rather, 'I won't punish you if you indulge your appetite for violence' . . ."[35]

Just as the reality and importance of altruism can be acknowledged, so also there is no need to deny the power of authority as a separate force in explaining the behavior of Milgram's subjects or of SS guards. We need not choose one kind of explanation to the complete exclusion of the other.

But neither need we take the ostensible subordination of the individual—Milgram's obedient subject or Koestler's altruistic patriot—simply at face value. The larger power can provide the individual with a channel for the expression of his otherwise inhibited impulses of destructive rage. What would be a dangerous vice at the individual level becomes enshrined by collective consensus as a noble trait.

Individual passions are transformed into collective ones. In the patriot, ready to defend Us against all the evils around us, "we have again

---

*Perhaps, indeed, constrained by fear of punishment by authority.

egotism, but so broadened as to become a virtue."[36] It is only the boundary that has been broadened, not the spirit. To those on the outside of the boundary, the quality of the energy still feels the same.[37] The individuals have made the best deal they could find: in exchange for surrendering their individuality, they are given license to discharge their pent-up passions. *

The social whole, meanwhile, has its own analogous dynamics. For, like the individual, the society operates in a hostile environment, and, also like the individual, it needs harmony within its boundaries. The challenges of achieving social harmony, and of maintaining security in an anarchic intersocietal system, might be addressed in a variety of ways. Some of these approaches might help foster genuine peace. But to the extent that the social whole has been suffused with the narcissistic and projective passions of its members, these coping patterns will tend to be ingrained also into the conduct of the whole. And as we saw in part 2, narcissism and projection are not the ways of peace. Both are at war with reality. They represent despair of the possibility of peace, and the choice to export evil and war.

At the boundary we make our war upon evil.

The anarchy that surrounds our nations thus combines with the unresolved war in our hearts to make the boundary between our societies a dread place. Across this line, we enact all the dimensions of the fragmentation and discord of our civilized human condition.

---

*It seems clear that it was important to Koestler to believe that it is altruism that leads people astray. He held on to this idea and reiterated it in various places in his writing. One might ask the question: what was the significance of this idea for Koestler? The facts of Koestler's own life suggest a possible answer.

Koestler was one of those who worshiped "The God that Failed," who embraced revolutionary communism and then came to repudiate it. (Indeed, one of his most brilliant writings was *Darkness at Noon,* a novel about the Stalinist purges.) He had been a fervent fighter for what he later realized was one of the more destructive movements of our century. Perhaps, I would conjecture, he had a need to see himself as contributing to evil not because of any evil in himself but because his altruistic desire to save humankind found misguided expression.

From my knowledge of revolutionaries, the role of unselfish devotion to humanity is less than they suppose, and the role of more selfish passions of rage and self-glorification rather greater than they admit. From what, by hearsay, I know of Koestler in daily life, it seems possible that he was a man who was not master of his aggressive impulses. And from what we know of his death—a double suicide of an aged, terminally ill Koestler and his younger and healthy wife—we have some basis for wondering how well in control he was of his own selfish passions.

12

A DANCE BEFORE THE MIRROR

T he boundary becomes a distorting mirror before which similar creatures—who, though very much alike, see themselves as opposites—perform a deadly dance.

In her book, *Beast and Man*, Mary Midgley recounts the libelous depictions of the wolf in human literature. The wolf is characterized as treacherous for creeping so secretly toward its victims. Of course, says Midgley in defense of the wolf, such criticism neglects the obvious, that "wolves would starve if they always gave fair warning . . ."[1] Unfair criticism, if one grants the wolf the right to live. But "wolves have traditionally been blamed for being carnivores," says Midgley, a condemnation she describes as "doubly surprising," "since the people who blamed them normally ate meat themselves . . ."[2]

What are we to make of this hypocrisy? One wonders how sincere can be the sympathy for the lamb displayed in the fables and fairy tales of us human carnivores. And one questions the sincerity of the moral outrage against the evil wolf expressed by people equally stained by blood. Are these moralistic feelings really only so much pretense, fabricated by one group of carnivores (the humans) to discredit another competitive group (the wolves)?

This question reaches far beyond the wolf, for the wolf stands here as the prototypical *enemy*. The enemy is always evil, and evil for doing much the same as one does oneself. We are challenged to understand this moral outrage, which plays so dynamic a role in the passions of war.

To dismiss these moral condemnations as pure pretense or hypocrisy would be to fail to meet that challenge. Somewhere long ago I came across the profound observation: "True insincerity is hard to find." This idea—the Sincerity Principle, we might call it—will serve us well in our present inquiry into the apparently hypocritical demonization of the foe. For however unfair may be the distortions involved, they are not truly insincere.

The Ever-Popular Double Standard

Earlier we saw how, for people obsessed with invulnerability, might can make right. Now we discover how, for people who need to use group boundaries to cleave the world into good and evil, "us" makes right.

In an experiment, two groups of employers in San Francisco were shown a photograph of a man. One group was told that the man pictured was treasurer of a local corporation. To the other group, the man was identified as treasurer of a local labor union. "The first group described this man as responsible, intelligent, thoughtful—generally a desirable person. The second group described him as ignorant, violent, aggressive, undependable—a very undesirable character."[3]

It all depends on what side of the boundary a person or a set of behaviors is located. The same face that looks desirable on our side of the border looks menacing and undesirable on the other side. What is a virtue when we do it is a vice when it is practiced by "them."*

Gandhi wrote that if the objects of Hitler's aggression practiced passive resistance, Hitler would recognize a courage "infinitely superior to that shown by his own Storm Troopers." But more credible is the dissenting viewpoint of another Indian, who wrote in response: "Courage to a Nazi, however, seems a virtue only when displayed by his own supporters; elsewhere it becomes 'the impudent provocation of Jewish-Marxist *canaille.*' "[5]

Justice may be blind, but human perception is not. We see our side through one prism, and the other side through another.

---

*Thus the power-motivated Agamemnon can speak derogatively of his adversary of the moment, Achilles, saying: "[H]ere is a man who wishes to be above all others, who wishes to hold power over them all, and to be lord of all, and give them orders."[4]

The implications of this for the challenge of achieving peace and justice are clear. Even in the world of sport, we display our penchant for bias. Although the contests of football are far removed from the wellsprings of hatred, even there the double standard is evident, as the same tactics that fans proudly call "tough" when their players practice them are furiously condemned as "dirty" when done by the other team. The attitude of the impassioned partisan toward impartial justice is well represented by the hallowed call of the baseball fan: "Kill the ump!" As exhibited blatantly and harmlessly in sports, so also more subtly and dangerously in the realm of war. In the "just war" doctrine, certain criteria of justification were developed to constrain the resort to violence by nations. But this doctrine is "vitiated by a radical weakness, a stone missing from its very foundations; it neglected the fundamental premise of effective justice, that no man can be a judge in his own cause."[6]

Righteous rage tends to mount on both sides of the boundary, as both sides prepare to wage war in the name of justice.

The predisposition to see ourselves as embodiments of the good and the just can only reinforce our sense that "they" are possesed by the most evil of intentions. For if we are good, they can have no just cause to fear us. And if they have no reason to be afraid of us, any maneuvering on their part against our power proves the aggressiveness of their designs.

Historians have found this double distortion among the roots of World War I. "England seeks no quarrels," said the English statesman Sir Eyre Alexander Crowe, "and will never give Germany cause for legitimate offense . . ."[7] Crowe assumed, says Robert Jervis, "not only that Britain was benevolent but that this was readily apparent to others." Neither England nor Germany, although each was exquisitely sensitive to any hostility directed toward itself, could grasp how its own behavior helped provoke the animosity of the other.[8] "Each government," noted Lord Grey, perceptively, "while resenting any suggestion that its own measures are anything more than for defense, regards similar measures of another government as preparation to attack."[9] Thus does the double standard help lead the dance toward war.

As in the movement toward World War I, so in many of the interactions of the Cold War. Reminiscent of Crowe's dubious reassurances are the words of an American secretary of state in the 1950s: "Khrushchev does not need to be convinced of our good intentions," said John Foster Dulles. "He knows we are not aggressors and do not threaten the security of the Soviet Union."[10] And reminiscent of Lord Grey's insight was an observation by George F. Kennan, early in the Cold War, of a strange resistance in the mind of official Washington to the idea that what were seen as Russian provocations might be reactions to American behavior.[11] Kennan was commenting on the establishment of American bases in Japan. But this same strange resistance persists in more recent developments, as in the American interpretation of the recent Soviet military buildup.

There is no disputing that during the 1970s, the Soviets substantially built up their military power in all categories. To the hawkish Committee on the Present Danger, this buildup was clear evidence of the Soviets' offensive intentions, of their plans to achieve such military superiority that, by use of force and blackmail, they could achieve their goals of world conquest. "Soviet military power and its rate of growth," declared the Committee in its founding document, "cannot be explained or justified by considerations of self-defense."[12] But, according to a different perspective on the historic unfolding of the arms race, the Soviets' drive to arm came directly after their humiliation by the United States in the early 1960s, and after a dramatic American military buildup in the same period. Former U.S. Secretary of Defense Robert McNamara has said that if he had been his Soviet counterpart, the unfavorable balance of forces in the 1960s, combined with the rumors that some in the U.S. military establishment wanted to seek a first-strike capability, "would have scared the hell out of me!"[13]

But this ability to put oneself in the position of one's adversary is rare in the dance that leads to war. One's own concerns are legitimate, while one's competitor's cannot be. In our competitor, the wolf, the taste for meat is a sign of evil. His teeth and claws are signs of his cruelty, while our knives and guns are required for our security.

Can the Soviets' buildup be "justified" by considerations of self-defense? It probably is the case that the Soviets have built far more than is rationally required for effective deterrence and self-defense. But the same people who could not imagine that defensive insecurities could explain Soviet behavior proceeded in the 1980s to direct a similarly excessive American escalation without which, they say, our defenses would be inadequate and our national security jeopardized.

The Sincerity Principle once again applies. To assert that their overkill is a certain sign of aggressive intentions while our overkill is required for a margin of security appears to be rank hypocrisy. One might wonder about the good faith of those who think we must make "worst case" assumptions about them in our preparations, while arguing at the same time that the Soviets must accept our own protestations of peaceful, or at least defensive, intentions. But good faith is not the issue; the double standard is maintained in all sincerity. With our persistent distortions across the boundary, it becomes a good deal easier to have a sincere appreciation of our own needs and fears than of those on the other side.

This double standard evidently has operated in the interpretation of "nuclear doctrine," a nation's approach to the use of nuclear weapons. In my interviews of experts, I found among American hawks a tendency to assume that it is in the most frightening of Soviet doctrinal statements that the real Soviet orientation is to be discovered. Thus, Soviet arguments for the winnability of nuclear war, no matter how obscure their source, have figured prominently in the assessment by these hawks of the requirements for American national security. These same people believed that the Soviets should know that American doctrine has been intended solely to achieve deterrence, and that any American arguments for more aggressive possibilities could be safely disregarded as merely hypothetical or peripheral.

Given the "worst case" interpretation of Soviet intentions, we transform ourselves into something more like the image (quite possibly distorted at that) of our enemy. Or possibly, with each making worse-case interpretations of the other, they simultaneously make themselves into images of what they most fear.

In preparing his book, *With Enough Shovels: Reagan, Bush and Nuclear War*, Robert Scheer had an opportunity to discuss with both the Republican presidential and vice-presidential candidates in 1980 the requirements for the strategic defense of the United States. In his conversation with Bush, Scheer asked if there didn't come a time when enough is enough, and more is just overkill. Bush responded, "Yes, if you believe there is no such thing as a winner in a nuclear exchange, that argument makes a little sense. I don't believe that."[14] But when Scheer reported this in the *Los Angeles Times*, Bush declared that he was just talking about the *Soviets'* adherence to the "ugly concept" of a winner in a nuclear exchange. He himself, he protested, did not believe anyone could win a nuclear war.[15] Shortly thereafter, Scheer interviewed Ronald Reagan. Reagan condemned the Soviets for believing in the possibility of winning a nuclear war, despite the fact that such a "victory" would entail enormous casualties. "We have a different regard for human life than those monsters do," Reagan declared. Yet, when the Reagan administration came to power, as Scheer shows, it began to transform American strategic doctrine and preparation in precisely that direction alleged to have been adopted by those godless monsters, and said to be contrary to our more godly values. *

To the actors on each side of the boundary, the interaction is one of opposites: on our side there is nobility, while on theirs is menacing evil. To an impartial observer, however, the boundary seems like a mirror, with each figure acting like the one across from it. If the double standard operates unchecked, the dance before the mirror will escalate until—uncomprehending of both their own threats and the other's fears—the two enraged actors leap at the mirror to fight.

The Polarization of Good and Evil

Underlying the double distortions of the double standard is the need to polarize the world into the good and the evil. We distort our image of ourselves because we cannot confront our own evil. We distort the image of those on the other side of the boundary because the evil we have denied in ourselves we are compelled to discover in someone else.

When the polarization between good and evil becomes extreme, the world is rent by an unbridgeable chasm, as if between two wholly opposite kinds of beings. In the medieval world, a Christian could write that "since it is most certain and undeniable that the happiness of the blessed shall continue forever without mixture of misery, so likewise shall the unhappiness of the damned continue forever without mixture of comfort."[16] The world is cloven into extremes, each justifying wholly opposite treatment. And as the principles of electromagnetism dictate that one pole of a magnet cannot come into being without its opposite, so is there a psychological principle that requires that there be a pole of evil to contrast with the pole of goodness. The deification of the Nazi leader, says Henry Dicks, is the other side of the coin of the dehumanization of the scapegoat.[17] One human being—the representative of "us"—is turned into a god to be worshiped, while the other—the hated "them"—is regarded as "vermin" to be exterminated. The mentality of the totalitarian, Edward Shils observed, whether Nazi or Bolshevik, includes this tendency to make "all or none" judgments of people in

---

*Issues surrounding nuclear war, nuclear deterrence, and nuclear doctrine are enormously complex, and in discussing this issue my point is not to dismiss any particular nuclear doctrine as self-evidently wrongheaded or monstrous. What I am trying to show, rather, is the way the double standard distorts our perception of ourselves and our adversaries, and how this distortion helps feed the preparations for war.

terms such as "capitalist hyena" or "red scum."[18] The world is at war between these poles of good and evil, and the totalitarian cannot envision the possibility of harmony except through the complete triumph of his own group.[19]*

Of course, not all of us are so extreme in our tendencies to polarize the world. But it would be a great, if somewhat ludicrous, error for us to allow ourselves to divide the world into two groups: into "them," the dangerous people who are polarizers (the totalitarians, the zealots, the paranoids), and "us," who refrain from such distortions. The tendency to polarize seems more universal than that. We good people like to contrast ourselves with the evildoers of the world.

In his book, *The Myth of the Good and Bad Nations*, Rene Wormser expressed his concern about the widespread tendency, in the wake of World War II, to demonize the German nation. To those who had for decades condemned the Germans for their imperialism, Wormser grants that the Germans were imperialists. But, he adds, "there were no innocents in Europe."[21] He reviews the history that shows that among the nations there has been plenty of evil to go around. The method of scapegoating is to focus all evil on a single object, and then to drive it off or destroy it. But Wormser combines his view of the universality of guilt with an understanding that to be tainted with evil does not warrant being condemned utterly. "Are the English people inherently wicked because they first used the concentration camp in the Boer War, where about ten per cent of the confined civilians died in the camps? Or because they massacred great numbers of East Indians, executing some by shooting them from cannon mouth? Or the French because of the terror and excess of the French Revolution?"[22] No, is his answer. "To believe that a whole nation is wicked is in itself wicked."[23]

It is precisely this act of utter condemnation that affords such relief to the polarizer. If all evil lodges in one place, that place can be damned or destroyed, leaving us in our unsullied purity. The land can be made *"Judenrein,"* clean of Jews. Scapegoating is a process of cleansing. Some in the United States take barely concealed moral pleasure in the crimes of the Soviet Union. When the Soviets destroyed the KAL airliner 007, it seemed as if to some among us the evil of their deed validated our

---

*In the words of an Iranian pamphlet of the early 1980s, entitled *The Great Satan*, "(T)he slogan 'Death to America' clearly defines the difference between good and evil in all areas."[20]

righteousness. If they are evil, we must be good. One pole implies the other.*

We see again the workings of psychic—and national—housecleaning.

Hypocrisy and the Warlike Morality

Because of this housecleaning, injustice is as blind as justice—just in a very different way. The problem is not that we ignore the beam in our own eye. We see it, but blindly insist on discovering it in the face of the other.

In his book *People of the Lie: The Hope for Healing Human Evil*, Scott Peck tells of the day

> when my wife was awarded her citizenship along with two hundred other new citizens at a celebration attended by their families and assorted dignitaries and officials in downtown Honolulu. The festivities began with a parade. Three companies of spit-polished soldiers with rifles gleaming marched around the field and then took their formation behind seven howitzers. The cannon were then used to offer a roaring twenty-one-gun salute to the occasion. At this point the governor of Hawaii stepped to the podium, just in front of the still-smoking howitzers. "Today is referred to as May Day," he began, "but our nation has designated it Law Day. Here in Hawaii," he quipped, "we might call it Lei Day. Anyway, the point is that here we are celebrating this day with flowers, while in the communist countries they are having *military* demonstrations." (p. 131.)

The Sincerity Principle would tell us that blindness, not true insincerity, is at work here. We see the flowers we display, but are blind to the smoke of our howitzers.

The blindness of our hypocrisy derives from our turning away from the war that rages within us, the war between the demands of our culture and the needs of our nature. When one always "acts according to precepts which are not the expression of his instinctual inclinations,"

---

*The same comforting polarization of good and evil is to be found also among the members of the peace movement. The more evil is located in the Pentagon, the more we are confirmed in our goodness. "They" are warmongers who want to blow up the planet, while "we" are lovers of peace. A close familiarity with the inner workings of peace organizations, however, suggests that the irrational passions of war—however denied—are at work there too.

Freud said, hypocrisy is the inevitable result.[24] So abundantly does this deep-seated internal war produce such blindness, says Freud, "One might venture to say that our contemporary civilization is built up on such hypocrisy."[25]

It was the civilization of Victorian Europe whose foundation Freud saw as resting upon hypocrisy. But wherever the demands of culture make intense war upon human nature, the psychic housecleaning of the hypocrite will be rampant. Among the Puritans, says Judith Shklar, a good deal of "unconscious hypocrisy" was the means by which people protected themselves from the fear for their own souls induced by the high standards of their religion.[26] Since one pole requires the other, hypocritical blindness to one's own sin requires external embodiments of evil. In medieval times, such externalization spawned a world of demons to rage in the Christian cosmos. In his book The Pursuit of the Millennium, Norman Cohn describes how, as the moral burden of Christianity grew increasingly intolerable, there was a simultaneous intensification of a sense of demonic forces threatening. Monks and nuns suffered most of all from these evil demons, he says, which were projections of forces tempting one "to irreverence and sacrilege, indiscipline and rebellion."[27] And sometimes, for medieval Christians, these demons would be Jews or other infidels, fit for killing.

And here lies the explanation of the unjust maligning of Mary Midgley's wolves. Midgley herself articulated the key insight:

> When an animal tries to eat you, or even to eat your dinner, you cannot be expected to like it, and only a very occasional Buddhist will cooperate. But why did man feel so morally superior? Could he not see that the wolf's hunting him was exactly the same as his hunting the deer? . . . The reason such parallels are hard to see is, I suggest, that *man has always been unwilling to admit his own ferocity* . . ."[28]

This insight into the hypocritical condemnation of the wolf by us human carnivores fits also the sanctimonious contrast, uttered before the smoking cannon, between *their* militaristic May Day and *our* lovely Lei Day.

That great philosopher of the swamp, Pogo, declared in his most memorable pronouncement: "We have met the enemy, and he is us." But, for the most part, that understanding eludes us still, for the reason that it is too painful to confront the reality of the war within. We would rather don the mask of righteousness, and look outward to the menacing face of the wolf.

This will remain so as long as we are compelled to internalize harsh cultural demands. Some say that the demands of *any* culture necessarily create intense internal conflicts in human beings. An element of paranoia, some suggest, is inherent in the human condition. Perhaps there is validity to these arguments. But surely, because the form that civilization has taken thus far has inescapably been structured by the requirements of the struggle for power, our history does not reveal the limits to the harmony of mind that humankind can achieve. In much of the world throughout history, and into our own times, our civilization has been in the grip of a morality that operates in the irreconcilable terms of war. It is a harsh morality in which the "good" (cultural precepts) demands the unconditional surrender of the "evil" (human nature).*

Thus do the cycles of war and rage feed each other. Our rage is the hidden wound from the war our culture wages against our nature, and that remains implanted to rage within us. And rage in turn is the passion of war. Too frightened to face our own ferocity, we create the mask of the wolf, whose cruelty embodies our secret rage, and whose treachery expresses our own hypocrisy. Stalin sits, drawing faces of wolves, emblematic of the forces by which he feels surrounded.[29] "We are in a dark jungle, surrounded by wolves," says Qaddafi.[30] From the denial of our rage comes the image of the wolf—the enemy against whom we must wage war.

The wolf is the part of our own face we cannot face. This suggests another reason why the dance of war is a dance before the mirror. It is not just that both sides are usually doing the same thing on different sides of the boundary, although using hypocritical double standards to deny their similarity. Also, what each side sees as so evil and menacing on the other side of the boundary is in fact largely a part of itself. Had we but the strength to endure the recognition, we would see that the evil "face of the enemy" is a part of our own countenance.†

---

*Not all the harshness of our socialization comes from specifically moral strictures. Any failure to meet the needs of our organism is likely to be interpreted as reflecting upon the worthiness of those needs. And the rage we derive from the frustration of our needs—due to neglect or hostility even when it does not wear the garb of morality—is likely to augment the harshness of the morality as we internalize it.

†Sometimes our enemy—like a Hitler—is indeed evil, and the dance is not symmetrical on both sides of the boundary. But in view of our overeagerness to cast all our conflicts as the struggle of our good against their evil, it behooves us to be skeptical of all our polarized perceptions. Look how our perception of "Uncle Joe" Stalin reversed from the good guy of the war years, when he was one of "us," to the devil of the Cold War years when we saw him on the other side of that boundary we called the Iron Curtain. This reversal clearly shows distortion, either in the first period or the second or, perhaps, at least some of both. And such distortion should certainly make us suspicious of the way "we," who are always on our side of the boundary, always remain such good guys in our own eyes.

Having been taught by the war waged upon us in the name of morality that the essence of the interaction between opposing elements is the struggle of good against evil, we see our opponent not just as a competitor but as an embodiment of evil. Our fellow carnivore—our lupine competitor—is thus diabolically treacherous in laying his snares. Our making the foe into the devil is imaged in the history of a word: "Satan" means "the adversary" but, as the figure evolved, the adversary became the foul-smelling Evil One. The evil of our foes serves to confirm the goodness of ourselves.

In a complex world, we will always have adversaries, for reason tells us that interests will conflict. But in the grip of unreason, we transform our adversaries into evil enemies. Thus does the warlike morality make the world still more dangerous than it must inevitably be. Unable to reconcile the elements within us, we turn outward to enact our drama of strife. Our injured warrior spirit spurred to excess, we wage our holy wars.

Thus again we see that our glorious image of ourselves—mighty and righteous—derives not from our strength but from our weakness. Too weak to confront the reality of our condition, we use the world to enact a fiction. This fiction is a war story—the story that says that conflict is an external matter, against the evil that lies out there. Waging war against our reality, we stand Pogo on his head: we go out to meet the enemy because he is not "us."

Confusions and Reversals

There is suggestive evidence to support the idea that we demonize our foes to escape from our experience with the war-type morality of our civilization. That evidence lies in the way our image of the evil on the other side of the boundary is beset by reversals and paradoxes and contradictions.

Earlier in part 3, the question was asked: what part of ourselves is thrown over the wall? A twofold answer was given. In the beginning, it is the persecutory introject—representing the antagonistic forces of morality—that is projected. But then, because the forces of persecution remain so entrenched in the world around us, and so much more powerful than ourselves, eventually we identify with our persecutor and project instead our forbidden natural impulses—our sexuality, our dependency, and especially the rage we feel from their frustration. But indeed, our identification with the morality that persecutes us can never be complete, for we never fully renounce our fundamental needs and passions. With our identification divided, so too is the substance of our projections. The result of this unresolved contradiction in ourselves is the pattern of contradiction in the way we demonize our enemies.

We already encountered this paradoxical quality of our projections in the discussion of the pathology of the will, in chapter 8. In the name of order, the abusive parent avenges himself for the injuries that he suffered from the forces of order. The child with the shattered skull is thus simultaneously child and parent—he is the child whom one teaches the necessity of obedience, and he is one's own battering parent who was too powerful for one to attack directly. The righteous cleavage of the world is beset by a paradox, merging tyranny and rebellion. The motives of those inflamed to punish the criminal, says the psychoanalyst Gregory Zilborg, "are the very same ones which lead man to commit a transgression of the law."[31]

The more extreme the polarity, the more contradictory the demonization. At war with themselves, the medieval Christians slaughtered Jews as Christ-killers. But underlying this scapegoating is an unacknowledged hostility to Christianity on the part of these defenders of the faith.[32] The Jew, hated ostensibly for being Christ's killer, also stands as a representative of Christ himself, hated as the source of an oppressive system of moral demands. In the name of the faith, the faith is attacked. Just as, in the name of the fatherland, the Nazis could attack the fathers. And in the United States, those who demonize the communists have represented them in both infantile and parental terms: infantile in that communism represents dependency, in contradistinction to the enforced self-reliance of the American ethic; and parental in that the communists will control and command everything one does.

Another paradox may underlie something we touched upon in an earlier chapter. Recall the observation—made in part 2—that we expect our enemy to be cowed into backing down by threats that, if directed against us, would provoke us toward greater aggressiveness in defense of our honor. Why, we wondered then, do we imagine that our enemy's response will be so different from ours? Why, if the Soviet buildup leads us to escalate the arms race in response, do we expect that our buildup will compel them to submit? Why, if our belief in Soviet strategic superiority is a reason (in the early 1980s) for us not to negotiate—never negotiate from weakness!—do we believe that our achieving superiority will "force them to the bargaining table"? The reason, perhaps, is that we are projecting another contradictory set of attributes onto our enemy: he is at once a creature of unbridled boldness and aggressiveness, and so fearful that he will be intimidated by threats. And again, the contradiction in our image of the enemy reflects our own internal split. We project onto him both our conflicting poles: our power and rage, and our weakness. We expect him to manifest the truth we deny about ourselves: that the outward bravado is but a mask for more fundamental feelings of weakness and fear.

Polarization represents an effort to relieve oneself of an excruciating inner split. But the effort is futile, since the split remains, with the two sides inextricably locked together in their deadly embrace. So enmeshed are they that even the process of projection sends both elements out. But just as the reality of the internal war is denied, so does the projector make himself blind to the contradiction in the demonized image. *"Opposites never contradict,"* is one of the rules propounded by Lloyd deMause for what he calls "Historical Group Fantasies."[33] And the reason for this, I suggest, is that at the root of these generally paranoid fantasies is the denial of contradiction.

Here we may see also the psychological reason for the fact, often noted, that extremists of both right and left tend to be similar, as if the political spectrum were not a straight line but a curve bending back toward itself. The reason may be that the political extremist himself embodies an intense polarization. Ernest Renan, the French historian, observed that "there seems to be a thin line between violent, extreme nationalism and treason."[34] About which Eric Hoffer says that "the opposite of the chauvinist is not the traitor but the reasonable citizen."[35] In the name of order, rebellion; or in the name of rebellion against tyranny, a new tyranny. In the name of preservation, radical destruction. In the name of justice, brute injustice.* Contradictions that do not

---

*This helps to answer that question, so compelling in the United States during the summer of 1987: how is it that Lt. Col. Oliver North—a man besieged by the forces of law for his role in a major illegal conspiracy—could emerge a national hero? He accomplished this in the country devoted to "a government of laws, not of men," a nation that has enshrined law (in the form of the Constitution) as the sovereign power in its political system. The answer is that the hidden side of the American relationship to the law is a hatred for the structures that bind us. The hero is the man who sets us free. Sometimes he is the one who frees us to express our forbidden impulses. Oliver North presented an irresistible package for those who both deify and hate the law. Piety on the outside and rebellion at the core. Only an Ollie North—impeccable in his uniform with its medals—can throw out the rulebook for us. In the name of defending civilization, Col. North frees us to answer the call of the wild. In this paradoxical reversal of piety and rebellion, Ollie was like Dirty Harry, the movie cop hero of the 1970s who brought criminals to justice by running roughshod over the legal system. Ostensibly enforcing the law, Dirty Harry was himself a law-breaker. Ostensibly running a Project Democracy, Ollie North was subverting the principles of our own democratic government.

contradict in the eyes of the extremist with his polarizing approach to human affairs. Hypocrisy that is not truly insincere.

In the name of————. The names are the faces we put on what we do, but they cannot be taken at face value. This was the problem with Arthur Koestler's interpretation of the altruistic patriot, and with Stanley Milgram's assumption of the primacy of obedience. When Milgram declares, "When you think of the long and gloomy history of man, you will find more hideous crimes have been committed in the name of obedience than have ever been committed in the name of rebellion,"[36] he neglects to attend to the fundamentally paradoxical nature of internally polarized creatures.

Polarization is a sign of reality denied. But what is denied does not go away: as we saw in part 1, it is what we run away from that can take possession of us. To the extent we are at war with ourselves and will not face it, we ourselves are the enemy, potentially ready to reverse ourselves and adopt his demonized image. Those who suffer from an inner split, writes the Jungian psychologist Erich von Neumann, actually already "belong to the enemy camp [opposed to] their conscious ideology." This is because "in them the shadow is more dynamically alive than the moral ego of the conscious system."[37] That is why often, at a crucial point, the extremist will "make a complete *volte-face* and go over to the enemy camp."[38]

It is a plunge through the looking glass, to the other side of the mirror—to embodying an opposite image that was already one's own.

Dance of Death

The relationship between enemies is, therefore, an intimate one. The enemy is the means by which we confront a part of ourselves. If the enemy did not exist, we would have to invent him—as indeed we do.

We need our enemy to provide us access to a vital part of our own being. The pious of the Middle Ages, in their words and images, railed against the sins of the flesh and their consequences. Alan Watts says that "the allure of [this] demonographic literature is, to a considerable extent, pornographic."[39] Only through the campaign against the flesh could these people express their attractions to the flesh. Something analogous occurs in that southwestern American subculture that Howard Stein sees as the heartland of American militarism. While this subculture's form of Christianity teaches "the sheer unacceptability of human anger," that same culture exhibits, says Stein, "a public fascination with brutality and perversion."[40] We need those evil wrongdoers "out there" in order to keep in touch with the reality "in here" that has been denied.

Were we clear in our relationship with ourselves, our boundaries would be like a clean window through which we could see the world around us. But to the extent that we deny parts of our own being, that window becomes silvered into a mirror onto which we project a partial image of ourselves.

Even if only one side begins the projective process, the power of the projection tends to bring the other into the dance. Jung writes of the "counterprojections" that are elicited from the object of another's projections, if that object is not conscious of the quality the other is projecting onto him.[41] Projection provides a "hook" to bring the other into an intimate connection. An "unconscious identity is established," says Jung, between him who projects and him who receives the projection. They become " 'one soul' and seem to need each other for their psychic existence and balance, even though in the process they may be destroying each other . . ."[42]

From this, destruction ensues, because what is projected is specifically an *antagonistic* element in the psychic system. The union of which Jung writes is thus a union of warring parts. The mirror, before which each dances, reflects an image of his own antagonistic spirit.

Through the intimate bond of projection, the actors induce one another to confirm their own worst suspicions. The Arabs, refusing to make peace with Israel, reinforce (indeed, they largely created) Israeli militancy. The postwar Soviet Union, regarding the United States as one more deadly rival from the West, helped draw the United States into the dangerous confrontations of the Cold War. In South Africa, the Afrikaners' belief that if they do not crush the will of the blacks the blacks will destroy them, has led the Afrikaners to adopt policies that prevent any middle ground from emerging. The hypotheses of projection are self-confirming: the paranoid makes enemies. * The dance before the mirror is thus a dance of escalation.

---

*With the rise of Mikhail Gorbachev to power in the Soviet Union, it appears that the paranoid pattern that has characterized Soviet leadership has been broken. Whether this change can endure remains to be seen. In the meanwhile, however, this break in the projective pattern has already had a major impact. I believe that Gorbachev's non-paranoid manner of relating to the United States is one major factor in the change toward the end of Ronald Reagan's administration, in the American president's posture toward the Soviet Union. Reagan himself has long been attached to a projective style of

There is another aspect of the projective process that is crucial to understanding its destructiveness. At the heart of the process is *fear*. Not only is the psychic element that is projected antagonistic in nature, it is also powerful. Were it not powerful, it could be confronted directly. Such a confrontation is too frightening precisely because the element that is denied is infused with so much psychic energy that it cannot be successfully subdued. Those who dance before the mirror, therefore, are looking at an image that is not only hostile but fearfully potent.

"In lunatic asylums it is a well-known fact that patients are far more dangerous when suffering from fear than when moved by rage or hatred."[43] Jung's observation helps explain the race toward destruction. One who is afraid requires more to make him feel secure than one who is not. When both sides are beset by excessive fears, mutual security cannot be achieved. Each side feels compelled to achieve superiority simply to feel secure. What each regards as its *defensive* requirements therefore appears extremely threatening to the other. The process thus escalates unceasingly or until, out of terror, we make ourselves bold and strike the first blow—in self-defense.

Now, when the escalation of the nuclear arms race has appeared—at least, perhaps, until recently—to be better entrenched than the stability of nuclear deterrence, an anthropological account of paranoid defenses bears relating. The story is told by Jules Henry, who studied a South American Indian society—the Kaingang—that suffered in the grip of severe paranoid anxiety about aggressive impulses. These anxieties were self-verifying, as their history was replete with cycles of killings. About the murder of one man, Kovi, Henry writes:

> They say that Kumblo, Kuven, and their hunting companion "found out" that Kovi wanted to kill them; but in an atmosphere of distrust and terror, where people do not sleep at night and an almost paranoid fear oppresses the mind, it is not necessary to "find out" anything. When fear swells beyond control, and they can stand it no longer, the Kaingang strike and they often "find out" afterward.[44]

The Kaingang are not the only ones caught in the grip of terror. Thus, convinced that these "monsters" think they can win a nuclear war, we

---

relationship with the "evil empire," but he—unlike some of his right-wing followers—seems to have been able to respond to a change in his adversary with a change in himself of a similar nature. As projection can ensnare, so also the abandonment of projection can release.

ourselves seek the superiority that will allow us to "prevail." Driven by the fears that come with projection, both sides see their provocations as mere reactions, and their threats and aggressions as acts of self-defense.

Out of Weakness

Our projective use of boundaries can bring death. But even if the dance does not escalate to destruction, there are other significant costs to this process of projection. Dying is not the only way of losing life.

Projection leaves us feeling weak and fearful not only because there is something powerful out there menacing us, but because we have weakened ourselves. The power we see in the mirror was, after all, our own. But we have sent it away, leaving ourselves diminished.

Of course, there are payoffs. The externalization of the war brings a kind of relief. That relief is the righteous sense of purity in which we can indulge ourselves. Whatever happens, we are blameless.

Blessed are the blameless, and it would seem that the world is filled with the blessed. It will be recalled that, on the eve of World War I, Kaiser Wilhelm told the Russian czar that if civilization plunged into the abyss then opening before them, the responsibility would not be laid at his door.[45] When the Soviets refused to apologize for the shooting down of the Korean airliner, Charles Krauthammer wrote of "a heart grown so cold that it had lost the capacity for remorse."[46] But the issue is not just coldheartedness, but an unvarying sense of blamelessness. The Soviets' reaction—in all sincerity, one may suppose—was not "What have we done?" but "Look what you made us do!" Someone else was at fault. The United States was at fault. In the modern world, it appears that no one is ever guilty. Public figures in the United States, going on trial, always protest their innocence. Even after conviction, far from displaying remorse, they are the victims of injustice. (Evidently, what Richard Nixon most regrets is that he did not destroy the Watergate tapes, not that he committed the crimes of which they are evidence.) Now the Austrians have elected as their president the unrepentant Kurt Waldheim, displaying their own lack of national repentance for their eager collaboration in some of the worst crimes in history.*

---

*The opposition candidate could not raise as a campaign issue the very clear evidence that Waldheim had consistently lied about his past, because this too was a national practice. In Austria—officially a "victim" rather than partner of Nazi Germany—an overscrupulous respect for honesty in facing the past evidently is not good politics.

We are all blameless. This capacity to maintain purity of conscience despite our committing the most impure of deeds is the benefit that comes with projection. The war was your fault; our shooting innocents out of the sky was forced upon us; what is outrageous is not what we did to the partisans and Jews, but the interference in our affairs by those alien people who intrude their documentary evidence into our election.

But what a cost we pay for this purity. Doubtless there is sincerity in the protestation that "I am an innocent victim." The paranoid is willing to experience himself as a victim, says W. W. Meissner, but not as a victimizer. He feels himself to be beset by alien forces that seek to persecute and destroy him.[47] The projective process, says Anthony Storr, leaves a person feeling that he "possess[es] little or no power and [is] therefore in a weak and helpless position."[48]

The natural power of the human being has become separated from its possessor. It reappears beyond the boundary, and in menacing form. It is the Other that has great power, and usually for evil purposes. For what we deny becomes demonized in the form of what Jung called the shadow. Because of our alienation from ourselves, we become but a shadow of our natural selves.

Projection thus leads to the loss of life: in an objective sense when, on the battlefield, we do battle with the enemy because we can not make peace within ourselves; and in a figurative sense when, by declaring a part of our own vital power to be Other, we banish our own living energy. Out of weakness, we weaken ourselves further.

To Separate and to Destroy

However we may try to banish a part of ourselves to avoid the war within us, we cannot escape the pull to reclaim ourselves. Like Aristophanes' image, presented in Plato's *Symposium,* of the creature divided into halves—for example, male and female—which thereafter are always seeking to cleave to each other, the dyads of projective enemies also cleave to each other. But they make war, not love.

Polarization creates a deadly embrace. A man, says Genesis, shall cleave unto his wife; but the enemies polarized by projection go at each other with a cleaver. "Cleaving" is a two-edged sword, meaning both union and division. The pious makes war upon the pornographer, barely concealing his own pornographic impulse. The believer is obsessed with the infidel, the superpatriot hunts for the traitor. The poles, inseparable and repelling.

Cleaving the world into good and evil is the way of destruction. Boundaries are a natural feature of civilization, emerging as it inevitably did in a fragmented condition. But for those compelled to polarize, boundaries become a vital necessity. In a world not yet emerged from anarchy, the problem of war across boundaries is inevitable. But those who banish a part of themselves would need to draw the boundaries and make the war even if the boundaries were not there.

An emblem of this is Melville's *Moby Dick*. Captain Ahab adopts the way of polarizing: he is "a man driven to confine all evil to the person of the white whale."[49] Having separated off a focus of evil, he is obsessed with the idea of destroying it. With relentless fury, he pursues Moby Dick. The tragedy of Ahab culminates with the white whale, bound to Ahab and his craft by the rope attached to the harpoon Ahab has embedded in the whale's flesh, pulling Ahab and those around him down to their death.

To separate and to destroy. This connection is embedded in the ancient Hebrew language. James Aho describes the Hebraic term *herem*, which derives from the infinitive "to separate." This is the term used by Yahweh in his admonition to the Israelites to "spare not the life of any living thing . . . Thou shalt utterly destroy them." We separate to destroy.

The way to peace, by contrast, is along the path of reunion.

13

THE TRANSCENDENCE OF BOUNDARY

Introduction: Make War or Love

I n two separate places, I have come across a most surprising connection. Two different thinkers about the anthropology of violence have noted a link between *warfare* and *marriage* among social groups. Rene Girrard, discussing a tribe called the Tupinamba, likens "the warfare ritualized into exchange" (the communities take captives from each other for cannibalistic rituals) to "the exchange ritualized into warfare" (the exchange of women for purposes of marriage is accompanied by ritualized violence).[1] Jacob Black-Michaud, in his study of feuding patterns in the Balkans and the Middle East, discerns the same intriguing linkage. Marriage and feud, he says, "are two aspects of precisely the same process. The ambiguities inherent in marital alliance often cause feuds, just as feuds are also frequently the 'cause' of marriages contracted to 'conclude' hostilities."[2]

War and marriage: this connection is doubtless subject to many interpretations. Let me propose that they stand as images of our ambivalent relations with the outside world, and of our correspondingly mixed feelings concerning what to do about boundaries.

War represents the negative side of this ambivalence. The world is a place of danger that evokes the fear and distrust that lead us to erect boundary walls for our preservation. Feud is a means of demarcating group boundaries, as Black-Michaud demonstrates. And since power is a threat to us if it comes from beyond the boundary, we want to bring that power inside—e.g., by the taking of prisoners—and then perhaps all the way inside by cannibalistic incorporation.*

Marriage is a contrasting mode of transacting across the boundary. It is a joining, and thus can serve to conclude the feuding. "Alliance" replaces "defiance." Life substance is joined not through destruction, as in cannibalism, but through procreation.

The groups express their ambivalence about their boundary by alternately fighting and marrying across it. Perhaps the cooperation involved in the conflict ("the tribes have come to an agreement never to agree," says Girrard) and the conflict that accompanies the cooperative marriage exchange are also signs of the fundamental, unresolved ambivalence.

In war and marriage as images of ways of dealing with boundary, the fundamental polarities are displayed. One is the polarity between good and evil. If the world out there is seen as evil, we deal with it as a threat, drawing and defending boundaries for our protection. If the world is seen as good, worthy of loving rather than fearing, then we allow our boundaries to disappear to create a new union. The world as we find it is an inextricable tangle of good and evil, and our boundaries are both an attempted solution to and an embodiment of our predicament. In the crucible of our ambivalence—shall we make love or shall we make war?—a link is forged between our conflicting impulses, with the result that the perceptive anthropologist can sense a connection between war and marriage as images for our relationship with the wider world.

The second polarity is of life and death. Seeing the world as evil, we create and defend boundaries. The wage of this way of division and strife is death. Seeing the world as good, we embrace in union, and the result of the way of union is the creation of new life.

As long as the world is plagued by the evils that make it dangerous, we will need our boundaries. But as long as we continue in the way of division, we will deal out death. The challenge for our species is to heal those evils, to make the world safe for the transcendence of boundary. For this is the way of life.

---

*"[B]y eating the flesh of their victims they assume that, at the same time, they absorbed their courage and their *imunu* ('spiritual power')."[3]

Realism and Neo-realism

To the realist, the idea of a world where humankind has transcended boundaries might seem like a utopian vision of little relevance in the real world. For millennia, the spiritual visionaries have exhorted humankind to love their enemies, but the whirlwinds of hatred have continued to swirl. They have appealed to the brotherhood of man under the fatherhood of God, but in the absence of an activist Father to hold us all in awe, the pattern of fratricide has persisted. And they have given us millennial visions of a world in which the lion can lie down with the lamb. But the lamb who consents to such company will be resurrected only as the flesh of the lion. In the real word, there *is* evil and there *are* enemies. We may pay in lives for the maintenance of our defenses, but without those defenses we might not survive at all. In the world as it is, therefore, the "way of life" entails the defense of boundaries.

Among the "defenses" required, the realist could argue, are psychological distortions like those described in part 3. As long as the world is divided into those who help us survive and those who threaten our survival, the double standard—although unjust—is adaptive. As Jules Henry observed, betraying the friend and helping the enemy are both perilous. The double standard corresponds to the cloven reality of allies and foes. We need strength to survive the genuine threats we face, and our moral blindness gives us strength. How could we bear the anguish of fully recognizing the humanity of those we must destroy to preserve ourselves? Our situation is morally anguished enough without having to plunge into our hearts the knowledge that our enemy is also our brother.

This is the view of the realist, and it is not to be dismissed. It is not, however, to be left unquestioned as if it adequately addressed our realities.

"Realism" almost always calls attention not to all reality but only to certain aspects of it. In the first place, the realist always calls attention to unpleasant realities: "realistic" novels are not about happiness and beauty. That is because when people are "unrealistic," it is almost always in refusing to face unwelcome truths. Beyond that, in the realm of international affairs, the realist is always concerned about unpleasant realities "out there," the threats to our well-being that come from external sources. It is not the realist who concerns himself with the realities underlying the statement: what does it profit a man if he shall gain the whole world and lose his own soul? When the realist notes how the world devours those who are armed only with love, and when the apostle notes how the passions of enmity corrode the human spirit, both are making valid observations of reality.

But there are new realities as well that must alter the ancient debate between those who are concerned with what must be rendered unto Caesar and those concerned with what must be rendered unto God. Our salvation in spiritual terms always required that we transcend the ways of strife and divisiveness. Now, increasingly, our physical survival requires it as well.

To some extent, the controversies about defense are battles of value systems masquerading as debates about the nature of reality. The warriors cling to their a priori disposition to seek security through armed might, and the spiritual sermonizers condemn the wielding of raw power as the means to protect what is held sacred. Both sides, in confronting the dilemmas of the nuclear age, seem ready to distort reality in preaching their versions of realism.

The warriors concoct scenarios of limited and protracted nuclear war that rest on assumptions that scrutiny suggests are anything but realistic. But those of us who are eager for humankind to progress beyond the war system have also been overeager to portray a "reality" supportive of our purposes. Some have declared that our entering the nuclear age has made all war obsolete as an instrument of policy, as if the existence of this technology had eliminated the continuing and very real struggle for power in the intersocietal system. And some condemn as "ineffective" every show or use of force, as if the lessons learned by nations through five millennia of history had suddenly been erased. And then there is the issue of nuclear winter. This scenario, it now seems, was developed by scientists on the basis of suppositions that may have been generated as much by ideological commitment as by scientific reality. The idea of nuclear winter was then eagerly adopted by those already opposed to the way of the warrior.

Reality, it turns out, is too complex to accommodate completely either faction in the debate. The "realists" are right that the world remains an arena in which interests conflict, and in which coercive power remains a major arbiter of how those conflicts are resolved. The world still is divided into "us" and "them." But the "neorealists" are also right. However likely or unlikely it is that any use of nuclear weapons would lead to an all-out exchange, however certain or uncertain it is that such a nuclear holocaust would mean the end of civilization, of the human race, or even of life on earth, one thing is clear: the presence of tens of thousands of nuclear warheads poised for delivery has fundamentally altered the realities of the age-old struggle for power. The magnification of power has itself eroded the utility of power as a guarantor of survival.

Just decades ago, major powers could resolve their conflicts by all-out war. But no more. World War II produced victors, and even the losers could rise again in a relatively short time. If World War III were just as total an effort, what would be left? What would a country look like after a thousand or more warheads larger than Hiroshima's had been detonated on its major targets? What would the planet be like after so much radioactive debris had been loosed into the atmosphere? Even without nuclear winter, the vastly magnified ratio between our exponentially increased destructive abilities and the constant scale of human and biospheric vulnerability has made the search for security truly planetary in a way that it has never been before.

Even while the old reality remains that each sovereign entity must have the power to protect its own national security, the need for "common security" has arisen as a new, transcendent reality. Even as boundary remains an essential fact of life, the evolution of power now compels our species to move toward the transcendence of boundary.

THE EXTINCTION OF DEMONS VERSUS THE EXTINCTION OF HUMANKIND

How do we begin to move in that direction? The thrust of part 3 points the way. What is required is to extricate from the real conflicts of interest across boundaries the distortive processes through which we make demons of those on the other side of the boundary. Satan as adversary one can deal with, but Satan as the foul-smelling focus of all evil means a Manichean world forever at war. With an opponent, one can coexist, but a "bad object" is something that must be destroyed. And, as Franco Fornari has said in explaining some of the psychological burdens of our era, the nuclear age does not allow us to kill the bad object.[4]

There is an image in C. S. Lewis's work that, in its contrast with Moby Dick, illuminates this necessary transformation of the enemy. Whereas to Melville's Captain Ahab the whale is the object of the most bitter and unrelenting hatred, the creatures (the *hrossa*) in *Out of the Silent Planet* regard their dangerous adversary—also a kind of leviathan called the *hnakra*—in an altogether different spirit. The realities of existence pit the two species against each other; but even as they take each other's lives, the spirit of enmity is absent:

> The *hnakra* is our enemy, but he is also our beloved [say the *hrossa*].
> We feel in our hearts his joy as he looks down from the mountain of
> water in the north where he was born; we leap with him when he

jumps the falls . . . We hang images of him in our houses, and the
sign of all the *hrossa* is a *hnakra*. In him the spirit of the valley lives;
and our young play at being *hneraki* as soon as they can splash in
the shallows.[5]

Ahab's relationship with his demonized whale must result in the extinction of one of them. But for humankind, it is necessary now to extinguish the spirit of Ahab or it will extinguish us. Our foe must become,
even while being a foe, also in our eyes a beloved expression of the same
life force that is in us. When our fellow human beings are no longer
demons, we will be able to move forward to transform those objective
circumstances that set us against one another. When the demonic spirit
of enmity ceases to haunt the boundaries between us, we will be able to
work toward an order in the world where boundaries are effaced.

But the thrust of part 3 also is that the heart of the problem lies
closer to home. The evil face of the enemy is an externalization of the
viciousness of the enmity that rages inside us. In order, therefore, to
reduce our conflicts in the outside world to what is realistically required,
we have to confront successfully the internal conflict that unleashes our
demonic energy. In order to move toward the transcendence of those
boundaries that fragment humankind, we must bridge the gulf that
cleaves the human psyche.

Embracing the Beast

To create a harmonious order on this planet would be to align ourselves
with the way of life. But we will be incapable of this as long as we
cannot embrace the living energy within us. The human animal, trapped
in the zoo of civilization as we have known it, is taught to renounce the
flesh-and-blood reality of his nature.

We become what Nietzsche called the "sick animal," disgusted with
himself. The very stuff of our being is rejected as evil. Alan Watts
observes that evil is associated "with slime, excrement, mud, worms,
and everything that might be described as 'goo.' "[6] Goodness, by contrast, is attributed to the realm of spirit, the structure of things abstracted from their dirty embodiments. In other words, the physical
animal body that has emerged from nature is evil, while the abstract
mental part of us on which civilization inscribes its commandments is good.
Child-rearing practices convey this message—e.g., those of the "intrusive" parents (the Puritans and others described by deMause) that teach

their children that their insides are bad by "using enemas to clean out the bad stuff . . ."[7]

But our animal being is inextricable from the life force within us, and to wage war upon that is to make war against life. There are some signs that some realignment of our allegiance is taking place in the modern consciousness. One sign of this from popular culture is the *Star Wars* Saga, in which the "Death Star" of the Empire is completely antiseptic, with hard, polished surfaces, cleansed of all goo; the Jedi, on the other hand, those who are serving the Force and struggling to preserve life, live in earthy environments, and are garbed not in shiny hard plastics but in homespun cloth. Perhaps our consciousness has grown readier to grasp that our survival requires us to nurture our animal being, not shunt it off as evil or disgusting. Lewis Mumford tells a story in his book *In the Name of Sanity* that seems a fitting image here:

> In a hospital I know of, a bright, efficient, immaculate place, visitors used to see a slovenly old woman, who wore no uniform, shuffling along the corridors, crooning tenderly with a baby in her arms. When questioned about her, the doctors would explain that, when one of their infants was seriously ill, and seemed to do poorly under normal nursing practices, they had learned to turn the little patient over to this old crone, and she would, often, by the magic of her body and her love, bring the child back to life.[8]

So too, if our species is to turn back from the abyss of extinction to which our raging spirit of enmity has brought us, we will have to open ourselves to the ancient body of our living energy, which alone can nurture us.

We must make peace with the animal, with our natural energy, if we are to make peace with one another. Another image is germane here, an image of the birth of the Peacemaker of Christianity as interpreted by the ethologist Lionel Tiger. It is significant, says Tiger, that the infant Christ is depicted "as lying in a manger of straw in a stable, like any other newborn mammal." This symbolism is not accidental, he says, and it accounts in part for the story's power. "The general distaste humans exhibit toward the animal-like aspects of their being is in this case entirely disarmed by the central fact of the account: that Jesus is, although an infant and an animal, the incarnation of God . . ."[9] At the birth of this creature, at once newborn mammal and embodiment of God, the angels sing of peace on earth and goodwill toward men.

Without such reconciliation, without this recognition of the indissoluble link between the natural and the sacred, the beast becomes demonized. It is a central insight of Jungian psychology that denial makes more sinister what is denied, and conversely that acknowledgment can transform the apparently sinister into something much finer, as the kiss of the princess in the fairy tale enabled the frog to become again a prince. In one striking dream, related by the Jungian Marie-Louise von Franz, when the dreamer gives appreciation to some criminal intruders, they are transformed into noble artists: "if the dreamer recognizes [the intruders'] gifts (which are her own) they will give up their evil intentions."[10] Likewise, how we treat the animal within us determines whether it will act as a force for good or for evil.

The animal in the wild is not the "wild animal" of our imaginations, the vicious force running amok, snarling and tearing flesh. It is the cage that drives the animal "wild," and when he breaks free he is dangerous indeed. As the storm of World War II was gathering, Jung wrote of "the 'blond beast' [to] be heard prowling around in his underground prison, ready at any moment to burst out with devastating consequences." This menacing blond beast was the fruit of centuries of repression in which "Christianity split the Germanic barbarian into an upper half and a lower half,"[11] and confined the lower half to that underground prison. It is this splitting, this denial, this cage that breeds the sinister passions of irrational destruction.

If we cannot embrace the beast, our animal being will be rendered demonic to haunt us, as sinister wolf or evil whale, as Jewish vermin or as imperialistic running dogs.

Sin Unacknowledged

The "central defect of evil," says Scott Peck, "is not the sin but the refusal to acknowledge it."[12] What we cannot face will catch us from behind. When we gain the true strength to acknowledge our imperfect moral condition, we are no longer possessed by demons.

Another contrast with Moby Dick. As Ahab's quest of the white whale is an emblem of the way of war, Joseph Conrad's tale of "The Secret Sharer" provides an emblem of the way of peace. This too is a story about a ship's captain, and how he deals with his own dark side.

Esther Harding, another Jungian psychologist, interprets Conrad's tale as a discourse on the shadow. The "secret sharer" in the story is a naked stranger who climbs aboard the ship while the captain is on watch. The stranger is an officer from another ship who has killed one of his men for shirking his duty. While the captain hides the stranger away, an aura of unease and danger lurks over the becalmed ship. At a crucial point, the captain himself comes close to committing a violent act like that of his secret companion. When he recognizes that he, too, could commit murder, Harding says, the tension is relieved. "Then and only then the shadow man slipped back into the ocean from which he had so mysteriously come, and we are given to understand that the strange tension that had hung over the whole ship and her untried captain dissolved, and they sailed home with a fair breeze."[13]

As long as we maintain that all the evil is out there, our ship, like Ahab's, is on the course of destruction. When we acknowledge that the capacity for evil lives within us as well, we can make peace with our shadow, and our ship can sail safely.

Of course, there *is* evil out there. We do have enemies, and they do threaten us. But just as war is cycled between levels of the human system, so can peace begin anywhere in the cycle. Change the chicken or the egg, and the bird can begin to evolve into a new species. Just as inescapable trauma in a fragmented world system has made us crazy, so can any movement in us toward sanity help us create a more whole world order. Overcoming the cleavage in the human spirit is one important step toward the transcendence of the boundaries that divide our endangered planet.

There is a Hasidic story.

> The son of a Rabbi went to worship on the Sabbath in a nearby town. On his return, his family asked, "Well, did they do anything different from what we do here?" "Yes, of course," said the son. "Then what was the lesson?" "Love thy enemy as thyself." "So, it's the same as we say. And how is it you learned something else?" "They taught me to love the enemy within myself."[14]

None Too Good

Loving the enemy within ourselves does not eliminate the enemy out there, but it can change our relationship with him. When evil ceases to be demonized, we are forced to deal with it in human terms. This is at once a potentially painful spiritual task and an opportunity for spiritual peace. This is the way it always is with humility.

The heart of darkness is our own heart. There is a comfort in demonizing the most monstrous and destructive among us, as if their being a different *kind* of creature made their example irrelevant to ourselves. Thus a German has written that all efforts to understand the character of the Nazi, Himmler, must fail "because they entail the understanding of a madman in terms of human experience."[15] A wiser voice is that of a German journalist, who reminds his countrymen, "We knew that [Hitler was one of us] from the beginning. We should not forget it now."[16] He was also one of *us*, a human being. In the dance before the mirror, we find a false inner peace by demonizing the enemy. But recognizing even a truly demonic enemy as made of the same stuff as we is part of the true path toward peace.

Our inner split makes us attached to the war of good against evil. But if we hold that the warring mode is itself the evil, then we are challenged to find a new moral dynamic that embodies the peace for which we strive. To the extent that morality takes the form of war, we will be compelled to choose sides, identifying with one part of ourselves and repudiating another. By this warlike path, we raise ourselves above ourselves, perched precariously above a void.

In our world, the "peacemakers" too often share with the war-makers this fundamental paradigm of morality. In the peace movement, the warriors are demonized into lovers of the bomb, while "we" are the good people who want peace: as if the warriors were not *also* protecting us against very real dangers, and as if we "peace lovers" did not *also* have our own need to assert our superiority over the "enemies" we have chosen. The mode of war continues to hold sway even under the banner of peace.

In *Gandhi's Truth*, Erik Erikson helps illuminate some of the moral pitfalls that lie on the path toward the making of peace. Gandhi is, of course, a hero of the ideological movement in our century to transcend the system of violence—and appropriately so. Gandhi clearly deserves the admiration he receives, and Erikson's book is itself a tribute: Gandhi in his loincloth embodying a simplicity of spirit; Gandhi teaching us not to demonize our adversaries but to appeal to their better selves; Gandhi showing how to stop the escalating cycle of violence by a courageous willingness to absorb the blow without returning it.

But there is a problematic side to Gandhi, one that Erikson addresses in an open letter to the Mahatma. This dark dimension stems from Gandhi's overzealous striving for moral perfection. Erikson sees in Gandhi's relationship with himself a kind of violence. Also, from the dynamic of that effort to triumph over himself in the mode of war, there grew tyrannical and exploitive relations between Gandhi and the people who were closest and most vulnerable to him.[17]* In Gandhi's very

---

*It is interesting that something similar is to be found in the life of Leo Tolstoy. In the later years of his life, just as Tolstoy was exhorting the world toward the perfection of Christian love and peace, he was apparently ruling over his wife and his household with a rather cruel tyranny.

striving for sainthood, Erikson discerns the toils that bind us to the cycle of violence.

The way of nonviolence (*Satyagraha*), says Erikson to Gandhi in his open letter, "will have little chance to find its universal relevance unless we learn to apply it also to whatever feels 'evil' in ourselves and makes us afraid of instinctual satisfactions without which man would not only wither as a sensual being but would also become a doubly destructive creature."[18] Figuring prominently in Erikson's argument here is Gandhi's war with his own sexuality, a war in which projection played a role and in which, partly in consequence, other people were injured. One is reminded here of George Orwell's reservations about the example of Gandhi: "No doubt alcohol, tobacco and so forth are things that a saint must avoid, but sainthood is also a thing that human beings must avoid."[19] Sainthood involves that overidentification with the "good" part, as irreconcilably opposed to the bad part. It connects with the warring mode: "Much of that excess of violence which distinguishes man from animals," Erikson goes on to say of Gandhi, "is created in him by those child-training methods which set one part of him against another."[20]

Perhaps there is another mode. Goodness can be conceived as health. The linguistic root of "health" connects with "whole." Evil is then sickness—to be cured, made whole, rather than destroyed in the way of the war-maker. Through making ourselves whole we find the way toward the goodness of peace, the fitting together of shalom. And at the core of that is coming to peace with our being the imperfect, sinful creatures that we are. Erich von Neumann speaks of the "moral courage not to want to be either worse *or better* than [one] actually is."[21] This, he says, is a major part of the therapeutic aim of depth psychology. And similarly, Erikson writes to Gandhi that to the Mahatma's path of *Satyagraha* should be added the therapeutic encounter with oneself, as taught by the psychoanalytic method. The two are kindred, Erikson says, because the latter teaches how to "confront the inner enemy nonviolently . . ."[22] The mode of war, which divides, is here supplanted by the mode of reconciliation, which makes whole.

Goodness will reign in the world not when it triumphs over evil, but when our love of goodness ceases to express itself in terms of the triumph over evil. Peace, if it comes, will not be made by people who have rendered themselves into saints, but by people who have humbly accepted their condition as sinners. It was in fact a saint—Saint Theresa of Lisieux—who expressed what it takes to allow the spirit of peace to reside in our hearts. "If you are willing to serenely bear the trial of being displeasing to yourself, then you will be for Jesus a pleasant place of shelter."[23]

Fruits of the Embrace

The U.S. Army advertises for recruits, using the slogan: "Be all that you can be!" It is a message of aspiration toward achieving an ideal, and such aspiration has a legitimate place in human life. But the way of peace we are discussing here calls for us to aspire to another ideal. Its slogan could be put, "Be all that you are!"

Embracing the whole of our being strengthens peace in a number of ways, not only in freeing us from the need for projection. Let us look at the fruits of this embrace.

Cut off from our own deep feelings, we are readier tools for others to use for whatever purpose. We have discussed the limits to Stanley Milgram's explanation simply in terms of "obedience" of those who willingly follow orders to do evil. But to the extent that it *is* blind obedience, and not unconscious impulse, that makes the willing Auschwitz attendant, such amoral readiness to obey is partly the fruit of the failure to embrace one's whole self. As Alice Miller articulates it, "Blood does not flow in artificial limbs; they are for sale and can serve many masters."[24] The deadness that Henry Dicks reported in the imagery of SS men (cited earlier in this book) is evidence of such "artificial limbs." Without access to the living energies of the core to serve as a compass, these men could be pointed in any direction, however inhuman, by the power system around them. It is different, however, with those who have so integrated themselves that what is at the core emerges freely into consciousness.

> [T]hose who have spontaneous feelings can only be themselves. They have no other choice if they want to remain true to themselves. Rejection, ostracism, loss of love, and name calling will not fail to affect them; they will suffer as a result and dread them, but once they have found their authentic self they will not want to lose it. And when they sense that something is being demanded of them to which their whole being says no, they cannot do it. They simply cannot.[25]

Bringing together all that we are thus provides a brake against the purposes of mechanical destructiveness in which our power systems may seek to enlist us. As my brother, Edward Schmookler, has written, nuclear winter begins with the coldness inside us.[26]

The embrace of our whole selves has other fruits as well.

Integrating ourselves is an essential step in bringing about the harmonious integration of humankind. The larger the gap in a person's relationship with himself, the shakier the foundation on which he can build solid bridges to other people.

The basis of human bonds is trust, and we can build trust with others only to the extent that we confront the truth in relation to ourselves. Once again Joseph Stalin can serve as a negative example. Throughout his life, writes Robert C. Tucker, Stalin "was in the position of attempting . . . to be something that he was not, yet of never being able to face this fact."[27] As a consequence of his own pretense, Stalin was "prone to perceive pretense all around him . . . Stalin's mental world was full of enemies wearing masks."[28] Just as the unresolved internal war creates enemies for wars outside, so also the pretense toward oneself places masks over the faces of others.

In addition to trust, another foundation for the bridges between people is compassion, the ability to identify emotionally with the experience of others. This ability to place oneself sympathetically in another's shoes is, after all, the psychological prerequisite of the Golden Rule: do unto others as you would have them do unto you. But, as Edward Schmookler says, we cannot have compassion ("feeling with") others, if we kill off feeling within ourselves.[29] The capacity to embrace our own true emotions is conversely a prerequisite of our being able truly to allow others into our hearts.

As long as we persist in banishing a part of ourselves, humankind will be exiled to a state of fragmentation. Only when we have the courage to be all that we are do we contact the brotherhood of our species. The "living relationship with the shadow," writes von Neumann, "brings home to the ego its solidarity with the whole human species . . . since it discovers within itself a host of prehistoric psychic structures in the form of drives, instincts, primeval images, symbols, archetypal ideas and primitive behavior patterns."[30] Overidentification with the ideal imposed upon us by our cultures not only engenders our need for boundaries, reflecting our own divided condition, but it also separates us from our essential being in which we discover our bonds with all humanity.

O'Connor's "Revelation"

A superb literary work by Flannery O'Connor provides us with a final image of the struggle over boundaries, and of the fruits of the embrace that overcomes the internal boundaries in which we invest.

In her story "Revelation," O'Connor depicts Mrs. Turpin, a white southern woman. The divisions of people into groups that are better or worse is vitally important to Mrs. Turpin. "Sometimes Mrs. Turpin occupied herself at night naming the classes of people."[31] At least on the surface, Mrs. Turpin is immensely satisfied with herself, and is pleased to place herself in a high-quality class of people. Jesus "had not made her a nigger or white-trash or ugly! . . . 'Jesus, thank you!' she said."[32]

But this apparently confident sense of her own goodness is precarious. During the course of the story, this precariousness becomes manifest. Most of the story takes place in a doctor's waiting room, where Mrs. Turpin interacts with other people, good-naturedly finding continual confirmation of her own moral superiority over the mass of humanity. One of the waiting patients, however, emerges as a threat to Mrs. Turpin's complacent feeling of superiority. She is a surly college student who, reading a book and saying nothing, glares hostilely at Mrs. Turpin as the conversation between Mrs. Turpin and the others unfolds. At the very apex of Mrs. Turpin's self-congratulation, the girl brings her low. Just as Mrs. Turpin is declaring to everyone how glad she is to be just as she is, the girl in fury hurls her book at Mrs. Turpin and then follows the book herself to clamp her fingers around Mrs. Turpin's throat.

That this girl's hostility represents a voice from Mrs. Turpin's unconscious is suggested in two ways. First, O'Connor writes that, although Mrs. Turpin had never seen the girl before this encounter in the waiting room, "there was no doubt in [Mrs. Turpin's] mind that the girl knew her, knew her in some intense and personal way, beyond time and place and condition."[33] And second, the girl is silent throughout the buildup of tension, like some repressed message from the unconscious. She has only one line in the whole story, delivered immediately after the assault, when Mrs. Turpin asks a question directly of her. " 'What you got to say to me?' [Mrs. Turpin] asked hoarsely and held her breath, waiting as for a revelation. The girl raised her head. Her gaze locked with Mrs. Turpin's. 'Go back to hell where you came from, you old wart hog,' she whispered."[34]

This revelation from the unconscious throws Mrs. Turpin's entire world into upheaval. Her world has long been polarized into the good, who are blessed by Jesus, and the not-good, who belong below. And she has always placed herself on the favorable side of the boundary. Now there are two images of herself contending, and she cannot see how they are to be reconciled. "How am I a hog and me both?" she calls out to God. "How am I saved and from hell too?"[35] The Jungian cleavage between conscious feelings of superiority and unconscious feelings of inferiority has come to consciousness, jeopardizing the neat polarization of the world that Mrs. Turpin has striven to maintain. "Call me a hog again," she challenges God. "Put that bottom rail on top. There'll still be a top and a bottom!"[36]

In one last effort to preserve her position on top, her righteous megalomania—threatened as never before—overreaches as never before.

> A final surge of fury shook her and she roared [to God], "Who do you think you are?"
>
> The color of everything, field and crimson sky, burned for a moment with transparent intensity. The question carried over the pasture and across the highway and the cotton field and returned to her clearly like an answer from beyond the wood. (p. 146)

Her question returns to her as a final revelation—who does she think she is!—and by the force of it her cloven inner world is finally healed. At last she sees herself for what she is, sinful and saved, righteous and unclean, all together.

With this new, whole relationship with herself comes a new vision of humankind, freed of the cleavage of boundaries.

> A visionary light settled in her eyes. She saw the streak [in the sky] as a vast swinging bridge extending upward from the earth through a field of living fire. Upon it a vast horde of souls were rumbling toward heaven. There were whole companies of white trash, clean for the first time in their lives, and bands of black niggers in white robes, and battalions of freaks and lunatics shouting and clapping and leaping like frogs. And bringing up the end of the procession was a tribe of people whom she recognized at once as those, like herself and [her husband] Claud, who had always had a little of everything and the God-given wit to use it right. She leaned forward to observe them closer. They were marching behind the others with great dignity, accountable as they always had been for good order and common sense and respectable behavior. They alone were on key. Yet she could see by their shocked and altered faces that even their virtues were being burned away. (p. 146)

This vision provides a clear contrast with another vision of Mrs. Turpin's early in the story. And the contrast between these visions reveals what is at stake for humankind on the issue of boundaries. Near the beginning of the story, we see the fruits of a world where divisions among people are all-important. The passage on Mrs. Turpin's night-time reveries on the classes of people concludes thus: "Usually by the time she had fallen asleep all the classes of people were moiling and roiling in her head, and she would dream they were all crammed together in a boxcar, being ridden off to be put in a gas oven."[37]

The paths are laid out before us. Division is the road to destruction, to Auschwitz, to hell. With the denial of the truth about ourselves come arrogance and the fires of hell. With the embrace of the truth come humility and the fire of purification. Wholeness is the path to salvation. The story ends with Mrs. Turpin hearing "the voices of the souls climbing upward into the starry field and shouting hallelujah."[38]

The Knitting Together of Shalom

The matter of war and peace is thus bound up with the cleavage or wholeness of human life at every level.

We recall the two meanings of shalom, as "peace" and as "fitting together." From the individual level to that of the globe, the elements of the human system must be fitted together in the harmony of reconciliation if we are to create true peace. We are aided in this task by what appears to be a natural impulse to transcend our boundaries, to achieve oneness with the world around us. Above all else, says Ken Wilbur, "man wants real transcendence . . ."[39]

Unless we achieve transcendence, death triumphs over life. If our boundaries are only around the self, death always wins because our individual selves are made of mortal stuff. The body of our kind, however, has potential immortality. The living stream that pulses through us goes on forever, winning over death.

True, war provides us a "transcendent" experience, and this dissolution of individual boundaries is part of the exhilaration of war. This brings us back to the problem of "phony altruism" with which part 3 began. In his book *All Mighty*, Horst-Eberhard Richter describes the transcendent rush that comes from war. He says that people

> are confused by the fact that this feeling of fellowship and solidarity, which they experienced as emotionally liberating, was linked to the vicissitudes of war and all its terrors. Why, they wonder, can't they feel this sense of community in peacetime. If they think about it, they are bound to conclude that the destructiveness, which in wartime is directed exclusively against an external enemy, has in peacetime been incorporated into all aspects of our "normal" social order. Everywhere we encounter boundaries between people; inequities and domination . . . [that] perpetuate the concept of egocentric and imperialistic power.[40]

To escape the trap of death, therefore, it is not enough for us to knit together the macro-selves of imperialistic communities. The transcendence that comes with war remains part of death's dominion, with the pattern of boundary and destruction simply manifested at the larger level. The path of life requires true shalom, a harmonious fitting together—a transcendence of boundary—of all the levels of the human system.

It is the erection of the boundary between self and other, in Wilbur's view, that subverts our achievement of real transcendence and gives death its dominion. "As long as there is boundary, there is *Thanatos*," he writes—*Thanatos* being the Greek word for "death." Just as the fire in O'Connor's "Revelation" can be either the fire of the gas oven and death or the fire of purification and salvation, so does *Thanatos* in Wilbur's view take either of two forms. If we persist in erecting a boundary that "isn't real in the first place," *Thanatos* will take the form of the "death wish," i.e., the search for *"substitute sacrifices."*[41] But if we allow the illusion of boundary to disappear, he says, the work of *Thanatos* becomes transcendence: it is our egotism, our separateness, that dies. In this view, our attachment to our separateness is purely a spiritual error.

But this view is only partially correct. Boundary is not *only* an "illusion." Wilbur speaks of "that prior wholeness which was lost when the boundary between self and other was constructed."[42] An understanding of how civilization emerged from the wholeness of nature, however, shows that it was not from the spiritual realm alone that boundary emerged. In the realistic realm of relations among societies, inevitably budding up as a fragmented system, boundary was an inevitable and objective reality. The spiritual condition that Wilbur condemns is thus not only illusion, but at least partially a reflection of the lamentable result of civilization's emergence as an uncontrolled living growth.

In the world as it is, the urge to transcend the self must of necessity be tempered by the need to defend the self. The image of marriage as a dissolver of boundaries goes together with the image of war as a means of protecting boundaries. The issue of boundaries is also tied up, as we recall, with the division between good and evil: were the world only good, we would have no need of boundaries.

The vision of the mystic reveals the Oneness and goodness of the Being of which we are part. But the world as we find it is neither all One nor all good. Through the cracks of our fragmented civilization, evil gushes in. As long as this remains so, boundary will play a role not only in fostering *Thanatos*, but also in protecting life.

And yet, and yet—the mystic's vision still points toward the most fundamental truth, toward the way of shalom. The evils of our civilized condition are a reflection of the *incompleteness* of our evolutionary process. The force of life is still struggling to find the way to knit together the greater harmony and unity. *Yoga*—literally, "union"—is the way of life. This is true for us at the global and the personal levels. The mystic vision, though inadequate as a map for traveling the world as it is, provides a guide to the world as it must become.

At the intersocietal level, it has been our inescapable fragmentation that has led to the paradox that makes the way of *Thanatos* a requirement for the preservation of life. Because of the lack of integration of the system, what serves the part degrades the whole. Conversely, an actor who devotes himself completely to the brotherhood of the whole species exposes himself to destruction by other actors. The mystic vision of human brotherhood can nonetheless inspire us to transform the intersocietal arena into an integrated system where the good of the parts and of the whole are in better alignment.

As individuals, as we have seen in part 3, we become attached to boundary because of our failure to complete our own integration. The way of war and death gains dominion over us to the extent that we are unable to bring our own personal evolution to fruition. By contrast, the vision of the mystic is gained by virtue of the openness of his own psychic system. Harmony within opens the windows of the soul to seeing how boundary ultimately is transcended.

The mystic says that we should experience the unity of all being. The realist says that there is evil in the world, and that we must resist, not merge with, that evil. Both are right. But, rabbi—as the line goes in the old Jewish story—how can they both be right?

There are different levels of truth. That of the realist is immediate, and can be disregarded only at our peril. But it is contained within the larger truth of the mystic. A core issue here is: does boundary aid or impair the triumph of good over evil? The answer is, both. But which is ultimately the truer answer depends upon one's understanding of the ultimate nature of evil. Our discourse on the war of good against evil thus returns to the need to transform the nature of our civilized morality.

The realist's view is like the perspective of the Manicheans, who saw the cosmos as the arena of unceasing struggle between two principles, one good and one evil. The realist treats evil as an irreducible element of reality: that which threatens us is evil, and since evil can not be transformed into something else, it must be defeated and destroyed.

But there is another way of understanding evil. The parable of the tribes shows the sources of evil in the evolution of civilization. Our systems, newly erupted, have not yet knitted together the harmonious fabric characteristic of other, more fully evolved living systems. Evil is a function of disorder, which is a sign of evolution's work being unfinished. The edifice of our civilization being unfinished, evil can leak in through the cracks.

And at the individual level, part 3 shows that evil in the human psyche comes from a failure to bring together, to reconcile, the pieces of our experience. When we embrace all that we are, even the evil, the evil in us is transformed. The way of shalom heals, removing evil from the world.

Evil is not an irreducible element. Dirt has been defined as matter out of place. The wine in the glass has value; spilled on the shirt it is worth less than nothing. Similarly, evil is a sign that some part of being still remains to be fitted into its right place in the whole.

There is evil in the world, and while it is there we must protect ourselves from it. But our belief that the only way to protect ourselves from evil is to make war upon it is itself a manifestation of the world's evil. Even as we defend ourselves, we must know that it is not the way of war but of shalom that will allow good to triumph over evil. The pieces out of order must be not swept away but brought together, bringing to fuller fruition the process that created us.

When the diverse living energies of the human system are harmonized, the present bloody face of the world will be transformed into an image of the face of God.

PART 4

God's Truth

It says in Genesis that God made man in His own image. But when the human being enters this world, he or she emerges as an unfinished creature. Of all those created for the Garden, we human beings are the ones whose form nature leaves indeterminate. This incompleteness is required for the chief evolutionary adaptation of our species: the capacity for culture. Every human baby comes from nature with the flexibility to allow its image to be completed by some culture. Although biological evolution has prepared it for a Stone Age life, it can learn to take its place in the modern world. It is as ready to learn Chinese as English or Hindi. The growing human being is capable of fitting into a social environment hospitable to human needs or, although not comfortably, to one that is hostile. It is not just God, therefore, who is our creator, but our many and diverse cultures as well. The human being thus presents not a single image, but many.

This diversity is a treasure, but history shows how little we have been able to rejoice in it. It is a treasure because in the many faces of man we can see—more deeply than in any single one of our renderings—the

---

*Of course, it is true that not all of us are equally infected with this pathology. But, once again, I think the inclusive "us" a more helpful way of looking at the problem than to orient the discussion toward the more pathological "them."

richness of the human seed of which we are expressions. But the chronicle of intergroup relations reveals how often we experience this diversity of human expressions as a threat. It is intolerable for us to see our own way of being as but one bloom in the rich bouquet of humanity. *Ours*, we insist, is the image of God. The truth as our culture has represented it is God's Truth. The other renderings of the voice are deviations, more or less unforgivable; their adherents are heretics, infidels, more or less deserving of destruction.

To explore why this is—why we need to regard our own truth as God's Truth—and what we may do about it is the purpose of part 4.

14

IRRECONCILABLE DIFFERENCES

U nless we understand why our differences are the occasion of so much intolerance and destructiveness, we will be unlikely to know where to look for the problem's solution. If, for example, we look at the problem as being only *between* us and not also, and indeed foremost, *within* us, we will look to false solutions.

Eliminating Differences: False Solution #1

"Come to us," said the Crusaders to the Jews, according to a chronicle of the time, "so that we become one single people."[1] The Jew who accepted baptism, who agreed to surrender his differences, could save himself. "On the other hand, it was said that whoever killed a Jew who refused baptism had all his sins forgiven him; and there were those who felt unworthy to start on a crusade at all until they had killed at least one such."[2]

If you are not like us, we will not like you.

There is a German proverb. *"Und willst du nicht mein Bruder sein, so schlag ich dir den Schadel ein."* (If you don't want to be my brother, [my buddy, i.e. from the same stock], I shall smash your skull.)[3]

If you are not kin to us, we will not be kind to you. *Hostis* in Latin meant "both the stranger and, as such, the enemy."[4]

Can we *like* only those who are *like* us? Is "affection" as dependent upon "similarity" as the linguistic connection implies? Does "having

269

differences" necessarily mean to quarrel, as the idiom in English suggests? Can we feel our kinship only with those of our fellow human beings whose ways are akin to our own?

Some think so. And the solution they propose to the problem of the intolerance of diversity reflects this belief. Peace, they say, requires the elimination of differences. The Chinese visionary Youwei proposed at the beginning of this century that racial conflict could be eliminated by having intermarriage on a global scale homogenize humanity into a single race. Others argue that peace will come only when the world's religions have converged upon a single religion for all humankind. These and other variants on this theme we might call here "Peace Through Homogenization."

If peace can be purchased only through the surrender of our human diversity, it will come at a very high price indeed. But before we even advocate or begin to work toward the cure through homogenization, we should examine more closely the evidence that the remedy fits the disease.

If the heart of the problem were simply that the differences among peoples were so great that there is no way the human spirit can peaceably bridge the gap, this might be a plausible solution. But a closer look at intergroup intolerance suggests that it is not necessarily where the gap between groups is greatest that the enmity is most intense. Do you cross yourself with two fingers or three? The difference of but one finger may constitute grounds upon which heads can roll.

Small differences can create great antagonisms. An image from Swift's Gulliver illustrates this. Swift portrayed us human beings as willing to go to to war against those who crack their eggs open at the "wrong" end—i.e., the other end from the one we use. Freud wrote of what he called "the narcissism of minor differences." "It is," he said, "precisely communities with adjoining territories, and related to each other in other ways as well, who are engaged in constant feuds and ridiculing each other—like the Spaniards and Portuguese, the English and Scotch, and so on."[5]

Protestants and Catholics spilled one another's blood far more avidly than they ever did that of Hindus or Confucians.* The Stalinists exterminated the Trotskyites.

From these examples, and from the general phenomenon of the narcissism of minor differences, we can see the futility of homogeniza-

---

*A study of students at the American University in Beirut discovered that Sunni Moslems felt far greater hostility toward Shi'ite Muslims than toward Christian organizations.[6]

tion as a solution. Surely it is vain to think that homogenization could ever make us *completely* alike. And if small differences are sufficient to provoke the furious spirit of intolerance, it is vain to hope that by eliminating differences we will be able to purchase peace.

By exploring this approach, we have uncovered a clue that the problem of intolerance does not lie only in the differences themselves. That what I am is different from what you are is not the only reason we fight. There is also, evidently, something about the way we *both* are that makes us willing to spill blood over our differences.

Increasing Contact: False Solution #2

To many, it is our ignorance that makes us intolerant of one another. If only we *knew* one another better, we would recognize and embrace our common humanity. We would see our differences as trivial compared with our fundamental kinship. The path toward intergroup peace, therefore, lies in increased intergroup contact. For example, many believe that the key to peace is for there to be more extensive contacts between the peoples (and officials) of the United States and the Soviet Union. People-to-people, cultural exchanges will create a bridge between these two immense tribes now threatening each other across half a planet and a chasm of ignorance.

Often, contact between peoples can serve to increase empathy and mutual understanding. But not necessarily. Ignorance is part of the problem, but not all of it. Not even the heart of it.

Consider the following image as a key to the inadequacy of the increased-contact solution to the problem we have with our tribal differences. Konrad Lorenz notes that while the wearing of local peasant costumes has largely disappeared in Central Europe, there are still places where it has been preserved. Those places are not, it should be noted, in the remote recesses where intergroup contact has failed to bring the illumination that melts tribalism. On the contrary. It is, for example, precisely "in those parts of Hungary where Hungarian and Slovak villages are close together [that local peasant costume] has been preserved. Here the costume is worn proudly and with the obvious intention of provoking members of other ethnic groups."[7]

Many are hopeful that the increased knitting together of the world's peoples will lead toward the greater tolerance and understanding and compassion that could provide a basis for peace. As we come to live in a "global village," it is hoped, we will love our neighbors in a way we could not love them as strangers. Growing interdependence will increase cooperation and create a growing ability to identify with one another. But the compression of our many diverse tribes is not an automatic panacea. The increased kinetic activity of cross-cultural contact is as apt to produce conflagration as to function as a melting pot.

Those who have assumed that knitting our tribes together is a sure road to harmony must be sobered by the example of tribalism in Africa. As long as the contacts between tribes were limited and circumscribed, writes Peter Marris, the problem of cultural disparity was confined. But with the end of the colonial regime, the contacts intensified, and with them the anxiety and hostility among groups also increased. Only then, writes Marris, did *tribalism* emerge, which he defines as a "pervasive defensiveness" toward other groups.[8] The massacres of the Ibo tribe, for example, in the Nigerian suppression of the Biafran independence movement, was fueled by a "hysterical defense of tribal integrity."[9] The need to deal extensively with people very different from oneself has provoked intense anxiety, and this anxiety has led to defensiveness and hostility. The African experience reveals a paradox: that the very forces of education and development that can help "promote a national consciousness" can also work in the opposite direction. The very processes that are employed to "disarm" tribal reactions, says Marris, end up reinforcing them.[10]

The past couple of decades have underscored this dilemma on a worldwide scale. Across the globe, there has been an upsurge of fundamentalism as an apparent defensive reaction against the intrusion of alien ways and beliefs. The Iranian revolution is perhaps the most conspicuous case. Khomeini was evidently able to ride to power on a great wave of feeling among some classes of Iranians that the Western influences encouraged by the Shah were from the Great Satan, and were to be extirpated root and branch. Many of us in the United States are gratified when our music and fashions and ideas are introduced into the Soviet Union, thinking that greater understanding and harmony between the nations will follow. But a clearer look shows that it is precisely this "invasion" of foreign elements that provokes the old Russian xenophobia and defensiveness. *

---

*In the United States, the confrontation between traditional culture and modernism has led to similar reaction. The rise to greater political prominence of fundamentalist Christianity has been part of the reaction of groups trying to defend their conservative culture from what they regard as the subversive influences of pluralistic society. It should be added that many Americans—both Christian and Jewish—have recently become more fundamentalist (or orthodox), seeking refuge from the increasing uncertainties of a stressed American society amid the certainties of fundamentalist belief.

All these images—Europeans defiantly wearing their peasant costumes, Africa's burgeoning tribalism, Khomeini's Iran, etc.—serve as clues to the need to look further into the problem of intolerance. We are, it appears, as likely to respond to greater intercultural contact by accentuating our differences as by bridging them. Thus the solution, proposed by those who imagine the problem to be one of simple ignorance, is as apt to exacerbate as to ameliorate our intertribal tensions.

Again the evidence suggests that the problem lies not only in the differences between our cultural identities. Rather, there is something in the way we wear the image of man given us by our culture that leads to our intolerant belligerence.

15

DIABOLICAL IMAGES
OF GOD

Boundaries and More

In part, this problem of intergroup intolerance is another manifestation of the problem we explored in part 3, "Boundaries." Intolerance of neighboring groups can help a group to demarcate the boundaries separating it from the outside world. Earlier, Jacob Black-Michaud proposed that intergroup feuding helps define boundaries; so also with the intolerance toward similar but nonetheless distinct groups.*

In part also, the explanation of intolerance can draw upon the same psychological analysis as was developed in part 3. And a psychological explanation is required, even to underlie the "boundary definition" hypothesis. For the rational needs of society seem inadequate to explain why the demarcation of boundaries would be infused with energy intense enough to lead to excessive hatred and gratuitous killing. Freud's term "the narcissism of minor differences" gives some intimation of a possible link between the psychology of boundaries and that of intolerance.

---

*Writing of the Arab world, Raphael Patai says that the closer two groups are to each other, "the greater the hostility . . . A village will relate to a neighboring village, rather than to a remote one, with the greatest hostility."[1]

Group boundaries are psychically vital because they are infused with narcissistic energy, securing the internal microcosm for approval and directing toward the outside the deep and painful currents of enmity. As we saw, there is something in the spirit of our lives in our civilized cultures that confers vital importance on the boundary between inside and outside. It is that the antagonism between cultural demand and natural need establishes a dangerous paradigm. According to this paradigm, the encounter of different elements is experienced as a clash between good and evil. And because we are unable to live peaceably with our own good and evil, we use boundary to polarize reality.

But the insights about boundary, while relevant, are not sufficient to illuminate the problem of God's Truth. For "Boundaries" is about our *need to create differences* with the other; while "God's Truth" is also about our *inability to tolerate differences* that are actually there.

The creation of differences is one way of characterizing the "housecleaning" we do with projection, the double standard, polarization, etc. To assume the righteous posture we need, we *require* that the other side be very different from our side. So, in addition to using projection to produce differences, we may magnify differences with peasant costumes or other expressions of tribalism.

But even as we may need to differentiate ourselves from "Them," so also does it seem clear that we find very threatening the fact that others *are* different from us. It is all very disturbing—that you don't believe what we believe about what's right and wrong; that you do not worship our God Almighty; that you look so different from us. These differences may help define the targets for projection. But projection, and the psychological processes connected with it, are not sufficient to explain the fear and hostility that often fill people when they encounter people whose ways are alien to them. To understand this, we need to look further into the discomfort that accompanies our own cultural identities.

Precarious Masks

What we defend most zealously, I suggested at the beginning of this work, are those beliefs about ourselves that we inwardly sense to be false. Our intolerance, too, is a manifestation of this kind of zeal. For the certainty with which we profess that *our* way is *the* way is a defense against our own more fundamental doubt and confusion.

Our cultural image of man sits precariously upon our faces like an ill-fitting mask. As with the problem of "Boundaries," our anxiety about the precarious mask is greater the more what is required of us conflicts with what by nature we truly are. It is what we hold least securely that we grasp most tightly. Thus, the harder it is for us to embody the cultural identity we are given, the more adamantly and rigidly we must cling to every contour of its features. *

The most zealous defender of the faith, it has often been observed, is the convert. The zeal of the convert, and his hostility to deviation, as Harold Lasswell suggests, derives from the fact that conversion experiences represent a resolution of a powerful *internal* conflict within the personality.[3] But to the extent that our belief systems are antagonistic to our inherent nature as human beings, every true believer is inevitably a convert. We came from the womb firm believers in the validity of our needs. Adopting beliefs hostile to our humanity is indeed a conversion experience. For true believers generally, therefore, their certainties are a face worn over smoldering conflict, and their fanaticism represents the zeal of the convert. That is why it is precisely those belief systems that are harshest whose adherents are most likely to be zealous or intolerant.

The more our cultural identity is organically integrated with our whole being, the less desperately we need to defend it. Our true face will not fall off, and other different faces pose no threat to us. It is the image that is not our own—the mask—that must be bolstered with the compensatorily inflated claim that it is the one true way.

It is to protect the image that will not fit that people feel compelled to destroy those whose faces have a different look. If faces can be allowed to be different, then one's *own* true face might break through. Thus, it is often those whose God-given mission is the saving of souls

---

*This may help to explain why *minor* differences are especially likely to arouse great antagonisms. The zealous defender of the right way is like a man walking a crumbling ledge on a sheer cliff. Any deviation from the straight and narrow path seems to threaten disaster. The smallest deviations are the most threatening because they are the most imaginable and tempting. It is easier to imagine taking a step to the left than leaping to another side of the mountain. It is easier to imagine crossing oneself with a different number of fingers than being a Taoist; a communist might more readily adopt a competing communist doctrine than a worldview of a wholly different nature. Since any movement is perilous for one on a crumbling ledge, the most likely movement is experienced as the most threatening. Perhaps this is why the most intense battles are between neighbors, not only because they share a common boundary but also because *one really might be one of them.*

(The German sociologist Georg Simmel observed that it is where "hostility has arisen on the basis of previous solidarity" that " 'respect for the enemy' is usually absent." And it is between groups whose convictions and beliefs are similar enough "to make confusions and blurred borderlines possible" that "points of difference" are emphasized to a degree "not justified by the issue but only by that danger of confusion.")[2]

who cause the most psychic damage to those they encounter. Thus, it is the bringers of "revolutionary justice" who have perpetrated some of the most unjust atrocities. In Pol Pot's Cambodia of the 1970s, the image of the liberated society was zealously protected from contamination. "If you wore glasses [according to the Khmer Rouge] you could read. If you could read, you were an intellectual. If you were an intellectual, you were an imperialist. If you were an imperialist, you should die."[4] Thus the Khmer Rouge killed everyone who wore glasses. To the true believer, there is only one right image for man, and in Pol Pot's Cambodia, this image did not include eyeglasses.

Differences are threatening because they imply that there is more than one way to be. Such indeterminateness—which we might see as a glory of our humanity—evokes intolerable fear in the one whose own identity is insecurely rooted in his being. Differences, therefore, cannot be tolerated.

Right Belief

In striving to embody the right image for a human being, one follows the design laid down by right belief. Those who see themselves as embodying the image of God hold their truths to be God's Truth.

While belief defines and defends the right way to be, that is not the only essential task that belief performs. Belief systems are the internal means by which we enable ourselves to feel at home in the world. As a suit of armor protects against external danger, so can a system of belief protect against the experience of fear. While much of our fear revolves around our self-image—how do we have to be so that we may feel good about ourselves?—we have many other fears as well. And the greater the fear, the greater the need for certainty.

Under conditions of high stress, social psychologists have found, perception and belief rigidify. "Untested hypotheses are fixated recklessly" under the most stressful conditions. Tolerance for ambiguity is reduced. And aggressive responses are accentuated."[5] Now, for many human beings in the course of history, life itself has imposed chronic conditions of high stress. The result has been that the "untested" (or at least unproven) hypotheses that have inevitably formed the core of our belief systems have been "fixated recklessly." The ambiguity concerning what a human being might be has been experienced as intolerable. And Inquisitors holding unambiguous certainties have aggressively put heretics to the torch. "When ye encounter the unbelievers," says the forty-seventh sura of the Koran, "strike off their heads, until ye have made a great slaughter among them."

The terrors of history, we see again, mold people who will make history more terrible still. Those in the grip of stress will burn with the fire of intolerance that inflames further the stress of intergroup relationships. The chicken's eggs grow into more chickens. *

The more dangerous the world, the greater our need to believe our maps of it to be wholly accurate and reliable. The need for certainty is the child of fear. But our fears, in turn, arise from our ignorance and uncertainty. It is not in the light of day but in the darkness of the dead of night that we meet our terrors. So, our claims to be illuminated with God's Truth are fueled less by the light of knowledge than by our fear of the dark.

Again we see how we don the armor of grandiosity out of weakness. As our assertions of invulnerability are compensations for our sense of weakness, so also is our insistence upon certainty a denial of our true experience of terrifying uncertainty and confusion. Perils both from outside and from inside drive us to our dogmas—perils from an outside world rife with hostile forces beyond our control, and from the precarious sense of identity that comes from internalizing cultural demands that cannot be reconciled with what we really are. †

---

*Some years before Germany helped initiate the decimation of Europe in two bloody world wars, a German (Mueller-Freinfels) said of political debate in his country: "In hardly any other country of the world do political opponents so regard each other as moral scoundrels as in Germany, hardly anywhere else is political opposition so saturated with hatred as among ourselves."[6]

†It is not alone because they challenge precarious and rigid belief systems that intergroup differences evoke fear and confusion. For example, when Peter Marris describes how tribalism is a response to intensified intertribal contact, he cites a different kind of problem with cultural differences. Dealings between people who do not share "the same symbolic code," he writes, create "anxieties of misinterpretation." Thus it is not just that your contrasting worldview calls mine into question that makes me uneasy, but also having to conduct important transactions across a chasm of possible misunderstandings. By creating a diversity of languages among those people building the tower at Babel, the Lord was able to make cooperation among them impossible, and to induce them to flee in all directions till they were scattered across the earth.

At the same time, however, our failure to understand people different from us may not be due solely to the substantive differences in the symbols and meanings by which we communicate. Perhaps the anxieties and rigidities with which we respond to our *sense* of difference put barriers in the channels of communication. Here is an illustration from Takeo Suzuki's book *Japanese and the Japanese.* Suzuki writes of a Belgian priest, Father Grootaers, living in Japan. The priest speaks Japanese fluently—i.e., he can deal with the Japanese in their own symbolic code. Nonetheless, "(W)hen he travels through the countryside, he has great difficulty communicating with people just because he looks

Making God into the Image of Man

It is when we are most stricken with confusion, then, that we most adamantly assert our certainty. As we have seen, it is when we deny our true experience that we are apt to become instruments of evil. Thus it is often when we are most sure that we are acting as the right hand of God that we are most likely to do the work of the devil.

King Ashurbanipal of the Assyrians saw himself as God's agent, and he treated his enemies accordingly. Because they "uttered curses against Asshur my god, and devised evil against me . . . his worshipper," King Ashurbanipal delivered them to the wrath of God. "Their tongues I pulled out." "I cut off their heads, I burned them with fire, a pile of living men and of heads against the city gate I set up, men I impaled on stakes, the city I destroyed and devastated, I turned it into mounds and ruin heaps." "By these things which were done," declared King Ashurbanipal, "I satisfied the hearts of the great gods, my lords."[8]

As those who recognize a different truth threaten our security, destroying the idolators brings a kind of calm to our hearts. This we readily identify as satisfying the heart of the true God. Having declared ourselves to be made in the image of God, the same compensatory arrogance leads us to make God into our own twisted image, full of the fear and wrath of intolerance.

Having deified our own demonic energies, we are loosed to wage our holy wars.

There is but one way. It is ours, and therefore it is God's. All other ways are evil, and therefore must be destroyed. "I am the way," said Jesus, "the truth and the life: no man cometh unto the Father but by me."[9] As the civilization that worshiped Christ grew in power, it sent armies on crusades against the unbelievers and, later, colonial missionaries to subjugate and shatter the cultures of the pagans.

The idea of one God has many ramifications, some of them very constructive (such as the universalistic understanding of the brotherhood of all people under the Fatherhood of God). But one of the less

---

different. Sometimes people he talks to refuse to recognize that he is addressing them in Japanese. They just keep repeating *Watashhi eigo wakermasen*, 'I don't understand English,' moving an open hand back and forth before their faces to emphasize their negative response, disregarding his very fluent Japanese."[7] The appearance of difference produced a response among Father Grootaers's would-be interlocutors that overwhelmed the reality of a common language.

fortunate consequences is that the oneness of God seems to reinforce the idea that there is but one way to be or to believe.* Says the Koran, "There is no doubt in this book."[11]

Among the Arabs, the coming of monotheism seems to have transformed the nature of war, imbuing it with a spirit of righteous intolerance that made their conflicts more bitter and destructive. In pre-Islamic times, says James Aho, the mode of warfare was the *gzaza*, or camel raid. This was a struggle over narcissistic scarcity: "the losers experienced temporary ridicule, while the victors took pleasure in an equally tenuous heightened self-esteem."[12] But Islam brought the *jihad*, the holy war, where more than pride was at stake. Allah's warriors, writes Aho, have gone beyond the arena where the contest is over honor and shame into a darker realm. In this realm of righteousness, he who fights for Allah is "ipso facto innocent [while] the infidel is not just shameful, but guilty."[13] Whereas in the *gzaza* the opponent might be a neighbor or brother, "in the *jihad* he is a *harbie*, a stranger with a being radically opposed to that of the believers."[14]

Islam not only transformed the quality of warfare but enshrined it as the essence of the relationship with peoples of different belief. To the believers, said Majod Khadduri, "all the states and communities outside the world of Islam" constituted "the world of war."[15] "In theory," at least, "the believers were always at war with the unbeliever."[16]

The one God seems to go along with the one way: you won't get to the Father except through me. In Khomeini's Iran, this connection between monotheism and righteous intolerance has manifested in what has been called "holy fascism": you cannot serve the fatherland except as I say. Marvin Zonis and Daniel Offer write of Khomeini's monotheism that he takes Islam's traditional "theism" but adds a new emphasis on the "mono." "He does this by incorporating the idea of *tawhid* or unity into the idea of monotheism."[17] The one God thus combines with "a single interpretation of the proper way of organizing the community of the faithful for carrying out God's will." And this combination serves to "justify the rigorous and, all too frequently, ruthless, application of Khomeini's interpretations of proper Islamic behavior."[18]

It should come as no surprise that this possessor of God's Truth chooses to perpetuate a vicious and bloody war, spurning all the efforts of others, including the secretary general of the United Nations, to find a

---

*The prophets of the Hebrews, says Jacobson, assumed that whoever disagreed with them did so because they were evil.[10]

peaceful resolution. At one level, it can be said that this war helps to maintain a Khomeini regime in Iran that might otherwise prove quite shaky. At another level, this political interpretation might also be seen as a macrocosmic embodiment of the shaky structure of the true believer himself. His own stability requires this holy war against those who stray from his sense of right belief and righteous conduct.

The peace of the righteous requires war against the unrighteous. Aho writes that "the Hebraic, Muslim, and Reformation Protestant soldier, in identifying his cause with the perfect righteousness of God, uses the very ferocity of his violence as a confirmation of his own purity."[19] It is not any single group that threatens to destroy the world, Stanley Windass saw, "but the virus of the 'Holy War' which still rages in our 'Christian' bosoms."[20] As long as our righteousness requires their evil, and our rightness their error, peace will escape us. As long as we insist on wearing our truths as divine certainties, much of what is done in God's name will make this earth as Luther saw it, a place whose master is Satan.

16

GOD'S TRUTH
AS DARKNESS AND
AS LIGHT

H oly wars have given religion a bad name. So much blood has been spilled in God's name that some regard the news "God is dead" as good news. In our contemporary secular society, one hears frequently in discussions of religion and war the idea that a world at peace will have to be a world without religion.

Abandoning Religious Truths: False Solution #3

One lesson history teaches, it is argued, is that people hold their religious truths in a way that often precludes their interacting harmoniously with others whose religious truths are different. Nowadays, those who regard religion as part of the problem of war will cite the example of contemporary Islamic fundamentalism. But there is no shortage of excellent examples from centuries of history, throughout the world. We human beings have shed much blood because others would not acknowledge the truths revealed to us or to our ancestors by God. If a world at peace requires people who are tolerant, this argument concludes, the religious orientation that has been at the heart of most human cultures will have to be left behind on the ashheap of history. Peace will be attainable only when human culture has universally been secularized.

This solution, although it rests upon some valid observations, is another false one. It is true that there has often been something

282

pathologically intolerant about the spirit in which civilized peoples have held their religious beliefs. But from this acknowledgment it does not follow that our moving further toward a civilization that is wholly mundane in its outlook will make the world a better, more harmonious place. We have already explored that dead-end path. In the past couple of centuries in the West, in the wake of chronic religious wars, systems of belief not only nonreligious but antireligious in nature were developed and were promulgated to bring peace and justice to the world. But it turned out that the secular isms were subject to the same "virus" of the holy war that had infected religions. In our own time, for example, true believers in the communist and capitalist systems have regarded each other with the same spirit of intolerance that in earlier ages imbued religious conflicts. Narrow dogmatism can characterize purely secular systems of belief, like Marxism. Clearly, the problem of intolerance adheres not to the beliefs themselves so much as to the believers. If there is anything about the beliefs that makes them eligible to be held as "God's Truth" (generically speaking), it is that they address fundamental questions about the world and our lives in it.

This proposed "solution" to the problem of intolerance, therefore, needs revision. Not religion alone, but all passionately held systems of understanding would need to be eliminated. Not just "truths" divinely revealed, but any truths that answer fundamental human questions can be contaminated by the virus of holy war. It is for this reason that some would welcome not just the eradication of religion but an "end of ideology" generally.

In its revised form, solution #3 would call for the evisceration of passion and coherence from human belief. Nothing should inflame us, according to this view; no ideological commitments should rivet and compel us. Then the world would be safe from wars over belief. Then the categories of heretic and infidel, of dogma and inquisitor, would dry up from the earth, and blow away with the fresh winds of a wholly mundane and unimpassioned stage of history. Differences might remain, but, as no one would be passionately committed to his own way, the differences would be of little consequence.

There is a problem with this solution, however: it removes from among the forces molding history one that is vital and potentially indispensable. It is not by coincidence that those who would celebrate an end of ideology believe that we have already arrived at some kind of promised land. Seeing the status quo as satisfactory, seeing the larger forces of history as assuring progress, these apostles of the evisceration of passionate belief are happy to leave the historical field to the play of the forces of systemic momentum.

But if one's view of history is less sanguine, if one sees our systems as shaped by the selection for power into forms often indifferent, and sometimes hostile, to human needs, then the removal of the fire of human passion could abandon us to a cold and cruel fate. To one who sees history through the prism of the parable of the tribes, the momentum of history is potentially catastrophic. Our systems, unfolding according to a logic of their own, speed onward like the driverless stagecoach in the Westerns that is heading toward a cliff. Only from us, the human component of the machinery of our civilization, can come the energy to wrest our destiny from the dangerous rule of power. And it is only from the force of our passionate commitment that we can gain the strength to divert our civilization from its course.

For all the dangers that grow out of our passions, for all the pathologies to which they are subject, those passions are a vital resource, and they come from a sacred source. To know how to redirect the course of our civilization, we need the good maps of clear and coherent understanding; and we need the drive that comes from deep and impassioned commitment. A planet of passionless, uncommitted people might be free from the virus of holy war, but the planet would be endangered nonetheless.

Solution 4: Passionate Belief with Tolerance

It is not passion but intolerance that is the problem. Are we to assume that the two are inseparable in the realm of belief?

To judge from Nietzsche, any deep attachment to one's own belief necessarily implies disrespect for other beliefs. "He who deeply and powerfully promotes his own ideal cannot believe in others without judging them slightingly, as being the ideas of creatures *lesser* than himself . . . Thus tolerance . . . is evidence of mistrust in or a lack of an ideal of one's own."[1] Those who deeply believe, it would seem, must disrespect those who disagree; and those who respect those who disagree must be shallow in their own beliefs. It seems to be an instance of the situation lamented by Yeats, that "The best lack all conviction, while the worst / Are full of passionate intensity." If Nietzsche is correct—and the conduct of our true believers would certainly seem to validate his assertion—then intolerance is the inevitable companion of deeply held belief, and holy war an inevitable cost of having a planet of impassioned believers.

Is there but *one* truth? Does the validity of my point of view necessarily imply the falsehood of yours? How does one see the relationship between one's truth and the Truth? These are the questions upon which depends the separability between deep commitment on the one hand, and intolerance and disrespect on the other.

Although these questions bear upon any kind of beliefs we may hold, they arise particularly with respect to a certain important kind of beliefs: those religious truths that are said to originate with divine revelation. It will be fruitful, therefore, to examine this aspect of "God's Truth" more deeply.

When God Speaks to Man

There are several factors, bearing upon different levels of our dilemma, that make the question of *revealed truth* particularly pertinent to our discussion here.

1. As just suggested, revelation provides a kind of limiting case for the notion of respect for diverse truths. If my beliefs were revealed directly to me (or to the founders of my religion) and they differ from what was revealed to you (or to the founders of your religion), what room is there for mutual respect? Or, put another way, if I can believe that my truth came from God, yet respect your truth although it differs from mine, then I can respect diversity of belief in any area.

The logic of "God's Truth" does not seem to allow this respect. And this same logic—used by the true believer to brand all different believers as infidels—can be used to discredit the whole idea of revelation. Bertrand Russell used the idea of One Truth to demonstrate the intellectual bankruptcy of revealed religion. Since the different religions say different things, each with perfect certainty, Russell argued, obviously at most one of them can be true. Either all, or all but one, must be false. So much for revelation.

A logic of a different and ultimately more sensible kind is available. According to this logic, my truth might come from God and so might your different truth. Exploring this logic may help show the nature of the cure for the virus of the holy war. For if there is a path of tolerance and respect about God's Truth, then there will be for any other beliefs we hold.

2. Exploring revealed truth is pertinent also because the experience of revelation seems to bring with it some of those qualities characteristic of people infected with the virus of the holy war: the inflaming of passions and the imbuing of belief with a sense of certainty. Not just logically, therefore, but also psychologically the reception of truth be-

lieved to be direct from God seems to provide the ultimate challenge for the task of achieving an appreciation for human diversity.

3. The question of revelation is important also because of the positive potential it represents. As suggested in the discussion of false solution #3, although intolerance of belief endangers us, so also does the lack of valid and powerful beliefs. To overcome the potentially destructive momentum of our systems, it was said, our passionate commitment is required. But passion alone will not help if it is misguided. For a species facing enormous dangers and uncertainties, it would be greatly reassuring if there were a possibility that we could receive guidance and understanding through revelation.

What we need, therefore, is not just tolerance, and not just passionate belief with tolerance, but *valid* beliefs held with passion and tolerance and respect for other beliefs. With respect to all these dimensions, therefore, the idea of revelation thus provides both the ultimate test and the greatest opportunity.

Let us begin exploring the third point, starting with the question: should there be any place in our epistemology for revelation? Can we human beings receive important truths from some sacred source?

It is not fashionable in our time to speak seriously of the possibility of receiving truth directly from some holy and transcendent realm. Not only is it considered gauche in sophisticated circles to dedicate oneself passionately to some sacred vision, but the epistemology of modern civilization allows no room for knowledge obtained through revelation. According to the dogmas of "scientism," knowledge can be gained only through the scientific method. The universe consists only of matter and energy acting in rigid obedience to natural laws. Knowledge comes from processing logically the data discovered through observation. We thus arrive at many little truths, falling logically into larger theories. But for the hypothesis of God, and for the idea of such illogical and nonreplicable phenomena as revelation, we have no room and no need.

The scientific approach to knowledge has indeed proved to be a tool of enormous power. Through the systematic study of natural phenomena, in a matter of a comparative handful of generations, our species has laid bare the workings of our world down to a very profound level in many areas. Science is providing increasingly accurate and elaborate "maps."

But in fact, the world according to science does not answer all questions. The complacent sense of having squeezed all mystery out of the universe is but another manifestation of that same problem that underlies the intolerance of the religious zealot: our overeagerness for certainty.

I am reminded of a series of lectures on Aquinas, delivered by Professor Roger Albritton, that I attended years ago. Attempting to prove the existence of God, Aquinas argued that any series of phenomena required a first cause, and that this first cause had to be God. Albritton proceeded effectively, it seemed, to demolish Aquinas's argument, largely by using a more scientific conception of causality. We undergraduates began to sink complacently back into our seats. But then, in an astonishing about-face, Albritton suddenly opened a trapdoor from under the seemingly solid underpinnings of science. Does science really "explain" anything ultimately? I recall him asking us. Do the natural laws inferred by science really eliminate the need for a first cause or prime mover? Where did the laws themselves come from, let alone the matter and energy that obey them?[2]

There is no way of escaping it. Inevitably, our understanding of the universe—however complex, effective, and empirically sound it becomes—ultimately rests upon a sea of mystery. There are the mysteries of existence itself, of origins, and perhaps of purpose. On these questions—at the very heart of an understanding of the cosmos—our empirical science is unable to speak.

Where science cannot illuminate, does it *necessarily* follow that we must remain wholly in the dark? It is not the validity, but rather the sufficiency, of the scientific way of knowledge that is in question: are alternative ways of knowing to be ruled out? In a cosmos mysterious at the core, are mysterious channels for the conveyance of knowledge inconceivable?

No complete science, I would argue, will utilize *assumptions* about the nature of reality to foreclose the very *possibility* of our learning something about reality that goes beyond those assumptions. A science that does so is simply reincarnating its old nemesis—dogma—from which the human mind had to free itself in order for science to be born.

If what might be true were in fact true, how could we know it? If, as the evidence of cosmic evolution suggests to me, we may be—or be becoming—part of some larger Being, how might we learn of it? If our own evolution were contributing to the emergence of a consciousness that transcends ours, would it be impossible for that larger consciousness ever to have an impact upon ours? As the cells of our own bodies receive chemical and electrical instructions from the larger Being of which they are part (but of which they presumably have no real understanding), could there not be some way that a transcendent Being might give messages to the creatures that constitute it, messages that help the Body of the Whole to function in health?

To some, such notions may seem implausible; but they are not a priori impossible. Ultimately, it is not common sense but arrogance, with the familiar flavor of defensiveness, that would reduce our epistemology to forms that preclude our contact with mystery.

In a universe whose very existence is at heart a mystery, the further mystery of revelatory experience cannot a priori be ruled out. But the question still arises: what reason is there to rule it in?

Arrayed against the supposed logic that dismisses revelation is the evidence of the revelatory experience itself. This extraordinary experience loses scientific standing because it is nonreplicable. But why should it be assumed that valid knowledge can be gained only from events that we can control, predict, or reproduce? Mystical experience comes with such a power and intensity that those who receive it find no room to question its nature. Those who dismiss the possibility of revelation are never, as far as I know, people who have experienced it. (Freud, for example, when he explored the future of an "illusion," indicated clearly that he was discussing experiences that were alien to him.) Thus, if the essence of the true "scientific method" is to give priority to experience, those who are willing to dismiss revelation without ever having experienced it are much like those men from the Church who declared Jupiter's moons nonexistent without ever having looked through Galileo's telescope.

The force of a revelatory experience transcends that of ordinary experience. By virtue of its vividness and intensity, it possesses—for the one who experiences it—a quality of undeniability. The truth received cannot be denied; nor can the extraordinary nature of its source.

Certainly, the quality of the experience does not *prove* the validity of the interpretations given it. There is room for valid skepticism: the sense of revelation, of Truth, of contact with a Great Other, might all be illusions. Perhaps Saul/Paul's experience on the road to Damascus was "merely" an epileptic fit. Perhaps Blake's visions were "just" an eruption from the unconscious. Through these telescopes, unlike Galileo's, others cannot be invited to look for themselves. And even for those who get these glimpses into mystery, the nature of the experience must inevitably remain itself mysterious. Nonetheless, having myself experienced such a mysterious infusion of knowledge, I find I cannot help but believe that revealed knowledge is both valid and important. Having been thoroughly trained in the rationalist mode by which such experiences would be *reduced* to terms wholly congenial with the image of the cosmos as mere machine, I have felt compelled to adapt my understanding of reality to take into account the mystery of that experience.

In addition to the compelling nature of the experience, there is one other important kind of evidence that argues for making room for the possibility of revealed truth: the power of the truths that have been received thereby. At the core of most if not all revealed religions—however encrusted they may become with elements possibly pathological—there seems to be a life-serving vision that helps people discover meaning and wholeness in their lives. Undeniable to the receiver of the revelation, these truths also possess an intrinsic power that leads others to adopt them as their own, and allows whole cultures to turn to them for guidance.

An infusion of some sort of illuminating energy, apparently from some sacred source, becomes a powerful ordering force in human life. Thus arises God's Truth, received and articulated by one, shared with others to whom it is articulated, and handed down as authoritative tradition for future generations.

That brings this discussion to its destination, to show: first, that revelation *may* be a valid way of human knowing; and second, that revealed truth might be part of the solution, as well as apparently part of the problem with which we are concerned, of the destructiveness of civilization. If there were such a thing as valid revelation, it could be the vehicle for a kind of power to enter human affairs that is separate from, and might be an antidote to, the kind of power that reigns in the anarchic conditions of civilization. Perhaps in our search for the spiritual condition that would enable us to make real peace, we may be given strength and guidance by some divine power.

But what of the problematic aspects of revelation? After all, we approached "God's Truth" initially not as a divine vehicle for our salvation but as a cause of our all-too-human bellicosity. If we grant that it is *possible* that we may have access to a source that conveys *valid* beliefs to us to which we *passionately* commit ourselves, there remains the problem of tolerance and respect for diversity.

Combining valid revelation with the need for respect and tolerance, as we saw, confronts us with two problems. There is first the logical problem, suggested by Bertrand Russell, that the contradictions among revelations call into question the validity of revelation as a way of knowing. And then there is the psychological problem, that revealed truths seem especially prone to infection with the virus of the holy war.

17

DIVINE TRUTH
AND HUMAN

I f revelation conveys valid knowledge, why does one person's—or culture's—revealed truth differ from another's? That is what Bertrand Russell's challenge requires us to ask. The solution of most traditional religions is not satisfactory: our prophets are true prophets, but all the others are false. It is not only contaminated with an all-too-recognizable ethnocentrism (every people is a Chosen People), but it also inevitably discredits the revelatory channel itself. If *most* experiences of revelation are declared to be invalid, it surely seems more sensible to suppose that revelation is not a valid way of knowing than that valid knowledge has been delivered only to a narrow stream among the many currents of human tradition. But neither is Russell's solution—that revelation per se can be dismissed—logically required.

There is another solution, and it is this solution that makes the issue of revelation so useful a key to the whole problem of intolerance. This solution entails making a fundamental distinction: that between the Truth and our apprehension of it.

The fact that the messengers give different accounts in no way demonstrates that no Message was given. A conclusion that is at least equally plausible is that the messengers are imperfect transmitters of the messages they received.

This should come as no surprise. Ask different people to describe a particular individual, and the portrayals vary. Does that mean the individual does not exist? If we have even expert artists do paintings of the same tree, the renderings will be very different from one another (and from the tree). Any teacher who has read student examinations based on his lectures is compelled to recognize that divergence among students' reports does not prove the absence either of a teaching or of a teacher. If this is the way we apprehend the realities of the everyday world, how much more would it be so with the Reality glimpsed in the moment of mystical revelation!

Mystics through the centuries have described their experience as overwhelming and ineffable. The ineffability of the experience—its being inexpressible in words—suggests immediately that whatever translation the experience is given will be inadequate. Whatever symbols the mystic brings back from the experience to embody it even to himself or herself will be but a shadow of the actual moment; even more so the means by which it can be articulated to others. That the mystic felt overwhelmed tells us that what he or she brings back will be just a portion of the sacred flood that flowed through. The human vessel is simply not large enough to contain the wave of Truth.

The overwhelming, ineffable experience is not wholly self-interpreting. Even when people interpret a film, each interpreter intrudes his or her preconceptions, conceptual categories, and concerns. So even more so would it be with the interpretation of an overwhelming Truth.

If there is some sacred well of Truth into which we human beings can dip upon occasion, what we bring up from that well will inevitably be contaminated by the impurities of the vessel. And impurities there surely are in all of us. Prejudices, vanities, rages—the same emotional distortions that pollute our relationships with one another will cloud whatever trickles of the divine stream that may flow through us. To these emotional limitations must be added the shortcomings of our minds. Even in the classroom it is clear that the structure of the receiving mind limits the extent to which the structure of the incoming message can be apprehended. All the more so if the incoming message is not itself limited by the human mind, but partakes of the ineffable, overwhelming mystery of the cosmic forces that have brought us into being.

If the reports of the mystics are themselves inevitably distortions of the divine Message, even more subject to human foibles are the cultural processes by which the core revelatory vision is overlayed as it is transformed into religious tradition. These excrescences are generally enshrined as God's Truth equally with the revealed core, although their origins seem no more to transcend human ignorance and corruption than do any human cultural creations. Thus it is that "God's Truth" as it is handed down in tradition often serves to perpetuate delusion, to buttress tyranny, to inflame base passions.

Russell's challenge thus does undercut the idea of "God's Truth" as it often appears with all its distortions and excrescences. When Ashurbanipal satisfies the hearts of his lords with the atrocities he perpetrates against his victims, we can imagine that the pathologies of a world embroiled in chronic war may have pathologically distorted the image of sacred power. When we read laws of painstaking detail in the Books of Moses, it seems more reasonable to suppose that it is cultural practice that is being enshrined as divine fiat rather than that Moses took extensive dictation on Sinai. When Muhammad closed the door of prophecy behind him— granting validity to some prophets of the past but declaring that he was the last prophet of Allah—we may suspect that what is being expressed is the wish of man, not of God. When we see God portrayed as wrathful and jealous, behaving in a way we would not expect even of a mature and wise man, we may surmise that impurities from the human vessel are being expressed, not a clear image of the divine Source.

There is a Sufi story of a sage who, finding he could speak the language of the ants, approached one and asked, "What is God like?" The ant replied, "God is unlike anything I have ever encountered. An ant has a single sting, but God, He was *two*!"[1]

Given what we human creatures are like, and the nature of our cultural and historical processes, it could hardly be otherwise than that different peoples would carry as "God's Truth" visions that diverge in significant ways. This would be so even if there were a single divine Truth being revealed at different times and places to different peoples. Thus, Russell's challenge helps highlight the inappropriately arrogant way we tend to hold our "God's Truth," but does not really undermine the idea that there is or may be a sacred source of Truth available to help guide us.

One source of ambiguity in the interpretation of revelation is the basic question: what is happening in this apparent reception of transcendent Truth from a source apparently beyond ourselves?

Thus far, we have been discussing revelation within the image of a Great Being that sends a single Message to lesser beings. This idea— conveyed through the images of a single tree to be rendered, or film to be interpreted—is consistent with the famous Sufi story about the men from different countries traveling together who get into a quarrel in the marketplace about what to get with their money.

"I want to buy *angur*," said the Persian.

"I want *uzum*," said the Turk.

"I want *inab*," said the Arab.

"No," said the Greek, "we should buy *stafil*."

Another traveler, passing, who was a linguist, said, "Give the coin to me. [I will] satisfy the desires of all of you."

At first they would not trust him. Ultimately they let him have the coin. He went to the shop of a fruit seller and bought four small bunches of grapes.

[Each of the travelers then exclaimed that this was what he had wanted.][2]

The different religions, the story seems to suggest, are prevented by their different "languages" from understanding that they are all really trying to express the same Truth.

But there are other ways of imaging what "revelation" might be, ways still consistent with the idea that human beings have access to a source of transcendent Truth.

A second image is that there is some Being sending messages to lesser beings, but that the message sent is not identical in each instance. As the first image led to the metaphor of the teacher whose lectures are distorted on the students' exams, this second way of understanding can utilize a different teacher metaphor. Just as a good teacher will give different lessons to different students—depending on their needs and their readiness for understanding—so also might that Being impart different lessons to different peoples at different times and places. A metaphor of this might be the famous story of the blind men and the elephant: the one who touches the ear is certain the beast is like a broad rug; the one who has felt the trunk knows the elephant is like a powerful, flexible pipe; and the blind man who has put his arms around the leg asserts that the beast is like a pillar.[3]

A third image is that we humans sometimes make contact with a different dimension of being. Revelation, rather than a message, may be a discovery of a realm of being into which some people occasionally step. The famous Platonic metaphor of the Cave is illustrative of this way of understanding the process of sacred illumination. Although most of us live in darkness, there is accessible to us a realm of light in which Reality rather than shadow can be apprehended.

And a fourth image is that revelation is an experience that occurs when our own being is in some special alignment. It is as though there is some sacred source of knowledge dwelling inside us, that becomes accessible to us when we have made ourselves receptive to it. Perhaps it is when we have found the magic combination that brings our various elements into harmony. As a vault will open its doors to let us into the treasure within when all the tumblers are brought perfectly into line, perhaps when we have brought the various dimensions of our being into alignment a sacred treasure within us becomes available. This treasure is a source of the most important and most valid truths. This fourth idea—that there is a special condition in which the mystical experience occurs—tends to be common to all interpretations.* Indeed, these four interpretations are ultimately not exclusive of one another. Revelation, indeed, might be best understood as a combination of all those images. The nature of that Being might include its being separate from us, its being a dimension of the cosmos, and its dwelling within us as a part of

---

*It is but a jump from seeing the experience of revelation as occurring under "special" circumstances to explaining it away as a function of the abnormal. And indeed, most *reductive* interpretations dismiss the mystical experience as a function of psychopathology such as psychotic states, or of neurological illness such as epilepsy, or of eruptions of repressed material from the unconscious. What are we to make of such dismissive explanations?

Empirical research into mystical experience in our time has yielded some interesting findings. First, that the experience is more widespread than the silence surrounding it in our society would lead us to expect. Second, that those who have had mystical experiences tend to be not crazier but psychologically better put together than those who have not.

Those among us who have had mystical experience tend to be "in a 'state of psychological well-being substantially higher than the national average' as measured by the Bradburn psychological well-being scale . . . The conventional notion that mystical experience is a neurotic escape common to unhappy and maladjusted people is certainly not supported by these findings."[4]

David Hufford argues that the reduction of mystical experience to psychopathology— far from being true science—has been part of the arsenal of those who, like Inquisitors of the past, seek to keep the flock in line: "the psychopathological 'explanation' has been primarily a mechanism of social control."[5] By intimidating people, the reductive explanation inhibits people from telling others about their mystical experiences, thus excluding the force of mystic revelation from the realm of respectable public discourse.

Andrew Greeley's survey found that 35 percent of us have had experiences akin to those described in the classic literature of mysticism.[6] But many of these have kept the experience to themselves, fearing, Hufford suggests, being exposed to the opinions of others taught by our society to dismiss these "special" experiences.

Even mystical traditions would acknowledge that mystical experience does not generally come under completely "normal" circumstances. Thus they deliberately cultivate "abnormal" conditions, e.g. sitting endlessly in the meditation of *zazen*, or going out into the wilderness and fasting for forty days and forty nights. But this "abnormality" does not invalidate the experience. If it is a special event for a human being to make contact with the sacred, why should not some special condition of the organism be conducive to it?

what we are. The message might be similar whenever any human being receives it, and it might be sent in a form varying according to the nature of the person by whom it is received. Revelation might be both a message sent to us and a discovery we make.

But whichever of those images we prefer, or whatever way we combine them, they have one essential thing in common. In all these ways of conceiving how we human beings might gain access to sacred Truth, that truth would be reduced and distorted by our own limitations. However pure the water, the impurities in the vessel will get into it. We may gain glimpses into God's Truth, but we ourselves are incapable of being carriers of that Truth unadulterated and in its entirety.

In presenting revelation as a limiting case for the issue of tolerance and respect for diverse truths, I asked: if we have received God's Truth, what room is there for other truths that differ? The answer is that even if we are handed God's Truth, all we are capable of possessing is a human rendition of it. We are wise to hold sacred our understanding of God's Truth, for it is likely to be the best guidance we can get. For this reason, our vision deserves our passionate commitment. But it is arrogance and folly for us to identify our understanding with the Truth itself.

Revelation, as a limiting case, thus demonstrates an essential aspect of the human condition: that our knowledge and understanding are inevitably imperfect and incomplete. To the questions at the foundation of our lives, there is no way that we—limited and fallible creatures that we are—will possess the Answer, even if it were handed to us on Mount Sinai.

18

EMBRACING
MYSTERY

What is true of Truth revealed can hardly be less true of the truths we gain by other means. Like the wave of Truth that overwhelms the mystic, Reality itself is way over our heads. The cosmos in which we float like mites on a speck of dust far transcends the two-dimensional maps we have the capacity to draw or to grasp. The complexity of the living systems that we embody, in which we are agents, and that surround us, is many dimensions greater than that of the models of them we construct. What a piece of work is man, in reason how like an angel! Yet we are but part of an infinitely greater work, and it is hubris to imagine that our reason gives us mastery over the mystery surrounding us.

"The most profound and honest reaction of a man to this world," writes David Bosworth, is "awe." Awe, he says, is what we feel when we experience the "discrepancy between what actually exists and what we can rationally know of existence, between the infinity 'out there' and the finiteness of 'me.' "[1] This awe is a central component of our embracing the truth of what we are.

The experience of awe can fill us with either exhilaration or terror. Which feeling predominates depends on whether we sense that the overwhelming and unmastered forces of the cosmos are friendly or hostile. Awe is an admission of weakness. And as the helplessness of the infant can be blissful or terrifying depending upon how securely loving is

296

his or her environment, so also is the awesomeness of Reality either exciting or frightening. If the world is benign, its mysteries are wondrous; in a world where murder lurks, mystery is sinister.

Fear, again, is both the child and the parent of our bellicosity. The pattern of strife which inevitably has accompanied the development of civilization has made the world unsafe for awe. Awe, the most profound and appropriate reaction to our position in the cosmos, is too terrifying for a creature traumatized by the dangerous systems evolving around him. Mystery becomes fearsome; only certainty gives comfort. We retreat from the truth of our condition, retreat from awe, to proclaim our certainty. Indulging our love of certainty compels us to hate the truth. Hating the truth, we must make war on whatever proclaims it. The diversity of the visions of humankind proclaims our finite condition and thus, having cut ourselves off from the fresh air of an honest confrontation with the awesome, we become infected with the virus of the holy war. Our war against the truth becomes a war against diversity. Our fears, born in part from the embattled condition of our world, engender still more strife.

The more a truth we hold deals with the core questions of our lives, the more our fear of awe and mystery and uncertainty will drive us to fight to eliminate different truths. Here again revelation poses the challenge of the limiting case. For revelation deals precisely with the most central questions, those about which uncertainty is most threatening. These truths may be the best we can get, and if they must be regarded as less than God's Truth itself, we are compelled to fall back onto the openness that is the expression of awe. If openness is experienced as opening the door to terror and injury, we will close our minds. Recoiling in weakness from the experience of awe, we will inflate our all-too-finite selves to identify with the Infinite. God's imperfect messengers declaim the One Truth as if they were God Himself. The armies of the righteous strike as if they were His right hand. Fear, making us war against the truth, converts God's Truth into the devil's.

The war against the truth turns everything into its opposite. The semblance of power, once again, is but an expression of weakness. The destroyer undoes himself; the jailor creates his own prison. Bosworth juxtaposes the artist and the tyrant, seeing them as natural enemies: while the artist opens himself to be the channel of immensity and complexity, the tyrant "must reduce the world to an idolatrous cartoon of perfect heroes and irredeemable foes, of ironclad moral certainties."[2] Then he turns to the example of Stalin, who illustrates the reversals that the war against the truth brings. Stalin, the murderer of Mandelstam, the imprisoner of Solzhenitsyn, and harasser of Pasternak—was in a curious way as much the victim as the benefactor of his imposed world view, scarcely freer of his own tyranny than those he ruled. Towards the end, he had reduced his environment to one basic room, a self-sufficient womb he rarely left, a womb he had recreated in all the cities he commonly visited so that no matter where he went, he always appeared to be in the exact same place. The same dimensions, the same furnishings in the same positions, day after day after day; no matter where he was, the same four walls greeted him; his own temple of Baal; his own Gulag cell, if you will; his own sentence of imprisonment.[3]

Once again, Stalin exaggerates what is a part of the rest of us. Although we are not just like Stalin, Bosworth says, "We [too] hide within our habits, within our inflexible moralities and acquired prejudices, wrap ourselves in a perceptual cocoon that blinds us from a reality we find too awesome to confront." Like Stalin, "we all to some degree condemn ourselves as he did to a prison-cell world."[4]

Reality may be frightening, but the attempt to escape from it only substantiates our fears. Trying to make the world completely safe, we make it more dangerous. Trying to be masters of our world, we make ourselves prisoners. Trying to possess certain truth, we compound and perpetuate our ignorance. Trying to play God, we make ourselves into lesser creatures than we are.

The war against the truth is one we can only lose. Reality as we now find it may be far from what we want. But it is all that we have.

The Treasure of Diversity

We cannot wish our fears away. But we can at least come to understand that allowing them to possess us only compounds our peril. We cannot simply by an act of will gain the courage to embrace the truth of our condition. But by exploring where the path of fear and falsehood takes us, we can learn that only through the truth shall we be set free.

That our species has many faces tells us something profoundly true about the human condition. Our running from that truth brings the scourge of our unholy wars. Embracing that truth can be the means of our liberation. As in the myths, to gain access to the greatest treasures one must first confront monsters, the embodiments of our fears.

We are born unfinished, and full of potentiality. As we grow to maturity, the unfinished becomes finished. It is a necessary process, but it has a cost: flexibility is lost in the hardening of habit.

Any culture leads the unfinished creature into a particular rendering of his or her being which inevitably expresses part of his nature to the neglect of others. Every culture strives also—with varying success—to transcend its narrowness and to provide routes for its members to contact the core of their being. This may be the chief function of religion and the arts, whose task is to deal with experiential depths. Yet, while trying to maintain contact with the depths, every culture also directs its members to spend a great deal of their time on the particular surface their culture fabricates ("Have a nice day!") And that surface—emphasizing some parts of human nature and ignoring and suppressing others—inevitably alienates people from themselves.

As human beings harden into adulthood, assuming the face their cultures mold, they are challenged to combine the fixity of being a particular kind of person with sufficient spontaneity and freedom from sterile habit to maintain the vitality of experience. It is the spirit which giveth life while the letter killeth. And the spirit is the basic human life-energy, while the letter is the cast that spirit learns to take.

A creature's fulfillment lies in the full expression of its nature. Because every culture restricts the range of human experience, as well as allowing some expression as well, people are imprisoned in their cultures. Culture, although necessary for our species, is thus burdensome to the human spirit—not just because of the Freudian war of restraint against instinct, but also because of the narrowing of human potential that any particular way of being entails. We need liberation from the confinements of culture.

A most essential kind of human freedom lies in contacting the source of our human potential, and in releasing ourselves from the worship of culturally sanctioned habit and prejudice. For this liberation, the multiplicity of human visions embodied in our diverse cultures can be key. As we see represented to us by the different cultures the many faces our humanity might have taken, we must stand in awe of the great expanses of the human soul. Through Greek tragedies no one in our own culture could have written, we learn more about our humanity; into the experiential spaces expressed in Japanese film, we too can expand. In the diverse forms of humanity, we can realize the distinction between what we have become and what we truly are, and can stop losing our souls in a debilitating idolatry of the one culture into which we happen to have been born. In this way, we come more fully into possession of the mystery at the core of our being.

As with the mystery that is within us, so also with the mystery that transcends us. As the many faces of man can help us regain the mysterious core of our humanity, the many forms that God's Truth takes among us can remind us that the truth of God surpasses our understanding. In the Torah is the insight that God's order is a lawful one; while Zen Buddhism conveys the limits of the human mind in its encounter with the flash of enlightenment. We are indeed like blind men around an elephant. The better we can listen to the testimony of others who have also encountered the beast, the better an image of the elephant we will be able to achieve. This stance is *not* one of complete cultural relativism: for not all blind men are equally good interpreters of the part of the elephant they are feeling and, more important still, not all are in touch with the elephant. But whatever is our best understanding, it deserves the devotion of our hearts: valid (albeit imperfect) belief, held with passion and with tolerance.

Our diversity reveals how limited are what we are and what we understand. Although experience of our limitation may be painful and frightening, only by achieving harmony with the truth can we ourselves become whole. "Except a corn of wheat fall into the ground and die, it abideth alone: but if it die, it bringeth forth much fruit."[5] Only in awe of how the potential of our species surpasses our particular form can we gain our own full humanity. And only when we acknowledge how incomplete is our own rendition of God's Truth can our hearts fill with the awe that is properly part of our knowledge of God's Truth.

Embracing the truth of our narrowness, we become more able to discover our unity in the family of humankind. Being at one with the truth of our limited understanding, we become more open to union with God.

EPILOGUE:

War and Peace in Evolutionary Perspective

The Chronic Condition

I llness of longstanding, it is said in medicine, is not healed overnight. For our species, war is such an illness. Warfare became chronic with the rise of civilization. With roots reaching so deeply into the structure of our systems and into the rifts in our psychological structure, our destructiveness will not be easily plucked out.

War is like the "original sin" of civilization. Sin has been defined by the theologian Paul Tillich as a matter of separation—the separation of people from one another, the separation of each person from him- or herself, the separation of man from God. The plague of our destructiveness, we have seen, grows out of our being in a state of sin at two levels.

At the macrocosmic level, we fell into the social evolutionary trap of the rule of power because civilization arose, as it would inevitably have to, as a fragmented system. Civilized societies formed a system because they, unlike the primitive hunting-gathering societies that preceded them, were compelled to interact together. But this system was in a "state of sin" because there was no integrative order holding them together. In this condition of anarchy, we were condemned to a war of all against all.

From this "original sin" of macrocosmic anarchy followed those sins on the human scale that we have explored here. That is, (largely) because of the agony of the war of all against all, we have striven to separate ourselves from several important dimensions of our true experience.

1. In a world where power rules, it is terrifying to be weak, for the weak are disregarded and destroyed. So we have separated ourselves from our real but unendurable condition as weak and vulnerable creatures; we posture as gods embodying the strength we worship; we cultivate narcissistic images of our own specialness, separating ourselves still further from our fellow human beings. In this world of fragmented humanity, competition not cooperation seems the essence of relationship, and security appears as a scarce commodity to be enjoyed by one at the expense of another.

2. Another aspect of power's reign has separated us still further from ourselves. Because the course of our civilized societies' runaway evolution has been dictated largely by forces indifferent to human needs, we have been compelled to internalize cultural demands that turn us against ourselves, teaching us to regard our nature as evil. To separate ourselves from the agony of the war we internalize, we separate ourselves from our own "evil" by discovering it instead out there, in those on the other side of the boundary.

3. The more dangerous the terrain, the more frightening it is to wander in it blind and disoriented. In a world where destruction lurks, therefore, we have felt an urgent need to believe our own "maps" infallible. We have consequently separated ourselves from our true experience of confusion and uncertainty, zealously making war on the unbelievers whose differences from ourselves call into question our possession of God's Truth.

Our destructiveness therefore is an outgrowth of a state of "sin" originating with the beginnings of history.

Such a perspective might seem, like the doctrine of original sin, to carry with it despair about our capacity to work our salvation. But it should not. For as chronic as our problem is by *historical* standards, yet in the perspective of our true origins it is but a recent crisis. Our story does not start with the beginnings of history, and in the larger evolutionary perspective it is not sin but wholeness that is our heritage.

In the Western world it was believed until recently that time began a mere six thousand years ago; and barely had it begun before we separated ourselves from paradise by eating of the tree that gives knowledge of the cleavage between good and evil. And, with the very first brothers, fratricide began. Such an image of time and of our inherent sinfulness fitted well a culture with no basis for seeing humankind separately from the civilized systems in whose toils we find ourselves ensnared.

During the past century and a half, new knowledge has made possible a wholly new understanding of our origins, and thus also of our nature. We now trace our ancestry back—not some six thousand years to the edge of civilization, but much further. Civilization, we now know, comprises but a tiny portion of the story of our species. Before civilization began, we lived as hunter-gatherers, whose societies apparently had little or no warfare (and it seems likely that such warfare as there may have been was of a wholly different nature from what we know as war— more ceremonial display than actual destruction).[1] But our origins go back much further than that. Even Lucy, the famous hominid whose several-million-year-old skeleton was uncovered in Africa, is not one of our early ancestors. Our ancestry goes all the way back, to the reptiles, to the fish, to the one-celled creatures in the seas where life began. The intellectual revolution begun by Darwin shows that the ten thousand years we call history is but a tiny period at the end of a shelf-ful of volumes of the story of life on earth. And the story told in all those volumes, and not just the period at the end, comprises *our* story.*

To know what in our condition is "chronic," therefore, and what is acute, it is important to understand the nature of the evolutionary process from which, after almost four billion years, our species has emerged.

Ancient Synergy

What is the salient characteristic of the evolutionary process? It is the knitting together of ever-larger wholes of ever-increasing harmony.

This was not immediately realized with the advent of the theory of biological evolution, partly because of the cultural context in which the Darwinian perspective was first developed. Darwin's was a society whose domestic economy was giving increasing rein to the forces of atomistic competition. This same Great Britain was engaged, with the rest of Europe, in a global process of predatory imperialism. The process of natural selection, viewed through the prism of such a cultural and historical context, was understood as a *struggle* for survival in which the *fittest* eliminated the losers. To justify their own predatory ways as a

---

*This scientific revolution in our understanding thus helps us overcome yet another dimension of our sinful condition: our seeing ourselves as separate from the rest of earth's living body.

continuation of the very process that had created us, the Social Darwinists thus portrayed the natural order as one of "sin"—i.e., of each separated from each, all warring against all. Projecting their own lusts onto nature, they saw our common mother as "red in tooth and claw," and gave to the destructive process that comes with anarchy the name "the law of the jungle."

But the law that operates in the jungle is really quite different. True, there is predation and there is parasitism. But the visibly conflicting interests are subsumed in a more fundamental harmony of interest in protecting the stability of the whole living system. Remember the fate of the strategy named HARRINGTON: those, like HARRINGTON, who try to win at the expense of the others eventually render first their prey and then thereby themselves also extinct. The success of TIT FOR TAT shows that only those whose interactions are characterized by mutuality can endure. Thus the wolves' falling upon the sheep is fundamentally different from the European powers' carving up Africa. The wolves' predation is necessary not only for their own survival but is part of the pattern of survival for the sheep as well. For with inadequate predation, the sheep would become overpopulated; the overpopulation of sheep brings overgrazing; and overgrazing exposes the precious soil to the erosive forces of weather, thus undermining the very foundation of the sheep's long-term viability. Win-lose eventually pushes both the winner and the loser under; only those who practice the pattern of win-win can ride the evolutionary wave into the future.

The four billion years that carried life up to the new experiment of civilization saw the creation of an ever more wondrous wholeness. From the tiny fragments of life in the primordial soup, the system grew in complexity, selecting not just for individual bodies and their descendants (as the Darwinists of the nineteenth century tended to see it), but for whole communities of interdependent species. Like a family around the dinner table, the creatures on earth pass around the precious stores of substance and energy of which life is created. Even nonliving parts of this planet became organized into this emerging whole, as living organisms turned rocks into soil and made of the gaseous envelope around the globe an atmosphere for the circulation of the oxygen, carbon, and nitrogen necessary for the ongoing chemistry of life.

The historical processes that engender our destructiveness go back scores of generations into our species' history. But as rulers of this world, the evolutionary processes that build life's synergistic systems have far greater seniority. The crisis of conflict is acute; it is the wholeness of which our life is composed that has been chronic.

But indeed, it may be that even the beginning of life does not mark the origins of this impetus toward the assembling of ever more complex and harmonious wholes. Since the very beginning of time, the very matter of the cosmos seems to have been unfolding in a similar direction.

According to the scenarios of cosmic history that cosmologists now find most consistent with the evidence, the universe began some sixteen billion years ago with the Big Bang.* In the very first instants of the universe's existence, because of the enormous temperature and pressure, matter could exist only as discrete quarks and leptons. The quarks then assembled into integrated structures, creating the subatomic particles like protons and neutrons. Then began the evolution of the elements, starting with the simplest—hydrogen, which still comprises most of the mass of the universe—and then helium. As the process of fusion continued, in the crucible of the interior of the stars, heavier elements formed from hydrogen and helium. In her book *The Unfinished Universe*, Louise B. Young traces this process through the assembling of atoms into molecules, even up to the extremely complex organic molecules that are the precursors of life, and on into the evolution of life itself. There is, she says, "a natural tendency for self-organized wholes to form."[2] The whole cosmos is composed of "organisms" in this sense of self-regulating units that maintain stability and even regenerate themselves when fractured.[3] Young quotes the famous scientific philosopher Alfred North Whitehead: "Biology is the study of larger organisms; whereas physics is the study of the smaller organisms."[4]**

Looking at the course of sixteen billion years of cosmic evolution, Young concludes: *"With the elapse of time Form has increased."*[6] By "Form" she means the sum of those assemblies of matter that "exhibit the characteristics associated with wholeness."

Our very existence, on a moment-to-moment basis, rests on wholeness more elaborate and more profound than we can comprehend. At the macro level (in terms of the earth), there is the intricate harmony of the biosphere. At the micro level, there is the organization of matter to create our bodies. "A single gene is constructed of at least a hundred thousand atoms; each chromosome contains somewhere between two thousand and twenty thousand genes; each species carries a characteris-

---

*I will use the figure of sixteen billion although among cosmologists there is a range of disagreement of several billions of years on this issue.

**Says Cyril Ponnamperuma, the head of the Laboratory of Chemical Evolution at the University of Maryland: "There is a characteristic of life in almost everything, and at a certain point it becomes recognizable."[5]

tic number of chromosomes—from two to several hundred."[7] This incredible complexity is coiled into the nucleus of every cell in our bodies. Each cell is by itself a small universe; each cell is an organism of a complexity that can boggle our minds. And each of us is a cosmos composed of a trillion such microcosms.

And those minds of ours, thus boggled, are founded upon what may be up to 10^{17} interconnections among the neurons in our brains (that is 100,000 times as many as a million million).[8]

Our bodies and our minds—they are the fruits of a process that goes back to the beginnings of evolution. Certainly to the evolution of life, but even beyond that to the beginnings of cosmic evolution.

In the very nature of the cosmos, apparently, there is something laboring to fit things together into ever-greater wholes.

An Unprecedented Disruption

The breakthrough made by our species into a new kind of living system—civilization—has (at least) temporarily upset the wholeness that has been growing upon this planet. Civilization, so far, constitutes an unprecedented threat to the viability of the biosphere. What is unprecedented is not the disruption per se, but rather the nature of the source.

The evolution of life on earth has encountered crises before. Previous crises have apparently been precipitated by developments originating *outside* the living system. Life's control of the terrestrial environment, although considerable, has been incomplete. Thus, the floating of the continents upon the earth's crust could have lead to a sudden joining of two previously separate biological communities when North and South America met, and the result was a wave of extinctions (primarily among South American fauna). The harmonies of living systems emerge through extensive interaction over time. A sudden meeting of organisms that have had no time to evolve a synergistic pattern is likely to be destructive, as in the sudden encounter (mentioned in part 3) between the American chestnut and the virus from China. Another, still greater cataclysm originating outside the biosphere is thought to explain the disappearance of the dinosaurs: the collision of a huge meteor with the earth, it is now believed, so upset the earth's climatic patterns for a while that the dominant dinosaurs were wiped out. So also with the extinctions that have accompanied the coming and the recession of the Ice Ages, caused perhaps by solar fluctuations well beyond the reach of the living system to regulate.

The current crisis in the evolutionary process is unprecedented because it emerges from the living system itself. We are the first of earth's children to threaten our mother. An extension of the biological process into civilization has spread deserts where there was green life, and now is extinguishing species of plants and animals at an alarming and accelerating rate. All this even without our using our growing stockpiles of weapons of destruction, weapons that could inflict grave injury upon the biosphere as a whole. Out of the harmony of biological systems has emerged a creature destructive of the natural foundation of its own existence, out of harmony with its own nature, and at war with its own kind.

The fall from wholeness into sin is the consequence of our inadvertent plunge out of order into anarchy. The human capacity for creativity that developed as an adaptive strategy for life within the regime of nature eventually took us out of that order into an unprecedented—and therefore disordered—situation. The evolutionary process, evidently, cannot look forward. In our case, the innovation in our cortical structure eventually led life into a new game, civilization. But the old game—biological life—is a continuing prerequisite of the new, and its requirements must still be met. The disorder of the new system undermines the integrity of the old.

Order takes time to create. What is suddenly introduced into a living system will be, at the outset, out of harmony with the rest of the system. This is true of that sudden invasion of South America by North American fauna; and it is true of civilization's precipitous emergence into the biosphere. But the case of civilization is different from the other. The fauna of North and South America could, in time, come to an accommodation of a familiar kind: an ecological balance in a biologically governed order. But civilization has carried cosmic evolution to a new stage, to what Jonas Salk calls the "metabiological" level. The discord it introduces is extraordinary in nature, and the restitution of wholeness will also have to be at an extraordinary level. The floating of the continents produced what might be called a regressive crisis, for it represented the intrusion of forces from an earlier level of cosmic evolution (i.e., the nonliving systems). Civilization has produced a progressive crisis, a disorder caused by the sudden emergence of a new kind of order—that created by the creative spirit of a living creature.

The progressive crisis caused by the emergence of civilization creates a new kind of problem, and further evolution along this line of life's development will require a new kind of solution. The new phase of evolution that is engendered by the creative spirit can be described in terms of the spirit. The disorder and damage we unleash we may speak of in terms of the notion of sin. The encompassing Whole we are challenged to create at a new level may have something to do with God.

Alignment in Evolutionary Architecture

We human beings are carriers of sin because we are pulled apart by two evolutionary processes: the one that created us, and the one of which we inadvertently became the creators. We are of divided allegiance, separated from ourselves by the conflicting pulls of the nature within us and the runaway cultures evolving around us. Unlike the jaguars seeking a niche in South America or the giant sloth falling out of its place in the jungle, we are the "sick animals."

Our being out of kilter with our environment is more dangerous than the jaguar's because conception in the mind is far less conservative than conception in the body. That is, with our creativity we can quickly—in the space of a few millennia—amass powers orders of magnitude larger than those embodied in the flesh. We become powerful before we become safe. In purely biological evolution, change is slow enough that new forms do not become general unless they work: no creature can win against its environment for long. Biological evolution may not look forward, but it discards what is not harmonious with its environment before it rules the planet.

But, again, the old game continues. No new level of organization can survive unless it conforms to the rules governing the levels below it.* The evolutionary process works toward the creation of wholeness, balanced harmonies stacked up from the lowest to the highest levels. It should not be surprising that a sudden eruption would create disruption. But the evidence of cosmic evolution suggests that we will not long continue in our disharmonious state. The wage of sin is indeed death. Civilization must repent—creating an order in harmony with all the orders below—or it is damned.

---

*"[I]n spite of the intense specialization and apparent subjugation of the individual cell to the needs of the larger whole, each cell still retains its own separate potentialities . . . Like the electrons in an atom, the molecules in a crystal, the amino acids in the protein chains, the units involved in this new level of matter do not relinquish their individual identity. Building of form has taken place at each stage without the loss of the ones before."[9]

The way of repentance is the way of shalom, of knitting together at all the levels not now at peace with one another. The natural wholeness of life must be reestablished.

At the macro level, the current anarchy of civilization's overarching order must be replaced with a new order which, like the old regime of nature, is so structured that what each actor does necessarily contributes to the viability and well-being of the system as a whole. At the micro level, the pattern of intrapsychic conflict that has been explored in this work must be replaced with an experience of harmony between what we are and what we feel we should be.

As in the regime of nature, so also in the new kingdom of shalom that we are now challenged to create: each creature could follow its own law yet be in harmony with the surrounding order.

Only the creation of a new, overarching order that fosters harmony and wholeness will enable the members of humankind to become whole. (Overcoming the structural fragmentation of our macrosystems is required to make the world safe for the consciousness that transcends boundary.) And only when the human elements of the system are whole can the greater Whole we need to create be established. (It is not sick cells but healthy cells that comprise a healthy body.)

Wholeness Built on Consciousness: The Bio-Civisphere

This new wholeness will emulate the ancient wholeness from which we arose, but it is a new kind of wholeness. This new whole might be called the "bio-civisphere." Like the biosphere that evolved by wholly biological means, the bio-civisphere will embody the harmonizing of relationships and the cycling of resources that safeguard the system's stability and long-term viability. But unlike the biosphere, it must incorporate the new dimension of consciousness into a central place in its harmonious order.

Consciousness—a creative capacity for awareness and choice that transcends genetic programming—is what lifted our species out of nature into civilization. Fragmented civilization has engendered a sick consciousness—in its cognitive, emotional, and spiritual dimensions. The whole civilization of the bio-civisphere will require a consciousness of a very different sort, a consciousness that is the expression of the harmony and integration that characterized the system of life before civilization.

The bio-civisphere, therefore, is like a biosphere governed by con-sciousness. Above all, the consciousness that is required to carry the evolutionary process forward to the new level of the bio-civisphere will be characterized by the spirit of shalom. As the problem of war is the most profound image of the destructiveness that we have introduced, through civilization, into the living system, so does our working for peace appear as the specifically human challenge in life's evolutionary unfolding. We, the animals whose creative minds have unleashed a time of division and destruction, are called upon for our very survival to align our consciousness with a new kind of wholeness.

In this work, we have explored both the consciousness that divides and leads to war and that which can bring humankind together.

Shattered by injury and by the fear of further wounds, we have donned protective armor, turning us each into a separate microcosm. Afraid of our real condition as small, vulnerable creatures, we adopt the posture of great and mighty gods. Now that such creatures have tens of thousands of nuclear warheads, it is clear that the evolutionary process will be able to continue through us, rather than terminate in us in a thermonuclear fireball, only if we turn away from this path of separateness. If, like the samurai with the flea, we are possessed by an impulse to destroy whatever discloses the truth of our condition, we will destroy ourselves. If we persist in posturing menacingly at each other, as "nuclear giants," this flimsy stage we have erected under ourselves will collapse. The defensive structures of narcissistic pride and denial that divide us from one another and alienate us from ourselves must be removed for us to become elements in some larger Whole.

What must replace our narcissistic structures is a spiritual quality that many religious traditions have sought to encourage. It is called *humility.* The evolutionary process now gropes to create through us a larger "organism." But only as we embrace the idea that we ourselves are but a very small part of the whole do we become suitable elements to be fitted into that emergent organism. The mystical traditions suggest that the experience of our oneness with the One requires this humility. It is a common thread running through the disciplines of these traditions: to prepare for the transcendent experience of mystical vision, cultivate humility.

Humility is intimately connected also with *tolerance,* for the intoler-ance we explored in "God's Truth" is a form of arrogance. To assert that one's own truth is *the* solution to the mysteries of human life and the cosmos is as false and prideful a posture as that of the flea-denying samurai. Conversely, the respect for difference that is the path of peace implies a (fitting) humility about the limits to one's own capacity as a vessel for truth.

With a humble consciousness, one is prepared to become a means for some transcendent whole to accomplish what needs doing and not just be an end in oneself. Humility thus connects with the idea of becoming a *channel* for something larger than oneself (or, as in the meaning of "Islam," of *surrendering* to the will of some Order infinitely greater than oneself). "There is no longer so much the feeling that I do this and this (I live my life, I pursue my career)," writes Genevieve Foster of the effect of her mystical experience, "as that life lives itself through me . . . When this happens, there is a true alteration of the psychic structure."[10] That alteration seems almost invariably connected with a spirit of peacefulness. For the force moving through the channel knits together in the way of shalom.

Essential to the fabric that we human beings knit together is *love*. Perhaps more than any other quality, it is love that characterizes the manifestation in our species of the spirit that must govern a harmonious bio-civisphere. It is love that stretches out the furry hairs that warm us against the cold and howling cosmic wind, melting the fear that separates us. It is the bonding force that dissolves the boundaries of the self. And it is love that liberates human relationships from the bondage of scarcity and leads the way to the promised land of abundance: for with love, giving and receiving feed one another, and so the land runs with milk and honey. To achieve the mutuality and abundance that characterize the biosphere, a system governed by human consciousness must be infused with the spirit of an open heart.

Part of this spirit is *forgiveness*. In the ecosystem of Robert Axelrod's contest, forgiveness is one of the virtues of a strategy that succeeds in the long run. (When the other player makes the cooperative move, the "forgiving" player also returns to cooperation, forgetting about past injuries and betrayals.) So also have our spiritual teachers understood the need to let go of the evil of the past ("as we forgive those who trespass against us"). Holding grudges merely perpetuates the separateness among us; retaliation perpetuates the unraveling of the wholeness of the world.

Forgiveness is the prerequisite for *reconciliation*. Forgiveness is letting go of the sense of evil. So long as we understand the world as an arena for the irreconcilable struggle of the two principles of good and evil, so long will we be condemned to our dangerous separateness, and so long will the emergence of the new wholeness of the bio-civisphere be prevented. Only when we can forgive ourselves for being what we are and let go of the sense of irreconcilability that makes our internal life unbearable, as we saw, will we be able to forgive one another. Such forgiveness, such reconciliation, would relieve us of our attachment to boundaries, boundaries that signify our inability to carry evolution to the next stage of wholeness. The more we can see evil as a manifestation of the incompleteness of our evolutionary process—as something more to be healed than to be warred against—the more able we will be to carry forward our evolution to a new completion. *

Time Again

We may regard these as old truths. For two thousand years and more, the teachings of the mystics have been with us: Buddha's compassion, Jesus's forgiveness, Chuang-tzu's example of humbly becoming one with the Way. But thinking of these as old truths shows again that our time perspective is in need of expansion. Buddha's time was but an instant ago in the context of the larger evolutionary process that has brought us into being. Amid the agonies of our fragmented civilizational process—in the throes of this new and disruptive upsurgence—the human spirit has become the channel for the creation of the new wholeness. Glimpses here and there have given us precious guidance in this evolutionary terra incognita. Perhaps the same process that melded quarks into nucleons, atoms into nucleic acids, and cells into the biosphere, now works to open the human spirit to merge with the new emergent Whole.

These "old" truths, therefore, are both very old and very new. They are very new in that they are adaptive responses to the very recent and especially tormented evolutionary situation in which we precipitated ourselves just millennia ago.† They are very old in that they are

---

*The healing of the human system must occur simultaneously at the micro and the macro levels. Crazy creatures cannot construct a sane order, and a disordered system will perpetuate our craziness. Healing at each level provides a basis for the other level to move forward. The knitting together of a more whole consciousness and of a more harmonious world order are thus like the two feet on which we walk: one foot cannot progress far until the other also makes a step; but together, they make a long journey possible.

This is the way the human system will be healed. Like the growth of an embryo, the whole will grow together. Wherever we are able to provide nourishment into the system, we are contributing to the unfolding of a viable whole.

†The spiritual insights of Moses and Buddha and Jesus and Chuang-tzu have been described[11] as healing responses to the evils that befell humanity as we became caught in a world ruled by imperial power systems. Out of an ancient world where new structures of

expressions—in terms meaningful to the human spirit—of the propensi-
ties characteristic of the cosmic evolutionary processes that stretch back
billions of years before the human mind began to assemble in our
mammalian skulls.

This time perspective, as I suggested above, helps free us from the
gloomy view of our species as being rooted in original sin. To see that
the destructiveness chronic to civilization represents a sudden crisis in
our evolution is to see ground for hope. Although the passions of war
have been ingrained in us for the millennia of civilization's development, it has been for eons that the spirit of shalom has governed the
cosmic evolutionary process that has brought us into being. The forces
that drive us to war are deeply entrenched, but the force in us that
craves harmony runs still deeper.

The principle of shalom governs the natural core of our being. As it
has created us, we in turn by nature strive to align ourselves with it.
Although what we most directly strive for may be our own fulfillment, it
seems clear that the more fully a person's needs are met, the more likely
that person is to act as a channel of harmony and goodwill. The
spiritual condition for which, by nature, we yearn not only fulfills us. It
also makes us peacemakers.

True, our history has made us sick. But that does not negate our
organism's natural tendency to work toward health. Too often, the
agony of the war that has been incited within us exceeds our strength to
overcome, and we can break down into channels for war's perpetuation
instead of its termination. But just as an oak tree will reach toward the
light of the sky if given the room, the human creature allowed to grow
naturally will open to the flows of wholeness. Every human being,
therefore, enters this world as a natural ally for peace. In this there is
hope.

There are many who despair. In our game, they see, there is little
time left on the clock, and the forces that would save us are many

---

coercion arose to enslave the mass of humankind, treating flesh and blood like so much
raw material for the machinery of power, these spiritual leaders taught that each human
being is a repository of the sacred, and stands in direct relation to a transcendent source of
Goodness. In a world where the apotheosis of man-made power threatened to rule
unchecked, these mystics taught that obedience to a power greater than any made by man
is the most essential human calling. This spiritual revolution swept across rather widely
separated parts of the world in a comparatively brief time. Perhaps in our time, the new
manifestations of power—ratcheting up both the dangers and opportunities that confront
us—are producing a new time of spiritual ferment. Perhaps from this will yeast up the
spiritual insights now needed for healing us to a new level of wholeness.

points behind those that would destroy us. They see that the world today, so much in the throes of sin, is very far from embodying the wholeness of peace. Feeling the breath of destruction panting on the backs of their necks, they have concluded that death must surely overtake us before we reach shalom.

But the larger time perspective may offer some hope here also. The stuff of which we are made is some sixteen billion years old. It was more than twelve billion of those years before that stuff began to assume the intricate forms of living organisms (here on earth, at least). Terrestrial life took most of the time since its beginning to produce a single nucleated cell.[12] Three-fourths of the four billion years of life on earth passed before the first multicellular organism appeared. By the time the first rudimentary mammalian cortex emerged, more than 95 percent of the time of life's evolution had gone by. A creature with the mental capacity for just the beginnings of culture—language and tool-use—did not evolve until only a couple of million years ago, and the time that creatures with a neo-cortex roughly as developed as ours have been around constitutes a period to be measured in tens of thousands of years, or at most a few hundreds of thousands. It is less than ten thousand years since the breakthrough into civilization. Although civilization has from its beginnings wrought its transformations with a speed unprecedented in all previous evolution, it is only in the last few centuries that the rate of change has been fast enough to be visible during the course of a single human lifetime.[13] And now in our own century, the rate of transformation—for better and for worse—has quickened still more.

The evolutionary process, in other words, has manifestly been accelerating. Or perhaps a more accurate way of interpreting this evolutionary pattern is this: laying the ground for the next stage of evolution takes a long time in comparison with the time it takes that new stage to emerge and blossom forth. Had we been observing terrestrial evolution up to five hundred million years ago, we might well have despaired of the possibility that life—having taken three and a half billion years to come that far—could knit together in the next half-billion years sufficient complexity to enable us to exist by now. Similarly, had we looked at the evolution of primates up to three million years ago, or even at the evolution of civilization in its first eight thousand years, we would not have imagined that at this point in history our species could so thoroughly hold this planet in its (albeit unsteady) grip as we do in the latter part of the twentieth century.

Perhaps that is the way it is now, as we see that the destiny of civilization must be either toward death or toward shalom, and as we sense that we have a long way to go and not so very long to get there.

It does seem reasonable to fear that the continuation of civilization's evolution according to the pattern that has governed its development these past millennia will lead to death. And the persistent play—in the relationship between the superpowers, and in smaller struggles around the world—of fear and mistrust, of overweening pride and unlimited ambition, of blind righteousness and intolerance, shows that the deadly patterns of the past are alive and keeping us unwell in the present.

But the evidence of previous evolution suggests that the new form, the new level of wholeness, the healthier spirit of human consciousness, may flower forth much more quickly than the previous apparent rate of change in the system might lead one to suspect. I say "apparent" because evolution suggests that laying the foundation is far more complex than it is spectacular: in some fundamental sense, creating a single nucleated cell *does entail most of the work* involved in creating us. Likewise, we should not judge our progress by how fully we have already created the global whole: the readying for the leap is most of the work, and the readying is very much under way.

This leap will not come tomorrow, or the next day, or probably even within our lifetimes. But perhaps in a matter of generations that could be counted upon the fingers of our hands.

Evolutionary Work in Progress

Our times, as troubled as they are, are manifestly full of activity to lay the foundation on which a new structure of civilization might be built. Where there is famine, food from around the world pours in; for problems of the global environment, international organizations have been formed; the very idea that war and conquest are glorious—dominant in civilization until less than a century ago—has been substantially eroded, and ideas of world order and international arms control have sprung up. The very basis of our despair—that growing sense of ours that our present ways of running our civilization are dangerously inadequate— may itself prove to be like the coiling of the spring for the leap.

But in the meantime, even as we may be laying the foundation for a new civilization, we may despair of our having the capacity to make fundamental change. We may see the destructive historical pattern of the old fragmented civilization stretching indefinitely into the future until it falls off the cliff. The idea of the wholeness of a bio-civisphere may seem impossibly utopian. But this should not be at all surprising.

There is a saying in Yiddish, never show a fool a half-finished work. And in these matters, we are fools. Had we been observers earlier in the evolutionary process, we could hardly have had the capacity to imagine what the next whole would look like. In a world of elements, we would be unable to envision something as magnificent as a strand of DNA. Nor could our minds have seen how the cell implied the possibility of a body like ours. Now, as we strain to begin to grasp the magnificent complexity of the biosphere at one level, and of our own brains on another, it is way over our heads to imagine the whole that might emerge through a harmonious alignment of human minds with one another, and with the living flows of the earth's biosphere.

Perhaps we are as little able to grasp the whole we might comprise together as the cells that together constitute us can comprehend the whole of which they are part. How overwhelmed one of our cells would be to glimpse the larger entity in whose living processes it is but a small channel. As overwhelmed, perhaps, as the mystics have been by their glimpses into the transcendence of God. *

The world as we now find it is riven with wounds and divisions. But it is laboring to heal itself. Even out of conflict and destruction, the way toward the new whole may be discovered.

In the evolution of the cells that are our ancestors, something like that took place.[14] As different types of bacteria preyed upon one another, swallowing one another for food, or invading one another to consume from within, something rather marvelous occurred. In some instances, the eater did not wholly destroy the eaten: genetic material from the "food" remained intact, and it happened that the two cells both moved into the next generation joined in one living package. As it turned out, some of these combinations could act synergistically to gain advantages neither kind could achieve individually.

> The ancestors of mitochondria [the oxygen-using parts of all our cells] invaded and reproduced within our other bacterial ancestors. At first, [some of] the occupied hosts just barely kept alive . . . The invaded victims and tamed mitochondria recovered from the vi-

---

*As I grope for the idea of God in this evolutionary perspective, I repeatedly encounter a node of my confusion. If this cosmic picture suggests something about God, is God something already there from the beginning? Or is God coming into being as the Whole to which the evolutionary process is moving? Or is God somehow both? An image comes to me: perhaps, as the story tells of God seeing that Adam in paradise was lonely with no mate, perhaps God was there from the beginning and has spent sixteen billion years using the process of cosmic evolution to create a mate to keep Him/Her company.

cious attack and have lived ever since, for 1,000 million years, in dynamic alliance. Time wreaked its changes on both parties. Animosity became interchange . . . [T]he prey was obligated to its oxygen-using guests because they protected its DNA from the poisonous oxygen prevalent in the outside world . . . The prey bacterium may have been a tough microbe able to protect the mitochondria from harsh environments . . . Cohabiting symbiotically, the archaebacteria and their eubacterial invaders did what neither could do alone. Their descendants became the foundation of the macrocosm ["the visible world of plants, animals, and fungi"].[15]

Perhaps the predation of our societies upon one another—after marring the face of civilization over the millennia to this point—will similarly bear the fruit of evolutionary advance. Perhaps as victims and victors share the patterns of their awareness and seek the basis for a harmonious and synergistic way of coexisting, the consciousness for a new kind of civilization will emerge. Perhaps out of the crucible of war will be forged the symbiotic kingdom of shalom.

The ways our minds are changing help prepare the way. Our increasing recognition that we have reached an evolutionary cul-de-sac unless we elevate our path to the next level is part of this. We are coming to understand that the "new" game of civilization must give way to the still newer game of a different kind of civilization, a newer game that better respects the rules of the old game that first breathed life into us.

Our very suffering is part of the process. If we can gain the strength not to be broken by our injuries, we can use them to grow wiser. The more we are able not to act *from* weakness, the more capable we will be to move *beyond* weakness. Our pain, if we have the courage to face it and to learn what it has to teach, can guide us to heal the deadly fragmentation of our systems and the dangerous cleavage in our souls.

Our yearning for transcendence is also part of the birthing process of the new Whole. The passions that drive us to deal in division and death are powerful. But human experience has shown that there is nothing in human life that more powerfully motivates and directs us than contact with the transcendent reality to which we have access through the life-affirming core of our being.

Which suggests one more ground for hope. Perhaps, in our efforts to create a kingdom of peace upon this splendid planet, we are not without some larger Ally. Throughout the millennia, people have had experiences that seem to reveal us to be part of or agents of something greater than ourselves. In our own time, in our own society, a large proportion of people have such experiences.[16] And these experiences guide their lives in the direction of love and wholeness.

It may be that the path toward peace is ultimately not so uphill as we fear. To struggle against the destructive currents of history may be, from a more fundamental point of view, to allow the still more powerful creative force of the cosmos to flow through us. Not war but peace is the way of life. Not anarchy but harmonious order is what the cosmic process creates. It is through us that this cosmic process now works, challenging us to use this time to heal our injuries. Then can the weeds of our historical fears give way to a garden of love. Then can the gargoyle that is now the visage of our civilization be transformed into an image of the face of God.

NOTES

Prologue

1. Sagan, Eli, *The Lust to Annihilate: A Psychoanalytic Study of Violence in Ancient Greek Culture* (New York: Psychohistory Press, 1979).
2. Rochlin, Gregory, *Man's Aggression: The Defense of the Self* (Boston: Gumbert's, 1973).
3. Jungk, Robert, *Brighter Than a Thousand Suns: A Personal History of the Atomic Scientists* (New York: Harcourt, Brace & Co., 1958).
4. Schmookler, Andrew, *The Parable of the Tribes: The Problem of Power in Social Evolution* (Berkeley: University of California Press, 1984), pp. 21–22.
5. Meissner, W. W., *The Paranoid Process* (New York: Jason Aronson, 1978), p. 617.
6. From James W. Prescott's address, "Developmental Origins of Violence: Psychobiological, Cross-Cultural and Religious Perspectives," before the American Psychiatric Association 136th Annual Meeting, May 4, 1983.
7. Rogin, Michael Paul, *Fathers and Children: Andrew Jackson and the Subjugation of the American Indian* (New York: Alfred A. Knopf, 1975).
8. Steele, B. F., and C. B. Pollock, "Psychiatric Study of Abusing Parents," in Helfer, Ray E., and C. Henry Kempe, *The Battered Child* (Chicago: University of Chicago Press, 1966), pp. 111–112.

Chapter One (pp. 35–41)

1. Storr, Anthony, *Human Destructiveness* (New York: Basic Books, 1972), p. 57.
2. Paul, Robert A., "Did the Primal Crime Take Place?" *Ethos*, vol. 4, no. 3, Fall, 1976.

3. This image comes from Robert Redfield, who, in *The Primitive World and Its Transformations* (Chicago: University of Chicago Press, 1941), contrasts the folk society of the Latin American Indian with the hierarchical society that replaced it.

Chapter Two (pp. 42–52)

1. Begin, Menachem, *The Revolt*, seventh English edition (Jerusalem: Steimatzky's Agency, Ltd., 1977).
2. Bennedict, Ruth, quoted in Sagan, Eli, *Cannibalism: Human Aggression and Cultural Form* (New York: Harper & Row, 1974), pp. 37–38.
3. Quoted in Erikson, Erik, *Gandhi's Truth: On the Origins of Militant Nonviolence* (New York: W. W. Norton, 1969), p. 225.
4. Romans 12:20.
5. Tucker, Robert C., *Stalin As Revolutionary 1879–1929* (New York: W. W. Norton, 1973), p. 434.
6. Waite, Robert G. C., *The Psychopathic God: Adolf Hitler* (New York: Basic Books, 1977), p. 44.
7. Ibid., p. 43.
8. Quoted in Miller, Alice, *For Your Own Good* (New York: Farrar, Straus & Giroux, 1984), pp. 71–72.
9. Sagan, Eli, *At the Dawn of Tyranny: The Origins of Individualism, Political Oppression, and the State* (New York: Alfred A. Knopf, 1985), p. 320.
10. Stein, Howard F., "Farmer and Cowboy: The Duality of the Midwestern Male Ethos—A Study in Ethnicity, Regionalism, and National Identity," chapter 9 in monograph vol. II *From Metaphor to Meaning: Papers in Psychoanalytic Anthropology*, from Series in Ethnicity, Medicine, and Psychoanalysis, edited by H. F. Stein and M. Apprey, University of Virginia Press (manuscript in progress), p. 7.
11. *All Mighty: A Study of the God Complex in Western Man* (Claremont, CA: Hunter House, 1984), p. xvi.
12. Patai, Raphael, *The Arab Mind* (New York: Scribner's, 1983), p. 89.
13. Brodie, Bernard, *War and Politics* (New York: Macmillan, 1973), p. 26.
14. Ibid.
15. Wills, Garry, *The Kennedy Imprisonment* (Boston: Little, Brown & Co., 1982), p. 236.

Chapter Three (pp. 53–65)

1. Thucydides, *The Peloponnesian Wars*, book V.
2. Quoted in Stagner, Ross, *Psychological Aspects of International Conflict* (Belmont, CA: Brooks-Cole, 1967), p. 28.

3. Leites, Nathan, *Psycho-Political Analysis: Selected Writings of Nathan Leites*, edited by Elizabeth Wirth Marvick (Beverly Hills: Sage Publications, 1977), p. 289.

4. Canetti, Elias, *The Conscience of Words* (New York: Farrar, Straus & Giroux, 1979), p. 155.

5. Leites, *Psycho-Political Analysis*, p. 283.

6. Campbell, J. K., "Honor and the Devil," in Peristiany, J. G., ed., *Honour and Shame: The Values of Mediterranean Society* (Chicago: University of Chicago Press, 1966), p. 152.

7. Miller, Alice, *For Your Own Good* (New York: Farrar, Straus & Giroux, 1984), p. 226.

8. See Schmookler, Andrew, *The Parable of the Tribes: The Problem of Power in Social Evolution* (Berkeley: University of California Press, 1984), p. 184.

9. Quoted in Stillman, Edward, and William Pfaff, *The Politics of Hysteria: The Sources of Twentieth Century Conflict* (New York: Harper & Row, 1964), p. 117.

10. Quoted in Fromm, Erich, *The Heart of Man* (New York: Harper & Row, 1980), p. 37.

11. Fromm, *Heart*, p. 40.

12. *Oedipus at Colonus*, lines 1382–83, 1387–89.

13. Ibid., lines 1417, 1426, 1440.

14. Sagan, Eli, *The Lust to Annihilate: A Psychoanalytic Study of Violence in Ancient Greek Culture* (New York: Psychohistory Press, 1979), p. 128.

15. Miale, Florence R., and Michael Selzer, *The Nuremberg Mind: The Psychology of the Nazi Leaders* (New York: Quadrangle, 1975), p. 281.

Chapter Four (pp. 66–76)

1. Lewis, C. S., *Out of the Silent Planet* (New York: Macmillan, 1967), p. 151.

2. Richter, Horst-Eberhard, *All Mighty: A Study of the God Complex in Western Man* (Claremont, CA: Hunter House, 1984), p. 157. Italics in original.

3. My attention was directed to the importance of this imagery by Ernst Becker's *Escape from Evil* (New York: Free Press, 1975), p. 119. As I no longer watch television at sign-off time, I do not know whether this kind of film is still used by stations, but I do recall seeing it often in earlier decades.

4. Waite, Robert G. C., *The Psychopathic God: Adolf Hitler* (New York: Basic Books, 1977), p. 43.

5. Ibid., p. 267.

6. Ibid., p. 394.

7. Ibid., p. 387.

8. Money-Kyrle, R. E., quoted in Fornari, Franco, *The Psychoanalysis of War* (Garden City, NY: Auction Books, 1966), p. 100.

9. Dicks, Henry V., *Licensed Mass Murder—A Social-Psychological Study of Some S.S. Killers* (New York: Basic Books, 1972), p. 38.

10. Quoted in Miller, Alice, *For Your Own Good* (New York: Farrar, Straus & Giroux, 1984), p. 71.
11. Odajnyk, Volodymys Walter, *Jung and Politics* (New York: New York University Press, 1976), p. 22.
12. Jacobson, Dan, *The Story of the Stories: The Chosen People and Its God* (New York: Harper & Row, 1982), p. 104.
13. Waite, *Psychopathic God*, pp. 237–38.
14. Ibid., p. 21.
15. Leites, Nathan, *Psycho-Political Analysis: Selected Writings of Nathan Leites*, edited by Elizabeth Wirth Marvick (Beverly Hills: Sage Publications, 1977), p. 272.
16. Richter, *All Mighty*, p. 120. Alice Miller, also from the Germanic culture, says similarly that "Those who persecute others are warding off knowledge of their own fate as victims." (p. 197.)
17. Quoted in Mitscherlich, Alexander and Margarete, *The Inability to Mourn* (New York: Grove Press, 1975), p. 19.
18. Sagan, Eli, *At the Dawn of Tyranny: The Origins of Individualism, Political Oppression, and the State* (New York: Alfred A. Knopf, 1985), p. 163.

Chapter Five (pp. 77–85)

1. Schmookler, Andrew, *Sowings and Reapings: The Cycling of Good and Evil in the Human System* (Indianapolis: Knowledge Systems, in press).
2. Smith, Lillian, *Killers of the Dream* (Garden City, NY: Anchor Books, 1961), p. 71.
3. Salk, Jonas, *Anatomy of Reality: Merging of Intuition and Reason* (New York: Columbia University Press, 1983), p. 57.

Chapter Six (pp. 89–97)

1. Caneiro, R., "A Theory of the Origin of the State," *Science* 169 (1970).
2. Leites, Nathan, *Psycho-Political Analysis: Selected Writings of Nathan Leites*, edited by Elizabeth Wirth Marvick (Beverly Hills: Sage Publications, 1977), p. 313.
3. Farrell, John C., and Asa P. Smith, *Image and Reality in World Politics* (New York: Columbia University Press, 1967), p. 7.
4. Schmookler, Andrew, *The Parable of the Tribes: The Problem of Power in Social Evolution* (Berkeley: University of California Press, 1984; Boston: Houghton Mifflin, 1986), p. 317.
5. Quoted in Jacobson, Dan, *The Story of the Stories: The Chosen People and Its God* (New York: Harper & Row, 1982), p. 45.
6. Wills, Garry, "The Kennedy Imprisonment," *Atlantic Monthly*, February, 1982, p. 61.

7. Burton, J. W., "The Philosophy of Disputes Resolution," September 1982, pp. 6–7 (manuscript).
8. Quoted in Sagan, Eli, *Cannibalism: Human Aggression and Cultural Form* (New York: Harper & Row, 1974), p. 37.
9. Waite, Robert G. C., *The Psychopathic God: Adolf Hitler* (New York: Basic Books, 1977), p. 44–45.

Chapter Seven (pp. 98–142)

1. Meissner, W. W., *The Paranoid Process* (New York: Jason Aronson, 1978), p. 618.
2. Mack, John, "Self-Esteem and Its Development: An Overview," in Mack, John and S. L. Ablon, eds., *The Development and Sustaining of Self-Esteem in Childhood* (New York: International Universities Press, 1983), p. 12.
3. Ibid.
4. Ibid., p. 10.
5. Quoted in Meissner, *Paranoid*, p. 620.
6. Ibid., p. 619.
7. Meissner, *Paranoid*, p. 618.
8. Quoted in Frank, Jerome D., "Nuclear Death: An Unprecedented Challenge to Psychiatry and Religion," *American Journal of Psychiatry*, vol. 141 (November 1984), p. 11.
9. Kernberg, Otto, *Borderline Conditions and Pathological Narcissism* (New York: Jason Aronson, 1975), p. 235.
10. Based on Kernberg, *Borderline*, p. 231.
11. Richter, Horst-Eberhard, *All Mighty: A Study of the God Complex in Western Man* (Claremont, CA: Hunter House, 1984), p. 192.
12. Rochlin, Gregory, *Man's Aggression: The Defense of the Self* (Boston: Gumbert's, 1983), p. 120.
13. Miller, Alice, *For Your Own Good* (New York: Farrar, Straus & Giroux, 1984), p. 59.
14. Ibid., p. 22.
15. Ibid.
16. Ibid., p. 60.
17. Ibid., p. 90, italics in original.
18. Ibid., p. 28.
19. Quoted in ibid., p. 29.
20. Sagan, Eli, *At the Dawn of Tyranny: The Origins of Individualism, Political Oppression, and the State* (New York: Alfred A. Knopf, 1985), p. 255.
21. Rougemont, Denis de, *Man's Western Quest* (New York, Harper, 1957), p. 78.
22. Rochlin, *Aggression*, p. 266.
23. Ibid.

24. Jacobson, Dan, *The Story of the Stories: The Chosen People and Its God* (New York: Harper & Row, 1982), p. 47.
25. Quoted in Waite, Robert G. C., *The Psychopathic God: Adolf Hitler* (New York: Basic Books, 1977), p. 287.
26. Quoted in ibid.
27. Waite, *Psychopathic*, p. 44.
28. Erikson, Erik, *Childhood and Society*, second edition (New York: W. W. Norton, 1963), p. 343.
29. Mitscherlich, Alexander and Margarete, *The Inability to Mourn* (New York: Grove Press, 1975), p. 64.
30. Quoted in Richardson, Frank, *Napoleon: Bisexual Emperor* (New York: Horizon Press, 1972), p. 22.
31. Richardson, *Napoleon*, p. 30.
32. Zonis, Marvin, and Daniel Offer, "The Psychology of Revolutionary Leadership: The Speeches of Ayatollah Khomeini," *Psychohistory Review*, winter 1985, p. 10.
33. "Soviets Said to Dislike Star Wars as Much as Reagan Likes It," *The Christian Science Monitor*, October 8, 1985.
34. Quoted in Tucker, Robert C., *Stalin as Revolutionary 1879–1929* (New York: W. W. Norton, 1973), p. 424.
35. Ibid., p. 425.
36. Genesis 4.
37. Genesis 37:5.
38. Canetti, Elias, *Crowds and Power* (New York: Viking, 1962), p. 169.
39. Meissner, *Paranoid*.
40. Genesis 37:19–20.
41. Pointed out to me by Nancy Kurilla, an undergraduate student in a course I taught at Georgetown University.
42. Becker, Ernest, *Escape from Evil* (New York: Free Press, 1975), p. 105.
43. September 1969, quoted in Barbara Rowes, ed., *Book of Quotes* (New York: E. P. Dutton, 1979), p. 81.
44. deMause, Lloyd, *Foundations of Psychohistory* (New York: Psychohistory Press, 1982), p. 95.
45. Quoted in Schoeck, Helmut, *Envy: A Theory of Social Behavior* (New York: Harcourt, Brace & World), p. 177.
46. Told by Kenneth Cooper in Givens, R. Dale, and Martin A. Nettleship, eds., *Discussion on War and Human Aggression* (The Hague: Mouton Publishers, 1976), p. 85.
47. Ibid.
48. Wills, Garry, "The Kennedy Imprisonment," *Atlantic Monthly*, February 1982, p. 41.
49. Rochlin, *Aggression*, p. 82.
50. Black-Michaud, Jacob, *Cohesive Force: Feud in the Mediterranean and the Middle East* (New York: St. Martin's Press, 1975).
51. Rochlin, *Aggression*, pp. 194–95.

52. Bordieux, Pierre, "The Sentiment of Honour in Kabyle Society," in Peristiany, J. G., ed., *Honour and Shame: The Values of Mediterranean Society* (Chicago: University of Chicago Press, 1966), p. 212.
53. Wyatt-Brown, Bertram, *Southern Honor: Ethics and Behavior in the Old South* (New York: Oxford University Press, 1982), p. 34.
54. Bhagavad Gita, verses 34–36.
55. Quoted in Augustine, and in turn by Walcot, Peter, *Envy and the Greeks* (Westminster, England: Aris & Phillips, 1978), p. 95.
56. Quoted in deMause, *Foundations*, p. 190.
57. Becker, Ernest, *Escape from Evil* (New York: Free Press, 1975), pp. 1–2.
58. Leites, Nathan, *Psycho-Political Analysis*, p. 313.
59. Sagan, Eli, *At the Dawn of Tyranny*, p. 335.
60. Quoted in ibid.
61. Canetti, Elias, *Crowds and Power*, p. 272.
62. Quoted in Sagan, Eli, *The Lust to Annihilate: A Psychoanalytic Study of Violence in Ancient Greek Culture* (New York: Psychohistory Press, 1979), p. 169.
63. Quoted in Fornari, Franco, *The Psychoanalysis of War* (Garden City, NY: Auction Books, 1966), p. 57.
64. Khomeini, "Message to the Pilgrims" (September 12, 1980), *Islam and Revolution: Declarations of Iman Khomeini*, translated by Hamid Algar (Berkeley: Mizan Press, 1981), p. 305.
65. Quoted in deMause, *Foundations*, p. 190.

Chapter Eight (pp. 143–177)

1. Quoted in Miller, Alice, *For Your Own Good* (New York: Farrar, Straus & Giroux, 1984), frontispiece and p. 11.
2. Stein, Howard F., "Farmer and Cowboy: The Duality of the Midwestern Male Ethos—A Study in Ethnicity, Regionalism, and National Identity," chapter 9 in monograph vol. II *From Metaphor to Meaning: Papers in Psychoanalytic Anthropology*, from Series in Ethnicity, Medicine, and Psychoanalysis, edited by H. F. Stein and M. Apprey, University of Virginia Press (manuscript in progress).
3. Sagan, Eli, *The Lust to Annihilate: A Psychoanalytic Study of Violence in Ancient Greek Culture* (New York: Psychohistory Press, 1979), p. 32.
4. Quoted in Miller, *Own Good*, frontispiece.
5. Ibid.
6. Dunn, Patrick P., "Childhood in Imperial Russia," in deMause, Lloyd, ed., *The History of Childhood* (New York: Psychohistory Press, 1974), p. 396.
7. Quoted in Miller, *Own Good*, p. 12.
8. Steele, B. F., and C. B. Pollock, "Psychiatric Study of Abusing Parents," in Helfer, Ray E., and C. Henry Kempe, *The Battered Child* (Chicago: University of Chicago Press, 1966), p. 112.

9. Quoted in Dunn, "Childhood," p. 396.

10. Quoted in Miller, *Own Good*, frontispiece.

11. Horace, *Epistles* I. x. 24.

12. Miller, *Own Good*, p. 65.

13. Stein, "Cowboy," p. 40.

14. Jacobson, Dan, *The Story of the Stories: The Chosen People and Its God* (New York: Harper & Row, 1982), p. 86.

15. Quoted in Halkin, Hillel, "The Wheel of History" (review of *The Story of the Stories*, by Dan Jacobson), *Commentary*, September 1982.

16. Waite, Robert G. C., *The Psychopathic God: Adolf Hitler* (New York: Basic Books, 1977), p. 305.

17. Peck, M. Scott, *People of the Lie: The Hope for Healing Human Evil* (New York: Simon & Schuster, 1983), p. 81.

18. Sagan, Eli, *At The Dawn of Tyranny: The Origins of Individualism, Political Oppression, and the State* (New York: Alfred A. Knopf, 1985), p. 332.

19. Sagan, *Dawn*, p. 333.

20. deMause, Lloyd, ed., *The History of Childhood* (New York: Psychohistory Press, 1974), p. 8.

21. Miller, *Own Good*, pp. 196–97.

22. Sagan, *Dawn*, p. 164.

23. Quoted in Stein, "Cowboy," p. 44.

24. Stein, "Cowboy," p. 44.

25. Quoted in ibid., p. 39.

26. Erikson, Erik, *Childhood and Society*, second edition (New York: W. W. Norton, 1963), p. 388.

27. From the film *Shoah*.

28. Quoted in Stein, "Cowboy," p. 39.

29. Thucydides, *The Peloponnesian Wars*, book V.

30. Meissner, W. W., *The Paranoid Process* (New York: Jason Aronson, 1978), p. 675.

31. Ibid.

32. Ibid., p. 669.

33. Ibid., pp. 548–49.

34. Storr, Anthony, *Human Destructiveness* (New York: Basic Books, 1972), p. 86.

35. Quoted in Bukovsky, Vladimir, "The Peace Movement and the Soviet Union," *Commentary*, vol. 73, no. 5 (May 1982), p. 25.

36. Lebow, Richard Ned, "Generational Learning and Conflict Management," *International Journal*, XL (autumn 1985), p. 581.

37. Ibid., p. 573.

38. Meissner, *Paranoid*, p. 669.

39. Ibid., p. 617.

40. Kernberg, Otto, *Borderline Conditions and Pathological Narcissism* (New York: Jason Aronson, 1975), p. 231.

41. Wyatt-Brown, Bertram, *Southern Honor: Ethics and Behavior in the Old South* (New York: Oxford University Press, 1982), p. 53.
42. Tore Nordenstam, quoted in Patai, Raphael, *The Arab Mind* (New York: Scribner's, 1983), p. 121.
43. Patai, *Arab*, p. 123.
44. Numbers 31:17–18.
45. Fornari, Franco, *The Psychoanalysis of War* (Garden City, NY: Auction Books, 1966), p. 103.
46. Ibid.
47. Ibid.
48. Ibid., p. 227.
49. *Newsweek*, August 12, 1985, p. 45.
50. Prescott, James W., "Body Pleasure and Origins of Violence," *The Futurist*, April, 1975, p. 68.
51. Quoted in Patai, *Arab*, p. 126.
52. Walcot, Peter, *Envy and the Greeks* (Westminster, England: Aris & Phillips, 1978), p. 18.
53. Patai, *Arab*, p. 125.
54. Ibid., p. 34.
55. Ibid.
56. Sagan, Eli, *Cannibalism: Human Aggression and Cultural Form* (New York: Harper & Row, 1974), p. 46.
57. Hyde, Lewis, *The Gift: Imagination and the Erotic Life of Property* (New York: Random House, 1982), pp. 11–12.
58. Fromm, Erich, *The Heart of Man* (New York: Harper & Row, 1980), p. 41.
59. Ibid.
60. Hyde, *The Gift*, p. 5.
61. Ibid., p. 4.
62. Senzaki, Nyogen, and Ruth Strout McAndless, *The Iron Flute: 100 Zen Koans* (Rutland, VT: Charles E. Tuttle Co., 1961), p. 53.

Chapter Nine (pp. 178–193)

1. Meissner, W. W., *The Paranoid Process* (New York: Jason Aronson, 1978), p. 618.
2. Rochlin, Gregory, *Man's Aggression: The Defense of the Self* (Boston: Gumbert's, 1973), p. 169.
3. Wilbur, Ken, *Up From Eden* (Garden City, NY: Anchor/Doubleday, 1981), p. 13.
4. Dreikurs, Rudolf, *Children: The Challenge* (New York: Duell, Sloan & Pearce, 1964), pp. 148–49.
5. Meissner, *Paranoid*, p. 675.
6. Fornari, Franco, *The Psychoanalysis of War* (Garden City, NY: Auction Books, 1966), p. ix.

7. Quoted in Wyatt-Brown, Bertram, *Southern Honor: Ethics and Behavior in the Old South* (New York: Oxford University Press, 1982), p. 38.
8. *Newsweek*, December 23, 1985.
9. Axelrod, Robert, *The Evolution of Cooperation* (New York: Basic Books, 1984), p. 117.
10. Ibid., p. 52.
11. Ibid., p. 112.
12. Schmookler, Andrew, *The Parable of the Tribes: The Problem of Power in Social Evolution* (Berkeley: University of California Press, 1984), p. 33.
13. Matthew 15:32–38.
14. Cf. Burton, cited on p. 191.
15. Sennett, Richard, "Symbols of Recognition," *The Atlantic Monthly*, February 1982, p. 20.

Chapter Ten (pp. 197–203)

1. Atkin, Samuel, "Notes on the Motivations for War," in Winnik, Heinrich, Rafael Moses, and Mortimer Ostow, eds., *Psychological Bases of War* (New York: Quadrangle, 1973), p. 142.
2. Meissner, W. W., *The Paranoid Process* (New York: Jason Aronson, 1978), p. 541.
3. Ibid.
4. Ibid.
5. Dicks, Henry V., *Licensed Mass Murder—A Social-Psychological Study of Some S.S. Killers* (New York: Basic Books, 1972), p. 25.
6. Ibid.
7. Rogin, Michael Paul, *Fathers and Children: Andrew Jackson and the Subjugation of the American Indian* (New York: Alfred A. Knopf, 1975), p. 9.
8. Smith, Lillian, *Killers of the Dream* (Garden City, NY: Anchor Books, 1961), p. 105.
9. Fornari, Franco, *The Psychoanalysis of War* (Garden City, NY: Auction Books, 1966), p. xviii.
10. Ibid., p. 102.
11. Stein, Howard F., "Farmer and Cowboy: The Duality of the Midwestern Male Ethos—A Study in Ethnicity, Regionalism, and National Identity," chapter 9 in monograph vol. II *From Metaphor to Meaning: Papers in Psychoanalytic Anthropology*, from Series in Ethnicity, Medicine, and Psychoanalysis, edited by H. F. Stein and M. Apprey, University of Virginia Press (manuscript in progress), p. 19.
12. Tucker, Robert C., *Stalin As Revolutionary 1879–1929* (New York: W. W. Norton, 1973), p. 458.
13. Fromm, Erich, *The Anatomy of Human Destructiveness* (New York: Holt, Rinehart & Winston, 1973), p. 384.

14. Holsti, Ole R., "Crisis, Stress, and Decisionmaking," *International Social Science Journal*, vol. 23, no. 1, 1971, p. 63.
15. *USA Today*, October 15, 1986.

Chapter Eleven (pp. 204–225)

1. Koestler, Arthur, "The Limits of Man and His Predicament," in *The Limits of Human Nature*, Benthall, Jonathan, ed. (London: Allen Lane, 1973), p. 51.
2. Edwards, Paul, ed., *The Encyclopedia of Philosophy* (New York: Macmillan, 1967), Vol. 3, p. 173.
3. Fein, Leonard, "A Man of His Words: Menachem Begin and the Golan Heights," *Moment*, Jan.-Feb., 1982, p. 38.
4. Ibid.
5. Hoffer, Eric, *The True Believer* (New York: Harper & Row, 1951), p. 137.
6. Rochlin, Gregory, *Man's Aggression: The Defense of the Self* (Boston: Gumbert's, 1973), p. 253.
7. Brodie, Bernard, *War and Politics* (New York: Macmillan, 1973), p. 267.
8. Dicks, Henry V., *Licensed Mass Murder—A Social-Psychological Study of Some S.S. Killers* (New York: Basic Books, 1972), p. 38.
9. Quoted in Mack, John, "Some Thoughts on Nuclearism and the Psychological Roots of Anti-Sovietism" (manuscript).
10. Rougement, Denis de, *Man's Western Quest* (New York: Harper, 1957), p. 78.
11. Simon, Neil, *Biloxi Blues* (New York: Random House, 1986), p. 67.
12. Mitscherlich, Alexander and Margarete, *The Inability to Mourn* (New York: Grove Press, 1975), p. 48.
13. Miller, Alice, *For Your Own Good* (New York: Farrar, Straus & Giroux, 1984), pp. 187–88.
14. Zonis, Marvin, and Daniel Offer, "The Psychology of Revolutionary Leadership: The Speeches of Ayatollah Khomeini," *Psychohistory Review*, winter 1985, p. 9.
15. Mack, John, "Nationalism and the Self," *Psychohistory Review*, vol. II, nos. 2 and 3 (spring 1983), p. 25.
16. Girrard, Rene, *Violence and the Sacred* (Baltimore: Johns Hopkins University Press, 1972), p. 12.
17. Ibid.
18. Ibid., p. 4.
19. *The True Nature of the U.S. Regime, the "Great Satan,"* no author, no publisher, no date, but evidently published in Iran in the early 1980s, p. 46.
20. See Frank, Jerome D., *Sanity and Survival in the Nuclear Age: Psychological Aspects of War and Peace* (New York: Random House, 1982). Also, Sam Keen has done work in this area—of which I saw a slide presentation in

1983—which culminated, too late to be a resource for this book, in his *Faces of the Enemy: Reflections of the Hostile Imagination* (New York: Harper & Row, 1982).

21. Henry, Jules, *A Kaingang Tribe of the Highlands of Brazil* (New York: Random House, 1964), p. 113.

22. Black-Michaud, Jacob, *Cohesive Force: Feud in the Mediterranean and the Middle East* (New York: St. Martin's Press, 1975), p. 234.

23. Ibid., p. 235.

24. Peristiany, J. G., ed., *Honour and Shame: The Values of Mediterranean Society* (Chicago: University of Chicago Press, 1966), p. 187.

25. Patai, Raphael, *The Arab Mind* (New York: Scribner's, 1983), p. 93.

26. See Adorno, Theodore, et al., *The Authoritarian Personality* (New York: W. W. Norton, 1982).

27. Mitscherlich, *Inability*, p. 92.

28. Fornari, Franco, *The Psychoanalysis of War* (Garden City, NY: Auction Books, 1966), p. 51.

29. Ibid., p. 52.

30. deMause, Lloyd, *Foundations*, p. 156.

31. Koestler, in Benthall, *Limits*, p. 51.

32. Milgram, Stanley, *Obedience to Authority* (New York: Harper & Row, 1974), p. 7.

33. Ibid., p. 166.

34. Miale, Florence R., and Michael Selzer, *The Nuremberg Mind: The Psychology of the Nazi Leaders* (New York: Quadrangle, 1975), p. 11.

35. Ibid.

36. Rougement, *Quest*, p. 164.

37. On this, see Hyde, Lewis, *The Gift: Imagination and the Erotic Life of Property* (New York: Random House, 1979), p. 180.

Chapter Twelve (pp. 226–244)

1. Midgley, Mary, *Beast and Man: The Root of Human Nature* (Ithaca: Cornell University Press, 1978), p. 382.

2. Ibid.

3. Stagner, Ross, *Psychological Aspects of International Conflict* (Belmont, CA: Brooks-Cole, 1967), p. 25.

4. Homer, *Iliad*, book I, translated by Richard Lattimore (Chicago: University of Chicago Press, 1951), pp. 287–89.

5. Gandhi, M.K., *Towards Lasting Peace*, edited by Anand T. Hingorani (Bombay: Bharatiya Vidya Bhavan, 1956), p. 46.

6. Windass, Stanley G., foreword to Regamey, P., *Non-violence and the Christian Conscience* (New York: Herder & Herder, 1966), pp. 16–17.

7. Quoted in Jervis, Robert, *Perception and Misperception in International Politics* (Princeton: Princeton University Press, 1976), p. 68.

8. Ibid.
9. Quoted in ibid., p. 69.
10. Quoted in ibid., p. 69.
11. Jervis, *Perceptions*, p. 352.
12. Scheer, Robert, *With Enough Shovels: Reagan, Bush and Nuclear War* (New York: Random House, 1982), pp. 48–49.
13. Ibid., p. 49.
14. Ibid., p. 29.
15. Ibid., p. 30.
16. Quoted in Watts, Alan W., *The Two Hands of God: The Myths of Polarity* (New York: George Brazilliers, 1963), p. 178.
17. Dicks, Henry V., *Licensed Mass Murder—A Social-Psychological Study of Some S.S. Killers* (New York: Basic Books, 1972), p. 247.
18. Quoted in ibid., p. 267.
19. Ibid.
20. *The True Nature of the U.S. Regime, the "Great Satan,"* no author, no publisher, no date, but evidently published in Iran in the early 1980s, pp. 73–74.
21. Wormser, Rene A., *The Myth of the Good and Bad Nations* (Chicago: Henry Regnery, 1954), p. 24.
22. Ibid., p. 5.
23. Ibid.
24. Quoted in Mitscherlich, Alexander and Margarete, *The Inability to Mourn* (New York: Grove Press, 1975), p. 89.
25. Ibid.
26. Shklar, Judith, "Let's Not Be Hypocritical," *Daedalus*, summer 1979, p. 4.
27. Cohn, Norman R., "Europe's Inner Demons," in Wolman, Benjamin B., ed., *The Psychoanalytic Interpretation of History* (New York: Basic Books, 1971), p. 73.
28. Midgley, *Beast*, italics in original, p. 27.
29. Image from TV show on Stalin in 1950s.
30. *Washington Week in Review*, April 18, 1986.
31. Zilborg, Gregory, *The Psychology of the Criminal Act and Punishment* (Westport, CT: Greenwood Press, 1986), p. 76.
32. Cohn, "Demons," p. 73.
33. deMause, Lloyd, *Foundations of Psychohistory* (New York: Psychohistory Press, 1982), p. 189.
34. Quoted in Hoffer, Eric, *The True Believer* (New York: Harper & Row, 1951), p. 85.
35. Hoffer, *Believer*, p. 85.
36. Milgram, Stanley, *Obedience to Authority* (New York: Harper & Row, 1974), p. 2.
37. von Neumann, Erich, *Depth Psychology and a New Ethic* (London: Hodder & Stoughton, 1969), p. 90.

38. Ibid.
39. Watts, *Hands*, p. 41.
40. Stein, Howard F., "Farmer and Cowboy: The Duality of the Midwestern Male Ethos—A Study in Ethnicity, Regionalism, and National Identity," chapter 9 in monograph vol. II *From Metaphor to Meaning: Papers in Psychoanalytic Anthropology*, from Series in Ethnicity, Medicine, and Psychoanalysis, edited by H. F. Stein and M. Apprey, University of Virginia Press (manuscript in progress), p. 26.
41. Jung, cited in Odajnyk, Volodymys Walter, *Jung and Politics* (New York: New York University Press, 1976), p. 74.
42. Ibid.
43. Jung, Carl G., *Collected Papers*, vol. 10 (Princeton: Princeton University Press, 1970), p. 232.
44. Henry, Jules, *A Kaingang Tribe of the Highlands of Brazil* (New York: Random House, 1964), p. 53.
45. Quoted in Holsti, Ole R., "Crisis, Stress, and Decisionmaking," *International Social Science Journal*, vol. 23, no. 1, 1970, p. 63.
46. Krauthammer, Charles, "Pacifism's Invisible Current," *Time*, May 30, 1983, p. 79.
47. Meissner, W. W., *The Paranoid Process* (New York: Jason Aronson, 1978), p. 544.
48. Storr, Anthony, *Human Destructiveness* (New York: Basic Books, 1972), pp. 80–81.
49. Becker, Ernest, *Escape from Evil* (New York: Free Press, 1975), p. 148.

Chapter Thirteen (pp. 245–263)

1. Girrard, Rene, *Violence and the Sacred* (Baltimore: Johns Hopkins University Press, 1972), pp. 278–79.
2. Black-Michaud, Jacob, *Cohesive Force: Feud in the Mediterranean and the Middle East* (New York: St. Martin's Press, 1975), p. 228.
3. Holmes, J. H., quoted in Sagan, Eli, *Cannibalism: Human Aggression and Cultural Form* (New York: Harper & Row, 1974), p. 9.
4. Fornari, Franco, *The Psychoanalysis of War* (Garden City, NY: Auction Books, 1966), p. 171.
5. Lewis, C. S., *Out of the Silent Planet* (New York: Macmillan, 1967), p. 78.
6. Watts, Alan W., *The Two Hands of God: The Myths of Polarity* (New York: George Brazilliers, 1963), p. 168.
7. deMause, Lloyd, *The Foundations of Psychohistory* (New York: Psychohistory Press, 1982), p. 111.
8. Mumford, Lewis, *In the Name of Sanity* (New York: Harcourt Brace & Co., 1954), pp. 221–22.
9. Tiger, Lionel, *Optimism: The Biology of Hope* (New York: Simon & Schuster, 1979), p. 82.

10. von Franz, Marie-Louise, in Jung, Carl G. et al., *Man and His Symbols* (Garden City, NY: Doubleday, 1964), p. 203.

11. Jung, Carl G., *Collected Papers*, vol. 10 (Princeton: Princeton University Press, 1970), pp. 12–13.

12. Peck, M. Scott, *People of the Lie: The Hope for Healing Human Evil* (New York: Simon & Schuster), p. 69.

13. Harding, M. Esther, *The "I" and the "Not-I": A Study in the Development of Consciousness* (Princeton: Princeton University Press, 1965), p. 91.

14. Quoted in *Tarrytown Letter*, April 1983, p. 16.

15. Quoted in Waite, Robert G. C., *The Psychopathic God: Adolf Hitler* (New York: Basic Books, 1977), p. xvii.

16. Ibid.

17. See Erikson, Erik, *Gandhi's Truth: On the Origins of Militant Non-violence* (New York: W. W. Norton, 1969).

18. Erikson, *Gandhi*, p. 251.

19. Orwell, George, *Collected Essays* (London: Heinemann, 1966), p. 456.

20. Erikson, *Gandhi*, p. 234.

21. von Neumann, Erich, *Depth Psychology and a New Ethic* (London: Hodder & Stoughton, 1969), p. 111.

22. Erikson, *Gandhi*, p. 433.

23. Quoted in Peck, *Lie*, p. 11.

24. Miller, Alice, *For Your Own Good* (New York: Farrar, Straus & Giroux, 1984), p. 85.

25. Ibid.

26. Schmookler, Edward Lynde, "Red Alert" (unpublished paper), p. 4.

27. Tucker, Robert C., *Stalin as Revolutionary 1879–1929* (New York: W. W. Norton, 1973), p. 459.

28. Ibid.

29. Schmookler, Edward, "Alert," p. 4.

30. von Neumann, *Depth Psychology*, p. 96.

31. O'Connor, Flannery, "Revelations," in *The Complete Stories of Flannery O'Connor* (New York: Farrar, Straus & Giroux, 1971), p. 491.

32. Ibid., p. 497.

33. Ibid., p. 500.

34. Ibid.

35. Ibid., p. 506.

36. Ibid., p. 507.

37. Ibid., p. 492.

38. Ibid., p. 509.

39. Wilbur, Ken, *Up From Eden* (Garden City, NY: Anchor/Doubleday, 1981), p. 13.

40. Richter, Horst-Eberhard, *All Mighty: A Study of the God Complex in Western Man* (Claremont, CA: Hunter House, 1984), p. 226.

41. Wilbur, *Eden*, p. 14.

42. Ibid.

Chapter Fourteen (pp. 269–273)

1. Quoted in Cohn, Norman R., *The Pursuit of the Millennium* (Fairlawn, NY: Essential Books, 1957), p. 70.
2. Cohn, Norman R., *Pursuit*, p. 75.
3. Erich Gumbel, in Winnik, Heinrich, Rafael Moses, and Mortimer Ostow, eds., *Psychological Bases of War* (New York: Quadrangle, 1973), p. 177.
4. Ibid.
5. Quoted in Volkan, Vamik D., *Cyprus—War and Adaptation: A Psychoanalytic History of Two Ethnic Groups in Conflict* (Charlottesville, VA: University of Virginia Press, 1979), p. xi.
6. Study, by Protho and Melikian, cited in Patai, Rafael, *The Arab Mind* (New York: Scribner's, 1983), p. 221.
7. Lorenz, Konrad, *Civilized Man's Eight Deadly Sins* (New York: Harcourt Brace Jovanovich, 1974), p. 66.
8. Marris, Peter, *Loss and Change* (New York: Pantheon Books, 1974), pp. 70, 76.
9. Ibid., p. 67.
10. Ibid., p. 70.

Chapter Fifteen (pp. 274–281)

1. Patai, Raphael, *The Arab Mind* (New York: Scribner's, 1983), p. 219.
2. Simmel, Georg, *Conflict* (Glencoe, IL, 1955), p. 48.
3. Lasswell, Harold, *World Politics and Personal Insecurity* (New York: Free Press, 1965), p. 35.
4. "All Things Considered," National Public Radio, May 19, 1983.
5. Postman and Brunner, quoted in Holsti, Ole R., "Crisis, Stress, and Decisionmaking," *International Social Science Journal*, vol. 23, no. 1, 1971, p. 59.
6. Quoted in Ginsburg, Morris, *Reason and Unreason in Society* (Cambridge: Harvard University Press, 1948), p. 142.
7. Suzuki, Takeo, *Japanese and the Japanese: Words in Culture* (Tokyo: Kodansha International, 1973), p. 144.
8. Quoted in Aho, James A., *Religious Mythology and the Art of War: Comparative Religious Symbolisms of Military Violence* (Westport, CT: 1979), p. 177.
9. John 16:6.
10. Jacobson, Dan, *The Story of the Stories: The Chosen People and Its God* (New York: Harper & Row, 1982), p. 18.
11. Second sura.
12. Aho, *Mythology*, p. 188.

13. Ibid.
14. Ibid.
15. Quoted in Wright, Quincy, A Study of War (Chicago: University of Chicago Press, 1965), p. 318.
16. Ibid.
17. Zonis, Marvin, and Daniel Offer, "The Psychology of Revolutionary Leadership: The Speeches of Ayatollah Khomeini," Psychohistory Review, winter 1985, p. 8.
18. Ibid., p. 9.
19. Aho, Mythology, p. 33.
20. Windass, Stanley G., foreword to Regamey, P., Non-violence and the Christian Conscience (New York: Herder & Herder, 1966), p. 28.

Chapter Sixteen (pp. 282–289)

1. Quoted in Mitscherlich, Alexander and Margarete, The Inability to Mourn (New York: Grove Press, 1975), pp. 229–30.
2. Based on my recollections of lectures for Humanities 5 at Harvard during 1963–64.

Chapter Seventeen (pp. 290–295)

1. Based on Shah, Indries, Thinkers of the East (Baltimore: Penguin Books, 1971).
2. From Shah, Indries, The Sufis (London: Octagon Press, 1983).
3. This story is told in many places, in different cultural traditions. See, for example, a Sufi version in Indries Shah's Tales of the Dervishes (New York: E. P. Dutton, 1967).
4. Hufford, David J., with quote from Andrew Greeley, Commentary on Genevieve Foster's The World Was Flooded with Light: A Mystical Experience Remembered (Pittsburgh: University of Pittsburgh Press, 1985), p. 95.
5. Ibid., p. 105.
6. Reported in Hufford, Light, p. 93.

Chapter Eighteen (pp. 296–300)

1. Bosworth, David, "The Literature of Awe," The Antioch Review, vol. 37 (winter 1979), p. 246.
2. Bosworth, "Literature," p. 248.
3. Ibid.
4. Ibid.
5. John 12:24.

Epilogue

1. See "Red Sky at Morning: The Dawn of Civilization and the Rise of Warfare," in Schmookler, Andrew, *The Parable of the Tribes: The Problem of Power in Social Evolution* (Berkeley: University of California Press, 1984), pp. 74–81.
2. Young, Louise B., *The Unfinished Universe* (New York: Simon & Schuster, 1986), p. 41.
3. Ibid.
4. Ibid., pp. 41–42.
5. Quoted in Young, *Universe*, p. 69.
6. Ibid., p. 55, italics in original.
7. Ibid., p. 93.
8. Allman, William F., "Mindworks," *Science 86*, May 1986, p. 24.
9. Young, *Universe*, p. 83.
10. Foster, Genevieve, *The World Was Flooded with Light: A Mystical Experience Remembered* (Pittsburgh: University of Pittsburgh Press, 1985), p. 47.
11. I have come across this idea twice over the years, but neglected to write down the quotations, and now cannot recall the sources.
12. Margulis, Lynn, and Dorian Sagan, *Microcosmos: Four Billion Years of Microbial Evolution* (New York: Summit Books, 1986), p. 116.
13. See, for example, Geoffrey Bibby's *Four Thousand Years Ago* (New York: Alfred A. Knopf, 1961).
14. This is compellingly described in Margulis and Sagan's *Microcosmos*, See especially chapter 8, "Living Together."
15. Margulis and Sagan, *Microcosmos*, pp. 130, 131, 133, 284.
16. David Hufford, in Foster, *Light*.

BIBLIOGRAPHY

ABC. *Nightline*, February 8, 1983.

Adorno, Theodore, et al. *The Authoritarian Personality*. New York: W.W. Norton, 1982.

Aho, James A. *Religious Mythology and the Art of War: Comparative Religious Symbolisms of Military Violence*. Westport CT: Greenwood Press, 1979.

Antonov-Ovseyenko, Anton. *The Time of Stalin: Portrait of a Tyranny*. New York: Harper & Row, 1980.

Atkin, Samuel. "Notes on the Motivation for War," in Winnik, et al.

Avineri, Shlomo. "The Begin Tragedy: Learning to Hate." *The Washington Post*, October 10, 1982.

Axelrod, Robert. *The Evolution of Cooperation*. New York: Basic Books, 1984.

Bakan, David. *Disease, Pain & Sacrifice*. Chicago: University of Chicago Press, 1968.

Barber, C. L. *The Idea of Honour in the English Drama 1591–1700*. Goteborg, Elanders boktr, 1957.

Baroja, Julio Caro. "Honor, Shame: A Historical Account of Several Conflicts," in Peristiany, J.G., ed.

Becker, Ernest. *Escape from Evil*. New York: Free Press, 1975.

———. *Denial of Death*. New York: Free Press, 1973.

Begin, Menachem. *The Revolt*, English edition. Jerusalem: Steimatzky's Agency, Ltd., 1977.

Benthall, Jonathan, ed. *The Limits of Human Nature*. London: Allen Lane, 1973.

Bernard, Viola W., Perry Ottenberg, and Fritz Redl. "Dehumanization: A Composite Psychological Defense in Relation to Modern War," in *The Triple Revolution*. Boston: Little, Brown & Co., 1968.

Bernstein, Jerome S. "Some Archetypal Dynamics in the Thermo-Nuclear Age," Manuscript.

Bibby, Jeffrey. *Four Thousand Years Ago*. New York: Alfred A. Knopf, 1961.

Black-Michaud, Jacob. *Cohesive Force: Feud in the Mediterranean and the Middle East.* New York: St. Martin's Press, 1975.

Bleibtreu, John N. *The Parable of the Beast.* New York: Macmillan, 1968.

Block, Kenneth. *Human Nature and History.* New York: Columbia University Press, 1980.

Bordieu, Pierre. "The Sentiment of Honor in Kabyle Society," in Peristiany, J.G., ed.

Bosworth, David. "The Literature of Awe." *The Antioch Review*, vol. 37 (Winter 1979).

Brewer, Garry D. *The War Game.* Cambridge: Harvard University Press, 1979.

Brodie, Bernard. *War and Politics.* New York: Macmillan, 1973.

Broyles, William, Jr. "Why Men Love War." *Esquire*, November 1984.

Bukovsky, Vladimir. "The Peace Movement and the Soviet Union." *Commentary*, vol. 73, no. 5. May 1982.

Burton, J. W. "The Philosophy of Disputes Resolution." September 1982, manuscript.

Bychowski, Gustav. "The Proletariat," in Wolman, Benjamin B., ed.

Callah, Hilary. *Ethnology and Society.* Oxford: Clarendon Press, 1970.

Campbell, J.K. "Honor and the Devil," in Peristiany, J.G., ed.

Canetti, Elias. *The Conscience of Words.* New York: Farrar, Straus & Giroux, 1979.

———. *Crowds and Power.* New York: Viking Press, 1962.

Carthy, J. D., and F. J. Ebling, eds. *The Natural History of Aggression.* London: Academic Press, 1964.

Cohn, Norman R. "Europe's Inner Demons," in Wolman, Benjamin B., ed.

———. *The Pursuit of the Millennium.* Fairlawn, NY: Essential Books, 1957.

Cousins, Norman. *Human Options.* New York: W.W. Norton, 1981.

del Vasto, Lanza. *Warriors of Peace, Writings on the Techniques of Non-Violence.* New York: Alfred A. Knopf, 1974.

deMause, Lloyd. *Foundations of Psychohistory.* New York: Psychohistory Press, 1982.

———. ed. *The History of Childhood.* New York: Psychohistory Press, 1974.

———. *Reagan's America.* New York: Creative Roots, 1984.

Dicks, Henry V. *Licensed Mass Murder—A Social-Psychological Study of Some S.S. Killers.* New York: Basic Books, 1972.

Dinnerstein, Dorothy. *The Mermaid and the Minotaur.* New York: Harper Colophon Books, 1977.

Douglas, Mary. *Purity and Danger.* London: Routledge & Kegan Paul, 1966.

Dreikurs, Rudolf. *Children: The Challenge.* New York: Duell, Sloan & Pearce, 1964.

Dunn, Patrick P. "Childhood in Imperial Russia," in deMause, Lloyd, ed.

Dunning, Eric, ed. *The Sociology of Sport.* London: Frank Cass, 1976.

Edwards, Paul, ed. *The Encyclopedia of Philosophy.* New York: Macmillan, 1967.

Erikson, Erik. *Childhood and Society*, second edition. New York: W.W. Norton, 1963.

————. *Gandhi's Truth: On the Origins of Militant Non-violence.* New York: W.W. Norton, 1969.

Fabbro, David. "Peaceful Societies," in Falk, Richard A. and Samuel S. Kim, ed.

Falk, Richard A., and Samuel S. Kim. *Toward a Just World Order.* Boulder, CO: Westview Press, 1982.

Farrell, John C., and Asa P. Smith. *Image and Reality in World Politics.* New York: Columbia University Press, 1967.

Fein, Leonard. "A Man of His Words: Menachem Begin and the Golan Heights." *Moment*, vol. 7, no. 2, Jan.–Feb., 1982.

Ferguson, John. *War and Peace in the World's Religions.* London: Sheldon Press, 1977.

Fornari, Franco. *The Psychoanalysis of War.* Garden City, NY: Auction Books, 1966.

Foster, Genevieve. *The World Was Flooded with Light: A Mystical Experience Remembered.* Pittsburgh: University of Pittsburgh, 1985.

Frank, Jerome D. "Nuclear Death: An Unprecedented Challenge to Psychiatry and Religion." *American Journal of Psychiatry*, vol. 141 (November 1984).

————. Commentary in Fromm, Erich, *War Within Man: The Psychological Roots of Destructiveness.* Philadelphia: Peace Literature of The American Friends Service Committee, 1963.

————. "The Nuclear Arms Race—Sociopsychological Aspects." *American Journal of Public Health*, vol. 70, no. 9 (September 1980).

————. *Sanity and Survival in the Nuclear Age: Psychological Aspects of War and Peace.* New York: Random House, 1982.

Fromm, Erich. *The Anatomy of Human Destructiveness.* New York: Holt, Rinehart & Winston, 1973.

————. *The Heart of Man.* New York: Harper & Row, 1980.

————. *War Within Man: The Psychological Roots of Destructiveness.* Philadelphia: Peace Literature of The American Friends Service Committee, 1963.

Gandhi, M.K. *Towards Lasting Peace.* Edited by Anand T. Hingorani. Bombay: Sharatiya Vidya Bhavan, 1956.

Gerove, Santiago. *Is Peace Inevitable? Aggression, Evolution, or Human Destiny.* London: George Allen & Unwin, 1970.

Ginsburg, Morris. *Reason and Unreason in Society.* Cambridge: Harvard University Press, 1948.

Girrard, Rene. *Violence and the Sacred.* Baltimore: Johns Hopkins University Press, 1972.

Givens, R. Dale, and Martin A. Nettleship, eds. *Discussion on War and Human Aggression.* The Hague: Mouton Publishers, 1976.

Gladstone, Arthur. "The Conception of the Enemy." *The Journal of Conflict Resolution*, vol. III, no. 2 (June 1959).

Glover, Edward. *War, Sadism and Pacifism.* London: George Allen & Unwin, 1935.

Green, Philip. *The Theory of Nuclear Deterrence.* Columbus: Ohio State University Press, 1966.

Gregg, Richard B. *The Psychology and Strategy of Gandhi's Non-Violent Resistance.* New York: Garland, 1972.

Grenier, Richard. "The Horror, The Horror." Review of *The Time of Stalin: Portrait of a Tyranny,* by Anton Antonov-Ovseyenko. *New Republic,* May 26, 1982.

Gumbel, Erich. "Notes on Some Psychic Motive for War," in Winnik et al.

Halkin, Hillel. "The Wheel of History." Review of *The Story of the Stories: The Chosen People and Its God,* by Dan Jacobson. *Commentary,* September 1982.

Hallett, Charles S. and Elaine. *The Revenger's Madness.* Lincoln: University of Nebraska Press, 1980.

Harding, M. Esther. *The "I" and the "Not-I": A Study in the Development of Consciousness.* Princeton: Princeton University Press, 1965.

Helfer, Ray E., and C. Henry Kempe. *The Battered Child.* Chicago: University of Chicago Press, 1966.

Henry, Jules. A *Kaingang Tribe of the Highlands of Brazil.* New York: Random House, 1964.

Heradsvtveit, Daniel. *The Arab-Israeli Conflict: Psychological Obstacles to Peace.* Oslo: Universitets Forlaget, 1979.

Hingorani, Anand T., ed. *Towards Lasting Peace,* by M.K. Gandhi. Bombay: Bharatiya Vidya Bhavan, 1956.

Hoffer, Eric. *The True Believer.* New York: Harper & Row, 1951.

Holsti, Ole R. "Crisis, Stress, and Decisionmaking," *International Social Science Journal,* vol. 23, no. 1, 1971.

Homer. *Iliad.* Translated by Richard Lattimore. Chicago: University of Chicago Press, 1951.

Horsburgh, H. J. N. *Non-Violence and Aggression: A Study of Gandhi's Moral Equivalent of War.* New York: Oxford University Press, 1968.

Hotchkiss, Marlow. "The Motzu Project: Personal National Peace-finding." *The CoEvolution Quarterly,* fall 1982.

Hufford, David J. Commentary in Foster, *Light.*

Hyde, Lewis. *The Gift: Imagination and the Erotic Life of Property.* New York: Random House, 1983.

Iacocca, Lee. "My Turn." *Newsweek.* December 23, 1985.

Jacobson, Dan. *The Story of the Stories: The Chosen People and Its God.* New York: Harper & Row, 1982.

Jampolsky, Gerald G. *Love Is Letting Go of Fear.* Millbrae, CA: Celestial Arts, 1979.

Jervis, Robert. *Perception and Misperception in International Politics.* Princeton: Princeton University Press, 1976.

Jung, Carl G. *Collected Papers,* vol. 10. Princeton: Princeton University Press, 1970.

———, M.-L. von Franz, eds. *Man and His Symbols.* Garden City, NY: Doubleday, 1964.

Jungk, Robert. *Brighter than a Thousand Suns: A Personal History of the Atomic Scientists.* New York: Harcourt, Brace, 1958.

Kernberg, Otto. *Borderline Conditions and Pathological Narcissism.* New York: Jason Aronson, 1975.

Kim, Samuel S. "The Lorenzian Theory of Aggression and Peace Research," in Falk and Kim, eds.

Koestler, Arthur. "The Limits of Man and His Predicament," in Benthall, Jonathan, ed. *The Limits of Human Nature.* London: Allen Lane, 1973.

Kohut, Heinz. *The Analysis of the Self: Systematic Approach to the Psychoanalytic Treatment of Narcissistic Personality Disorders.* New York: International University Press, 1971.

The Koran.

Krauthammer, Charles. "Pacifism's Invisible Current." *Time,* May 30, 1983.

Krebs, Caroline W. *Breaking the Silence Barrier.* Manuscript. A presentation to the Second World Congress of Organization Development Professionals. October, 1981.

Kull, Steven. "Nuclear Arms and the Desire for World Destruction." *International Society of Political Psychology,* vol. 4, no. 3 (1983).

———. "Nuclear Nonsense." *Foreign Policy,* no. 58, Spring, 1985.

Lasswell, Harold. *World Politics and Personal Insecurity.* New York: Free Press, 1965.

Lebow, Richard Ned. "Generational Learning and Conflict Management." *International Journal,* vol. XL (autumn 1985).

———. *Between Peace and War: The Nature of International Crises.* New Haven: Yale University Press, 1981.

Leites, Nathan. *Psycho-Political Analysis: Selected Writings of Nathan Leites,* edited by Elizabeth Wirth Marvick. Beverly Hills: Sage Publications, 1977.

Leng, Russell J. "Misapplying Lessons from the Cuban Missile Crisis." *The Christian Science Monitor,* October 27, 1982.

Lewis, C.S. *Out of the Silent Planet.* New York: Macmillan, 1967.

———. *The Abolition of Man.* New York: Macmillan, 1978.

Loewenberg, Peter. "Theodor Herzl: A Psychoanalytic Study in Charismatic Political Leadership," in Wolman Benjamin B, ed.

Lorenz, Konrad. *Civilized Man's Eight Deadly Sins.* New York: Harcourt Brace Jovanovich, 1974.

Mack, John E. "But What About the Russians?" *Harvard Magazine,* March-April 1982.

———. "Nationalism and the Self." *Psychohistory Review,* vol. II, nos. 2 and 3 (spring 1983).

———. "Self-Esteem and Its Development: An Overview," in Mack and Ablon, eds.

———. *Nightmares and Human Conflict.* Boston: Houghton Mifflin, 1974.

———. "Some Thoughts on Nuclearism and the Psychological Roots of Anti-Sovietism." Manuscript.

———, and S.L. Ablon, eds. *The Development and Sustaining of Self-Esteem in Childhood.* New York: International Press, 1983.

Margulis, Lynn, and Dorion Sajan. *Microcosmos: Four Billion Years of Microbial Evolution.* New York: Summit, 1986.

Marris, Peter. *Loss and Change.* New York: Pantheon Books, 1974.

Meissner, W. W. *The Paranoid Process.* New York: Jason Aronson, 1978.

Marvick, Elizabeth Wirth, ed. *Psycho-Political Analysis: Selected Writings of Nathan Leites.* Beverly Hills: Sage Publications, 1977.

Miale, Florence R., and Michael Selzer. *The Nuremberg Mind: The Psychology of the Nazi Leaders.* New York: Quadrangle, 1975.

Menninger, Karl. *The Crime of Punishment.* New York: Viking Press, 1968.

Milgram, Stanley. *Obedience to Authority.* New York: Harper & Row, 1974.

Midgley, Mary. *Beast and Man: The Root of Human Nature.* Ithaca: Cornell University Press, 1978.

Miller, Alice. *For Your Own Good.* New York: Farrar, Straus & Giroux, 1984.

Mitscherlich, Alexander and Margarete. *The Inability to Mourn.* New York: Grove Press, 1975.

Money-Kryle, R.E. *Psychoanalysis and Politics.* London: Gerald Duckworth & Co., 1951.

Moss, Norman. *Men Who Play God.* Middlesex, England: Penguin Books, 1972.

Motzu Project. "The Motzu Project: Personal National Peace-finding," by Marlow Hotchkiss. *The CoEvolution Quarterly,* fall, 1982.

Mumford, Lewis. *In the Name of Sanity.* New York: Harcourt, Brace & Co., 1954.

———. *Human Development.* New York: Harcourt Brace Jovanovich, 1966.

National Public Radio. "All Things Considered." Report on Cambodia, May 19, 1983.

Nisbet, Robert. "Boredom." *Commentary,* September 1982.

Nisbett, Richard, and Lee Ross. *Human Inference: Strategies and Shortcoming of Social Judgment.* Englewood Cliffs, NJ: Prentice-Hall, 1980.

Nitobe, Inazo. *Bushido: The Soul of Japan.* Tokyo: Teilei, 1907.

O'Connor, Flannery. "Revelation." In *The Complete Stories of Flannery O'Connor.* New York: Farrar, Straus & Giroux, 1971.

O'Flaherty, Wendy Doniger, ed. *Karma and Rebirth in Classical Indian Traditions.* Berkeley: University of California Press, 1980.

Odajnyk, Volodymys Walter. *Jung and Politics.* New York: New York University Press, 1976.

Orwell, George. *Collected Essays.* London: Heinemann, 1966.

Patai, Raphael. *The Arab Mind.* New York: Scribner's, 1983.

Paul, Robert A. "Did the Primal Crime Take Place?" *Ethos,* vol. 4, no. 3, Fall, 1976.

Peck, M. Scott. *People of the Lie: The Hope for Healing Human Evil.* New York: Simon & Schuster, 1983.

Peristiany, J.G., ed. *Honour and Shame: The Values of Mediterranean Society.* Chicago: University of Chicago Press, 1966.

————. "Honour and Shame in a Cypriot Highland Village," in Peristiany, J G., ed.

Pettman, Ralph. *Human Behavior and World Politics.* New York: St. Martin's Press, 1975.

Pryce-Jones, David. "The Palestinian Pattern." *The New Republic,* November 8, 1982.

Prescott, James W. "Body Pleasure and the Origins of Violence." *The Futurist,* April, 1975.

————. "Developmental Origins of Violence: Psychobiological, Cross-Cultural and Religious Perspectives." Invited Address before American Psychiatric Association 136th Annual Meeting, May 4, 1983.

Pulliam, H. Ronald, and Christopher Dunford. *Programmed to Learn: An Essay on the Evolution of Culture.* New York: Columbia University Press, 1980.

Rapoport, Anatol, and Albert M. Chammah. *Prisoner's Dilemma: A Study in Conflict and Cooperation.* Ann Arbor: University of Michigan Press, 1965.

Redfield, Robert. *The Primitive World and Its Transformations.* Chicago: University of Chicago Press, 1941.

Regamey, P. *Non-violence and the Christian Conscience.* New York: Herder & Herder, 1966.

Richardson, Frank. *Napoleon: Bisexual Emperor.* New York: Horizon Press, 1972.

Richter, Horst-Eberhard. *All Mighty: A Study of the God Complex in Western Man.* Claremont, CA: Hunter House, 1984.

————. "Our Children and the Problem of Peace." Draft paper.

————. "Psychological Effects of Living Under the Threat of Nuclear War." Draft paper.

Rochlin, Gregory. *Man's Aggression: The Defense of the Self.* Boston: Gumbert's, 1973.

Rogin, Michael Paul. *Fathers and Children: Andrew Jackson and the Subjugation of the American Indian.* New York: Knopf, 1975.

Rokeach, Milton, et al. *The Open and Closed Mind.* New York: Basic Books, 1960.

Rosenstock-Huessy, Eugen. *Out of Revolutions: Autobiography of Western Man.* New York: Morrow, 1938.

Rougemont, Denis de. *Man's Western Quest.* New York: Harper & Row, 1957.

Russett, Bruce M. "Cause, Surprise, and No Escape," in Falk and Kim, eds.

Sagan, Eli. *At the Dawn of Tyranny: The Origins of Individualism, Political Oppression, and the State.* New York: Alfred A. Knopf, 1985.

————. *Cannibalism: Human Aggression and Cultural Form.* New York: Harper & Row, 1974.

————. *The Lust to Annihilate: A Psychoanalytic Study of Violence in Ancient Greek Culture.* New York: Psychohistory Press, 1979.

Salk, Jonas. *Anatomy of Reality: Merging of Intuition and Reason.* New York: Columbia University Press, 1983.

Scheer, Robert. *With Enough Shovels: Reagan, Bush and Nuclear War.* New York: Random House, 1982.

Schmookler, Andrew. "Assassinations: The Problem Is Not that the World is Sick." *Terrorism: An International Journal,* winter 1982.

————. "The Authoritarian/Totalitarian Dichotomy." *International Issues Series* (CSIS), 1981.

————. "International Ramifications of the Israeli Raid on the Iraqi Reactor." *International Issues Series* (CSIS), 1981.

————. *The Parable of the Tribes: The Problem of Power in Social Evolution.* Berkeley: University of California Press, 1984; paperback, Boston: Houghton Mifflin, 1986.

————. "The Promised Land," *Environmental Action,* 15th Anniversary Issue, April 1985.

————. Review of Eli Sagan's *At the Dawn of Tyranny, New York Times Book Review,* June 30, 1985.

————. *Sowings and Reapings: The Cycling of Good and Evil in the Human System.* Indianapolis: Knowledge Systems, in press.

————. "Three Troubled Areas of the World." *Washington Quarterly,* fall 1981.

————. "To Invade or Not to Invade: Factors the Soviets Must Weigh [in Poland]." *International Issues Series* (CSIS), 1981.

————. "Understanding U.S.-European Differences on Defense and Detente," Center for Strategic and International Studies, *International Issues Series,* 1982.

————. "U.S.-U.S.S.R.: Are We Angling Toward a Shoot-out at the O.K. Corral?" *Political Psychology,* summer 1985.

Schmookler, Edward Lynde. "Red Alert." Unpublished paper.

Schoeck, Helmut. *Envy: A Theory of Social Behavior.* New York: Harcourt, Brace and World, 1966.

Schurmann, Franz. "From Nazi Death Camps to Assam—An Obsession to 'Cleanse' the Homeland." Press release by Pacific News Service, San Francisco, February 28, 1983.

Schweitzer, Albert. *The Philosophy of Civilization.* New York: Macmillan, 1960.

Scott, John Paul. "Biology and Human Aggression." *American Journal of Orthopsychiatry,* 40, no. 4, (July 1970).

————. "Agonistic Behavior of Primates: A Comparative Perspective," in *Primate Aggression, Territoriality, and Xenophobia, A Comparative Perspective.* New York: Academic Press, 1974.

Sennett, Richard. "Symbols of Recognition." *The Atlantic Monthly,* February 1982.

Senzaki, Nyogen, and Ruth Strout McAndless. *The Iron Flute: 100 Zen Koans.* Kutland, VT: Charles E. Tuttle Co., 1961.

Shah, Indries. *The Sufis.* London: Octagon Press, 1983.

————. *Tales of the Dervishes.* New York: E.P. Dutton, 1967.

————. *Thinkers of the East.* Baltimore: Penguin Books, 1971.

Shklar, Judith. "Let's Not Be Hypocritical." *Daedalus*, summer, 1979.

Simmel, Georg. *Conflict.* Glencoe, IL: Free Press, 1955.

Simon, Neil. *Biloxi Blues.* New York: Random House, 1986.

Smelser, Neil J. *Theory of Collective Behavior.* Glencoe, NY: Free Press, 1963.

Smith, Lillian. *Killers of the Dream.* Garden City, NY: Anchor Books, 1961.

Smuts, Jan C. *Holism and Evolution.* Westport, CT: Greenwood Press, 1973.

Somit, Albert, ed. *Biology and Politics.* The Hague: Mouton, 1976.

Stagner, Ross. *Psychological Aspects of International Conflict.* Belmont, CA: Brooks-Cole, 1967.

Steele, B.F., and C.B. Pollock. "Psychiatric Study of Abusing Parents," in Helfer et al.

Stein, Howard F. "Farmer and Cowboy: The Duality of the Midwestern Male Ethos—A Study in Ethnicity, Regionalism, and National Identity." Chapter 9 in monograph vol. II *From Metaphor to Meaning: Papers in Psychoanalytic Anthropology,* from Series in Ethnicity, Medicine, and Psychoanalysis, ed. by H.F. Stein and M. Apprey, Virginia: University Press. Manuscript in progress.

Stillman, Edmund and William Pfaff. *The Politics of Hysteria: The Sources of Twentieth Century Conflict.* New York: Harper & Row, 1964.

Storr, Anthony. *Human Destructiveness.* New York: Basic Books, 1972.

Suzuki, Takeo. *Japanese and the Japanese: Words in Culture.* Tokyo: Kodansha International, 1973.

Tarrytown Letter, April 1983.

Tiger, Lionel. *Optimism: The Biology of Hope.* New York: Simon & Schuster, 1979.

The True Nature of the U.S. Regime, the "Great Satan." No author, no publisher, no date, but evidently published in Iran in the early 1980s.

Tucker, Robert C. *Stalin As Revolutionary 1879–1929.* New York: W.W. Norton, 1973.

Ulam, Adam. "Lust for Power." Review of *Stalin's Secret War* by Nikolai Tolstoi. *Commentary*, September 1982.

Volkan, Vamik D. *Cyprus—War and Adaptation: A Psychoanalytic History of Two Ethnic Groups in Conflict.* Charlottesville: University of Virginia Press, 1979.

von Franz, Marie-Louise. *Shadow and Evil in Fairy Tales.* Zurich: Spring Publications, 1974.

von Hendig, Hans. *Punishment.* Montclair, NJ: Patterson Smith, 1973.

von Neumann, Erich. *Depth Psychology and a New Ethic.* London: Hodder & Stoughton, 1969.

Waite, Robert G.C. *The Psychopathic God: Adolf Hitler.* New York: Basic Books, 1977.

Walcot, Peter. *Envy and the Greeks.* Westminster, England: Aris & Phillips, 1978.

Watts, Alan W. *The Two Hands of God: The Myths of Polarity.* New York: George Brazilliers, 1963.

Wheeler, Harvey. "The Role of Myth Systems in American-Soviet Relations." *Journal of Conflict Resolution*, vol. IV, no. 2 (June 1960).

Wilbur, Ken. *Up From Eden*. Garden City, NY: Anchor/Doubleday, 1981.

Wilensky, Harold L. *Organizational Intelligence: Knowledge and Policy in Government and Industry*. New York: Basic Books, 1967.

Wills, Garry. *The Kennedy Imprisonment*. Boston: Little, Brown & Co., 1982.

———. "The Kennedy Imprisonment." *The Atlantic Monthly*, February 1982.

Windass, Stanley G. "Foreword" to P. Regamey.

Winnik, Heinrich, Rafael Moses, and Mortimer Ostow, eds. *Psychological Bases of War*. New York: Quadrangle, 1973.

Wolman, Benjamin B., ed. *The Psychoanalytic Interpretation of History*. New York: Basic Books, 1971.

———. "Postscript: Psycho-Historical Speculations," in Wolman, Benjamin B., ed.

Wormser, Rene A. *The Myth of the Good and Bad Nations*. Chicago: Henry Regnery, 1954.

Wright, Quincy. *A Study of War*. Chicago: University of Chicago Press, 1965.

Wright, Will. *Six Guns and Society: A Structural Study of the Western*. Berkeley: University of California Press, 1978.

Wyatt-Brown, Bertram. *Southern Honor: Ethics and Behavior in the Old South*. New York: Oxford University Press, 1982.

Young, Louise B. *The Unfinished Universe*. New York: Simon & Schuster, 1986.

Zilborg, Gregory. *The Psychology of the Criminal Act and Punishment*. Westport, CT: Greenwood Press, 1968.

Zonis, Marvin, and Daniel Offer. "The Psychology of Revolutionary Leadership: The Speeches of Ayatollah Khomeini." *Psychohistory Review*, winter 1985.

ACKNOWLEDGMENTS

It is my brother, Edward Schmookler, whom I wish to thank first of all. His love and wisdom helped me to learn the lesson that is at the core of this book.

If the human condition is one of insecurity, that of one who tries to write a book like this in the absence of institutional support is especially human. I am especially grateful, therefore, to those individuals who expressed their belief in my work by volunteering financial help.

The generosity of Lloyd and Ellen Wells of Falmouth, Maine, gave me assurance at an early stage of this work that the maligned wolf was far enough from the door that I need not let it distract me.

Then L. and J.M.—whose desire to avoid publicity I hereby respect—offered further support that allowed me to complete this book without imposing undue sacrifice upon my family. The M.s' unflagging commitment to making a better world is an inspiration, and my gratitude for their encouragement is enduring.

The Wellses and the M.s have been like pillars holding up the edifice of my continued work.

Several others have also given material as well as moral support. The very first was Walt Hayes of Rutledge, Tennessee, whose gesture was magnified in my eyes for coming so clearly from the heart, and for coming at a moment when the encouragement was especially needed. John Cox of Gaithersburg, Maryland, has been a fellow seeker as well as a helper along the path. W. H. and Carol Ferry of Scarsdale, New York, also gave some much-needed support.

The gifts of two members of the older generation of my family expressed a vote of confidence that supported me in ways beyond the financial: my aunt, Evelyn Gallagher, of Chapel Hill, North Carolina; and my mother, Pauline Schmookler, of Takoma Park, Maryland.

I am indebted also to my agent, Patricia van der Leun, who first found me because she resonated to the words I had written and who has the courage to pursue her business as a means to serve such ends. Her unswerving belief in the value of this work helped it to find a way into the world.

I would also like to thank John Marks and Bonnie Pearlman of the Search for Common Ground in Washington, D.C., who provided me with a base to visit when I needed a respite from the solitude of writing.

With the book itself, I have had valuable help from several people.

My wife, April Moore, and Patricia van der Leun read early parts of the manuscript and gave me much needed encouragement. Both subsequently read the completed draft of the book and helped me to improve it.

Also helpful readers of the completed manuscript were Don Williams of Boulder, Colorado; Mary Colemen of Washington, D.C.; Robert Fuller, of Berkeley, California; and my mother, Pauline Schmookler. They were generous with their time and their intelligence. I want to make special note of the help, at the same stage, of David Landau, of Arlington, Virginia, to whom I turned for his good counsel in weighing some final decisions about presentation.

Of course, all the responsibility for the imperfections that remain is my own.

There was one other, very important and very helpful reader of the manuscript I want to single out for special acknowledgment: my editor at Bantam, Tobi Sanders. Her enthusiasm for the project gave the book a good home; her deft editorial pen challenged me to make it as good as I could. Her untimely and lamentable death—as well as being a shocking reminder of the fragility of our existence—is a great loss for a great many, and for me as well. I regret that she could not be here to see our labors come to final fruition.

It was my great good fortune that Toni Burbank was there at Bantam to take this book under her wing. Her solidity, her reliability, and her goodwill have contributed more than she probably imagines to my peace of mind during the months the book has been in production.

Finally, there are those whose love is the center of my life.

My children, Aaron and Terra, nourish me just by being who they are. And though they do not yet concern themselves with what I say in my writing, they convey in a profound way their delight that I am saying it.

It is customary for authors to thank their wives for putting up with so much in the production of their books. My own has not had to put up with so much, but she has given a great deal. With her great gentleness of spirit and with her sweet caring for me, April Moore, companion of my heart, has given me much of what I know of peace.

INDEX

A

abundance, 110, 188–89, 191, 192–93, 313

Achille Lauro (ship), 124n, 131n

Achilles, 10, 45, 132, 164, 227n

Adam, 62, 63, 114

adaption, 3, 4–5; boundaries as, 215, 247; and fear, 4; narcissism as, 109; and traumatic overlearning, 56–59; worship of strength and, 55–56

Africa, 39, 46n, 109n–10n, 137, 139, 272, 273

Afrikaners, 112–13, 240

Agamemnon, 132, 164, 227n

aggression, 20, 37; authority and, 224; and identification with aggressor, 69–70, 69n, 150–51, 150n, 151n, 152, 158, 236–37; individual, channeled through group, 207–10; and narcissitic rage, 103; as paranoid elaboration of mourning, 201–2, 202n; sex hormones and, 36

Ahab, Captain, 244, 249, 252

Aho, James, 244, 280

Albania, 135, 140, 142

Albritton, Roger, 287

Alexander the Great, 9

all-can-win game, 91–92; *see also* TIT-FOR-TAT strategy

All Mighty (Richter), 260

all-or-nothing, 157, 158, 161, 231–32

altruism, 204–5, 222–25, 222–25, 225n, 239, 260

ambiguity, 18, 245, 277–78, 292

ambivalence, 63, 217–18, 245–46

American: South, 84n, 133n, 165, 166; West, 6, 120, 134–35, 134n, 148–49, 239–40

Amin, Idi, 12

anarchy, 6, 303; boundaries required by, 215–17, 224, 244; and contest of wills, 145, 146, 156; and distortion of male power, 38; and emergence of culture, 99, 107; and human destructiveness, 20; vs. integrated world order, 23–24, 26, 32, 77–78; and intrapsychic war of good and evil, 18–19; king as survivor and, 137–38; males and, 41; and narcissism, 107, 109, 112; and rise of civilization, 14, 15–16, 26, 145; of societies, 56n, 57; vs. tyranny, 145–46

anger, suppression of, 239–40

ABOUT THE AUTHOR

ANDREW BARD SCHMOOKLER is the author of the prize-winning book THE PARABLE OF THE TRIBES: THE PROBLEM OF POWER IN SOCIAL EVOLUTION. He has focused his work on the search for an integrated understanding of the problems facing our species and of the challenge of creating a more humane and viable civilization in the future. A *summa cum laude* graduate of Harvard College, Dr. Schmookler went on to earn his doctorate at Berkeley in a program specially created to accommodate his comprehensive perspective on cultural evolution. His commentaries on social and political issues have appeared in such journals as THE CHRISTIAN SCIENCE MONITOR and have been heard on National Public Radio. In 1985, Andrew Bard Schmookler was selected by ESQUIRE MAGAZINE as one of the "Men and Women Under Forty Who Are Changing the Nation."

He lives near Washington, D.C. with his wife and two children.